Pursuing the Good Life

While Restoring Its Intrigue

J.W. Phillips

All Scripture quotations, unless otherwise indicated, are taken from the New King James Version of the Bible. Copyright © 1979, 1980, 1982, Thomas Nelson, Inc. Publishers. Used by permission. All rights reserved.

King James Public Domain

Revised Standard Version of the Bible, copyright 1952 [2nd edition, 1971] by the division of Christian Education by the Council of the National Council of the Churches of Christ in the United States of America. Used by permission. All rights reserved.

Front cover picture: furnished by Oleksii Olkin

Cover design: Shayna Kusumoto (www.9thavestudio.com)
Copyright © 2017 by J. W. Phillips. All rights reserved.

Editor: Linda Chiu

Printed in the United States of America.

No part of this publication may be reproduced, stored in a retrieval system or transmitted in any way by any means, electronic, mechanical, photocopy or otherwise, without prior permission of the author except as provided by USA copyright law.

ISBN: 978-0-9968545-2-8

Dedicated to my brothers, Daniel and Michael Phillips, who have walked with the Lord for many years

Table of Contents

Chapter 1—Why Good Is Better	7

The Mystery: Finding Treasures and Traps

Chapter 2—The Good Life—Part I	21
Chapter 3—The Good Life—Part II	35
Chapter 4—What God Says about Being Good—Part I	47
Chapter 5— What God Says about Being Good—Part II	61
Chapter 6—Tracking Sin	77

The Adventure: Danger Ahead!

Chapter 7—An Autopsy of Sin—Part I	99
Chapter 8—An Autopsy of Sin—Part II	115

The Biography: Mistakes and Recovery

Chapter 9—The Consequences of Sin	133
Chapter 10—Defective Obedience—Part I	147
Chapter 11—Defective Obedience—Part II	159
Chapter 12—Motivations for Goodness—Part I	171
Chapter 13—Motivations for Goodness—Part II	185

The Hero: Overcoming All Odds

Chapter 14—Consistent Goodness—Part I	205
Chapter 15—Consistent Goodness—Part II	215
Chapter 16—Consistent Goodness—Part III	231

The Romance: United At Last!

Chapter 17—Rewards for Goodness—Part I	251
Chapter 18—Rewards for Goodness—Part II	267
Chapter 19—The Reaping of the Rewards—Part I	283
Chapter 20—The Reaping of the Rewards—Part II	303
Chapter 21—Losing the Rewards	317
Chapter 22—What If	333
Subject Index	347
Scripture Index	355
Endnotes	359

Chapter 1

Why Good Is Better

The good life! These three words convey what we all want. The aspirations we have, the commitments we make, the energy we expend are all related to this one overriding goal. But to arrive at our destination, and to do so with GPS-like accuracy, requires first mapping an itinerary. So that's the agenda of this book.

As with any meaningful goal, clarity is certainly important. But with this subject, clarity is impeded by its controversial nature. Proof of this impediment is easily discerned by asking yourself: What images come to mind whenever the "good life" is mentioned? Material abundance? Enjoyable activities? An idyllic atmosphere? Congenial company? What doesn't come into view as quickly is a life vigorous for virtue. And should the concept of morality be introduced later, this introduction will be deflected—pronto!—by reducing "good" to an innocuous term that means little more than being polite, cheerful, and nice.

Not too deeply embedded in this verbally-facile deflection is the assumption that moral goodness is bland, that it is not worthy of our attention and therefore shouldn't claim our devotion. This isn't a perspective that has always been believed. Nor is it the perspective of God.

Other generations were less dismissive of moral goodness. There was even a day when virtue intrigued and character inspired. We see, for example, Sir Lancelot coming on the scene with aspirations to join the Knights of the Roundtable. As you recall, selection in this highly revered group required more than bravery in battle; there also had to be impeccable moral credentials. Accordingly, while making his case in the musical "Camelot," Lancelot sings:

> And here I stand, as pure as a prayer,
> Incredibly clean, with virtue to spare,
> The godliest man I know!

This sounds like the autobiography, *How I Became the Most Humble Man the World Has Ever Known*. Large pictures of the author were on both inside flaps and on the back of the book as well.

Equally enamored with himself, Lancelot later sings:

> I've never strayed from all I believe;
> I'm blessed with an iron will.
> Had I been made the partner of Eve,
> We'd be in Eden still.

Such effusive praise, especially about one's own morality, is a bit hard to take, so a backlash was bound to occur even in Camelot. No matter how celebrated its ideals and commemorated its virtues, moral goodness has always had its detractors. Hence, "The Seven Deadly Virtues" are lampooned in this same musical with observations like: "It's not the earth the meek inherit but the dirt ... If charity means giving, I give it to you! And fidelity is only for your mate!"

The Middle English word "fie," repeatedly used in this musical, expresses disgust at the sheer boredom of goodness.

> It's been depressing all the way
> And getting glummer every day
> No one repents for any sin now
> Every soul is immaculate and trim
> No one is covered with chagrin now
> Gad, but it's grim
> Oh, fie on goodness, fie
> Fie, fie, fie!

All this contempt for goodness isn't exactly common today, but it isn't unknown, either. In the eyes of some people, the only thing worse than moral goodness is a personal testimony about moral goodness! How gagging some of these self-eulogies can be!

Little wonder, then, that there's an abrupt U-turn, a redirection of focus to what does intrigue: obtaining all that represents frivolity, festivity, sensuality, and indulgence. All that pampers and scintillates. All that comforts and delights. Never mind the shallowness of this life. And never mind how it turns real people into well-dressed mannequins robotically tinkling wineglasses as they move among the guests with nothing important to say.

Cultural Corrosion

Perhaps in no other way is "the good life" more encouraged, but also more distorted, than during that time of life that follows childhood. Older cultures envisioned two stages in life: childhood and adulthood. Modern societies, however, have invented a third stage, adolescence. Whereas in older cultures there was a determined effort to increase responsibility after one's twelfth birthday, just the opposite is true today. Adolescence has been zoned off as a time to enjoy youth, to party, to play, to sow your oats, to get these sanctioned "wild times" out of your system.

But what overly permissive parents indulge, and what society has come to expect, has contributed enormously and erroneously to modern perceptions of the good life. By making these allowances for adolescence and then turning away so as not to see what's really going on, the world's imprimatur has been given to hedonism and narcissism run amok.

Predictably, the recipients of this relaxed morality later reciprocated by extending their bad behavior yet another decade or so, far beyond the previous postponement of adult years. And in some cases, adulthood was avoided altogether as plastic surgeons help grandmothers named Bambi join the jet-set crowd by wearing the same make-up and fashions their granddaughters use. Even morticians get in on the act!

The product of their work is a formally-dressed corpse with blush loaded on to look like a perennial attendee of a never-ending cocktail party. Horizontal, to be sure, but that was also true when too much of the good stuff had been imbibed during one of these parties.

There is a price for this kind of life, though! One simply can't ignore morality and still be a pleasant person to live with. People who live by their glands and operate on their instincts may find a following in the tabloids, but their children may not want to follow them!

It has been said that each society is only one generation removed from barbarism. Columnist George Will wrote about the slow-motion barbarization of America, a dehumanizing of society that worsens in successive generations. As products themselves of this widely extended adolescence, many parents today, through their leniency-is-love approach, are allowing their children to grow up like weeds. It is this type of parenting that provides the needed breeding ground for a sociopathic inability to care for others, which is the passive side of barbarism.

To see life rendered more hollow than hallowed by people fascinated with what is shiny, fast, loud, and expensive is to see a shriveled soul without inner beauty. Such people may occupy vast real estate and dine at the most exclusive clubs; yet, the interior life of these people is slovenly, gaunt, cramped, and crabbed. There's simply nothing there that intrigues, beyond the question of how sane people could ever do this to themselves.

Amoral people like this never blush—not even when caught in gross wrongdoing! Thomas Watson said of such people, "They cannot endure a serious thought, nor do they love to trouble their heads about sin."[1] Though the words "sham" and "shame" may rightly describe their behaviors, these words never seem to connect with whatever conscience they have left. Tozer wrote, "There has never been a time in history when people were good, but there have been times when the masses were ashamed of being bad."[2]

That day, however, seems long gone, because we see from these people: not a hint of guilt, not a syllable of regret, not a sign of reflection—nothing! The hiding Adam did when he first sinned isn't even contemplated by many moderns. Instead, they are determined to wring out of life everything self wants, right or wrong. It is in this regard that Dorothy Sayers' observation bears repeating, "... life takes revenge on those who make it a god."[3] Huxley echoed this sentiment, declaring "a man's worst difficulties begin when he is able to do as he likes."[4]

Centuries earlier, Pascal succinctly observed what history has now amply confirmed, "It is not good to have all one wants."[5] Weighing in on this issue as well, British novelist George Kingsley wrote, "There are two freedoms—the false, where a man is free to do what he likes; the true, where he is free to do what he ought."

It is this false freedom that has proven to be an addiction to many moderns.[6] The intensity of their pursuit persists until that last day when eternity's light reveals their utter folly. Only then do they see that what was chased and cherished throughout a lifetime was only the product of false advertising.

It should be noted that it isn't just tabloid fascination that framed our modern view of the good life. Because for many years now, literature—more cultured in its tastes and refined in its skills—has had this fascination with the "complex" person; and, conversely, has found the consistently good person to be simple, boring, a cliché, entirely too predictable and therefore not worthy of consideration. Noting this pattern, A. W. Tozer wrote:

> The world has divided men into two classes, the stupid good people and the clever wicked ones.
>
> This false classification runs through much of the literature of the last centuries from the classics to the comic strip, from Shakespeare's Polonius, who furnished his son with a set of good but dull moral platitudes, to Camp's Li'l Abner, who would never knowingly do a wrong act but who would rather fall on his head than on his feet because there is more feeling in his feet than in his head.[7]

Much more interesting to devotees of literature is that one who steals off in the middle of the night to do what those who know this person during the day could never imagine. The mystery, the secrecy, the compartmentalization, the inner conflicts—all these richly reward rapt attention! So say the experts in literature. Yet, isn't this complexity, this bundle of inner contradictions, really quite common? Of greater interest one would think—precisely because it is so rare—is the person who spotted all the traps, resisted all the pressures, followed a different path, and remained strong to the end.

It is the life that didn't indulge self, didn't follow the crowd, but chose courage over convenience and principle over expedience that glows stronger and longer with its own inner radiance. Far more so, to be sure, than any of those brief, bright flashes that come from sequined worldlings parading themselves on stage. The glitter there illumines the gutter, and not the higher life to which God summons us.

Clarifying Contrasts

The good life, as the Bible sets this forth, may not seem exciting. But it is actually far more intriguing than what might be suggested by the vapid stares and wide yawns that initially greet this subject. With characteristic insight, C.S. Lewis said, "Good, as it ripens, becomes continually more different not only from evil but from other good."[8] The variety embedded in goodness—rich in its hues, intriguing in its configurations, inspiring in its glow, and rewarding in its glory—fascinates in a way evil could never do. G.D. Watson tells us, "There is a mine of wealth, untold treasures, inestimable jewels, hidden away in the saints of God."[9]

By contrast, the more one observes evil at work, the clearer it becomes that evil shrivels and shrinks a person, producing a monotony that eventually reduces the damned to almost nothing. C.S. Lewis referred to this phenomenon as "ex-man"—these worse-than-worthless souls from whom even God walks away.

Lewis further asserted, "Bad cannot succeed in being bad as truly as good is good."[10] There is an inverse capacity for the two to be what they are. Evil contracts, restricts, depletes, and drains; whereas good does precisely the opposite: expands, blooms, replenishes, and rewards. "There is," remarked one of the old Puritans, "a straightness, slavery, and narrowness in all sin; sin crumples up our souls; which, if they were freely spread abroad, would be as large and wide as the whole universe."[11]

Contrary to the false advertising of this world, experience teaches that evil diminishes in its appeal, becoming more boring with time and less satisfying with usage. It is the very nature of evil to contract and reduce. Peter Marshall said of sin: "It has no originality, no creativity, no being in itself. Sin lives off that which is good."[12] It doesn't create; it only corrupts.

Another contrast between good and evil manifests in the visibility of each. One may think it is evil that hides, and not good. But according to Faber, the sixteenth-century French mystic:

> It must be observed that evil, of its own nature, is more visible than goodness. Evil is like the world—loud, rude, anxious, hurried, impetuous and ever acting on the self-defensive; goodness partakes of the nature of God and imitates the ways of God, of quietness, unobtrusiveness, slowness, non-combativeness, meekly suffers instead of defending itself ....[13]

While evil may be more noticeable than goodness, it is never more desirable, at least in the final analysis. Because what may fast gain our attention will inevitably lose its appeal.

Still another difference between good and evil is made evident by their perceptions of truth. Both good and evil have a directional antenna. The direction of each antenna, however, is opposite from the other. While civility, charm, and intelligence may exist in both groups of people, their length of acquaintance will not be long before a string of opinions reveals the direction of each person's antenna, differences that can be as wide as one hemisphere is from another.

G.D. Watson said of those whose antenna is wrongly directed:

> They may not be criminals, and may pass in the world for fairly good people, but they are the serpent's brood, sleek, oily, treacherous, unreliable, deceitful souls, with double motives, double intentions, that love a lie, that hanker for error, that always take the wrong side, that instinctively apologize for Cain, and Jezebel and Judas ....[14]

In subject after subject, their views are predictable—and wrong! Again, what they think to be right, and argue for vociferously, is altogether accounted for by their antenna.

Analogies from Literature

Challenging the world of literature where it needs to be challenged, let me throw the gauntlet down. The good life set forth by Scripture has more intrigue than a mystery book, more daring than an adventure story, more honesty than a biography, more inspiration than a heroism tale, and more wonder than a dream-come-true fantasy. As we shall see in this book, the life of goodness far surpasses what even the most creative minds have imagined.

To amplify this point, consider further each genre of literature cited in these five comparisons, as we begin to introduce these differences.

The first reason the good life is intriguing is because, like a well-crafted mystery story describing a search for hidden treasure, this treasure is exceedingly difficult to find. Philosophy certainly couldn't find it, whether ancient or modern. Summing up their efforts, Horatius Bonar said, "Philosophy was helpless in its encounters with human evil, and in its sympathies with human sorrow. It looked on and spoke many a true word; but it wrought no cure, it healed no wounds, it rooted out no sin."[15]

Professor Arnold Toynbee, the historian and humanist, spent a lifetime studying the human condition. His massive

History of the World, published in twelve volumes, is impressive in detail and rich in insight. Yet, what Toynbee said in his last book when he was an old man conveyed his disillusionment about the progress of man.

> There is a morality gap in the development of mankind. Man constantly extends his physical power over the environment, but he is unable to improve his social arrangements correspondingly; still less to subdue his destructive passions. Technology is the only field of human activity in which there has been progression.[16]

Aldous Huxley, a scientist and humanist, once thought that science provided the needed answers to improve humanity. But when he eventually saw this wasn't the case, he turned to mysticism and Buddhism, which likewise left him disappointed. Toward the end of his life, this very brilliant man was finally compelled to acknowledge the dead-end he had reached when he wrote, "It is a bit embarrassing to have been concerned with the human problem all one's life and at the end one has no more to offer by way of advice than 'Try to be a little kinder.'"[17]

Only that? Yes, only that—nothing but feeble words that darker forces will resist with a sneer and overwhelm with a grin.

As with every philosophy, so with every man-made religion: Sin remained stubborn in its presence and well-fortified in its defense. Worshippers prostrated their bodies, vocalized their chants, wafted their incense skyward as their leaders, dressed in religious regalia, convened councils, presided over assemblies and made officious pronouncements. Yet, sin—obvious in its manifestation, sometimes—remained elusive in its cure, always.

There can be little doubt that evil has gained many a victory through deceit. At least in modern warfare there are rules limiting this deceit. Under article 39 of the Geneva Convention it is illegal for a combatant to disguise himself in apparel worn by the enemy. In spite of that dictum, a subterfuge very much like this is seen in our day through highly sophisticated disinformation that attempts to pass off evil as good and good as evil.

All this blurring and blinding has disoriented society to the fact that good has been stripped of most of its content. However, once this "public-consumption" model of modern-day ethics is duly analyzed, it becomes clear: God's commands have been abandoned so that only a few hints of its existence remain. According to Scotland professor, James S. Stewart, this distortion has had its adverse effect. Stewart said of people today, "They pursue the trivial as though it were eternal." Unfortunately, the reverse of this is seen in church, where "the Christian too often pursues the eternal as though it were quite trivial."[18] Such calamitous confusion!

Even worse, no rescue appears forthcoming because of something else that has occurred: "Good" has been robbed of its appeal, and by an ever-widening consensus has been deemed boring. Well! The popular preachers aren't going anywhere near a subject thought to be boring! That's why all these preachers who advertise the gospel as "fun" insert entertaining dynamics each week, supposedly to benefit the assembled.

It sometimes seems that the great god Entertainment is omnipresent in our world. Just as entertainment corrupts the news, and reality shows corrupt entertainment, so also the shallow and sensational corrupt the pulpit. It seems that the boring factor has to be dislodged before the pulpit can be enlisted for help! But, as it turns out, introducing intrigue to this topic is not difficult to do.

Talk about a mystery. Paul admitted he didn't know how to be good. Now, most Christians today have never had that problem, at least in their own minds. So they can't imagine why this exceedingly brilliant man, well tutored in the Scriptures, should ever be stumped by a problem that has never been a problem for them! But what Paul eventually discovered, which is later disclosed in this book, is shocking to unbelievers (since none, as it turns out, has even one good work to his or her name); yet surprising to believers, too, (since true holiness is fully inside them right now).

The good life is intriguing, then, first because it solves mysteries. There are many hidden traps in this life—

locations where the treasure appears to be hidden but isn't there. People will visit these locations, and, satisfied by what they see, they often stay. It is there that the counterfeits sparkle, deceiving and delighting. So for these people, the search soon ends and the real treasure is never found.

Second, the good life is daring because, like an adventure story, dangers lurk all along the way. Grave dangers! You can talk about members of the mob, bosses in a drug cartel, gang members in the streets all you want—each dangerous and cruel; none soft in demeanor or kind in disposition. But not even these people, whose paths none of us want to cross, pose the threat of Satan's vast empire of demons. All organized! All trained! All endowed with supernatural powers! All dedicated to individual and global ruin! Little wonder, then, that big beads of sweat populate frightened faces when facing forces like these. Nerve sweat in this setting is altogether understandable!

Third, the good life is honest because, like a bibliography, harsh realities present and heartwarming outcomes emerge. Biblical biographies tell of wrong decisions bearing painful consequences, but they also tell of noble aspirations that lead to gratifying experiences.

How easily we can identify with a good biography! Yes, *Pilgrim's Progress*—a story that evokes feelings from us, and a story that offers instructions to us—is one with which we can easily resonate. This story connects with what we know, yet charts a course we don't know.

Fourth, the good life is inspiring because, like a hero story where great courage is summoned and keen insight is put on display, traps designed to harm are cleverly avoided, roads meant to lead astray are astutely bypassed, pleasures meant to be enjoyed are fully experienced, virtues meant to acquire are impressively accumulated, while the race that appears so grueling is run without even a stumble.

It is true that most stories like these are creations of the imagination. James Bond, after all, is fiction. Spider Man is fiction. The Terminator is fiction. But while Sean, Toby, and Arnold all play characters from fiction, the Apostle Peter is real! And think of how far he came! Who more than Peter—especially during his early days of bonehead blunders—could have said: No one is perfect ... We all make mistakes ... I may not want to, but I sin every day ... I just can't help it! To err, is what? Oh, yeah—human! Yet, it is this same fallible Peter, even after his documented past of legendary defeats, who became a spiritual hero!

What Peter later said would have resulted in snickers and sneers had they been said during his earlier years. But because there was so much credibility to his later life, Peter could say: "Be holy, just as God is holy ... Purify your souls ... Show forth the praises of him who has called you out of darkness ... Sanctify the Lord God in your hearts ... Be partakers of the divine nature ... Giving all diligence, add to your faith virtue ... You shall never fall."

In the end, Peter became more of a hero than any of those revered in fiction books. All the zigzags of his early life gave way to a straight line with an upward trajectory. The life people today say is impossible, he lived!

Finally, the good life is like a fairytale romance; for there is a wedding to celebrate, a banquet to attend, crowns for coronation, rewards for past service, a vast kingdom to rule, and that never-ending happiness with loved ones to enjoy. Good ... boring? Hardly! British-born scholar Arthur W. Pink pointed out, "The original Saxon meaning of our word 'God' is 'The Good.'"[19] So since good is a derivative from God, how could good possibly be boring? Is there anyone, anywhere, more fascinating than God?

I submit that the good life will intrigue anyone who enjoys mysteries, adventure, biographies, hero stories, and fairytale romances. To see the good life as it really is, is to see yawns turn into gasps and elitist' smugness turn into shock.

Reflection Questions

1. Identify two contrasts between good and evil that prompted further thinking for you.

2. Of the five genres of literature discussed, which one appeals to you the most, and which one the least?

The Mystery: Finding Treasures and Traps

When the obvious is wrong ...
When the problem isn't perceptible ...
When everybody else seems satisfied ...
When the object of your search seems not to exist ...
When the search runs into dead-ends ...
When traps ensnare and the treasure is elusive ...

**Alas, we have a mystery!
But unlike other mystery books,
this one isn't fiction!**

Chapter 2

The Good Life—Part I

There are many twists and turns in one's search for the good life. What seems promising at first, often fails; and where one least thinks to find the good life, there it shows up.

False leads and dead-ends are common throughout this search, especially if the search is undertaken with an undue confidence in the mind's ability to discern. When pursued this way, the discovery of the good life becomes as elusive as a cure for cancer. By trusting our own thoughts too much, all the treasures to be found, and all the traps to be avoided, become *more* imperceptible, not less.

Any meaningful search for the good life will want the location of this life in one's heart and not just in one's bank account. While most people do want their life to be good, they also want others to *think* of them as being good. Their circumstances, their character, their situation, their soul—they want all these areas of life to be good not just in the sense of being above average, but actually *very* good!

On the character side of this equation, "good," for most children, was encouraged from their first day in kindergarten. It was there they got on an assembly line where "good" was the word of the day—everyday! Happy-face stickers were routinely placed on their papers; and beside these happy-face stickers the word "good" was written with bold letters and an emphatic exclamation point!

Upon arrival at school each morning, hugs from the teacher were always followed by immediate reminders of "Let's be a good boy and put our backpack in the right cubbyhole." And should the class get a little noisy later in the day, the teacher instructed one and all to use their "inside voice" and be good children.

As school years passed, the notion of "good" changed. It was in teenage years when the vernacular flip-flopped as kids said "that's baad!"—and by that they meant the exact opposite, that it was really good. In other ways, too, this flip-flop exhibited, for no one wanted to be "goody-goody." Instead, other behaviors won peer approval—like sex, drugs, and do-whatever-your-peers-do lockstep imitation.

By the time we became adults, "good" underwent another change, for now it meant life in an upper-class suburb—preferably one with a large house, manicured lawn, large deck, heated pool, a tennis court off to the side, and an expensive membership at the country club.

The "good" life also included a glamorous job, one with more pleasure than pressure and more perks than jerks. This life afforded the best seats at popular restaurants, frequent vacations to exotic locations, pricey automobiles for chauffeurs to park, private schools for the kids to attend, and—to stick religion in there—occasional visits to an Episcopalian church where rich people wore expensive clothes and short sermons never disturbed.

In all these ways, the "good" life has been badly distorted by marketers of materialism and corrupters of morality. If the truth be told, the life of "goodies without God" can never satisfy a man, despite what secularism says. Tozer wrote, "Man is bored because he is too big to be happy with that which sin is giving him. God has made him too great, his potential is too mighty."[1] According to Pascal, "All the miseries of man prove his grandeur." The "good" life, as the world fashions it, is bound to disappoint.

So what, then, is the good life?

Mistaken Worldly Ideas about Good

Those with a more "spiritual" bent may envision long stays at a monastery with dark rooms, hard beds, lit candles, and Gregorian chants to induce meditation. New-Agers may pursue "good" by following their local guru to some isolated spot where they squint, mutter, exercise, and seek magical powers found in mantras and crystals. Poets pursue "good" as they find beauty in nature. Singers pursue "good" as they write songs about love. And fundamentalists pursue "good" by going to church three times during the week, and three more times on Sunday!

Whichever path one takes, assurance is given by our mental health practitioners that each person is already good. According to these earthly custodians of the soul, we live in a world where only judging is wrong and nothing else is. As such, morality doesn't matter; only "appropriate" behavior does. But then again, we all make "mistakes" and no one is "perfect." Of utmost importance, these teachers of tolerance will exhort us, is that we all have a good sense of self-esteem. Therefore, even when it comes to putting people in prison, retribution isn't the issue; remedial training is.

Indoctrinated by this deeply entrenched and widely extended community crusade, many citizens exhibit little concern about their moral standing, or what's going to happen to them after death. One might assume that considerable consideration would be devoted to this subject; eternity is a long time, after all! But, no, only an occasional thought passes through their minds, a momentary blip on the radar of rational reflection that never triggers a second thought or affects their emotions in any way.

So how are we to account for this astounding degree of security, for this widely-accepted notion that goodness is innate and that rewards in heaven await us all? We account for it by noting man's careless conclusions in the areas of anthropology and theology. In anthropology, man considers himself good, or even in the words of the Creator, "very good." That anything happened *after* man's creation seems not to be on our minds; and that God's assessment drastically changed *later* seems not to be an issue.

As for theology, man is a little less sure about this, although he suspects there might be a god. What Alistair MacIntyre said of English' belief, may well describe people's attitude today: There is no god, but it's still wise to pray to him from time to time.² And if it turns out there is a god, blind optimism assumes he will welcome us into heaven (or some equivalent of heaven) so our lives there will be even better than they were on earth.

At funerals, therefore, even the raunchiest rock singer is envisioned to be in heaven, as is the man who never went to church but also never kicked his dog. Tozer observed, "The man who knows himself least is likely to have cheerful if groundless optimism in his own moral worth."³

All this optimism is a rather recent development in man's history. In former days—from the Golden Age of Greece to the European Renaissance—serious reflection was given to this subject of good. In fact, were these people alive today, they would shake their heads in collective puzzlement at this culture of ours that barely produces a mental hiccup when it comes to ethics and the afterlife.

Even those less refined in philosophical thought—the villager in India, the native in Africa, the mountain person in Brazil—had distinct and revered ideas about good, and exactly what was required to be accepted by god or the gods. So deeply engraved were these ideas, parents passed them on to their children with rigor and uniformity. Free thinking in a cafeteria of ideas was hardly an option.

It is *our* generation and *our* culture that sticks out as an oddity in the history of man. To assume what we do with so little thought, to journey toward the afterlife without ethical considerations producing a single crease in our brains, is stunning, to say the least. How can anyone consider one's self intelligent if he or she zones out eternity and acts as if this brief time on earth is all there is?

Reflecting on the afterlife, the brilliant mathematician, physicists, and philosopher Pascal wrote:

> When I consider the short duration of my life, swallowed up in the eternity before and after, the little space which I fill, and even can see, engulfed in the infinite immensity of spaces of which I am ignorant, and which know me not, I am frightened, and am astonished at being here rather than there; for there is no reason why here

rather than there, why now rather than then. Who put me here?[4]

Such creature frailty! Such imponderables bearing down on one so human! Who, I ask, has not had sentiments like these? Who among us can fathom how vast this universe is, how limited our understanding is, and not stoop to ponder in primitive silence or creature fear? I'll tell you who! Modern man—chummy and chatty and full of smiles! The man fascinated by trifles yet unaffected by truth! The man of fashion, trends, technology, and anything else that helps him keep pace with others zipping down the fast lane of life. This man who notices everything but sees nothing, who moves speedily but goes nowhere, who is determined to get to the top but stoops ever so low to get there!

Isn't it about time that we stop this mad race where all that should have meaning darts by as a mere blip, and all that should have value recedes into the background as an unfocused blur? We need to *stop*, and to *think*, and to make some decisions about the good life—even if we are Christians and think we are already well-acquainted with this subject.

Mistaken Church Ideas about Good

The Bible says that God's ways are not our ways and his thoughts are not are thoughts. So has this Grand Canyon gap closed for you? Would *you* say that you are on now God's wavelength in this matter of understanding what good is?

Ask many Christians to define this fruit of the Spirit, and the definition offered will strongly resemble one of Satan's counterfeits. Most Christians will acknowledge they don't always do good, yet they believe they can do good, once they set their minds on doing so. Is this what you think?

The rich young ruler approached Jesus one day, saying, "Good master ..."—but Jesus immediately interrupted him to say there is none that does good, except God. In saying this, Jesus wasn't distancing himself from this appellation; he was simply clarifying it.[5] Yes, he was good! And yes, he was the Master! But that word "good" needed clarification.

You may reason that "good" in this sense means the *full* measure of good, what some would call perfection. But get this: Without God at work, man is incapable of *any* good—not one deed, thought, or aspiration! Adam at his pious best is still going down to a tragic fall! Moreover, the shame that will greet him there will send him into hiding once more, this time with an agonizing awareness that his goodness is much more than tainted; it is irreparably ruined.

Many Christians think, "Well, now that I read my Bible, worship, pray, give, and fast, I am making considerable progress." However, didn't Paul do all these things, and do them with a diligence that far exceeds the zeal of anybody else? Yet he found himself on the wrong road in this pursuit of good, and therefore he wasn't nearly as optimistic as others seem to be.

After the rich young ruler declared that he had kept all the Sinai commandments since his youth, he then asked Jesus, "What lack I yet?" In reality, this rich young ruler had never kept any of these commandments! Apparently, religion had done to him what mental health sloganeering has done to us—it anesthetized him from having any consciousness of his real condition.

Perhaps, to you, this triggers thoughts of coming short, of missing by degrees, of a careless reflection offered in dim light. But that isn't what this means at all. *Everything* about this man's goodness was false! He didn't just come short; the rich young ruler's efforts were in another category entirely. Making that very point, A.B. Simpson described what happened next in this conversation.

> Then the Lord presses the keen edge of the sword of truth into his hypocrisy that had so longed deceived him. It was as if he had said, "You think you have obeyed the second table of the law and loved your neighbor as yourself, for that is the real spirit of the law. Well, I'm going to apply a simple test. If you love your neighbor as yourself, it will not be difficult for you to share with him your wealth; and if you love the Lord with all your heart, it will be no sacrifice to you to give up all and follow him. Therefore, as a simple test of your love to your neighbor and your love to God, go,

sell your possessions and give to the poor, and you will have treasure in heaven. Then come, follow me."

And, lo, that man's castle of righteousness crumbled into dust ... the illusion was gone, his dream of righteousness and eternal life melted into air ....[6]

The morality of this man, as with every man who comes into this world, wasn't just defective, having only an imperceptible flaw here and there; it was a complete counterfeit, coming nowhere close to the qualities the Holy Spirit releases in a man.[7]

When Paul began to see this issue more clearly, he, this brainy brain whose spirituality soared stratospheres above other religious men (even the theologians of his day), came to abject despair. Could it be, then, that there is something immensely important about the good life many people *haven't* seen? And could it also be that their assessment of their own spiritual progress is without scriptural foundation?

Some will counter this thought with a theology that talks about our "position in Christ" and his righteousness credited to our account. Well, that's true, but isn't it also true that an *observable* goodness is expected from us on earth? Doesn't Scripture exhort believers to exhibit good deeds (I Timothy 2: 9, 10; 4:12; 5:10; 6:18) that will bring glory to the Father in heaven (Matthew 5:14-16; John 15:8)? And doesn't it do so with the view that this isn't just an idealistic goal but is actually doable?

Agreeing that good deeds are a part of God's standard, these Christians will quickly pivot from this acknowledgment to point out that even the Apostle Paul said he was the chief of sinners, that he had not yet obtained what he was aspiring to. And in saying this, these Christians expose the fact they have never understood the problem, nor understood its solution. What Paul discovered is still beyond them.

There are important discoveries that will expose all the wrong answers about what the good life is, and, if made, will put us on a course that lifts life, here and hereafter, to all the robust significances that the word "good," as the Bible uses it, fully implies.

That the world lacks understanding about the good life is no surprise, given its diminished capacity to access and process spiritual truth. But the degree misunderstanding exists in the church *is* surprising, given Scripture's complete explanation about these things. To think one's aspiration for moral goodness frequently entails frustrating defeats is a big mistake. So, desiring to overcome this deficit, we must seek clarity from the only source where it can be found, Scripture.

The Deep Imprinting of the Moral Imperative

It is commonly believed that we ought to be good. No matter which nation we live in, or which generation we belong to, there is this almost-universal consensus that decrees the necessity of pursuing good and decries any intent to pursue evil. This fact says something most profound about both our makeup and our Maker. In reflecting on this studied and observable tendency, we have to ask ourselves why a moral "oughtness" exists to such a remarkable extent.

Theoretically, a different scenario could be true. History could show an evolutionary trend where man, in the beginning, was inclined toward evil but eventually became good. Or, as we contemplate alternatives, history could show considerable variations among individuals and cultures, wherein certain personality types pedestal evil and certain cultures unabashedly admire wickedness. But this is precisely what both the sociologist and the anthropologist will tell you do not exist.

In his book, *The Abolition of Man*, C.S. Lewis delivers a stinging rebuke to our education system's attempt to reconfigure moral values through subterfuge and illogic. Lewis writes:

> There never has been, and never will be, a radically new judgment of value in the history of the world ... The human mind has no more power of inventing a new value than of imagining a new primary color, or, indeed, of creating a new sun and a new sky for it to move in.[8]

The philosopher Will Durant spoke nonsense when he declared that morals "are changing today like clouds before the wind."[9] Morals are hardly a puff of transient vapor, interesting in their formations, while having no standing over the earth. Yet, the progressives among us remain determined in their efforts to inculcate their notions of morality as widely and deeply as they can. That they do so in supposedly moral terms is profoundly necessary, since a moral code is embedded in us all.

Even the few who are hellbent in their lifestyles—gang members, for example, who will kill for drugs—have their own version of a moral code. And should this code be infringed upon, an immediate indignation will flare, and a speedy enactment of supposed justice will result! Convoluted though this thinking is, the idea, "this isn't right," appears even among this group, though the logic of their lifestyle would require commending what isn't right, and certainly not condemning it.

It seems, then, that this obligation to right and repudiation of wrong is inescapable, even among the worst of us. This reality surfaces something profound in the constitution of man. Pascal, taking note of this fact, wrote, "It is a singular thing to consider that there are people in the world who, having renounced all the laws of God and nature, have made laws for themselves which they strictly obey ...."[10]

Since ethical standards—internally perceived and externally codified—vary little in man's history, it might be assumed there is no need to define what goodness is. However, definitions *are* necessary, since the devil isn't going to keep his hands off an issue as important as this.

George MacDonald seemed to deem such defining unimportant when he said, "Could Jesus by one word have set to rest all the questionings of philosophy as to the supreme good and the absolute truth, I venture to say that word he would not have spoken."[11] True, a point-counterpoint philosophical debate may have been bypassed, but not the topic itself. After all, goodness was the issue that most divided Jesus from contemporary Jewish thought.

Nevertheless, MacDonald further expounded his own objections by writing:

The Lord cared for neither isolated truth, nor for orphaned deed. It was truth in the inward parts, it was the good heart, the motivation of good deeds that he cherished. It was the live, active, breathing good he came to further. He didn't care for any speculation in morals or religion.[12]

Speculation, no; but definition, yes. Eternal values will vaporize if clear and concrete definitions are withheld.

There is considerable difference between philosophical speculation and biblical revelation. Throughout Scripture, especially in the wisdom literature of the Old Testament, extensive explanations are offered to differentiate the good God can bless from the counterfeits he denounces. So contrary to MacDonald, Scripture does indeed sanction this kind of defining.

Where Scripture is silent, and where definitions aren't forthcoming and distinctions aren't made, the proper protocol is to respect this absence of information without substituting speculation for revelation. But because Scripture isn't silent on this subject, the defining we will now undertake is warranted.

Philosophical Definitions of Goodness

Down through the years, there have been several criteria advanced for determining what constitutes good. John Stuart Mill defined this attribute as "that which does the greatest good to the greatest number." But the problem with this definition is that it allows such evil as euthanasia to be implemented if it is perceived that distinct minorities like the aged or the infirmed have become too much of a burden for the rest of society to bear.

Actually, Hitler could have functioned quite well under this definition when arguing that the elimination of Jews, the subjugation of blacks, and the propagation of a superior Arian race served the ultimate good of his mostly all-white society.

Other people, such as Immanuel Kant, related good to that which produces happiness. Without ever denying religion outright, the deism in Kant reduced religion to morality, thereby removing from the believer the only reliable and effective ability to obey.

Elton Trueblood said of Kant: "He argued for the necessary union of virtue and happiness, which he called the *Summum Bonum* ...."[13] And while Kant's view of happiness isn't as shallow as it sounds, what's to keep it from degenerating into precisely that as others employ this same criterion? For example, let the Freudians, with their view of pleasure, get a hold of Kant's definition; and soon enough this view will get elasticized into gross immorality.

The existential view of goodness, crassly stated by Ernest Hemingway, declares: "Good is what I feel good after, and bad is what I feel bad after."[14] But if unguided by a properly functioning conscience, this perspective can quickly degenerate into hedonism, a way of life that makes pleasure a god.

A popular song during the 1970s expressed Hemingway's view in a slightly different way, stating, "It can't be wrong if it feels so right." Really? One's *feelings* are an accurate judge of morality? To the contrary! Feelings are an unreliable source, deserving all too often to be thrown out of court!

Solipsism says that good is whatever self says it is. According to this view, since religion and tradition are unreliable, only self is the arbiter of good. This is a philosophy that presupposes self to be what the Bible clearly says it is not—full of wisdom and always accurate in its discernment. But anyone possessing an optimism like *this*, despite an avalanche of evidence that proves quite the opposite, can never be taken seriously.

Secularism says that good is whatever society says it is. In his book, *Knowing Man*, J.I. Packer notes:

> The word "secularism" was coined by G.J. Holyoake in a fine flush of Victorian indignation to mean "the doctrine that morality should be based on regard to the well-being of mankind in the present life to the exclusion of all considerations drawn from belief in God or a future state."[15]

Consistent with this perspective, Will Durant said, "Nothing is immoral unless it injures one's fellows"[16] This view, you will notice, is nothing but horizontal morality; the vertical has been obliterated! And can morality exist apart from God? Jean Paul Richter wrote, "Take God out of the world and everything is annihilated, every higher joy of the mind, every love, and only the wish for mental suicide would remain ...." It is in this kind of world, he said, that "only the devil and the beast would still desire to exist."[17]

With much justification, then, A.W. Tozer declared, "The idea that God exists and that he is sovereign in the heavens is absolutely fundamental to human morality."[18] Attempts to construct morality apart from God make as much sense as attempting to plant a garden in midair. But how? *There's no ground!* Likewise, moral definitions based on a brief consultation with self are groundless. The Greek sophists, believing man is the measure of all things, concocted morality this way. But on so flimsy a foundation, morality is utilitarian, transitional, and relative.

People determined to view morality as the sophists did seek to diminish the ethics of Jesus, even if they have to impose their premises on history in order to do so. For example, some relegate the ethics of Jesus to the time he lived—and that's it. Paying tribute to his ethics while dismissing its relevance for today, these enlightened ones inform us (with professorial smugness) that the morality Jesus taught was fine for the first-century Palestinian world but should not be binding on our more modern and sophisticated world.

G.K. Chesterton took to task these critics, saying, "The truth is that when critics have spoken about the local limitations of the Galilean, it has always been a case of the local limitations of the critics."[19] They impose the dubious standards of their age (as if assured of the superiority of these standards) onto the ethics of Jesus, which their own declarations prove they never understood in the first place.

G.K. Chesterton then argued, "Whatever else is true, it is emphatically not true that the ideas of Jesus of Nazareth were suitable to his time but are no longer suitable to our time. Exactly how suitable they were to his time is perhaps suggested in the end of his story."[20] Now, had these critics shown *any* skill of observation, they would have seen that the standards of righteousness taught by Jesus transcended the time he lived. They neither mirrored the culture, nor reflected the age. Thus, Chesterton correctly asserted, "It is not the morality of another age, but it might be of another world."[21]

Indeed! What Jesus said was not limited by first-century Palestinian thought. It is really the rival opinions of the critics that are limited by specious thought floating smoothly in the stream of modern opinion.

By dismissing Jesus and by eliminating Scripture, "good" then becomes whatever consensus opinion or ruling authority says it is. Such thinking, though, gets dangerously close to what was true at the time of the Judges, wherein it was said that each man did that which was right in his own eyes (Judges 17:6; 21:25).

The verdict of history regarding the usage of this moral barometer is that it resulted in utter corruption. Scripture declares people did evil in the sight of the Lord (Judges 3:12; 4:1; 6:1; 13:1)—constantly! And for that they paid an enormous price! In his *Pensées*, Pascal provided an explanation for what occurred, saying "… since man has lost the true good, everything can appear to be equally good to him, even his own destruction …."[22]

Others today, less philosophical in their approach, say "good' is what their parents say it is, or what their conscience says it is, or what culture says it is, or what tradition says it is, or what religion says it is. But Mom and Dad can be wrong, and one's conscience can be contaminated, and culture can be corrupted, and both tradition and religion can be out of sync with the Word of God.

So what constitutes a good work? And more precisely, what are its components? And what are its characteristics? These questions, deserving answers more reliable than what we have thus far considered, will claim our attention in the next chapter. There, we will see both clear criteria and precise definitions, each which is knowable to a believer, yet scarcely known by most believers today.

So the mystery continues.

Reflection Questions

1. List two observations in this chapter that resonated with you about the way culture anesthetizes us to the real condition of our soul. Explain why.

2. Have you given much thought of what will happen to you after you die? If so, suggest the direction of these thoughts and the motivation that triggered them. And if not, indicate why you haven't.

Chapter 3
The Good Life—Part II

Definitions matter, especially when the needed outcome depends on accuracy. Just as the pharmacist has to be precise when filling a prescription, and the aeronautical engineer has to be precise when constructing an aircraft, and the accountant has to be precise when entering numbers on a spreadsheet, so, too, theology has to be precise when defining goodness.

Many people think otherwise. To them, the idea of defining morality with certitude is both impossible and undesirable. Far preferable to them is people making their own choices, for in this way individual opinion is honored and a variety of views are protected.

That may sound good, but are these views correct? And are the people who make them able to understand good and evil by simply taking counsel with themselves? To say that they are is to say there's no need for Scripture to provide a standard; man already knows it. Really? Well, the whole of Scripture's wisdom literature casts doubt on that idea!

How naïve to think that "enlightened" man doesn't need God's revelation, that contaminated thinking isn't a problem today, that Satan's guile has never deceived, that an impure heart was never tempted, that righteousness was never watered down by personal preferences.

Proverbs 21:2 speaks of the rationalizations of men and how—lo and behold!—all that they do is right in their own eyes. But Isaiah 5:21 pronounces woe against those wise in their own eyes. The previous verse claims they call evil, good and good, evil. Indeed, Proverbs 26:12 says of such a man, there is more hope for a fool than for him! So do you think a little more humility might be in order here?

Since goodness is rooted in God, and since he alone knows all its ways and ramifications, turning to *the* expert is really not a bad idea—especially when taking into account man's proclivity to rationalize moral choices, warp ethics, and plunder holiness. Such ineptitude on *man's* part necessitates a good God revealing the standards by which man will be judged. Just here, you must know that, contrary to secular thinking, a trustworthy standard *does* exist. And because God is good, he isn't going to stay silent about a subject where the stakes for us are sky-high.

The Need for an Authoritative Standard

To avoid ethical relativism (which declares that moral clues are embedded in the situation and that our ability to perceive them is limited only by our cerebral capacities), God provided a standard beyond human genius and beyond the fluctuations of time and space. This standard, rooted in his nature (and not in our opinions), is revealed, not by a new generation's way of thinking but by the eternal Word of God.

Can you see how this criterion dispenses with the obfuscations of philosophy and the inadequacies of other competing standards? Francis Schaeffer observed, "There is no Law behind God, because the furthest thing back is God. The moral absolutes rest upon God's character."[1]

The title of one of Schaeffer's books, *He is There and He is Not Silent*, gets to the heart of his work in apologetics. Confronting secular philosophies, Schaeffer presented compelling reasons for affirming Jesus is God and that the Bible is God's unique and authoritative revelation to man.

One might wonder why the Bible should be trusted to this extent. Declarations from a faith perspective may satisfy people who share this faith, but what about the people who don't? Why should these people accept Scripture as *the* standard for moral decision making? The Bible doesn't mean anything to them.

This question is certainly a fair one, and therefore deserves a thoughtful response. For any notion that posits faith as the ultimate guide may appear dangerously close to Russian roulette. What spares Christians this risk, however, and what keeps us from taking a blind leap into the unknown, is the fact Scripture offers objective, verifiable evidence for authenticating its truth claims.

Actually, God gave man a revelation that doesn't require a big leap of faith to trust. There are, for example, hundreds of minutely-detailed prophecies in the Bible, impressive in both number and fulfillment. So do the so-called scriptures of other religions have this feature? No, they do not. They may offer poetry, philosophy, and an array of moral teachings, but what these revered religious writings don't offer are specific prophecies that can be confirmed or rejected by historical investigation.

One importance of biblical prophecies, then, besides the inspired content of each, is the statistical evidence they collectively provide to authenticate Scripture. In his book, *Science Speaks*, Professor Peter Stoner employed established principles of mathematical probability to assess the viability of these prophecies. Assigning probability factors to each prophecy according to the age of the prophecy, the specificity of the prophecy, the number of components in the prophecy, etc., Dr. Stoner calculated that the fulfillment of eight of these ancient prophecies by a single person who lived many centuries later is 10 to the 17th power.

Professor Stoner further stated that the equivalency of this number can be conveyed by covering the entire state of Texas with silver dollars, two feet high, and then having a blind man pick, on his first attempt, the only silver dollar previously marked for selection. This, of course, would be a highly improbable accomplishment.

Professor Stoner also helped us to understand the probability of one man fulfilling forty-eight prophecies given hundreds of years before. This, he said, would be numerically equivalent of an almost incomprehensible number, 10 to the 157th power. So large is this number in fact that Professor Stoner likened it to all the known electrons in all the known mass of the entire universe. Now, if one of these electrons could be marked, and if a blind man had access to all these electrons, the likelihood of choosing the right one on the first try would be the same as the probability of Jesus fulfilling forty-eight Old Testament prophecies.

The astounding fact, though, is that Jesus fulfilled more than six times that number of prophecies! The actual number of minutely detailed prophecies he fulfilled is three-hundred twenty-four. In such a stunning and astonishing way, then, the predictive prophecies in Scripture confirm with unequaled certitude that Jesus is who he said he is and that the Bible is what it claims itself to be. Scripture is the breathed out Word of God, altogether trustworthy in its teachings and wholly reliable in its reports.

An objective study of predictive prophecies is more than sufficient to silence all doubters. According to Pascal, "The prophecies are the strongest proof of Jesus Christ."[2] For they convincingly credential the one book that uniquely proclaims his deity. Verification of these biblical prophecies gives strong assurance that Scripture, and Scripture alone, has authority for moral decision making.[3] Scripture has been forever esteemed and established by God as his reliable guide for daily life and eternal faith.

Biblical Definitions of Goodness

It was the Puritan theologian John Owen who said: "That good which the mind cannot discover, the will cannot choose, nor the affections cleave unto." Correctly defining good is therefore imperative, if the respective capacities of mind, will, and heart are to rightly align. Unless good is defined by Scripture, that which camouflages and counterfeits will find its voice and propagate serious errors.

With little reflection and a lot of opinions, a campaign of ethical confusion has been unleashed upon our culture, disseminating the view that man is not nearly as flawed as God says he is. The chirpy optimism of our world is hardly a reliable guide, because the surface view that marvels at modernity and acts as if achievements in technology translate into positive assessments about our soul is extraordinarily naïve. Exposing this fact, Disraeli astutely observed that too often "comfort" is mistaken for "civilization." The substitute of one for the other transacts, seemingly, by sudden impression, but could never endure a full examination. A pleasant environment means all is equally pleasant inside a person's heart? The exterior discloses the interior? Oh, my! Such discombobulated thinking!

Horatius Bonar talked about society's penchant for minimizing sin by supposing that these deeds can be "toned down into goodness" and that they deserve "no expulsion from Paradise, no deluge, no Sodom's fire." Society's view of sin, Bonar pointed out, concludes that sin "is not a thing for the judge, but for the physician; not a thing for condemnation, but for pity. It deserves no hell, no divine wrath, no legal sentence. It needs no atonement, no blood, no cross, no substitution of life for death."[4]

To this line of thinking, F.J. Huegel answered, "If God's wrath toward sin were something which could be lightly turned off, there would be no sure foundation for true moral order; the moral integrity of God would be shaken."[5] Properly understood, morality rests on the character of God. There can be no other sustainable basis!

Professor Paul Copan wrote:

> ... if God doesn't exist, then we simply do not have an adequate foundation for objective ethics—including intrinsic human dignity and rights, personal responsibility and moral obligation. Furthermore, if the divine grounding for morality is lacking, then (as Nietzsche argued) it is not a far step to undercut moral motivation as well.[6]

By definition, morality must reflect the holiness of God and not the slipshod performance of man. Moreover, this morality must be rooted in the life of a holy God, which, due to his grace, is posited even now in our new nature. G.D. Watson noted:

> There is a difference between a moral life and a spiritual life. A moral life has its eye on duty and

depends on our views of law. But a spiritual life has its eye on the life of God and can be produced only by faith ....[7]

The very power that draws us to this life produces qualities that will be approved in the Judgment. Everything else there will be passed over or punished.

Sin minimized in its consequence is sin minimized in its definition. Jacques Bossuet, a seventeenth-century orator in the court of Louis XIV, boldly set forth clear differences between God's virtue and the kind of virtue the world prefers. Of Christian virtue, he said it is "severe, constant, inflexible, always keeping closely and steadily to its rules of conduct, incapable of being turned aside from them by any influence, however powerful." And is this the virtue of the world? "No, the world will hear nothing of this sort of virtue," Bossuet insisted.

Extending his commentary on the supposed virtues practiced and paraded by the world, Bossuet wrote:

> There is quite another kind which the world fashions for itself, much more accommodating and plastic; a virtue adjusted, not to rules that would be too austere, but to the opinion, to the humors of men. This is commercial virtue; it will take care to not always break its word, but on certain occasions it will not be in the least degree scrupulous, and it will manage to keep up a good appearance at the expense of others. This is the virtue of the worldly-wise ... it is the specious mask behind which they hide their vices.[8]

Convenient morality like this may transact with broad smiles and hearty handshakes, but it cannot serve as the model we purpose to follow.

Often, even when a more serious attempt to display goodness is examined, the results prove disappointing. The kindhearted Richard Baxter had to admit as much when he wrote: "And now I see that good men are not so good as once I thought they were ... that nearer approach and fuller trial make the best appear more weak and faulty than their admirers at a distance think ...."[9] And have not others among us also observed the same thing?

Wanting to get past surface impressions so we're neither too rigid nor too charitable in our view, we must allow Scripture to accurately define what is morally good. Tozer said, "To be good a deed must pass three tests: What? How? And Why?"[10]

In his book, *Truths That Transform*, Dr. D. James Kennedy set forth three scriptural criteria that answer these questions. According to Scripture, no deed done by man is ever going to be deemed good in the eyes of God unless all three of these components exist.

First, the deed, if it is truly good, must coincide with the commands of Scripture. This criterion answers the question, what? And by answering this question, all excuses and equivocations are dismissed outright. G.D. Watson observed:

> A great many say, "I want to do better," and think that religion means to do better. You may do better and do better and go to perdition. Suppose a man tells ten lies a day, and says he will do better and tells only five, he does do better, but, he is a liar still! The Bible does not say "Do better," but "Do right."[11]

And because the Bible is unequaled in its authority, it makes total sense to state the obvious: Any deed contrary to what Scripture sets forth is not good, regardless of what tradition, religion, and popular opinion have to say.

The kind of thinking that talks about the morality of the twenty-first century makes as much sense as comparing an elephant with a tube of toothpaste on the basis that neither one rides a bicycle. Really? What do any of these things have to do with each other? Ethics doesn't vary with time! Just as God doesn't change, his laws never change.

C.S. Lewis was correct in his observation: "God may be more than moral goodness; he is not less. The road to the Promise Land runs past Sinai."[12] Therefore, good is what God says it is.[13] New decades and new polls determine nothing—except perhaps the extent of our ignorance and the fact of our rebellion.

The second criterion of a good work is that it must be achieved through the exercising of faith. This criterion answers the question, how? Hebrews 11:6 says that without faith it is impossible to please God. Romans 14:23 insists that whatever is not of faith is sin. John Hunter writes, "Even a quality of 'goodness' independent from God is sin!"[14]

The Bible tells us the just are to live by faith. For the Christian, all of life is to be a series of faith transactions. The believer isn't to depend on his own efforts, which Jesus said profit nothing (John 6:63), but should depend on the workings of the Holy Spirit to honor his promises.

The Old Testament illustrates this principle in a clear but shocking way. Proverbs 21:4 says that the plowing of the wicked is sin. To understand what is being said here, get a picture in your mind of "Silent Sam," a hardworking farmer who gets up before the sun does and labors under its heat, day in and day out. Then, long after the sun sets, this hardworking man comes home, eats a bite or two, then tumbles into bed and into the arms of sleep.

Sam isn't a Christian, mind you, but he is diligent in taking care of his family, and often helps his neighbors. Nevertheless, though the hard work Sam does is consistent with the first criterion (Scripture's command for a man to work), the fact he does this without faith in God means he is only sustaining his rebellion, and therefore his isn't a good work! Even if Sam were a Christian but undertook this labor independent from God, it still wouldn't be a good work. Having done this work with human energy and not divine, it will be rejected by the Lord on that last day (I Corinthians 3:12-15).

Oswald Chambers exclaimed, "I wonder how many of us are living on the virtues of our grandparents! The natural virtues are remnants of what the original creation of humankind once was ...."[15] At first glance, these virtues, like the virtues of Sam, may appear to be commendable. But not so, according to the criteria set forth by Scripture! A closer inspection uncovers their flaws.

The third criterion of a good work is that it be done for the glory of God. This criterion answers the question, why? I Corinthians 10:31 says "... whatever you do, do all to the glory of God." Similarly, Colossians 3:17 says, "... whatever you do in word and deed, do all in the name of the Lord, giving thanks to God ...." Colossians 3:23 offers a similar point of view, "And whatever you do, do it heartily, as to the Lord and not to men." F.B. Meyer declared, "The service may be great or small, conspicuous or obscure, but the glory of God must be the supreme passion."[16]

With regard to this criterion, Dr. Kennedy offered this clarifying comment:

> It makes no difference how beautiful a deed may be in itself. It makes no difference how highly polished, how magnificent and extraordinary, how much effort and energy goes into the work, if its direction is not right, it matters not at all and the work is not good; it is sin.[17]

In illustrating this point, Abraham Kuyper, the Dutch theologian, invited us to picture two very expensive yachts. One yacht may appear just as valuable as the other. But what would happen if the rudder of one of the yachts were wrongly directed? Well, if not corrected, this yacht would smash on the rocks! So, given this eventuality, it is the other yacht that is much preferred.

Similarly, when others view what appears to be a very splendid ministry, they may not see what God sees—the real motive inspiring it. Just know that motive is always critical to God's definition of a good work. If motive isn't directed toward the glory of God, that ministry will smash on the rocks of God's judgment.

Thomas Boston, the early eighteenth-century Reformed pastor from Berwickshire, Scotland, summed up this point well: "A man's most glorious actions will at last be found to be but glorious sins, if he hath made himself, and not the glory of God, the end of those actions." With probing insights, F.B. Meyer pressed this point, determined that we should see if our work really is for God's glory: "For if not—if in your secret soul you seek the sweet voice of adulation, if you are conscious of a wish to pass the results of your work into newspaper paragraph or the talk of men—be sure that deterioration is fast corrupting your service, as rottenness the autumn fruit."[18]

Do you see the dilemma the person trusting good works to save him has? He is hoping that somehow the good will outweigh the bad and that on that basis a God of mercy will save him and then sandpaper rough edges off his soul just before the Judgment.

But the fact is this man doesn't have one good work to his name! Not one! Affirming this truth, Jesus said that a bad tree cannot produce good fruit (Matthew 7:18). *Cannot*, it must be emphasized. The desire and the ability to be good, and to do good, simply don't exist within the nature we were born with.[19]

To those who think otherwise—that is, to those who still don't know the Lord—A.B. Simpson said:

> You are trying to be good with a bad heart. You are trying to serve God with a nature utterly depraved and fallen. You are trying to bring a clean thing out of an unclean. As well you might try to develop a dove out of a hawk, or a fawn out of the groveling swine.[20]

The morality coming from those who are not Christian is qualitatively different from the morality coming from those who are Spirit-filled Christians.[21] In fact, so different are these two types of morality, G.D. Watson was led to say, "... all the morality—be they ever so moral—of a million unregenerate souls would not equal the life of the humblest believer truly born of God."[22]

And should a non-Christian, in a dispensation of enlightened awareness, attempt to produce this higher morality, he would encounter the deep-seated reality C.S. Lewis observed: "No man knows how bad he is until he has tried very hard to be good."[23]

John Gerstner, a twentieth-century professor of church history, was even more blunt when he wrote, "The main thing between you and God is not so much your sins; it's your damnable good works."

To the thinking person, questions have to be buzzing the brain at this point as he or she comes to the edge of their thinking and begins to see how different God's thinking on this subject really is. Voltaire argued, "There is but one morality, as there is but one geometry."[24] Little did this atheist understand how profoundly wrong he was![25] Obfuscations like Voltaire's blur dramatic distinctions; accordingly, they are much like the worldly maxim:

> There's a little bit of good in the worst of us,
> There's a little bit of bad in the best of us,
> So it little behooves the best of us
> To say anything about the worst of us.[26]

What minimizing! And all for a purpose, too—so nothing much will be said about good and evil! Perhaps George Bernard Shaw shed light on this avoidance tendency when he remarked, "A nation's morals are like its teeth: the worse they are decayed, the more it hurts to touch them." This is exactly why we in the decadent West don't want to touch the subject of personal morality—because it would be painful to do so! Nevertheless, more needs to be said— particularly about the problem, when it comes to complying with God's moral standards, but also about the solution, which Paul never would have found on his own.

In the next two chapters we will see both: the problem clearly defined and the solution correctly set forth! So, get ready! Because this part of the mystery is about to be solve

Reflection Questions

1. List two observations you thought were helpful in the discussion of adequate and inadequate authorities for moral decision making.

2. What thoughts do you have about "Silent Sam"?

Chapter 4

What God Says about Being Good—Part I

Unlike some of the older mysteries where "shoe leather" and hard work eventually broke the case, today's mysteries involve extensive use of modern technology. CSI investigations will feature computer databases for DNA testing, engineering-based projections for determining bullet-entry angles, and chemical analysis of, say, a paint chip left at the crime scene. It can be quite fascinating to observe how science contributes to solving a mystery.

Regarding the mystery of the true identity of "good," let's see, then, what kind of help we can get from the lab. In one sense, divine revelation functions like both a microscope and a telescope.

Ask a child if the desk his books rest upon is solid, and he will assure you that it is. Yet, high-powered microscopes render a very different conclusion. Actually, the composition of that desk includes all manner of molecules floating around with high mobility and loose connectivity. This, the human eye could never see—except through a microscope.

Norman Grubb further explains: "... for years people surmised that the ultimate form of matter was the atom—hard, round, indivisible particles like minute billiard balls. Not a scientist believes that today."[1] Erich Sauer says the atom "is now seen to be a world of frantic, whirling movement."[2]

Well, in much the same way high-powered microscopes reveal interior dynamics of matter invisible to the natural eye, divine revelation reveals the interior dynamics of a behavior that otherwise would have gone undetected. G.D. Watson wrote, "... the microscope will take us down into the finest details of nature, and show us in a drop of water, or in the eye of an insect, marvels of wisdom and precision of workmanship ...."[3] We see this wisdom also on display when we inspect, with the assistance of Scripture, the interior intricacies of a good work.

By contrast, the telescope enables us see things in outer space that the squinting eye could never see, with or without glasses. Look upward, and we will see a few stars twinkling above. But what we will never see on our own are spheres of burning gas much larger than the earth. And what we will also never see is how far away these planets are, and the spectacle of trillions of them spanning the universe. Only a telescope will reveal what G.D. Watson called "the magnitude of astronomy, which tells us of countless worlds and solar systems ...."[4]

Likewise, divine revelation exercises a telescopic function by enabling us to see into faraway worlds, and even into the far-off future. This longer and more distant perspective is necessary if the whole story of goodness is to be understood.

When it comes to defining good and the life this quality produces, we dare not trust the natural perspective when forming our opinions, no matter how sensible and plausible these conclusions appear to be. A vision-enhanced perspective is needed! And this comes best from the God who created both protons and planets. Moreover, because he did all with his word, it is to his Word that we will turn again with an intent to discover what God established in the moral realm of life.

Thus far, we have used the microscopic function of God's Word for seeing what we never would have seen in the natural, an up-close view of what constitutes a good work. Having seen that, we will now use the telescopic view of God's Word to understand, from a broader and longer perspective, what goodness and righteousness really are. J.I.

Packer said, "If the Christian community does not teach righteousness today, nobody will. But the Western Christians today are scarcely able to teach righteousness, because they themselves have scarcely learned it."[5]

They have been diligent to learn a lot of other things, as they sought advanced degrees from the universities and the highest credentials applicable to their chosen profession. But no such effort is expended to learn what God means by good. George MacDonald wrote, "How the earthly father would love a child who would creep into his room with a troubled face and sit down at his feet, saying, when asked, what he wanted, "I feel so naughty, papa, and I want to get good."[6]

So is this an expression of your heart? Is your heart tender and teachable? When it comes to learning how to be good, is there enough humility to revise your views?

Prompted by Packer's warning, we will now seek to remedy the discrediting deficit accounting for our moral ineptitude. As we shall see next, there are four kinds of righteousness the Bible identifies. The first of these might be called innate righteousness.

Innate Righteousness

When Adam was fashioned by the hand of God, he began life on this earth as no other man has since. Having been created in the image of God (Genesis 1:26), he began a little lower than the angels (Psalms 8:5), and thus represented the pinnacle of God's creation (Genesis 1:31). Offering a summary statement, A.B. Simpson said of Adam:

> Man is the special handiwork of God. He is not the blind result of fortuitous elements and atoms, not a mere evolution from lower forms of light. He is created by the very hand of God himself, as a distinct order of existence, and the object of the most deliberate counsel, and all the resources of the divine wisdom and power.[7]

Unlike ourselves, Adam was born with a nature totally inclined toward good, having no propensities for evil. He was not the pathetic primitive of evolutionist construction.

Instead, impressive in every way, he was the prototype of all that God desired man to be.

In fact, if we at the time had a confirming role about who should represent the human race, that vote would have been enthusiastically unanimous—for Adam, perfect in every way, was the logical choice! In him, there was no trajectory of gradual improvement; he *started* life mature and moral.

But then—irrationally but not inevitably—Adam sinned. You should know that nothing in the biblical account suggests Adam was overwhelmed, or, for that matter, even deceived. So why did he fall? The Bible doesn't answer this question fully, except to say that Adam exercised his will in known disobedience. A.B. Simpson wrote, "... Adam was not deceived but being tempted by his fallen wife he yielded consciously, perhaps from many a plausible consideration of love for her and partnership with her in her fall ...."[8]

Extending this view, Jack Taylor added: "If Satan can't defeat you by frontal attack, he will defeat someone whose defeat will defeat you."[9] This is, perhaps, what happened to Adam.

The Bible makes it clear that Eve was deceived by the serpent, and therefore partook of the forbidden fruit. This outcome obviously presented a dilemma to Adam. For now—suspecting, maybe, that Eve would be banished from the garden—Adam had to choose between life in the garden without Eve, or a separation from God with Eve.

Although the alternatives may not have been that clearly defined in Adam's mind, what is known is that Adam allied himself with Eve and not with God. And thus, by choosing Eve, Adam sinned into existence what had never existed before—a nature that was totally depraved. According to Romans, chapter 3, this nature was so depraved, not only did it have no interest in God, it had no capacity for God.

The doctrine of total depravity, as articulated by the Reformers, doesn't teach that every man is as evil as he could possibly be. This doctrine actually speaks to the *extensiveness* of evil (it adversely affects every part of a man's life) and not to the *intensiveness* of evil (it corrupts every man in the most extreme way possible). There are admirable qualities even in fallen man, but none of these are sufficient for salvation.

As far back as Genesis, the Lord recognized the total depravity of man, saying every inclination of his heart is evil from childhood (Genesis 8:21). When David said, "in sin did my mother conceive me," he wasn't casting aspersions on his mother. He was simply acknowledging that he was born with an Adamic nature that didn't have to go to school to learn the ways of evil. This evil came naturally to him, as it does for everyone else, since they too possess an Adamic nature.

The way Tozer characterized fallen man is accurate: "We inhabit a world suspended between heaven and hell, alienated from one and not yet abandoned to the other. By nature we are unholy and by practice we are unrighteous."[10] Hence, E.M. Bounds declared: "No tinkering on the old heart can make it right. It is as hard as a stone and crooked as the Jordan. No melting it can make it soft, and no human effort can make it straight."[11]

This is the state into which mankind fell, but it is not the state in which mankind began. The importance of Adam's beginnings relates to its theological and psychological implications. The necessity for examining our heredity was rightly affirmed by A.B. Simpson, who said:

> The human mind requires an answer to the question concerning the origin and nature of things. The world as we find it must be accounted for in some way. Philosophers and scientists have sought to account for it, the one by speculation, the other by observation, and in their labors they have come upon many useful and inspiring facts. But they have not found the final truth. That comes by revelation and inspiration.[12]

Pointing out a major difference between observation and revelation, Samuel Chadwick noted, "In the scriptural account man was made a little lower than God and fell; in the scientific account he is made a little higher than the brute and is rising all the time."[13] Enormous implications stem from these very divergent views.

Theologically, it can be stated that Adam was "very good" when God created him, since he was capable of an unhindered intimacy with God. Now, if man never had this beginning, and instead entered the world with gorilla grunts and stupid stares, the psychological impact on us would be huge!

In the same way adopted children desire information about their biological heritage so they can better understand their own identity, we feel a compulsion to know more about the beginnings of mankind. But if this heritage is one of slime and chance combustion, it is exceedingly difficult not to be negatively influenced by that, despite all this humanistic blather about man's unlimited potential and other such things pontificated at graduation ceremonies (which only cause the eyes to roll in deserved disdain).

If not for the testimony of Scripture, we would have to accept a view of man's beginnings that J.W. Dawson described in his book, *The Story of the Earth and Man*. The primitive model, Dawson said, depicts the ancestral specimen of the race as:

> ... a coarse and filthy savage, repulsive in feature and gross in habits, warring with his fellow-savages, and warring yet more remorselessly with every living thing he could destroy, tearing half-cooked flesh, and cracking marrow bones with stone hammers, sheltering himself in damp and smoky caves, with no eye heavenward, and with only the first rude beginnings of the most important arts of life.[14]

The poet Edwin Markham once asked, "Who blew out the light in this man's brain?" Though posed in a different context, this question could hardly be asked of first man. For if this profile of primitive man is true, he seems to have made his entrance into this world with more motor skills than mental skills—and without the slightest hint about a God in heaven! But, again, Scripture disallows this imaginary depiction by describing first man as the apex of creation and not the ape of evolution.

Imputed Righteousness

In contrast to the original assessment that man was "very good," the Bible declares of fallen man that "there is none righteous, no not one" (Romans 3:10). And just two verses later it repeats this point, using a staccato rhythm for emphasis, "... there is none who does good, no, not one."

In attempting to reinforce this truth, three very revealing questions are rhetorically asked in the book of Jeremiah (Jeremiah 13:23): Can a leopard change its spots? Can an Ethiopian change his skin? Can you do good who are accustomed to do evil? Here, the likelihood of man doing good is said to be the same as a leopard becoming spotless and a black man turning white—not very good odds!

As Pascal observed, "Nature always begins the same thing again, the years, the days, the hours ...."[15] Nature repeats! This is the same problem with human nature, too: It cannot contradict itself; it cannot act in any other way than what it is. Eventually, it repeats even what it disavows.

Given this degradation of the human heart, which the Bible says is "desperately wicked" (Jeremiah 17:9), the question is repeatedly asked in Scripture, how can a man be right with God? Job asked it (Job 9:2). Bildad asked it (Job 25:4). The rich young ruler asked it (Matthew 19:16). The Publicans asked it (Luke 3:12). The lawyer asked it (Luke 10:25). One crowd asked it of Jesus (John 6:28) and another crowd asked it of Peter (Acts 2:37). As well, Saul of Tarsus asked it (Acts 9:6) and the Philippian jailer asked it (Acts16:30).

This recurring question is actually the most important question anyone can ask. A person can make a mistake about a lot of things for which there may not be any grave consequences. But if one answers this question the wrong way, devastating consequences will come long before the grave, and certainly after it.

How the Bible answers this question differs radically from the answer given by every other religion, and even from the answers given by people of no religion. Contrary to the Bible, these other religions (and, as I say, even the people of no religion) unite in their view that acceptance into heaven (if heaven, or some equivalent of heaven, exists) will be granted on the basis of good works. According to this perspective, if the quantity and quality of these works merit approval, then heaven is gained.

This proves that all religions aren't different buses going in the same direction. The Christian "bus" is going in an entirely different direction. Christianity alone affirms that our goodness will never be good enough and that's why all of us need a Savior. But other religions, other philosophies, don't believe this at all.

With respect to these alternative approaches to salvation—the law way and the grace way—the Bible compares two mountains: Mount Sinai, which represents the law approach; and Mount Zion, which represents the grace approach (Hebrews 12:18-24). Consider the differences between these two approaches.

The rugged heights of Mount Sinai—dark red granite peaks as high as 8,000 feet—were literally on fire when God descended to give his law. Violent tremors repeatedly shook Sinai when this theophany occurred! And chances are, you'd be all shook up, too, once you understood what the law way to salvation required!

II Corinthians 3:7 declares that the Sinai way, the law way, is a "ministry of death," since no one could approach God in this manner and have it turn out well. Hebrews 12:19 speaks of a trumpet, and then a voice that sounded forth from Sinai. The trumpet was a summons to judgment (Revelation 11:15). The voice articulated condemnation that all those hearing it begged to cease.

Verse 20 says they couldn't endure what was commanded. The "they" in this verse is universal, for no man could endure it! Romans 3:19 says the law was given so every mouth would be stopped and all the world would become guilty before God. How excruciating to be horribly wrong and not have one valid excuse! But this is what the voice from Sinai was declaring—that everyone was guilty, guilty, guilty!

In contrast to the lightening, thunder, and smoke that belched its fury from Sinai is the grace way, the gospel way, the Mount Zion way to approach God. Mount Zion, once a Jebusite stronghold, was conquered by David in the seventh year of his reign and renamed Zion. It is interesting that while the temple was built on Mount Moriah, the people's affection was particularly strong toward Mount Zion. Indeed, so great was this affection that the intensely loyal Jew today isn't known as a Moriahnist but as a Zionist. "The joy of the whole earth is Zion!" the psalmist declared (Psalms 48:2).

The reason for this joy is partially rooted in history. Zion was the last citadel relinquished by the Canaanites. Concerning this citadel, A.B. Simpson wrote:

> All through the days of Joshua and his successors, the Canaanites succeeded in holding it. Throughout the centuries of the judges, all through the days of Saul and all through the early days of David they held it.
>
> The fortress was so impregnable that the haughty Canaanites bragged to their enemies that they would only need to garrison it with the blind and the lame. They even challenged their enemies to capture it from such handicapped defenders. David met that challenge, and Moab executed it by a glorious assault, taking by storm the heights of Zion from the last chieftains of Canaan.[16]

It was there that David reigned, that Solomon reigned; and it is there that one day, Jesus will reign.

There is, you should know, great significance in the fact that Zion isn't even much of a mountain. It's really more of a hill, at best a gentle slope, a terrain that is very accessible and approachable. It isn't intimidating, as was the thundering Sinai. The point, then, is clear: If we march up to God with our good works, we will experience the fire and fury of God's rejection. But if we come the grace way, the gospel way, we'll find the wide open arms of the Father.

What actually occurs during the grace approach is this: When we come to Jesus confessing our sin and seeking as a gift what Jesus obtained for us on Calvary's cross, the very righteousness of Jesus is imputed to us (Romans 4:22). Now, this word "imputed" is a lawyer's term, or a banking term; it means to put into one's account. Amazingly, what gets put into the believer's account is complete credit for the perfect life that Jesus lived! This imputing isn't something we experience. The Bible simply tells us that at the precise moment Jesus comes into our heart, God makes this all-important entry into the record books of heaven.[17]

In setting forth what the Bible says about imputed righteousness, we must be careful not to isolate this truth from the reality of a newly regenerated heart. Imputed righteousness should never be discussed as if it were an independent operation undertaken prior to, or unrelated to, conversion. A.W. Tozer strongly warned against zoning off imputed righteousness when he wrote:

> The commonly held idea seems to be that I can be as vile as the inside of a green, mucky sewer, but if and when I believe, the Lord drops a mantle of judicial righteousness upon me and immediately I am accepted by God as perfectly pure. It is my conclusion that a holy God would have to contradict himself to perform an operation like that.[18]

This mantle of righteousness does come upon us, but it does so only when Jesus comes into our heart and gives us his new nature. It is that transforming reality which makes imputed righteousness possible.

Attempts to classify the different types of righteousness can be useful, if we don't do so in a way that is a little too glib, a little too neat. Perhaps you have seen this kind of thing play out in real life. Just say you believe in Jesus, the evangelistic prospect is told, and—what do you know?—instantly, on heaven's big computer, the term "righteous" pops up by your name.

Such a version of high-tech bookkeeping may be convenient (though crass), but rattling off an explanation like this is very misleading. Imputed righteousness is not mechanical and procedural. It is rooted in the reality of the indwelling Christ. Learn that first, and then we can more profitably discuss other characteristics of righteousness.

Remember, while the blood took away our sin, entrance into heaven isn't singularly premised upon the absence of sin. Also required is the presence of absolute perfection—a perfection that none of us can come anywhere close to obtaining by ourselves! Therefore, being saved by his death, and now by his life, God imputes the righteousness of Jesus to us. This means that when we stand before God on that last day, God won't decide our entrance into heaven on the basis of *our* life, but will do so on the basis of *Jesus'* life.

Charles Spurgeon stated it this way:

> On a life I did not live
> On a death I did not die
> I stake my whole eternity.[19]

This is imputed righteousness. In the words of Martin Luther, "Oh, Lord Jesus, thou art my righteousness—I am thy sin!"

One might easily think that since the grace way is so much better than the law way, people would gladly make this transition. But the reason this hasn't been the case is because men want approval and not grace.

Grace says we're so bad off that we have to have it! This is the "offense of the gospel." It is what some might call the dark side of grace. The law way imagines there is something in our own dear, darling self that brings a twinkle to the eye of God. In our vanity, we see commendation being deserved and surely not condemnation.

A.W. Tozer tells of the self-assessment of a Jewish rabbi who triumphantly declared, "If there are two righteous men in the world, they are myself and my son; if one, it is myself."[20]

Accolades like this, however inaccurate these may be, motivate people to establish a righteousness of their own. And given this mindset, they simply will not leave the path of law and good works, even though this path necessitates eagle-eye detection for any flaw in their performance, and bulldog tenacity for pursuing perfection every step they take.

Because the Pharisees were so fastidious in their attempts to keep the law, they became a well-respected voice in Jerusalem more than a century before Jesus was born. As inheritors and articulators of the moral law, they felt compelled to spell out various implications of the law, which in their assessment, lesser minds could never discern. It was decreed, for example, that a woman could not look in a mirror on the Sabbath because if she saw a gray hair, she would exert forbidden energy to pull it out.

Also, no one was allowed to swat a pestering fly on the Sabbath because to do so was tantamount to "hunting."

With uncharacteristic tolerance, the Pharisees did say it was all right to eat an egg that had been laid on the Sabbath, as long as you killed the chicken that had sinned the next day. Ridiculous, right? But the Pharisees weren't the only ones who came up with this stuff. Even the great Reformer, John Calvin, that brilliant theologian whose intellectual abilities deservedly rank him at the top of most people's "the brainiest brain" list, fell into this trap of post-New Testament Pharisaism.

In an attempt to "Christianize" Geneva, the city in Switzerland he was charged to govern, the following prohibitions, according to William Manchester, were enacted:

> ... feasting, dancing, singing, pictures, statues, relics, church bells, organs, altar candles; "indecent or irreligious" songs, staging or attending theatrical plays; wearing rouge, jewelry, lace, or "immodest" dress; speaking disrespectfully of your betters; extravagant entertainment, swearing, gambling, playing cards, hunting, drunkenness; naming children after anyone but figures in the Old Testament; reading "immoral or irreligious" books.[21]

While the ethical and theological issues behind some of these forbidden diversions are considerably more worthy than their absurd conclusions, nevertheless, these conclusions do strain credibility. Such concerns hardly justify preposterous decisions! One has to wonder how any man steeped in Scripture could ever think this way? Should not conclusions like these have alerted, if not alarmed, the great John Calvin? Surely, in one lucid moment he would have seen what the end of this road looks like and then discarded these views with haste! But no, according to Philip Yancey:

> A Father who christened his son Claude, a name not found in the Old Testament, spent four days in jail, as did a woman whose hairdo reached an "immoral" height. The consistory beheaded a child who struck his parents. They drowned any single woman found pregnant. In separate incidents, Calvin's stepson and daughter-in-law were executed when found in bed with their lovers.[22]

One can only imagine what Calvin would do in a country as immoral as the United States! Talk about curbing our population growth! Once Calvin got through, there might not be enough people left to populate an average size town!

Whether it is the Pharisees of old or the mistaken John Calvin, the issue of holiness and how to be right with God were badly misconceived. The Pharisees believed that a man could obtain and sustain a right standing with God by keeping the law. James S. Stewart noted: "Pharisaism found its watchword in such sayings as this from Deuteronomy 6:25—'It shall be our righteousness if we observe to do all the commandments before the Lord our God, as he hath commanded us.'"[23]

But the Bible says that "by the deeds of the law shall no man be justified" (Romans 3:20). Keep in mind here that God's requirement for entering heaven includes total righteousness; so *our* goodness will never be good enough! And equally perilous to us is this fact: God refuses to grade on a curve! Hence, our desperate need for salvation—and for grace!

The standard by which we'll be judged is as high as heaven, and will never be lowered. Consequently, any attempt to meet this standard on our own is doomed at the outset. What should be painfully obvious to everyone, then, is that we need help! Exactly how this help was subsequently given will be addressed further in the next chapter.

Reflection Questions

1. What was the impact on you when you learned that your goodness would never be good enough?

2. Is there still a tendency in you to want to earn approval rather than to seek grace?

3. The A. W. Tozer quote on page 57 challenges a widespread misconception in the church. How has this quote helped you?

Chapter 5

What God Says about Being Good— Part II

Righteousness, like holiness, is one of those words that has an antiquated ring to it. This word often triggers images like the ones John White identified: "thinness, hollow-eyed gauntness, beards, sandals, long robes, stone cells, no sex, no jokes, hair shirts, frequent cold baths, fasting, hours of prayer, wild rocky deserts, getting up at 4 a.m., clean fingernails, stained glass, and self-humiliation."[1]

Caricatured in this way, it is little wonder that the popular preachers of our day are in no hurry to offer teachings on this subject. But by marginalizing righteousness, they have come to accept ideas contrary to the Bible, and have even used the Bible to do so. For example, when reminded by some worldling that there are "none righteous, no not one," preachers and church members alike will hang their heads and let silence prevail. Assuming that righteousness is an impossible ideal, they further assume that Christians and these worldlings stand on common ground. Of course, this isn't true.

This failure to understand righteousness has caused many Christians not to aspire to it, and therefore not to achieve it. *Achieve* it? The untaught believer will immediately protest this idea! "It's not *our* works that matter," they say. "Only the righteousness of God matters— and this comes to us as a gift." As support for their error, they'll quote Bible verses taken out of context (verses that deal with salvation and imputed righteousness), never realizing that there is another kind of righteousness that God gave. And once this other kind of righteousness is explained, the head-hanging in our churches will stop.

Although God did give us this righteousness, what he gave must *behaviorally* manifest! There is to be a difference, a tremendous difference, between the lifestyle of a Christian and that of a non-Christian. But to see this as we should, certain errors have to be dispelled first. Among them:

- The idea that righteousness refers only to certain record books in heaven and not to life on earth
- The idea that we are weak when it comes to temptation, and powerless when it comes to sin
- The idea that we'll continue to flounder in our faith and be in daily need of God's forgiveness

All these accepted-but-untrue ideas find correction when righteousness is more fully explained.

Imparted Righteousness

The third kind of righteousness we will now consider differs from imputed righteousness, in that it is something experienced and not just explained. In contrast with the righteousness put in a book, this righteousness, what we might call imparted righteousness, was actually put inside us. Professor James S. Stewart of Edinburgh said this about the term righteousness: "It stands for both the divine nature itself, and for a status given to men."[2]

There is righteousness in the *forensic* sense of a judicial judgment rendered; this is imputed righteousness. But there is also righteousness in the *essential* sense of divine life released; this is imparted righteousness. Samuel Chadwick explained, "A sacrifice at the right hand of God secures our standing, but unless righteousness be implanted as well as imputed, we should still be in the bondage of sin."

To be free from the power of sin we need a new life indwelling us, a life possessing capacities beyond what we've possessed before. To supply this need, Chadwick said, "The Christ who laid down his life for our sins took it again that he might impart it to us in the person of his Spirit."[3] Amplifying this thought, Andrew Murray wrote, "The life of Christ in you is your holiness."[4] Similarly, G. Campbell Morgan said, this holiness is:

> ... that inward grace of character which is not weak, soft, anemic, able only to sing songs of spiritual experience and to see visions of the heaven which is not yet. It is that inner refinement of heart and life and soul which comes from the indwelling Christ, and makes the life strong in its relationship to the world.

According to A.B. Simpson, this holiness, this righteousness, actually *became us*! In his book, *Portraits of the Spirit-Filled Personality*, Simpson speaks of "an interior, intrinsic and personal righteousness ... not the result of self-culture but the infusion of the very life and spirit of Jesus."[5] In his book, *Wholly Sanctified*, A.B. Simpson said, "The sanctified spirit is filled with the presence of the Spirit of the Lord."[6] Simpson rightly concluded that "the spirit born of God is separated in its own divine nature."[7]

Holiness resides in the born-again spirit, in man's new nature, and is not something we crank out on our own while asking God to bless our feeble efforts. Holiness is a quality of life that has already been given, Simpson said. "It is the inflow into man's being of the life and purity of the infinite, eternal and Holy One, bringing his own perfection and working out in his own will."[8]

Evan H. Hopkins wrote, "Practical holiness is not something that begins by *doing* but by *being* ...." Quoting Bishop Huntingdon, Hopkins described holiness this way: "It is not a mosaic of moralities, nor a compilation of merits, nor a succession of acts."[9] Even with the utmost sincerity we can try to crank out such a life, but will that work? It will not. G.D. Watson declared, "The ruin of spirituality among modern Christians is putting the fussy doing of religion ahead of the deep, divine inward being like Jesus."[10]

Yet, it must still be asked, in what precise sense is imparted righteousness like Jesus? Is similarity implied? Or equivalency implied? Or exactness implied? Or is something else implied? These are questions that must be answered if imparted righteousness is to be understood.

Since the heart of the human problem was the problem with the human heart, God told Jeremiah and Ezekiel he was going to give man a new heart and a new spirit (Jeremiah 31:33; Ezekiel 36:26). This new heart, though, couldn't come to us by fiat; instead, certain stages were consecutively and successfully undertaken by our Lord when he came centuries later to live among us. Without describing these stages here, the point that does need to be made is that this process culminated in the very life of Jesus coming inside us (Colossians 3:4).[11]

The resurrected life of Jesus—fully human, perfected on earth, glorified by the Father, inhabited by the Holy Spirit (Romans 8:2)—is our new nature. A.J. Gordon said, "... it is no mere external morality, no garment of righteousness to be assumed and worn as a covering of a yet unsanctified nature, but a divine life, penetrating, possessing and informing the soul ...."[12] Supporting this point, A.B. Simpson wrote:

> God does not demand of us eternal obedience merely, but he puts in us the nature, the principle, the disposition to obey. He makes his law the law of our being, and we as naturally follow it as a material body falls to the ground by the law of gravitation, or, as an acorn develops into an oak because the law of the oak is in the heart of the acorn.[13]

Some people have made the words "grim" and "glum" synonyms for holiness. F.B. Meyer acknowledged as much when he wrote: "I know men who talk of holiness as if it meant that it was wrong to laugh, be bright, engage in manly sports, play the piano, read any book but the Bible, or follow certain pursuits for which we have aptitude."[14] According to this perspective, a frowning deity is against all that and is more than a little suspicious of even the slightest smile.

But how could this description be right? Does not our new nature, the imparted righteousness of God, include all nine parts of the fruit of the spirit? And that means love and joy and peace (Galatians 5:22, 23). While discipline and sacrifice are certainly worthy concepts, to extract adoring love, glowing joy, and blissful peace from holiness is to seriously distort the definition. The new heart, promised to the prophets centuries before the manger, is now inside every born-again believer—and it is appealing in every way![15] Indeed, the new nature given to us by God is critical to our ability to obey God.

Holiness will seem utterly unreal to us, if not altogether impossible, as long as the doctrine of the new nature is not understood. Affirming this point, Tozer said, "We have learned to live with unholiness and have come to look upon it as the natural and expected thing."[16]

Perhaps this acquiescence to a lower standard of living is unwittingly reinforced by the kind of reasoning J.I. Packer set forth when he wrote:

> The Christian who thus walks in the Spirit will keep discovering that nothing in his life is as good as it should be; that he has never fought as hard as he might have done against the clogging restraints and contrary pulls of his own inbred perversity, that there is an element of motivational sin, at least, in his best works; that his daily living is streaked with defilements, so that he has to depend every moment on God's pardoning mercy in Christ ....[17]

Well, conclusions like this hardly inspire an ongoing pursuit of holiness! Yet these are the conclusions that inevitably come from a theology that doesn't understand the new nature. With greater theological awareness, Tozer said that God has now given to his children his holiness "by imputation and by impartation, and because he has made it available to them by the blood of the Lamb, he requires it of them."[18] Given this very formidable fact, Tozer declared, "We Christians ought to be the cleanest, purest, most righteous, holiest people in all the world."[19] Our example should convey the extraordinary difference imparted righteousness makes.

Did you know that what you have just read represents a huge paradigm shift from traditional thinking? Most Christians envision a principle-by-principle staircase climb, which, after much learning and obedience, results in a conforming of our life into the image of God, at least to some degree. But this approach is nothing less than a carnal attempt to re-create, feebly and fallibly, the life Jesus already put inside us. So why reinvent the wheel, especially when it is impossible to do so?

The real need is for the life of our Lord already inside us to be *released*, and not for us to try to produce through diligence and desire what God has already created. This is where the filling of the Spirit is critical, and why a correct understanding of this filling is imperative.

The holiness in our new nature gets released with the Spirit's filling. A.B. Simpson declared, "... Christ himself must be the substance and supply of our new spiritual life and fill us with his own Spirit and holiness."[20] When inaugurated, this filling is sudden, not gradual. However, it isn't a one-time event; it does and should repeat. The main point to be underscored, though, is this: When this filling occurs, the imparted righteousness of Jesus flows out.[21]

With regard to our holiness fully supplied in the new nature and subsequently released by the Spirit's filling, A.B. Simpson said:

> It is God's great elevated railway, sweeping over the heads of the struggling throngs who toil along the lower pavement when they might be borne along on his ascension pathway, by his own Almighty impulse. It is God's great elevator, carrying us up to the higher chambers of his palace without our laborious efforts, while others struggling up the winding stairs faint by the way. It is God's great tidal wave bearing up the stranded ship until she floats above the bar without straining timbers or struggling seaman ....[22]

Of those strugglers below, trudging ever so slowly the morality path, G. D. Watson observed, "Many seek for only partial holiness; they seek it merely as a cure for some besetting sin."[23] The anger outburst, the drinking binge, and other such sins that offend society and embarrass the family—only that needs to be trimmed away. The result of such thinking is a lifestyle much less than what Jesus gives. The higher life isn't desired, or even thought possible.

Contrary to the opinion that the higher life is difficult, if not unobtainable, Simpson said, "... it is easier to live the high life than to drag along the lower plane ... It is easier to stand on the mountaintop than to stand with one foot on the heights of grace while with the other we are dragging our life along the lower plane."[24]

Remember, it is upon takeoff that the bird rapidly flaps it wings as it gains ascendancy. But once it reaches that higher plane, the bird glides with ease. The parallel point is this: The power that comes from the sudden surge of the Spirit's filling gains this ascendancy for us, without which we will live our entire lives furiously flapping our fleshly wings, unable to gain the height where the spiritual life becomes easier.

Many Christians think the believer has two natures. Therefore, by failing to recognize the old man doesn't exist in the believer (Romans 6:6), and by failing also to distinguish between the old man and the flesh (which are not the same), the believer has been deceived into thinking that something much less than what really happened is true about his current status and true identity.[25]

The Bible says we are a new creation—period! There is nothing hyphenated or bifurcated about this new nature. Martin Luther's phrase, *simul justus et peccator*, simultaneously just and sinner, is wrong.[26] The Christian isn't part sinner and part saint. Scripture never says anything like that. The New Testament calls believers saints, a designation true of all believers.

In his book, *What God Wishes Christians Knew about Christianity*, Bill Gillham points out that: "Paul addresses his epistles to 'all the saints,' never to 'all the sinners saved by grace.'" We are either saints or "ain'ts," a Christian or a non-Christian, a regenerate man or an unregenerate man, but we aren't a combination of the two. According to A.B. Simpson, "The purpose of Christ's redeeming work is to make it possible for bad men to become good—deeply, radically and finally."[27]

Now, while the Bible is honest in dealing with the sins Christians commit, it never describes their essence as that of a sinner. This is because the new heart within a believer is *totally* who he or she is! And it is *already* perfect! The new heart satisfies every demand and command of God's law, because the life within this heart is already ready for heaven!

This is the lesson Paul learned. The civil war described in Romans, chapter 7, finally ended when the Spirit of life in Christ Jesus (the new nature), set this man free (Romans 8:2). Thereafter, Paul repeatedly prefaced any call for behavioral change by insisting this change come from the new nature. For only the life that comes from the new nature is capable of complying with God's commands. Well-intentioned flesh—with Bible in hand, fellowship group surrounding, prayers offered, discipline exerted—will fail. Scripture's solution calls for a release of the new nature!

Many evangelical Christians convey confusion when they explain imputed righteousness but not imparted righteousness. Listen to what Miles J. Stanford had to say as he explained imputed righteousness by making this distinction between performance and position.

> The spiritually minded believer is conscious of sin in him, but he is fully assured that there is no sin on him; all of his sin has been laid on the Lord Jesus. Although his condition is needy, for he is indwelt by the principle of sin, he lives in his position in Christ.[28]

Now, while this distinction between *position* (the person who has the imputed righteousness of God) and *performance* (how the Christian is now living) is valid, missing from this description is *presence,* the impartation of the Lord's life within. Though sin is said to dwell within, the imparted righteousness of God is marginalized right out of this discussion. In this way, the supposed neediness of a Christian is discussed without identifying God's remedy for it—the new nature, the imparted righteousness of God released whenever the Holy Spirit fills us.

Leslie D. Wilcox points out in his book, *Be Ye Holy*, that positional righteousness "... denies any real or actual deliverance from sin."[29] The two-nature theory does the same thing. According to both theories, indwelling sin remains—and its power over the believer is formidable![30]

Another factor that keeps believers from ever experiencing their new nature is the idea that we were all filled with the Spirit the moment we became a Christian. This is patently false. If we check out scientific studies of the church, we will see conclusions that daily observations continually confirm: namely, that most Christians *aren't* exhibiting the behavioral evidence of being filled with the Spirit.

In his book, *The Way to Pentecost*, Samuel Chadwick asked the rhetorical question, "Is the character of the average Christian anywhere near the standard of a Spirit-filled soul?"[31] Indisputable evidence indicates that most church attendees are dominated by flesh. So how did that happen if all these Christians were gloriously filled with the Spirit?

Andrew Murray explained the dilemma of many:

> In our days, just as in those first ages, the great danger is living under the law, and serving God in the strength of the flesh. With the great majority of Christians it appears to be the state in which they remain all their lives. This explains the tremendous lack of true holy living and power in prayer. They do not know that all failure can have but one cause: Men seek to do to themselves what grace alone can do in them, what grace most certainly will do.[32]

This grace, which is a drawing on the resources of the Holy Spirit within them, is crucial to spiritual growth. So be clear on this point: Although all Christians have the Holy Spirit inside them (Romans 8:9), there is a tremendous difference between the *receiving* of the Spirit (which happens at conversion) and the *releasing* of the Spirit (which happens subsequent to conversion). At conversion, we drink from the well (John 4:14); but when the Holy Spirit is released, there's a river flow that carries us in its currents (John 7:38). In conversion, the Holy Spirit comes inside us (Romans 8:9). When released, the Holy Spirit comes upon us (Acts 8:16; 10:44; 19:6). These are two different realities, and we need them both.

The filling of the Spirit is always depicted in Scripture as a punctiliar, point-in-time event; it was never gradual. Anyone thinking that I'm a little more filled today than I was yesterday isn't filled at all. What may be happening is a progression from "disgusting" flesh to "USDA Prime" flesh, but this hardly constitutes a filling of the Spirit.[33] Flesh is flesh! All attempts to improve it find their inspiration in false religions and not in the Gospels. A.B. Simpson said of the flesh, "It is past improving. Our patching and repairing is worse than waste."[34] In fact, the more learned and dedicated flesh is, the farther one is walking down the wrong road!

This is what Paul eventually discovered. Although he loved the law and willed to do what it commanded, still, he failed—and failed miserably, even to the point of crying out for deliverance (Romans 7:24)! This deliverance never came to Paul by trying harder and harder, and by becoming more dedicated and consecrated. It came when Paul learned how to operate out of his new nature (Romans 8:2), which is the Holy Spirit indwelling our re-created spirit, the imparted righteousness of God.

Again, what God demands of us has already been put inside us! This righteousness, however, will flow out *only* when faith lays hold of grace (Romans 5:2) with an expectation that the Holy Spirit will supply. Moreover, this supply isn't for ministry only, or even primarily. A.B. Simpson clarified this truth when he wrote:

> The baptism of the Holy Spirit is not given to us primarily as an enduement of power for service. This is one of the mistaken teachings abroad today. Undoubtedly power for service is one

result of this blessing, but it is primarily given to us for personal character and holiness ....[35]

The baptism, the filling, the releasing of the Holy Spirit propels outward the very righteousness that resides in our new nature. This is why Scripture repeatedly tells us to put on the new man (to operate out of the new nature) before then telling us to make certain moral and ethical changes in our lives.

Unless we operate in new nature capacities, we will fail just as often as the man in Romans 7 did, no matter how hard we try. Yet many believers today will give rapt attention to some moral principle, and will diligently pursue some worthwhile instruction, but never give the first thought about the necessity of the new nature for compliance.

The notion that faculties of the soul, such as intellect and willpower, can be activated to achieve godliness is misleading if it assumes capacities of the soul have this ability. They do not. Godliness originates in our *spirit*; it is only by the resources of our re-created spirit that godliness is even possible.

Remember, Word-to-soul dynamics failed in the Old Testament and they will fail today. That's why the New Testament taught a fundamentally different message when it conveyed the necessity of the new birth.

To us, the new birth is a requirement for entrance into heaven. But it is more than that! The new birth is essential for living the saved life! If a believer bypasses the new nature, which is often the case, then the wrong source (the soul, and not the spirit) is being utilized for godly living. And will that work? Many who have tried it will tell you it won't. A.B. Simpson helped us to understand this truth when he pointed out:

> The Christian life is not a wonderful state or a marvelous experience, but a perfect union with Jesus, the living and perfect One. We do not merely receive grace, but the God of all grace; not merely holiness, but the Holy One ... The secret of divine holiness is union with Jesus, abiding in

Jesus, depending upon Jesus every moment and for everything.[36]

Those who don't understand the imparted righteousness put into the new nature will stay in Romans 7 defeat and think that's just the way it is in this life—when it isn't! As for Paul, he got free and stayed free! Scripture provides extensive biographical details about Paul to prove how free from sin's downward pull he was. Paul didn't just say, "... sin will have no dominion over you" (Romans 6:14), *he experienced that*! And Paul didn't just say, "... walk in the Spirit and you will not fulfill the lust of the flesh" (Galatians 5:16), *he experienced that*!

Yet, while the Spirit's filling is sudden, there is still a progressive dimension to spiritual growth. This is so because, while the new spirit within us is perfect, our soul is not. How we think, feel, and act, may be far from perfect. Therefore, our spirit must progressively impact our soul.

As the Lord's life within us is subsequently released, it will dramatically impact our soul—to the extent that our soul will not sin. Forever? Well, for as long as we are being filled with the Spirit! And that can be for a sustained period of time.

There are two views that need to be avoided in this discussion. The idea of reaching some stratospheric level of spirituality, where we cross a threshold into "sinless perfection," is, it must be pointed out, an ill-conceived idea.[37] Perfection lies at the end of the "glory to glory" journey; no Christian is going to get there in this life.

We set a false standard by telling people that a state of sinless perfection is possible. The perfection Scripture sets forth has qualifiers that are well-recognized by many in the holiness movement. Spurgeon commented wryly that he always thought a certain man was perfect until one day this man said that he was.[38]

Besides, perfection shouldn't be defined in only a negative way, the ceasing of sin; it should also be defined in a positive way: the fuller apprehension of fervent worship, breakthrough prayer, and yoke-directed service. A.B. Simpson said, "It is possible to be free from sin, utterly sanctified and walking with God as his children, and yet be living a very narrow, circumscribed life."[39] The challenge now is one of enlargement, where these splendid qualities extend more widely—like the stream that flows into the river, and the river that flows into the ocean—touching more people in more ways for God's glory.[40]

More ill-conceived than this idea of sinless perfection, are the arguments frequently raised against it. When set forth, these arguments reflect too low a vision of what God has made possible for the believer. Challenging this low vision with deserved reproach, A.J. Gordon contended:

> If we regard sinless perfection as a heresy, we regard contentment with sinful imperfection as a greater heresy. And we gravely fear that many Christians make the apostle's words, "And if we say we have no sin in us, we deceive ourselves," the unconscious justification for a low standard of Christian living.[41]

Charles Finney called this low standard "a ruinous accommodation to the experience of carnal people who profess religion."[42] Languishing in the "I-sin-every-day" mentality is squandering the imparted righteousness of God implanted in our new nature. This new nature, you see, has the power to dominate our soul to the extent aspiration becomes accomplishment.

The Inherited Righteousness of God

The last kind of righteousness we will consider is the righteousness every believer will be given when he or she goes to heaven. This is not a righteousness different in kind from that which was given on earth. Nor is it a righteousness different in quality—for how can the imparted life of our Lord be improved upon?

The chief difference between the imparted righteousness on earth and the inherited righteousness of heaven is the degree of its release, not the quality of its essence or the extent of its original deposit in our new nature. In heaven, the release will be complete. This due, not to spiritual discipline faithfully exercised but to a gracious bestowal from the Lord instantly undertaken upon arrival in heaven as a part of the believer's inheritance.

When comparing the righteousness given to us on earth with the righteousness given to us in heaven, F.F. Bruce said, "Sanctification is glory begun; glory is sanctification completed."[43] On that wonderful day, the Lord who called us to holiness will generate the release of his holiness in a freer, fuller way. In his book, *The Holiness of God*, R.C. Sproul helps us to understand the uniqueness of this holiness when he said:

> Only once in sacred Scripture is an attribute of God elevated to the third degree. Only once is a characteristic of God mentioned three times in succession. The Bible says that God is holy, holy, holy. Not that he is merely holy, or even holy, holy. He is holy, holy, holy. The Bible never says that God is love, love, love, or mercy, mercy, mercy, or wrath, wrath, wrath, or justice, justice, justice. It does say that he is holy, holy, holy, the earth is full of his glory.[44]

This glory will become a shared glory when God enables a gracious release of his holy nature in the lives of those who love him. To this, George Whitfield rightly said, "The anthem of heaven will be, what God hath wrought!"[45]

In heaven, there will be no flesh to contend with, no devil to defeat, and no absence from him who is our source of holiness, the Lord God of the universe. Unlike what could ever be on earth, there will be in heaven a glory emanating from us so bright in its glow and awesome in its effect that if we could see it now, our eyes would pop, our jaws would drop, and we, blinking and gulping, would say, "Me? Could that possibly be me?"

Oh, my! The glorified believer arrayed in his inherited righteousness helps to explain the marriage with Jesus that will one day occur in heaven. What seems incomprehensible to us now—this union between sinners and the Savior—will not be so bewildering once the holiness embedded in our new nature is fully released. For then the stunning similarity will be evident, and our place in the Throne Room of the universe will be heralded.

Perhaps a further clarification of righteousness can be expressed in this way. Imputed righteousness frees us from the penalty of sin. Imparted righteousness frees us from the power of sin.[46] Inherited righteousness frees us from the presence of sin and from all that restrained the bursting forth of God's glory.

Unmixed with any internal contaminants, and unchallenged by any competing intrusions, the goodness experienced and expressed in heaven will signal the end of the roller-coaster days and all those backsliding episodes. Self-doubting and self-loathing, unnecessary on earth, will finally and forever be replaced by a heart always at peace with itself, and by a commendation from the Lord that will never lose its thrill.

So, having examined the Bible's evidence about these four types of righteousness, we are now able to say that another part of the mystery just got solved.

Reflection Questions

1. Why are teachings about imputed righteousness and inherited righteousness not enough? Why is a correct understanding about imparted righteousness critical to obedience?

2. How would you characterize the gap between imparted righteousness and inherited righteousness? Is this an almost infinite gap? Or is this gap smaller than most people think?

Chapter 6

Tracking Sin

There are plots and there are subplots. The main plot of our story, "the mystery of godliness," deals with the dynamics of good (I Timothy 3:16). The subplot of our story, "the mystery of iniquity," deals with the dynamics of evil (II Thessalonians 2:7).

To understand the dynamics of good, which is the primary purpose of this book, it is necessary to examine its exact opposite, evil. The obvious reason for this being: Evil often masquerades as good in an attempt to keep people from discovering what good really is.

In most mysteries, false leads and dead-end clues hinder an investigation, and may even result in putting it into the cold case files. In the mystery of good and evil, this is exactly what Satan wants! So incorrect information is constantly disseminated by the forces of evil, a fact the Bible predicted thousands of years ago when it said that men would call evil good and good evil (Isaiah 5:20).

And what kind of men will do this? Well, not just the deranged mind of the career criminal, or the delirious mind of someone locked away in a padded cell, or the propagandized mind of a cult follower. Instead, it's the venerated minds of academia that do the most damage. The university shovels mounds of obfuscations onto a society all too willing to be deceived. Unless we are able to unscramble this deceptive information and start tracking sin with due diligence, a supportable conclusion that differentiates good from evil may continually elude us.

If we could restrict our focus to the good life alone by contemplating only those positives that encourage, our task would certainly be more pleasant. However, Scripture steers in another direction when it says in I Peter 3:10 "... he that will love life and see good days ..."—and that includes most of us, I suspect, for loving life is a common goal; and seeing good days is a desirable outcome. But, as stipulated by this verse in the words that follow, the preconditions for the good life involve refraining the tongue from evil, speaking no guile, and eschewing evil. This is the negative side coming into view, a side that warrants our utmost attention.

Now it would be nice if this word "eschew" was an onomatopoeic word that took its meaning from its sound: *eschew*, as in a sneeze. If only evil *could* be vacated this way! Pascal's observation of the soul being absorbed by sneezing is interesting, yet the obvious has to be acknowledged: The soul can never be liberated so easily. A fiercely contested conflict is always required.

Most of us who love the Lord do want to obey him. Indeed, this very basic desire—stressed by Jesus while he talked in the Upper Room, and stressed again that night while he walked to the Garden of Gethsemane—has long resonated with the believer's heart. But every believer has also known the precise opposite: what it is not to obey God— even for a protracted period of time!

Our memories of this experience, and our subsequent motivation to get free from a repeat performance, compel a clear understanding of exactly what it is we're trying to escape. In this pursuit, all must be brought into the light! Sin's essence, symptoms, implications, triggers, and consequences must be revealed.

Seventeenth-century Puritan writer John Owen rightly said, "To labor to be acquainted with the ways, wiles, methods, advantages, and occasions of the success of sin, is the beginning to this warfare."[1] In this chapter, therefore, and in the two chapters that follow, we will identify dynamics contrary to obedience, hoping as we do so to advance our ability to see and be good.

There is one word that accounts for inconsistent obedience, and that word begins with the serpentine sound—s-s-sin! Sin, undetected and seemingly dormant, may seem inconsequential at first, but then comes the day when it manifests with stark terror. Like a jet-black nuclear sub moving with stealth on the ocean floor, sin, like that sub, will suddenly surface from dark waters, producing an eerie chill in all those who see it. Breaking into the light as it vacates its place of hiding, this submarine will thrust upward through the water, and then into the air with daring and imposing aggression.

For a long while, this evil had been lurking unseen underneath. But then the decision was made to end the hiding and to lunge into the open with nose-in-the-air superiority. When this occurred, the serenity of the scene where it occurred was instantly terminated.

The Display of Sin

We see a display of lurking, lunging evil when Jesus walked first to Gethsemane and then to Golgotha. The evil that emerged that night included outright betrayal by one of his disciples, the infighting of the other disciples, the failure of even the most promising disciples to pray, a subsequent scattering of the sheep, their hastened descent into despair, the conspiracy of religious leaders, the marshalling of government forces, the illegal tactics of a corrupt and scheming judiciary. Indeed, all that was supposed to be the best of humanity got exposed that night as evil surged forth where one would least suspect it to operate.

Orchestrating all this evil was Satan himself, whose legions of demons were about to unleash every weapon in their artillery to defeat the Son of God. Their intense hatred for heaven, and their ambition for their own empire to dominate, seethed in them until that day they danced in glee, thinking they had finally made Jesus their captive and their prey.

During the course of this operation, hell seared the highest offices of the land, deeply staining its most respected people. But what occurred that day also occurs today: in that a once-tolerated holiness is being attacked with a vengeance!

Speaking to this point with needed clarity, Watchman Nee wrote:

> When the world meets in us a natural human honesty and decency, it appreciates this, and is willing to pay us due respect and place us in its confidence. But as soon as it meets in us that which is not of ourselves, namely the divine nature of which we have been made partakers, the hostility is at once aroused ... A so-called Christian civilization gains the recognition and respect of the world. The world can tolerate that; it can even assimilate and utilize that. But Christian life—the life of Christ in the Christian believer: that it hates, and whenever it meets it will assuredly oppose it to the death.[2]

Stephen Charnock stated this bottom-line truth, "The new creature is the delight of God, though the scoff of men; the pleasure of him that commands the world, though reproached by them that shall fill hell with their souls."[3]

Yet in our day—when evil has retreated to its hideouts of camouflage and counterfeits—how crude and uncouth that word evil seems! More than two centuries ago, Horatius Bonar observed the world's inclinations to minimize evil when he said, "The tendency is to underestimate sin and to misunderstand its nature."[4] God's estimate of sin, Bonar pointed out, is unspeakably dreadful. So, giving voice to God's perspective, Bonar declared:

> It is the abominable thing which I hate; it is an evil that I cannot bear; it cast the angels out of heaven; it ruined the world; it brought the deluge; it drew down the fire and brimstone; it slew my Son; it will yet set the world on fire; it will kindle hell.[5]

Paul clearly saw the vile nature of sin, even in the most impressive city of his day. When traveling to Rome, Paul wasn't much interested in a tourist's agenda, for he had come to win souls to the Master. In doing so, Paul witnessed firsthand the mastery sin had over a corrupt culture! Commenting on this fact, Leonard Ravenhill wrote:

> Paul saw the Roman populace as it really was—a mass of blind souls, practiced in perversity, clever in their conceit, lounging in their lust, defiant in their destiny, violent in their vice, senseless in their sensuality—an empire of souls against whom the wrath of God was about to be outpoured.[6]

You should know that the Spirit of God that enabled Paul to see this outcome will also enable us to detect evil, and to do so with the instinct of a mother hen. G.D. Watson observed, "A hen with a brood of chickens will detect the flight of a hawk in the sky faster than any hunter."[7] By contrast, the world's lack of moral discernment ranges somewhere between puny and pathetic. To the modern mind tutored by university elites, a more sanitized civilization is thought to exist. By imagining, as they do, that more noble aspirations reside in man, our contemporaries have been so anesthetized to evil that any judging that uses moral terms offends their sensitivities.

This sophisticated culture of ours has invested itself in tolerance, in understanding, in the assumption that words like "weaknesses," or "differences," or maybe even "mistakes" are more "appropriate" than the word "evil." In this regard, Vance Havner said, "The devil never had a greater ally than this modern atmosphere of genial, amiable, pleasant tolerance, in which nothing is bad, everything is good, and black and white are smeared into an indefinite gray."[8]

G.K. Chesterton spoke caustically on this point, saying: "Tolerance is the virtue of the man without convictions." This flight from moral categories (which is really pride denying the undeniable) cannot be allowed to stand. "Mistakes," after all, are made in math; they do not describe our offenses against the holy God of the universe. We should never sanction, even passively, what God forbids.

Especially in a day like ours—when the concept of sin is not in vogue and the concept of obedience is thought to be oppressive—being clear about moral terms is exceedingly important. Attempts by mental health gurus to exorcise morality from our thought processes, and to reclassify evil behavior with more civil and clinical terms, are far more pernicious than many people realize. For once moral thinking is replaced, and the right kind of judging is displaced, evil personified is emboldened—and for obvious reasons, too! This will transact because our culture, thought to be humane and nonjudgmental, is now providing the masking that helps evil to flourish.

Capitalizing on this self-imposed blindness, evil surges more boldly than before, fully aware that denied evil only increases evil. And can anyone deny that there is a noticeable deterioration in our culture, that evil men *are* acting worse and worse, just as Scripture predicted they would?

Although obedience does have a pivotal importance not easily overestimated, the mere mention of this topic will produce a potpourri of shrugs, yawns, and vapid, turn-out-the-lights stares. Other topics—such as miracles, marriage, and the millennial kingdom—will fill auditoriums and sell a lot of books. But in modern-day America, obedience school has become a concept for poodles and not people.

The word obedience doesn't exactly exude goose-pimple euphoria, or generate an appeal that gains headline-grabbing attention. Why, to measure the sensationalistic impact of this topic is to see that the seismograph needle doesn't even move!

The indifference we have toward morality is indicative of a population stumbling around in a stupor. Moral sensibilities in our day have become too numb to detect the danger caused by stripping moral language from our daily lexicons. Those in the highest seats at the university and at the most prestigious roundtables of public discussion are calling good, evil and evil, good. And, unfortunately, our culture has found much agreement with many of these pronouncements.

That our culture has been conditioned to disinvest in moral concerns is so obvious that the documentation supporting this conclusion isn't needed. The title of a Karl Menninger book puts it well: *Whatever Became of Sin?* That word sin was, for hundreds of years, employed in both public discourse and private reflection. But ever since Freud substituted a medical model for the moral model, the concept of sin—at least personal sin—has lost currency in today's marketplace of ideas. Noting this change, British author, David Watson, wrote, "We talk about inhibitions, complexes, twists in our nature, mistakes and temperament. We do not like using the word the Bible uses and Christ frequently used: sin."[9] Because doing so wouldn't be "nice."

It was not uncommon during the sixties to see Hollywood types take to the soapbox and shout their shrilled denunciations against the government (back then their favorite word was "obscene"). But the same people who lectured the country about public morality had no such convictions when it came to private morality.

Illicit sex, illegal drugs, and the wild-party scene were flaunted in their "flower child" lifestyles, even as traditional values were either ignored or deliberately disdained with sneering contempt. Seeing these dynamics at work prompted Elton Trueblood to write: "One of the marks of irrationality on the current moral scene is the separation of social from personal values, which amounts to a denial of integrity."[10]

While the decibel level of the sixties has dropped noticeably since then, morality has still been retained as a weapon, mostly against business conglomerates and the government. Other than that, morality is pretty much a nonissue. Accordingly, Arthur W. Pink wrote:

> We are prone to regard sin lightly, to gloss over its hideousness, to make excuses for it. But the more we study and ponder God's abhorrence of sin and his frightful vengeance upon it, the more likely we are to realize its heinousness."[11]

Hence, there is a definite need to track sin, to rip away its facades, to investigate where it hides, to expose its many counterfeits, and to reveal its true nature. Arnold Toynbee was right when he said that "the answer to the problem of history is the answer to the problem of evil."[12] Any attempt to understand our past (as a predictor of our future) requires a rigorous assessment of evil. Objectivity will go out the window if evil is overlooked! Overlooking evil is like outlining a picture but omitting every essential detail.

The Debate about Sin

Alcoholism, gambling, homosexuality—these used to be well-known sins. But taking their cue from Vienna and not Galilee, psychology either normalized these life-dominating behaviors or diagnosed them as diseases. This attempt to blur distinctions, to shift blame, to disguise sin as a more respectable phenomenon than we previously thought, has had a widespread influence.

The spillover effect today is a toned-down language that speaks of an "affair" and not what the Bible calls it, fornication; a "shrewd business" deal and not what the Bible calls it, stealing; a "neurosis" and not what the Bible calls it, the sin of unbelief. But to disguise a sin by renaming it will only deter the needed recovery from its debilitating effects.

What psychology calls a maladjustment, and biology calls a disease, and ethics calls a lapse of judgment, and philosophy calls a mere slippage in the evolutionary dynamic of progress, the Bible calls "disobedience" (Romans 5:1). And if this fails to make the point sufficiently, consider these much stronger biblical modifiers: "lawlessness" (I John 3:4), "iniquity" (Exodus 34:7), and "wickedness" (Genesis 6:5)!

In his book, *The God Who is There*, Francis Schaeffer—the Reformed scholar from L'Abri Fellowship in Switzerland—refused to minimize this point:

> ... Christianity does not look over this tired and burdened world and say that it is slightly flawed, a little chipped, but easily mended. Christianity is realistic and says the world is marked with evil and that man is guilty all along the line.[13]

While the elites of our day can continue to disguise sin—or, if they choose, to deny it (I John 1:8), laugh at it (Proverbs 14:9), and even enjoy it (Romans 1:32)—it is nevertheless true that what the Bible calls sin isn't just a weakness, a mistake, or a deficit in one's knowledge. Remember, false labeling—be it in the medical world, the business world, or even the spiritual world—can prove fatal. So we mustn't—for the purpose of pampering pride and elevating ego—accept the misdiagnosis being merchandised today.

I say merchandised because there *is* a financial incentive for mental health professionals to define behaviors the way they do. For example, if alcoholism can be called a disease (which for decades the AMA steadfastly refused to do), then the insurance companies will pay for treatment. But if alcoholism is not diagnosed as a disease, then insurance companies won't pay and that cash cow will be put out to pasture.

Don't be confused about this. A genetic predisposition is one thing, but a disease, in the conventional sense, is quite another. This is why a person with a genetic predisposition to alcohol may never consume a single drop of it. The real issue, for those who do let alcohol control them, is primarily one of character and not genetic makeup.

Be honest. No clear thinking person puts muscular dystrophy in the same category with alcoholism. People instinctively know that alcoholism is not a disease, unless the concept of disease is elasticized beyond recognition. This, when the pressure was on, the AMA capitulated to do. And if you want to know why, just follow the money trail!

In his book, *Homosexuality and the Politics of Truth*, Jeffrey Satinover (holding degrees from both Harvard and M.I.T., and having also served as a former professor of psychiatry at Yale) provides extensive documentation on the way the APA (the American Psychiatric Association) and the NASW (the National Association of Social Workers) attempted to ramrod the normalization of homosexuality through their respective governing bodies.

Dr. Satinover writes: "The APA vote to normalize homosexuality was driven by politics, not science. Even sympathizers (to the gay agenda) acknowledged this."[14] Dr. Satinover also details the role the National Gay Task Force played in both duping and intimidating APA members.

Interestingly, four years after the APA capitulated on this issue, the *Medical Aspects of Human Sexuality* journal surveyed psychiatrists and reported that the normalization of homosexuality vote "... was not a conclusion based upon an approximation of the scientific truth as dictated by reason, but instead was an action demanded by the ideological temper of the times." The survey also showed that 69 percent of psychiatrists disagreed with the vote and still considered homosexuality a disorder.[15]

The significance of this point couldn't be more crucial. Because in I Corinthians, chapter 6 (verses 9-10), the Lord throws the gauntlet down, saying that certain life-dominating behaviors will mean that their practitioners will not go to heaven (while repentance can reverse this destiny, nothing short of that will). Included in this list of damnable sins is alcoholism and homosexuality. So if alcoholism is a disease and homosexuality is normal, why would God send people to hell for that?

Do you see the problem? If we conclude that Scripture is wrong and that these experts are right, we've got a major problem with the nature of God on our hands. But if we agree with the experts, then the resulting fallibility-of-Scripture problem leaves no reliable resource for saying anything about what God will and will not do.

One might be predisposed to homosexuality, just as one might be predisposed to other evils embedded in the nature we all inherited at birth. The fact such tendencies appeared early and later became strong proves nothing, except the axe must be laid to the root for all of us.

The focus must be on destroying the root of that nature we were born with. This is done most effectively—whichever destructive behavior is in view—through the cross of Christ. Trying to deal with the fruit of the old nature without dealing with the root of the old nature is bound to fail.

In contrast to the sophisticated delusions of our day, envisioning as they do a noble humanity without any heart-gravitation toward sin, Thomas Guthrie wrote: There were places in nineteenth-century Africa where "no straggling ray of revealed truth had ever fallen." No Bible. No missionary. No church. Nothing! And yet, citing David Livingston,

Guthrie said of the natives there, "... they hold almost everything to be sin which, as such, is forbidden in the Word of God." So how did Livingston account for this?

Livingston concluded "... that the ten commandments received from God's own hand by Moses on Mount Sinai are but the copy of a much older law, the law that the finger of the Maker wrote on Adam's heart."[16] This certainly concurs with what Scripture itself says about the internal witness, conscience (Romans 1:19), which makes every man accountable before God. There *is* a moral compass in humanity, sufficient to guide, and therefore sufficient for one being accountable.

It was conscience that almost drove Martin Luther crazy. Indeed, even after Luther became a priest, he still went to the confessional every day. For others? No, for himself! So lacerated was Luther's conscience by what the Spirit of God was revealing that he once spent six hours just confessing the sins of the previous day.[17] Excessive, you say? Then you have no idea how the conscience tuned into God works.

John Bunyan, the author of *Pilgrim's Progress*, said this about himself: "When God showed me John Bunyan as God saw John Bunyan, I no longer confessed that I was a sinner, but I confessed that I was sin from the crown of my head to the soul of my feet. I was full of sin."

A.B. Simpson declared, "Conscience is the dread accuser of the wrongdoer, and conscience, without the restraint of divine mercy, is a terrible tyrant."[18]

John Owen, perhaps the greatest of England's theologians, graduated from college with distinction and was pursuing his course in life with discipline, when God showed him his sins. According to J.I. Packer, "... the torment of convictions threw him into such a turmoil that for three months he avoided the company of others and, when addressed, could scarcely utter a coherent sentence."[19]

What God revealed shattered the sense of moral goodness John Owen once had. This fact, typically true of the born-again believer, prompted A.J. Gordon to write, "The difference between the regenerate and the unregenerate man is that the unregenerate man lives in sin, and he loves it; but that the regenerate man lapses into sin, and he loathes it."[20] He does not rationalize it.

King David knew all too well what it was like to be accused by an unrelenting conscience. In Psalm 51 he cried out, "My sin is ever before me." Contemplating this horrendous reality, Australian pastor F.W. Boreham wrote:

> To be haunted, summer and winter, sleeping and waking, by that ugliest and most hideous of all specters, its ghostly finger continually pointing relentlessly and accusingly into the contrite penitent's face! It was with him in the night, and he drenched his pillow with his tears. It rose with him every morning. It tracked him through every day. His whole life was a sob. "Ever before me! Ever before me!"[21]

The memory vivid! The stain permanent! The wound yet open! One has to wonder how any man of conscience can bear such a burden. Regrettably, this burden is one with which many believers are well acquainted. With words of empathy, F.B. Meyer wrote:

> We, too, may be traversing at this very hour battlefields which have been sadly marked by defeat. Again and again we have met the foes of our peace in mortal combat, only to be repulsed. Our hopes have been dashed to the ground and our banners rolled in dust and blood. We meant never to yield again, but we did yield. We meant that the solemn vow should be kept, that holy resolution carried into effect; but they were shivered in pieces. We have been overthrown by our adversary, and overpowered in spite of all our efforts by our besetting sin.[22]

Do understand that when God reveals our sins, his purpose isn't to humiliate us or to get us to grovel in self-degradation. His greater purpose is disclosed in this fact: God knows that before the gospel can really become a gospel to us, there must first be a radical unmasking, without which we'll only be parroting the *mea culpa* words of the church, devoid of moral anguish as we do so, and therefore devoid of an exhilaration of soul that compels worship and makes witnessing contagious.

Granted, conscience can be hushed; and, as the Bible reports, the truth can be turned into a lie. But the price of this deception may very well be a reprobate ruin that causes even the Omnipotent One to give up. It is to be remembered that three times the book of Romans repeats these dreadful words: "God gave them up" ... "God gave them up" ... "God gave them up" (Romans 1:24, 26, 28). And is this what the sophisticated dodger of truth really wants?

The Defining of Sin

In setting forth what good is, and how it should be undertaken, it is important to define what we're attempting to avoid. In undertaking this assignment, let's first seek to uncover the very essence of sin. G.D. Watson declared, "Sin is no legitimate part of our being: it is an intrusion, a fungus on the soul, a poisonous parasite planted in us by an enemy ...."[23] At its bedrock core, sin—first and foremost—is a rejection of Jesus. In John, chapter 16, verses 8 and 9, Jesus himself defined it this way when he said that the Holy Spirit "will reprove the world of sin ... of sin, because they believe not on me."

The distinction that needs to be made here is between "sins" in the plural and "sin" in the singular. "Sins" in the plural include the infractions we typically think of—lying, stealing, adultery, and murder (and just here it should be noted that heaven will be full of people who did all those things). But then there is "sin" in its singular form, the sin of stiff-arming the Lord of love and saying one "no" too many to his offer of saving grace.

Oswald Chambers pointed out that, "Jesus Christ never says that a man is damned because he is a sinner; the condemnation comes when a man sees what Jesus came to do and will not let him do it."[24] It is this sin, and this sin alone, that excludes a person from heaven. The amount of sin, and its various ramifications, was never the issue.

When John the Baptist heralded the Messiah's coming, he spoke of him as the Lamb of God that will take away the sin of the world. This seems rather startling, does it not? Millions and millions of people but only one sin? Yes, only one! Because when it comes to eternal destiny, the deciding issue isn't showing moral improvement or moderating formerly troublesome habits. *The* issue is Jesus! To reject him, therefore, isn't just one mistake to be listed beside many others. The greatest moral blunder in all of human history was clearly identified by the Scripture, "He came unto his own, and his own received him not."

Rejecting Jesus is in a category all by itself! As such, it is altogether determinative of where someone will spend eternity. Thomas a Kempis said, "To be without Jesus is a grievous hell, and to be with Jesus is a sweet Paradise." According to Tozer, it really doesn't matter how high one's office and how splendid one's reputation, "God has a hell for people who do not want to serve him—from the covering cherub that walked up and down the stones of fire, to the bishop or the pope or the pastor who would rather serve his own flesh and the devil than serve God."[25]

There is indeed a choice, and there is indeed a consequence. Spurgeon hammered this point with needed force when he wrote: "... be as moral as you can be, be as honest as you will, walk as uprightly as you may—there remaineth the unchangeable threatening: 'He that believeth not shall be damned.'"[26]

Anyone who stacks their supposed good works and then presents one's self to God on *that* basis will learn, too late, that the issue is Jesus. Not to believe in *him*, and not to turn to him as Savior, is to consign oneself to the vulnerable, indeed damnable condition of unremedied guilt.

The connection between "sin" and "sins" is closer than what may appear to be the case. And here's why. The law, which sin transgresses, is a reflection of God's nature. These laws were never set forth in a capricious manner, whereby the Great Lawgiver slapped down some arbitrary rules to cramp our style and make our life on earth harder. Instead, these laws reveal the heart of God, and in so doing reveal his ideals for a blessed and happy life. To transgress these laws, then, repudiates God himself, and further: repudiates his right to determine how we ought to live. Alexander Maclaren said, "Every sin bribes us to forget God."[27] This is why David ended one of the worst episodes in his life by telling the Lord, "Against you and you only have I sinned."

Now, to those who know the story well, it may have appeared as if David had sinned against Bathsheba, and certainly against Uriah her husband, and even against Israel, that had been put in harm's way because of their king's immorality. So why would David say that his sin was really against God?

Because the laws David transgressed uniquely find their source in God and not in these other people David did sin against.

Consider, for a moment, what kind of person we would be if we obeyed every principal set forth in God's law. A perfect person! Very much like Jesus! Beautifully manifesting God's image! And, again, this would be true because the law is a reflection of God's nature, a transcript of his holiness, a suggested summary of his goodness.

The laws inextricable relationship to God is further disclosed by examining the responses of people ushered into the immediate presence of God. For example, when Isaiah saw the Lord in the temple that day, how did he respond? By taking a nonchalant stroll over to God and striking up a lively conversation?

No way! Nothing like that occurred! For Isaiah completely unraveled, crying out, "Woe is me! For I am undone, because I am a man of unclean lips ..." (Isaiah 6:5). In explaining these words, G.D. Watson wrote that "we must remember that it is not the confession of a man living in open and actual sin ...."[28] At the time of this confession Isaiah may have been the most righteous man in the nation—an example of moral rectitude, a person greatly admired by his countrymen! But once Isaiah saw his righteousness alongside the whiter, purer righteousness of God, Isaiah was absolutely horrified! Never before had he ever realized how corrupt and contaminated his real condition was!

Similarly, when Job finally got past the religion of hearsay and at last saw God for himself, it wasn't exactly the uplifting "feel good" experience one might have supposed. Instead of bubbly euphoria and intoxicating glee, Job said, "Wherefore, I abhor myself and repent in dust and ashes" (Job 42:6).

You will notice here that in neither instance—with Isaiah or Job—did God say a single word about their sins. Instead, making no attempts to persuade or prosecute, the Lord marvelously revealed himself—and, suddenly, these men knew what they never knew before: just how badly they were complying with God's law!

Why? Because, unlike those writers who write books that don't disclose their heart, the laws God wrote *do* reveal his heart. To see God, therefore, is to see, vividly and painfully, where we stand in relationship with not only him, but also with his law.

Another way to understand sin is to understand how it first came into the world. Adam intruded on the center of the garden, which up until that time had been reserved for God alone. From the very beginning, God wanted life to revolve around himself, just as he continues to desire today. Therefore, to enter where God tells us not to enter is to put self where God wants to dwell—and, in effect, to take the place of God!

In his book, *The Power to Bless*, Myron Madden comments on the objections people offer about this fact.

> Any man will deny that he wants to be as God. He will say that it is a very ridiculous notion. He will deny that he has ever in the slightest degree entertained the idea of such a thing. If this be true—that man does not fall into temptation trying to be as God—then Adam is different, his problems are different. Hence, the story in the Scripture would have nothing to do with man today.[29]

Yet, as we know, the fall that took place in Eden has everything to do with us! This is because the Adamic instinct to let life revolve around self, and not around God, is still active in most people today.

When reflecting on peoples' relationship with God, John Owen pointed out, "... all of us know enough of him to love him more than we do ...."[30] So what causes our love to be so cramped and crabby? Is not self at the center of the problem? In Owen's words, "Do I account communion with him of so little value that for this vile lust's sake I have scarce left any room in my heart?"[31]

We must remember that every deliberate sin is an echo of the crucifixion crowd that yelled, "Away with this man!" (Luke 19:14). "We will not have this man rule over us" (Luke 23:18). How hideous, then, is this Adamic instinct! Sin first seeks to dislodge God from the center of our lives, and then it seeks to exile him far from his place of rightful rule.

Eventually, sin will slander the very integrity of God by calling into question the veracity of his words. Hence, at sin's prompting, the command of God will become a subject for debate. Remember how it all began? The Shiny One slithered over to Eve and asked, "Has God said ...?" This was a sinister question designed to create doubt. Of course, Satan knew what God had said. But he also knew how doubt can dangerously grease the pathway to sin; for once doubt sneaks in, confusion starts to deceive.

While some people see doubt as an innocent phenomena (and in some instances it is), we must be mindful of Scripture's words that speak of unbelief as being evil (Hebrews 3:12). And why evil? Because hidden in all the alternatives we present to God, and in all the rationalizations we present to others, is the view that the Omniscient One doesn't know what he's talking about and that the Dependable One can't be trusted. We may never say that, or even in such blunt terms think that. Yet, this is the logic of our unbelief, a belief that may be embedded more deeply in our soul than where our conscience wants to probe.

How easy it is to rationalize sin away as the unbeliever does, or to tolerate its presence in our life, as all too many believers do. John Murray warned, "Sin does not change its character as sin because the person in whom it dwells and by whom it is committed is a believer."[32] Be it in a believer's life or in an unbeliever's life, the predictable pattern that follows is this: First, we allow sin to *exist*, then we allow it to *expand*,

and finally we allow it to *expel* the very blessings from God that make life worth living. And if not reversed, this pattern will end in permanent *exile*.

F.B. Meyer, the eloquent British pastor, wrote these sobering words about the outcome of sin.

> It cannot be too deeply pondered by the wrongdoer, whether he be a child of God or not, that sin carries in itself the seed of its own fatal penalty; that there is no need for God to arise and take a thunderbolt in his hand; if only he keeps still and allows sin to work out its own result, according to the constitution of his world, the wrongdoer will be abundantly punished.[33]

Echoing this thought, A.B. Simpson declared, "It is an awful truth that evil men and women grow worse and worse, and the power of sin to hurt them and hold them increases with every repetition."[34] As things now stand, Erich Sauer observed, evil is everywhere. "We see not ethical nobility but moral degradation, not success but failure, not progress but collapse, not hope but despair."[35]

Had we first examined sin in a more biblical light, perhaps this takeover never would have occurred. But it was because we moved away from the light and into the shadows (where sin wasn't likely to be exposed) that evil's encroachments made devastating inroads into valued relationships and core beliefs.

True, this erosion of character didn't happen all at once. But in time what we formerly detested defined us more horribly than we ever imagined it could. Charles Spurgeon described the final stage of sin when he wrote: "Men die by sin, as men die when frozen to death upon the Alps—they die in a sleep; they sleep, and sleep, and sleep, and sleep on till death closes the scene, and then in hell they awaken in torments."[36]

C.S. Lewis spoke of how numbing and imperceptible sin can be as it leads us to destruction, "Indeed the safest road to hell is the gradual one—the gentle slope, soft underfoot, without sudden turnings, without milestones, without sinposts."[37] For precisely this very reason, the sin debate must not be lost! The characteristics of sin must be made constantly clear!

Sin—the rejecting of Jesus, the setting aside of his law, the doubting of his Word, the slandering of his character, the challenge of his right to rule—oh, my! Once assembled for inspection like this, we can see that sin is considerably more hideous than what we first imagined. Moreover, the enthronement of self embedded in each sin, and the distancing from God that inevitably results, puts sinners in league with him who started a war in the heavens and has now brought his rebellion to earth. Don't you see? The coarsening of culture in our day isn't singularly caused by some carelessness of modernity; Satan is on the loose! Forces from another world are clearly involved!

Wherever sin lurks or lunges, the desire to be free from its oppression, and free from offending our most holy God, must become the strongest motivation that determines our response. Lucifer—or the Lord? Each of us must now choose whose side we are on.

Perhaps our choice would be clearer if Lucifer hadn't flooded the landscape with so much deception. Because he did, however, the story of good and evil is like a mystery. A mystery that features clever disguises, false appearances, a blurring of distinctions, and the calculated use of counterfeits—actually, anything that will cover up, delay discovery, or allow further wrongdoing perpetrated before, as the outlaws of cowboy days put it," getting out of Dodge."

Satan doesn't want these bedrock truths about sin made known, for this would stop his ingenious disinformation campaign. With increasing zeal, he wants his campaign to widen, and deepen, until it climaxes with supernatural fraud.

G.D. Watson wrote:

> According to Scripture, the Anti-Christ will be the perfection, the culmination, the climax of all the sin of the universe bound into one bundle of a living man, and that this perfection of all the sins of the universe will be in the name of religion, for

the Anti-Christ will assume to be the most religious man who ever lived.[38]

And just think: The whole world will be fooled! But not until that last day, when the Glory shines and the Anti-Christ is revealed, will this confusion finally end. It will be at that moment the Savior splits the skies and holiness beams a brighter light than what the world has ever seen before when suddenly, in a flash, the days of scholarly quibbling and erudite equivocations will be over. Then, instantly, the propagators of moral delusion—the university, the media, the entertainment industry—will be utterly exposed. At that hour, appointed and anointed by God, no one with a brain will rush to Satan's defense. Because by that time, with that revelation, one's brain would have to be fried or scrambled to welcome even one more word of sophisticated foolishness.

Truth manifesting, evil exposed—oh, what a day! He that deceived the nations will be brought to judgment at last. All the ruination he sponsored, and all the devastation he achieved, will be exposed in cosmic contempt. Endless retribution will finally engulf him who stood stout against God.

A cold case file? Not anymore, because where this guy is going isn't cold.

Reflection Questions

1. How do you react toward our culture's minimizing of personal sin?

2. After considering the various ways sin gains entrance in our lives, which of these ways has been more prevalent in your life?

3. Have you ever received a revelation of your sin? If so, share this experience (without recounting forgiven sins).

The Adventure: Danger Ahead!

The big, bad wolf blew houses down ...

The Wicked Witch of the East terrorized little Munchkins ...

Hannibal stalked his victims with diabolical cunning ...

Freddie whacked his victims with flesh-shredding vengeance ...

But no one is as fierce a foe as the enemy of God—Satan!

Other dangers may be avoided. But no deliverance is possible for those who consistently reject the Savior. It will be to those deluded souls that one day these eerie words will be spoken ...
Welcome to Hell!!!

Chapter 7

An Autopsy of Sin—Part I

Adventure stories provide their thrills, especially when an adrenaline surge follows an escape from danger. These dangers are no less real in the battle between good and evil. In fact, the more virtuous one becomes, the more quickly Satan devotes head-snapping attention and schemes with black-hearted evil. However, the trigger to such danger (a life of consistent righteousness) should not be avoided; we just need to find the right way to defense the danger.

As in stories from fiction, so also in this war for our souls—knowledge is the key. Being lucky won't cut it, no matter how favored and righteous we are. We must *know* how the enemy plots our destruction.

There are at least two ways to learn life's important lessons. One can either learn by experience through attending the University of Hard Knocks; or, far preferable, one can learn by bringing a teachable heart to God's Word.

In this modern day—when the idea of "learning from a book" is thought to be inadequate and gaining firsthand experience is assumed to be the best of all options—the source of learning we select may to be the wrong one. Yes, learning from experience does have its appeal, but it often results in needless failure.

The rugged individualism of the Hemingway spirit can be quite enticing to the young, especially when the high-noon adventure begins. The sunshine, the gentle breeze, the broad and easily traveled path, dazzles the mind with exciting prospects, and fills the imagination of successes to be gained. So—with hair blowing in the wind, shoulders thrown back in courage, eyes scanning the horizon with intrigue—our traveler takes one last look around as a spirit of adventure wells up inside. A quick swallow of intoxicating bliss follows. And then—he's off!

Ah, the adventure! Euphoric as he begins it, his strides are long, his steps are rapid, his eyes are riveted on that horizon of hope, beyond which await challenges to be conquered, qualities of heart to be tested, and, if all goes right, a strength of soul to emerge triumphant.

Each advance toward this triumph will have as its only witnesses an open sky at day and peering stars at night. Even so, the appeal of this adventure insists that the only way is forward, and that the only expectation warranted is one brimming with optimism.

In this setting of daring and discovery, a map is thought to be a drag on all that is enchanting. Marked as it is by cold and calculating notations, the map induces a fog over the mind, causing once-gleaming eyes to become glassy. Hence, the retort: Why turn to the past for guidance? Who needs paper? Is there not a new way calling—a summoning to spirit that defies risks, that throws off warnings, that cares little about walking paths others have already walked?

The voice of adventure speaks on—and does so with escalating boldness! Chart a new course, for goodness sake! It's not a map you need to follow—follow your heart! Trust it implicitly! Let it take you to places unknown! Don't you see? To delay the call of destiny by plotting points on a map only puts a padlock on whim and a noose on impulse. I tell you, spontaneity will suffice! It is this willingness to try the untried that will gladden the day!

Sometime later, though, after leaving town and losing the light of day, the scene dramatically changes. Oh, my! What the adventurer wanted, the adventurer got! The most severe challenges (which weren't there before) now confront him: a treacherous terrain, menacing sounds, the constant stalking of predators, a sun that blisters at day and those blustery winds that chill to the bone at night. The isolation now engulfing him threatens to dehumanize him. Hence, the body stiffens! The face grimaces! Fists clench! Eyes widen!

So will the thrill of this adventure continue to sustain its charm, or will this traveler, like the great Hemingway himself, begin to entertain despairing and even life-terminating thoughts? The outcome hangs in the balance! Because once a pitiless and peerless night begins to fall, the passion that initiated this journey will be challenged to its core.

Vexing questions are bound to surface, commencing a rapid-fire interrogation: How long will *this* go on? Will the next day bring relief at last? Or will the inhospitality of this journey become even more severe?

Forcing an interlude in this interrogation, hope may ask its own questions: Will scenes that entertain await you? Times of respite ... invite you? Happier thoughts ... occupy you?

Refusing to be brushed aside, though, the sponsor of more ominous outcomes jumps in to ask: Or will the grind and monotony continue until jolted by sudden danger and vain thoughts of a rescue?

Questions! And not hypothetical questions, either. These questions bear down on you, for your very life is at risk! Oh, how valued the map is now!

As sanity returns and reason escorts it, it becomes clear that the lust for experience validates the map; it doesn't discredit it. A map is really a compilation of other people's experiences! And are they not needed? Hard enough are the challenges of life; so why handicap ourselves by putting on the blind folders of ignorance?

It was this fact, remember, that prompted the Lord's lament, "My people are destroyed by a lack of knowledge" (Hosea 4:6). Correspondingly, F.B. Meyer correctly said of the Lord, "He would rather convey his lesson in sunshine than in storm."

What should have been obvious at the outset to our traveler is that truth learned by the light of God's Word comes much easier than truth discovered in the torrential downpour of a harsh and hostile environment. So much *could* have been avoided if only truth were known earlier on.

Just like a geographical journey to an uninhabited land, the journey into obedience is beset with both obvious obstacles and hidden dangers. To negotiate around these we do need a map. Success in this journey involves what should be a welcomed assignment: studying the map of God's Word.

In undertaking this assignment, we notice from the Word of God two kinds of statements—didactic statements that set forth principles, and historical statements that set forth a chronology of experience. Interestingly, when the Bible describes the formidable danger of sin, it uses both kinds of statements. From James, chapter 1, we see a succinct description of the six stages of sin (James 1:14, 15). And from the book of Numbers, we see every one of these stages fleshed out in the life of Balaam.

Moral dangers, I submit, must always be taken into account, for the last thing any adventurer wants is failure to complete the journey. To venture forth bravely, only to see long-held dreams crushed and sources thought to be reliable overwhelmed, is a calamity that provokes understandable anxiety.

Changing the metaphor from land to sea, A.B. Simpson described such anxiety when he said:

> It is one thing for the ship to weigh her anchor and spread her spotless canvas to the breeze, and sail away with pennants flying and hearts and hopes beating high with expectation. It is another thing to meet the howling tempest and the angry sea and to enter the distant port. The first experience many—perhaps most of us—have begun, but what will the issues be? And what promises do we have for the voyage and the haven? How will all this seem tomorrow, and tomorrow, and six months from now, when the practical tests of life will have proved our theories and measured the real living power of our principles of life and action?[1]

So many questions! Reasonable questions, too! Questions demanding the best answers possible! For unless we have God's provision, the "awful awful" of being found motionless in the mud is a distinct possibility.

In such a case, autopsies are often ordered. But when it comes to spiritual death, Scripture has already provided an autopsy report *in advance*! So it is this report we must now examine as we check out not just one man, Balaam, but any person who allows himself to be caught in the gargantuan grip of sin. Talk about a man found face down in the mud of immorality, let me introduce you to Balaam.

In seeking to learn more about Balaam, we quickly discover this isn't a man easily pigeon-holed. Usually, the Holy Spirit provides a cameo-sharp picture of people. However, as J. Vernon McGee correctly points out, we don't always get this clear delineation of character, this refined and focused profiling that helps us to know what a person is really like. Among the most mysterious people Scripture talks about is this man Balaam. Balaam, a Midianite from Aram, uttered some of the most wonderful prophesies in God's Word. And yet, there was something about this prophet that was disconcerting, to say the least.

While most of the people Scripture parades come and go, never to be heard from again, this isn't true of Balaam. There was something about Balaam that required continual retrospectives, even as late as the book of Micah in the Old Testament and the book of Revelation in the New Testament. For some reason, the focus, again and again, keeps reverting to this man.

But why did Scripture do this? Because there were qualities in Balaam so insidious, yet so pervasive in human nature, we dare not ignore him. In fact, the Bible has more to say about Balaam than it does about Mary, the mother of Jesus, and more about Balaam than it does about ten of the twelve disciples.

When Micah said to "... remember what Balak, king of Moab, devised and what Baalam, the son of Beor, answered him ..." (Micah 6:5), Micah was drawing our attention to the important dynamics that transacted between these two men.

So, heeding Micah's call to remember, let's scrutinize every stage of their transaction with a resolve to gain all that the Spirit of God intended for us to receive.

The Drawing

Purposing to superimpose the description of sin found in James chapter 1 onto this story of Balaam in the Old Testament, we are first compelled to consider the words: "every man is tempted when he is drawn away ...." Here, we're made to know that just as fishermen have lures, Satan has lures. Thomas Watson once said of Satan, "Though he cannot force the will, yet he can, by temptation, draw it."[2]

To cast the alluring appeal, Satan, the consummate craftsman, knows exactly which lure will work to draw one kind of person and which lure will work to draw another.[3] But to see how this principle gets activated in Balaam's life, we will first need to set the scene.

The children of Israel, under the leadership of Moses, were on their way to the Promised Land. As they approached the east bank of the Jordan River, Balak, the king of Moab, experienced increasing fear that Israel might want to colonize his kingdom.

Desperately wanting to keep his kingdom, but at the same time not wanting to go to war with Israel, Balak devised this little scheme. He thought by sending messengers to bribe Balaam that this prophet with a wide and a well-deserved reputation would agree to curse Israel, thus ensuring there wouldn't be any encroachments on Moab.

So why would Balak attempt a bribe? Was he thinking that Balaam was a prophet for profit? Whatever was in Balak's mind at the time, just know that if the believer today has a price, Satan will pay it. The drawing!

This tempting to do evil began long before Balak, and for sure it has continued long afterward. While the human heart can generate its own evil without any direct participation from an outside source, Scripture is replete with evidence that there is an outside source much greater than King Balak. A seducing spirit, deviously engaged in devising temptations, *is* at work. According to E.M. Bounds:

> He is presented without introduction or ceremony as the Evil One, a graduate in the school of deception and evil. The curtain is drawn

and the chief actor is in full dress. A world is at stake, man is to be seduced, Eden is to be corrupted ... Eden does not date his birth. It is not the first chapter of his history or the first test of his hellish art.[4]

What happened in Eden had its beginnings in heaven.

One might well dismiss this notion of evil personified were it not for the fact Jesus himself believed it! To validate this fact, one need only ask the question: Where did the Matthew 4 account of that titanic struggle between the Son and Satan come from? No one else was present when these wilderness temptations occurred, except a dispatch of angels who showed up at the end.[5] Is it not obvious? This detailed account of wilderness warfare had to have come from Jesus!

Moreover, it was the Holy Spirit, freshly introduced at the baptism of Jesus, who led Jesus into this encounter—and not with a leisurely, meditative walk, mind you, but with a swift, impetuous march! Because from the Spirit's perspective, there was an enemy to be confronted! A victory to be won! And not an inconsequential victory, either!

So what we have in this account is an involvement of each person in the Trinity. It was the Holy Spirit who led Jesus into this battle, it was Jesus who engaged the Anti-One in this fiercely contested conflict, and it was the Father who provided comfort (through these dispatched angels) once the battle was over.

So was all this delusional? Are we to suppose the Spirit didn't lead Jesus, that no battle took place, and that no angels appeared on the scene afterward? Inquiring along similar lines, F.J. Huegel asked these questions about Jesus' temptations in the wilderness:

> Was it really 'the prince of this world' he had to face—a terrible supernatural being whose hate for God was as dark and deep as hell? Or was he deluded?
>
> That he believed in a personal devil whose dominion he came to shatter; that he commanded

demons to come out of their victims, that he was convinced that if he were to save man he must show up the Prince of Darkness in his true light, and break his power over human hearts; that he really believed these things, no student of the Scripture would for a moment pretend to deny.[6]

Satan isn't an invention of certain Persians, as the mythological proponents are fond to say; he actually exists! And to say otherwise is to doubt the veracity of Scripture and the workings of the entire Trinity.
A.B. Simpson noted:

The agent of the temptation is called the devil. This name is passing out of some of the modern theological dictionaries, but you will also find that with the passing out of the devil, there will come the passing out of the blood, the cross, the Savior and even God himself.[7]

So, apparently, this mindset that discards the reality of a personal devil isn't as harmless as some people suppose.
Nevertheless, as concerned as Scripture is about Satan, it is much more concerned about the human heart, converted or unconverted. According to the Bible, we have propensities within that do not bode well for our future. In fact, from our very first day on earth this has been true.
People talk about innocent little babies, but J.C. Ryle correctly observed that "... as it lies smiling and crowing in its cradle, that little creature carries in its heart the seeds of every kind of wickedness."[8] The potential for wickedness is so unfathomable Jeremiah 17:9 says, "... the heart is deceitful above all things, and desperately wicked; who can know it." The intent and extent of this evil cannot be comprehended.
Very much sobered by what one's self-life can do, Andrew Murray breathed this prayer:

Lord God, self changed an archangel into a devil, and self ruined my first parents and brought them out of Paradise into darkness and misery. Self has also been the ruin to my life and the cause of every failure; oh, discover it to me.[9]

As Scripture astutely contends, every man is tempted when he is drawn away *of his own lusts*. A.W. Tozer added: "It is doubtful whether any sin is ever committed until it first incubates in the thoughts long enough to stir the feelings and predispose the will toward it favorably."[10]

Yes, there is a Tempter who wants to exploit our weaknesses within. And yes, as E.M. Bounds described the Tempter, "The air is heavier by his breath, the night is darker by his shadow ... Judas is falser still and Peter is more cowardly, because Satan is there."[11] Nevertheless, even if Satan were never there, there would still be major problems due to a self-determined to get its way even if it offends a holy God and incurs his deserved and devastating wrath. Accordingly, we do well to examine both—the tempter and the one tempted.

The Desiring

Having introduced us to the dual agents in this drawing, self and Satan, Scripture next focuses on the sequence of the temptation itself by saying that what follows the drawing is the desiring. The word in James used to describe this next dynamic is the word "enticed."

Of course, once someone has been enticed, sin's appeal—whether it comes from self or Satan—has been warmly welcomed. Deep in the inner chambers, in the theater of this person's mind, the imagination is being entertained by images so enchanting the outcome is almost certain. Let's see how all this played out in Balaam's life.

The messengers from King Balak arrive on the scene to make their proposal. With imploring urgency, they first state their proposition, and then dazzle their money before the wide eyes of this easily-tempted prophet. So what does Balaam do? Incredibly, he goes into his secret chamber and prays about it!

Now, how could anyone possessing even a scintilla of wisdom think this was a subject meriting prayer? Balaam knew God would never sanction his people being cursed! So what was this religious charade all about? It was about a double-minded man so enticed with what sin was offering, he couldn't turn it down, at least not immediately.

Maturity will confirm, and many years of experience will testify, that the easiest time to defeat temptation is in the beginning. But if for one reason or another this doesn't happen, if the door to temptation isn't shut and therefore the enemy manages to get his foot in the door, temptation will gain a momentum exceedingly difficult to stop. Delay in matters like these only makes it worse!

The twelfth-century writer, Bernard of Clairvaux, described this disastrous momentum.

> The first steps in sin are taken apprehensively and no blow falls from the dreaded judgment of God. Pleasure in sin has been experienced. Sin is repeated and the pleasure grows. Old desires revive, conscience is dulled, habit tightens its grasp. The unfortunate man sinks into the evil depths, is tangled in his vices and is swept into the whirlpool of sinful longings while his reason and the fear of God are forgotten.[12]

A.B. Simpson reminded us, "Sin does not come to us full born. It is nursed by foolish words, worldly scenes, suggestive pictures and unholy glances."[13] Such dynamics are always part of the enticing stage, a stage that excites desires as a start-up to the whirlpool of sinful longings.

Willing to risk this outcome, Balaam goes through this little prayer routine, hoping that somehow—miracle of miracles!—God will say something that will enable him to get his hands on all that money. This, as you can easily anticipate, never happens. Instead, the messengers are sent home with no prophet in tow.

So does that stop the king—a refusal is voiced, and that's the end of the temptation? No, for as with Jesus later, and as with us today, the enemy will pursue with increased vigilance. This is just the way the enemy is. Even when a believer takes that final step across the threshold of heaven, Satan's bloody jaws are going to come crashing down.

When word comes from these messengers that the prophet is not for sale, the king, not easily deterred, decides to "up the ante." Therefore, commissioning an even more impressive coterie of communicators, Balak plots another visit to the prophet's home.

Accordingly, after a journey of several miles, there comes another knocking at Balaam's door. And what do you know? The prophet, ever available, is totally receptive to their presentation! Upon then hearing every enticing word, Balaam says two things that indicate his spiritual decline.

First, Balaam says, "Though Balak was to give me his house full of silver and gold, I could not go beyond the word of the Lord my God, to do less or more" (Numbers 22:18). Now, forgetting the piety part of this little speech, we have to ask ourselves: Where did this business of a house filled with silver and gold come from? The king never said that. The messengers never said that. So where did this thought come from?

It came from Balaam, and more specifically from the heart, Scripture says, that devises mischief. Outwardly, you see, Balaam seems to be saying all the right things. But there is something else going on, which—at this stage, anyway—is scarcely noticeable. As events later unfold, though, what at first was ever so subtle and not at all detectable, takes on very different proportions.

We see yet a further indication of spiritual slippage by what Balaam says next. "Now therefore, please, you also stay here tonight, that I may know what more the Lord will say to me." Again, forget the pious stuff; what should more earnestly get our attention is this decision by the prophet to get his tempters to stay. Instead of an outright refusal to meet with them (which is what should have happened), this prophet wanted to hear everything they have to say! And instead of showing them the door once they said it, this man insists they should remain on the scene.

Now what kind of a strategy is this? To deal cordially with temptation—accommodating it and begging it to stay—is proof enough that defeat is immanent. And as for the supposed prayer meeting that followed, it was as many prayer meetings today: filled with words that never should have been spoken. Had there been any alertness to God's Word, any discernment of the situation at hand, not one syllable of these words would have been uttered.

Let's face it: Too many people today are telling God what the devil told them—and then, because their heads were bowed and their eyes were closed, they think the sum of their words is the essence of prayer. But if the source of prayer is an enticed self instead of the inspired Word, that disqualifies the prayer. Infinitely better than prattling utter nonsense to God, is a silence that muzzles doubt and hides perplexity.

With Balaam, you'll notice, the temptation was getting stronger during what was supposed to be prayer. As Balaam said what he said, he only deceived himself more. Because, with every mention of money, the tantalizing image flashed bigger and brighter—and that constituted the enticing!

A.W. Tozer said it well, "No Christian ever fell into sin who did not first allow himself to brood over it with increasing desire." F. B. Meyer similarly observed, "All who have carefully watched the processes of the inner life bear witness that a long period will often intervene between the first germ of sin, in a permitted thought or glance of evil, and its flower or fruit in act."[14]

What some would call harmless, or simply being human, amounts to opening the door of a furnace so hot a blast of heat soon flashes and flares. Be warned, my friend! Wrong desires, if cultivated, will open the door of hell!

J.C. Rile writes:

> We are too apt to forget that temptation to sin will rarely present itself to us in its true colors saying, "I am your deadly enemy and I want to ruin your life forever in hell." Oh no! Sin comes to us like Judas, with a kiss; and like Joab, with outstretched hand and flattering words. The forbidden fruit seemed good and desirable to Eve; yet it cast her out of Eden. The walking idly on the palace roof seemed harmless enough to David; yet it ended in adultery and murder. Sin rarely seems sin at first beginnings.[15]

And that's why we need to develop a discipline for early detection *and then let that be the cutoff point*! Without a clear strategy like this, we will succumb to sin.

Writing to her son, John, Susannah Wesley offered clarity to this issue when she pointed out: "Whatever weakens your reason, impairs the tenderness of your conscience, obscures your sense of God, or takes off your relish of spiritual things; whatever increases the authority of your body over your mind, that to you is sin."[16]

Should one goes beyond the point—where discernment detects sin by welcoming further contemplation of that sin— defeat is at hand. What happens in the inner chambers, in the realm of images and desires, is so determinative the Bible tells us to guard our heart with *all* diligence. All diligence, because a tardy turning away won't work! The compromise that alternately permits God *and* Satan to participate in our lives lacks the diligence demanded for a protected heart.

The affections of our heart must be set with riveting focus and preoccupying meditation on things above. Anything less than this makes the battle far more difficult, and our chances of success dangerously diminished. Remember, the heart secretly negotiating with the enemy has forfeited victory already. Even if the enemy doesn't win this time, he has gained an advantage for next time.

In telling us to guard our heart with all diligence, a warning is given that we must well consider. Referring to this heart we ought to protect, Scripture says, "... for out of it are the issues of life." This means that the quality of our inner life, whatever it is, will eventually manifest! And when it does, forces that direct, determine, and drive will have been successfully launched.

At one stage, true enough, we are in control. At another stage, however, these forces take over. And when they do— when attitude becomes action, and one action sets up further actions—the seed sown eventually comes to harvest, whereupon consequences bear down more harshly than we ever imagined! At which point, we do have "issues"—issues that label us, limit us, deprive us, and burden us.

Perhaps we find ourselves in the grasp of welcomed temptation even while we are trying to present to the world, as Balaam did, an entirely different image of ourselves. If so, this cultivated image we love to project is going to be shattered. Like a car spinning out of control at the racetrack, our life will drastically swerve and catastrophically crash.

Given this fast acceleration into danger and all that it forebodes, it is imperative that we *immediately* reverse course. This may not be easy, because, like a drunk in detox, the misery of being cut off from that which is rapidly destroying us is not a welcome prospect. The sweat, the chills, the shaking, the terrible torment the body has to suffer ... Is this the way it has to be when stopping sin? No, it isn't.

Let's go back to the beginning in order to discover the pivot point where sin gained access. Why does a person choose sin in the first place? The choice is initially made because sin has something to offer, in that it fills a void; it gratifies a pleasure. But important for us to see here is this: The pivot point for entrance is also the pivot point for exit.

The Bible says, "Set your affections on things above" (Colossians 3:1). The principle being: The best way to escape temptation is to focus on what's *better*! Despite what we may be feeling, there's a gospel here—because *God always meets needs in ways far superior to Satan*!

So the best exit strategy from sin is this: Instead of focusing on denial (what you must give up), focus on fulfillment (what you will gain). This very simple and practical step will help to offset the illusion of loss.

It must readily be admitted that the grip sin has on one's life is not always broken easily. A person may want to get free, but the resources to do so may not be apparent. What then? Well, instead of focusing on how hard temptation is (which through your own grit and guile you must give up), focus on how great the grace of God is (which through expectant faith you subsequently receive).

F.B. Meyer tells how he learned this lesson one night while sitting around a campfire with other ministers. The host of this meeting asked him to give a brief update on his walk with the Lord. In sharing a recent experience, F. B. Meyer mentioned giving up something for the Lord; and it was at this point, Meyer writes, that he was kindly interrupted.

An old clergyman on the other side of the room then got up, the light falling upon his reverend face. He said he was quite surprised to hear me talk about giving up. For his part he was always taking in. He said that formerly, when he was a very impetuous, impulsive man, he was about to lose his temper with a number of children, when suddenly he turned to Christ, and said, "Thy patience, Lord!" and instead of losing his temper he said he could have borne with twice the number of children, and twice the amount of noise, because he met it by the nature of the risen Christ.[17]

Is this not the best way to face temptation, to turn to our ever-present Lord and allow the temptation to be an occasion for released grace?

Let this be the guiding and governing principle you activate: As soon as temptation strikes, *that's* your cue! Turn immediately to the Lord for a giant supply of grace! Remember, your assignment isn't to give up; it is to take in.

What God offers and heaven supplies is always better than what Satan is selling, and is certainly sufficient to withstand his salesmanship. But, like Balaam, we won't see that if we allow the seducer of our soul to make his repeated appeals to an enticed heart, to a heart that welcomes these appeals and considers each with intrigue and fascination.

Thomas Watson described what often happens: "The sinner thinks there is danger in sin, but there is also delight, and the danger does not terrify him as much as the delight bewitches him."[18] This is exactly what happened to Balaam. And it is so sad, because all that later occurred could have been avoided.

In the next chapter we will see the ensuing steps Balaam took, which in turn led to that final and fatal outcome. Understanding each of these steps is certainly necessary if we're going to avoid the trap Satan sets, to which the seduced self frequently succumbs.

Reflection Questions

1. In reviewing your life, assign percentages and explanations to these two options: a) Have you been teachable before the Lord? And b) have you been a perennial attendee at the University of Hard Knocks?

2. Upon making this review, what decision, if any, are you willing to make now? Be as specific as you can be when answering this question.

3. Given that Satan knows which lures are effective for one person and which are effective for another, which lures have been effective for drawing you?

4. In following Scripture's directive to set our affections on things above, what precisely is it that heaven offers that would offset and displace the lures Satan has used against you?

Chapter 8

An Autopsy of Sin—Part II

Sin doesn't just happen. Never has. Never will. There are stages that link, a processing that builds, certain factors that always kick in prior to the deed itself. The plot Satan conceives against us may actually take years to administer: with a weakness perceived here, faulty judgment exposed there; yet, behind the scenes there's a fiendish brilliance at work. Unaware of what's happening, though, too often we strut toward our defeat with clueless confidence.

Samuel Johnson once observed, "The chains of habit are too weak to be felt until they are too strong to be broken." Even when we do become aware of Satan's plot, our clever and calculating adversary will persist anyway. So mere awareness isn't enough; determined conflict is required.

Like the first round of a boxing match, our opponent will search for our weaknesses, test our defenses, strategizing all the while for the destructive blow that will strike in a later round. To us, what may seem inconsequential as he feints right and moves left is far more significant than we know. For during this time, information is being gained and the process of breaking us down is under way.

We may appear formidable—to ourselves, anyway—but that impression may also contribute to our undoing! Because as we set our defenses for one attack, and succeed each time we do so, suddenly the attack comes from an entirely different direction—and down we go for the count!

That this attack against us *develops*, and that distinct stages are necessary before cruel cunning can achieve its victory, is encouraging in one respect; because instant defeat won't occur in in the moral realm as easily as it might in the physical realm. Satan's desired outcome takes time, time that *could* be used to exercise a proper alertness and a suitable defense. If we'll just do that, we can prevent these further stages of destruction from occurring. F.B. Meyer noted:

> Before temptation comes we almost always have a warning of some kind. The barometer falls; the sea birds come in to the shore; the leaves of the trees are bent back. The Spirit of God contrives to give the soul some signal that at any moment it may expect an assault.[1]

To be sure, a strong enough signal can come straight out of the Word of God, *if* believers will daily consult it.

As we saw in the previous chapter, the book of James identifies six stages of sin, each stage functioning like a trigger to a nuclear bomb. Before devastation can occur, each trigger has to be tripped in succession. In this chapter, we will continue to track these stages by focusing on Balaam.

The first two stages—the drawing and the desiring—are beginning to adversely affect Balaam, a fact Scripture has enabled us to see. As with Balaam, the deterioration in our lives may not be outwardly apparent. This is why others, not knowing any better, may view us with much admiration.

More ominous than their mistaken perceptions is the distinct possibility that *we* don't know the real condition of our soul. One by-product of moral decline is a muted conscience, whereby the alarm doesn't go off; or, if it does ring, its ring is too soft and too short. Consequently, we remain oblivious to what should be obvious: the continual degrading of our soul due to its receptivity of sin.

To get the alarm to ring louder and longer, the conscience must be programmed to detect and defense each stage of temptation. With this goal in mind, we'll see what happens next in the life of Balaam, who is Exhibit A for every stage of sin set forth in the book of James.

The Decision

In sequencing the stages of sin, James next mentions this thought, "... and when lust has conceived ...." These words refer to the point of decision. At this point, no one else may know because nothing has happened yet. Nevertheless, for Balaam, it is now a done deal. It's only a matter of time before this already-made decision will be carried out.

When Balaam exits his little prayer meeting, he has what he wants—or at least a little bit more of what he wants—the "go-ahead" from God to travel with these messengers to see their leader. But why would God give Balaam this much slack? Granted, the Lord was totally clear about what Balaam was permitted to do. But, still, doesn't letting him go put Balaam even closer to the powers that will overcome him?

While the Lord's response is not entirely clear in this instance, the questions we're tempted to ask will keep backing us up, backing us up, until finally what we're really calling into question is the wisdom of God for giving any person any slack, lest by a wrong choice that person brings on his own condemnation.

By way of contrast, D.A. Carson described what a different arrangement might look like.

> Suppose, for argument sake, that God gave instant gratification for every good deed, every kind thought, every true word; and an instant jolt of pain for every malicious deed, every dirty thought, and every false word. Suppose the pleasure or pain were in direct proportion to the measure of goodness or badness God saw in us. What kind of world would result? ... Such a system of enforced and ruthlessly "just" discipline would not change our hearts. We would smolder with resentment. Our obedience would be external and apathetic; our hearts and devotion would not be won over. The jolts might initially gain protestations of repentance, but they would not command our allegiance. And since God examines the heart, he would constantly be

administering the jolts. The world would become a searing pain; the world would become hell. Do you really want nothing but totally effective, instantaneous justice? Then go to hell.[2]

In matter like these, when examining the freedom extended to Balaam, it is best to trust the wisdom of our omniscient God, keeping in mind that God did give specific instructions to Balaam to speak only what God inspired him to speak. Moreover, there wasn't any possibility of God sanctioning a curse so Balaam could get that money.

No sooner had Balaam departed, when God, somewhat surprisingly, gets angry. But why was he angry? Hadn't God just given him permission to go? Yes, but somewhere in the interval between permission granted and trip begun a decision was finalized—a decision only God could know, since he alone sees all hearts (I Samuel 16:7). Apparently, the motive Balaam had in his heart in the morning wasn't the same motive he expressed to God the night before. Moreover, this change in motive was about to be disclosed by Scripture.

A careful reading of what God actually said to Balaam provides one clue. God said if the men of King Balak come to call you, rise and go with them (Numbers 22:20). But that's just it! The men of Balaam *didn't* come to call! It was Balaam who took it upon himself to launch this trip! Why, he's so pumped, no further temptations were necessary! So as one might imagine, this daybreak departure provoked a fast response from heaven! Thus, en route to King Balak, the Angel of the Lord (meaning not just any angel, but God himself) stood in the middle of the road to stop Balaam.

Now the notion of God being our friend is widely shared within the family of God, but what about this depiction of God being our adversary? Are there not times when God, with a steeled insistence, will impose himself against us, determined to thwart our plans and head off further foolishness? We may answer that we've never seen an angel sent to block our path, but remember: I Peter 5:5 says God resists the proud. And isn't pride a sin that has plagued us all? So is it not likely that we *have* experienced God resisting us? Helmut Thielicke, the German professor and pastor, said, "As long as you have not met God as one who opposes you, you have not met God at all."[3]

Yet, even when God stood stout against what we were pursuing, perhaps we, like Balaam, didn't have the spiritual sensitivity to recognize this divine barrier.

Keep in mind that the decision to sin had already been made by Balaam (after a welcomed incubation of considerable enticement), but the deed itself hasn't occurred. So even at this late hour, heaven is still seeking to reverse Balaam's decision—and is going to great lengths to do it!

This, you will recall, the Lord also did with Abimelech many years before. Abimelech, the king of Egypt living in Gerar, was about to take Abraham's wife and make her his own. The Lord then appeared to Abimelech in a dream one night and told him Sarah was already married. During this dream, the Lord also told Abimelech "... For I also withheld you from sinning against me; therefore I did not let you touch her" (Genesis 20:6).

What? God stopping sin? God making sure that wrong actions weren't undertaken? Yes, sometimes (not very often, it must be admitted) God will intervene to just this extent—which is exactly what he does with Balaam.

The interventions of God may have been just as effective for us, but far less obvious. God may have shepherded us away from certain situations which, had we remained, would have ruined us. Or perhaps he removed certain people from our lives in order to protect us from their influence. Only when we get to heaven will we learn how God intervened many more times than we knew. And each time he did so, his purpose was to keep us from temptations which, at the time, were too great for us to handle. Again, the eventual escape from temptation was his doing, not ours.

As we examine the divine intervention in this story, we note Balaam's donkey having considerably more insight than his master does. Seeing what Balaam doesn't see (this angel standing in the road), the donkey seeks to avoid him by darting off into an adjoining field. This sudden bolting away, though, triggered not gratitude but a burst of Balaam's wrath. What followed was nothing short of animal cruelty.

Balaam dismounted his donkey and then attacked it. In doing so, there was no hint of discipline being enacted; for the rage unleashed that day had no motivation higher than the petulant passion of an infantile tantrum.

Unfortunately, a second attempt to get around the angel, which Balaam still doesn't see, fares little better. This time, while attempting to avoid the angel, the donkey accidentally crushes Balaam's foot against the wall.

Well! Incensed by this injury, the prophet strikes his donkey even harder than before. Take that! And that! And that! This swiftly unloosed fury—with whip and fists and kicks—called into question the sanity of this man.

What followed this vitriolic thrashing was even more absurd! Squaring himself in front of the donkey, while holding its head with his large leathery hands, Balaam stood nose-to-nose with this animal in order to address it eye-to-eye. Determined that this donkey should know exactly how he felt, Balaam denounced his donkey in a tirade of verbal abuse.

Can you see this scene in your imagination: the man of God heaping scorn, condemnation, retribution, and wrath?

On the third time the prophet's travel resumed, the donkey, seeing the angel with his imposing stand, decides to lie down in the middle of the road. Whereupon, Balaam—by now livid with rage—whacks his donkey repeatedly. With arms flailing and voice screaming, this last beast-beating culminated with another barrage of scalding speech.

Balaam's anger—at first irritation, but now a volatile eruption—was a sure sign of fury losing control. Swarming, and ever ready to sting, was a disturbed beehive of hellish hornets—*Balaam is mad*! This highly-provoked prophet, with red face and "crazy-with-spite" eyes, launched blistering, biting words Scripture decided to omit.

Perhaps we've never experienced an episode like this where we became emotionally unhinged and allowed vile, reprehensible forces to take over. Yet, this scene may not be as foreign to us as we would like to believe. For there have been other times in our life when we had our heart set on a certain outcome, but then, when deterred, we didn't like it one bit! Though we knew our desire was wrong, we, with great vehemence, didn't want any interference—not even if it came from the Lord. So we bristled with resentment as we shunned the Lord's unwanted prompting.

F.B. Meyer told of a time in his own life when he experienced a hypersensitivity that wasn't exactly godly.

> There were things in my heart and life which I felt were questionable, if not worse. I knew that God had a controversy with respect to them; I saw that my very dislike to probe or touch them was a clear indication that there was mischief lurking beneath. It is the diseased joint that shrinks from the touch and the tender eye that shudders at the light.[4]

Most of us have some familiarity with this aggravation of soul, but Balaam had reached an advanced stage. For him at this point, there was no impulsivity control, no semblance of rational behavior—for all pretenses of religiosity, or even respectability, were gone!

With each frustration vented, we are made to see in this dissembling of the man a desire flushed into the open that was carnal to the core. Balaam, it is now clear, *wants that money*! In fact, he wants it more than he has ever wanted anything else! Indeed, Balaam is so intent on what he wants, and is so full of himself as he pursues it, that even when his donkey speaks—saying, "What have I done to you that you have struck me these three times?"—Balaam hardly takes notice of his talking donkey!

Talk about being removed from his senses! Balaam doesn't spend two-seconds processing the fact *a donkey has just spoken*! Now, put this miracle in perspective, if you will: In all the ages of recorded history, an animal has never constructed a sentence, much less carried on an extended conversation! So, given what just occurred, any sane man would have the good sense to be shocked! But, no, Balaam is so possessed by his desire, is so consumed by what has overcome his interior life, that nothing in this objective world can stop him. Without a moment's hesitation, therefore, he verbalizes an immediate rebuttal to his donkey, and does so with such volatile, vituperative words that those around him must have questioned his intelligence.

Wanting to kill his donkey and send him straight to donkey hell, Balaam lamented the lack of a sword. But it was then, just then, that God opened Balaam's eyes and caused him to see the Angel of the Lord standing there with—guess what?—a sword! A sword not to be turned over to Balaam for use against his donkey, but a sword that was drawn against him!

This had to be a very scary moment! Think of it—an attacking angel? How incongruous is *that*? Aren't angels supposed to guide and guard, or sing a song maybe, or perhaps deliver some poignant, inspiring message? What about those cute, cookie-cutter angels we see on the Christmas cards today, those fat, sissy cherubim whose mouths are shaped in the form of a perfect 'O'?

Well, not at all looking like a Christmas-card angel, the supernatural being confronting Balaam that day was far more terrifying than anything Balaam had ever seen before! This, you might guess, caused Balaam to calm down real fast and to start repenting like crazy.

Do you see the irony here? In one moment, Balaam wanted a sword to kill his donkey, and in the next moment he sees a sword drawn against him! Now Balaam may not have been the smartest guy around, but in a millisecond of time it was, for him, message received! The message? Balaam was being more of a jackass than his donkey—and God wasn't going to put up with this much longer!

There comes a time, you know, when patience isn't God's highest priority. At such times other virtues will manifest, such as love giving a warning, or God declaring judgment. Now, with respect to how God dealt with Balaam here, we see an aspect of the Lord dealing with his own that we should appreciate.

A.B. Simpson wrote:

> How thankful we ought to be that he is judging us now that we may escape the judgment when he comes. It is like the judge taking you into his office and pointing out your fault, and giving you

a chance to rectify it before the court shall be convened.⁵

It is with this insight in mind that the psalmist invited God to search him and see if there be any wickedness in him. The motivating principle for this? To discover sin in a timely way *before* it brings eternal harm. The ultimate purpose? To disallow a calamitous construction: erecting a barrier against God around which no escape is possible.

Interestingly, this discourse between the prophet and his donkey surfaces another irony difficult to ignore. At one point in their discourse, the donkey asks another question, actually two other questions—"Am I not your donkey on which you have ridden, ever since I became yours, to this day? Was I ever disposed to do this to you?"

Such thoughtful questions! And such a high level of grammar—with perfect sentence syntax, too! Why, the very eloquence of a prophet comes from the mouth of the donkey!

And do you see how the prophet answered? According to Scripture, Balaam said, "Nay." Ironic, right? At this point, Balaam sounds like a donkey and the donkey sounds like a prophet!

The reason God allowed Balaam to continue his journey that day was because, in light of this dramatic confession, God was determined to use Balaam for his glory. This is often the way God works. Meeting us where we are—in the middle of an ill-conceived journey—God will seek to save us from ourselves and, by involving himself in our lives, yet use us for a greater good.

At last, Balaam arrives onsite and is greeted by the king. Hurriedly, even frenetically, the king escorts Balaam to view the Israelites camped in the valley below. Fully expecting the uttered curse, the king waves Balaam into action. But instead of cursing these people, Balaam, in a foiling of the plot, does the opposite by blessing them!

This unexpected outcome caused King Balak to go ballistic, at least inwardly. "What have you done to me? How could you come at my bidding and then do the opposite of what I had asked you to do!" But instead of blasting Balaam with the bombastic speech bouncing around in his brain, the king, realizing too much was at stake, was forced to restrain himself.

Much like the Seducer himself, Balak wasn't one to give up easily. So, taking deep breaths and clasping his hands tightly with much restraint, the king brought Balaam to another mountain, hoping that by this new vantage point, Balaam could be persuaded to curse the people of God.

This, too, is much like the Seducer, in that Satan will keep turning the kaleidoscope of images until one finally casts its swaying charm. Satan actually has many viewing places for us to visit, and many visuals for us to consider.

But, after once again consulting God, Balaam goes to the edge of the mountain where Balak had brought him and, of all things, does a replay of the first blessing! Well! King Balak unravels! This time outwardly, as he immediately calls for the curtains to come down on this sorry show! "If you can't curse them," Balak declares with clenched-teeth restraint, "then for goodness' sake don't bless them!"

Frustrated beyond words, the king is then forced to contemplate his next move. Utterly perplexed, he's trying to find a way to draw the man of God into sin—and not just intended sin, but *demonstrated* sin.

Reduced to begging and pleading, the Moabite king compels Balaam to accompany him to yet another vantage point. However, at this juncture, Balaam, sensing time was running out, decides not to consult God as he had done before. Instead, he rushes to give his prophecy, thinking he can get this curse over with—and quickly collect the money!

But contrary to his wishes, *another* blessing was given on Israel's behalf, as a spirit of prophesy once again came over Balaam. Do you see the glory God brought to himself by steadfastly speaking blessing over his people? Count on that in your own life, too! God is devoted to blessing you more than any eye can see, ear can hear, or imagination can conceive (Ephesians 3: 20).

With all these supernatural interventions from God, it would seem that this sin would have been averted and that Balaam's ministry would have continued. That assessment, however, minimizes the perversity of the human heart, as we shall see when we examine what Balaam did next.

The Deed

James says that when lust has conceived it brings forth sin, and this is exactly what happened to Balaam. Instead of aborting the abominable evil conceived within, what was inside Balaam finally manifested. The precise way this occurred, though, has to be pieced together from strands of Scripture's testimony.

The twenty-fifth chapter of Numbers informs us that eventually the local Moabite girls invited local Jewish guys to their wild, licentious parties; and not too long after that, these Jewish men began to worship the gods of their foreign lovers. The thirty-first chapter of Numbers adds an important detail to this narrative by informing us that it was "through the counsel of Balaam" that Israel committed trespasses against the Lord.

Splicing the two accounts, we can conclude that Balaam, wanting that money, said something like this to wicked King Balak. "Look, it's obvious I can't curse the Children of Israel, but I have another way to defeat them. Here's what I want you to do. Send your most attractive Moabite women into the camp to do you know what. And I guarantee you that after harlotry will come idolatry."

This, the Bible reports, is exactly what happened. Consequently, despite considerable efforts from God to stop this, the deed at last was done. But before wagging a bony finger of accusation at Balaam, we should remember that believers today have advantages Balaam never had: a completed Bible, the indwelling Spirit, a new nature, a fellowship group to encourage us, and biographies like Balaam's to show us what not to do. Nevertheless, haven't we, at times, been just as obstinate as Balaam, and just as determined in our sin-pursuits as he was in his?

To see rebellion in the raw does take our breath away. But if nothing else, it also alert us to the way acts come from attitudes, and how being is attributable to seeing. These images from within (manufactured by the soul), and those images from outside (sent by the seducer), eventually sealed the decision for Balaam until it finally manifested as a deed of undeniable evil. But, again, doesn't such vivid viewing work similarly in our life?

The Destiny

James next tells us "... and sin when it is finished ...." Let's stop there as we ask the question, just one sin? No, if sin has its way, it's not going to be just one sin. Because one sin will beget another, then another, and then another, until that sin becomes a habit. And when propelled further, this habit will become a character; and that character—once sin has run its course and the toehold has become a stronghold—will become a destiny.

Now hold onto that thought as the scene changes. Let's go back in time when we are much younger, to a time when we were more innocent and less aware. Someone approaches us. Conscious of a certain transgression in our life, this person asks us outright where we think this sin will lead us.

We stare blankly; the question doesn't exactly register. Lead us? "Yes," this person says, "if you do this wrong thing today, and again tomorrow, what will the final outcome be?"

Umm. Strange question, we can't imagine how this behavior leads us anywhere. Thomas Watson was correct, however, when he said, "Sin first courts, and then kills. It is first a fox and then a lion."[6] We may not see this when conscience is muted and self-deception is increased. Consequently, evil will increase its advance so long as we remain desensitized to it.

Even when evil is later engaged, the environment where this occurs may not excite alarm. Alexander Maclaren observed: "A man may break all the commandments sitting in an easy-chair ... Von Moltke fought the Austro-Prussian war in his cabinet in Berlin, bending over maps."[7] Witches didn't chant, devils didn't spook, gangsters didn't gather. The fact is: Foul smells, eerie sounds, and dim lights need not be present for serious sin to occur. The setting we're in may be perfectly normal! So the impression easily gained is that what's transacting is equally normal—when it isn't! Our environment is actually masking the deception!

Deception also increases when we put a small frame on a picture, thereby failing to see the big picture. By looking at isolated deeds and not overall designs, we allow ourselves to take one step and then another, with little thought about where the road we are walking is taking us. It is only when the day is spent that we finally see the ironclad habit, the corrupted character, and that damnable destiny we have unwittingly embraced. By that time, though, it is too late.

"When it is finished"—these ominous words from James speak of a well-conceived plot, the devising of strategies we never suspected, a record of ruination we never wanted. All along, we were deluded to think *we* were in control. A compromise here, a clever cover-up there ... you know, little things, ordinary things—from which a chain was being fashioned and with which we were being enslaved.

"Finished"—how dreadful this word sounds! It has the intonation of scriptural finality: "What is written is written." "Let him who is filthy be filthy still." Reinforcing the fact of an inevitable judgment that *will* come, Galatians 6:7 declares "... whatever a man sows, that he will also reap." These words—communicating certainty, exactness, proportion—have become an axiom for the ages, offering no caveats, contingencies, or exceptions!

Somewhat unsettled by the precision of this axiom, someone once asked, "But couldn't God be a little more flexible?" That's a good question. Our lives, like pencils, do need erasers, but there isn't that much flexibility when it comes to sowing and reaping.

As we now contemplate the destiny of Balaam and the legacy he left behind, we are presented with three New Testament references, each serving as a peg upon which we can hang our thoughts. Jude talks about the error of Balaam (Jude 11). Peter talks about the way of Balaam (II Peter 2:15). And the book of Revelation talks about the doctrine of Balaam (Revelation 2:14).

Do you see an escalating evil depicted in these three designations? An error is one thing; we all make them. "The way," it should be noted, is quite another thing; it suggests a frequently traveled path, a defined pattern of living that became a habit. "The doctrine," however, is still worse; it suggests something that has been formulated for propagation, a philosophy cleverly crafted for dissemination.

An error, a way, and a doctrine. Three points that plot the damnable destiny of Balaam. Can you locate yourself in this journey? And upon doing so, are you ready to turn back?

The Denouement

James concludes this six-stage description of sin by saying "... it brings forth death." So what does this mean? For the lost person it means a final banishment from the presence of God, a departure from the Eternal that can never be reversed! But for the saved person it means a discrediting deterioration of life God meant to be abundant. It is an insipid sameness with the world, one blending instead of blessing. It is a lukewarmness no one even notices, except God—and it makes him sick!

Here, death has to mean more than the stopping of the heart or the ceasing of the brain. Death, in this instance, includes debilitating disappointments, dead-end roads, a distancing that isolates, a degradation that humiliates, a coming to life's end filled with regret because we lived life as a consumer—a "taker" rather than a "giver," a "scatterer" rather than a "gatherer," a trivializer of time and a fritterer away of opportunity.

To go through life with an increasing exterior and a dwindling interior is death. To hobby away our life in shallow entertainments is death. To become possessed by our possessions is also death, especially if the whirlwind of getting and gaining gets us. To be ravaged and savaged by death long before our body greets the grave is the desire of hell, the design of the devil, and the damnable denouement of every life where sin has its way.

In this respect, it is instructive that the Bible tells *how* the people of God killed Balaam. Apparently, the sword the angel had taken up against Balaam was finally taken up again (Numbers 31:8)—this time, not as a warning but as a judgment from God.

Here, in this story of Balaam, we see a man chosen by God, gifted by God, protected by God, and forgiven by God. G.D. Watson wrote, "Balaam was really a prophet, and wonderfully endowed with both natural and spiritual gifts, yet they did not make him holy."[8] Even though he walked with God, talked with God, and came to receive remarkable revelations, Balaam came to a bitter, detestable, end-of-life experience no believer could possibly want. For him, the light of revelation was covered by his own sinful desires.

One might wonder how this could have happened, especially to a man who once knew God on such intimate terms. The mystery begins to fade, however, once the light of God's Word shines on Balaam's life. Actually, Balaam took that downward turn the same way any life takes a downward turn. The drawing became a desire, the desire became a decision, the decision became a deed, the deed became a destiny, and the destiny became death.

At any point along the way Balaam could have radically reversed this downward decline. He could have repented, gotten right with God, and continued his ministry. But as another attendee at the University of Hard Knocks, he experienced what God never wanted him to experience—and, in doing so, became a despised and despicable figure, denounced by both of Scripture's Testaments, Old and New.

Offering a conclusion to this story, A.B. Simpson sounded a warning that needs to be both heard and heeded: "Oh! Let us beware how we tolerate a single sin, how we leave an enemy in the land, how we make terms with any forbidden thing, how we enter into alliances with the world, or let its spirit touch our fondest affections."[9]

Extending this counsel, F.B. Meyer wrote:

> God would lead us back to the moment when a tiny seed, borne on the breeze, floating through the air, found a lodgment in some crevice of our heart; and, although the soil was scanty, succeeded in keeping its foothold until it had sunk down its tiny roots, and gathered strength enough to split the rock which had given it welcome.[10]

This story of Balaam, while hardly a testimony to obedience, is a testimony, nevertheless. Because Balaam, by representing a contrast to the good life, helps us see, more clearly than it is comfortable to see, what the alternative to the good life is like, and why we should never choose it.

All the stages of disobedience are on display in Balaam's life to warn us, even generations later, what these stages are, exactly how each links to the other, and how each stage accelerates the path downward, until judgment finally comes. This anatomy of sin—given not in clinical terms but as a narrative from history—presents a clear picture.

So have you now seen enough to dissuade *you* from living a life that welcomes sin?

Reflection Questions

1. How does the story of Balaam affect you?

2. Upon reviewing the six stages of sin, which stage resonates with you the most?

3. How do the three designations—the error of Balaam, the way of Balaam, and the doctrine of Balaam—relate to your life? Consider the meaning of each and make connections.

Two roads diverged: There is the broad way—

*At first it made sense ...
The attraction seemed irresistible ...
The moment was now...
I didn't think anything bad would happen ...
Everybody else was doing it ...*

And there is the narrow way—

*It took me so long to see ...
I didn't know it could be like this ...
Life is so much better now ...
I wish I had done this many years ago ...
I want other people to benefit ...*

Chapter 9

The Consequences of Sin

An adventure story wouldn't offer much appeal if formidable opposition didn't exist. Many people think the most daunting opposition facing us today is terrorism. Ever since September 11th, warnings of suspected terrorist attacks have become familiar to U. S. citizens. And in the beginning, we took these warnings seriously, but after a while our capacity to remain on alert diminished—due, most likely, to the normalcy of our daily routines.

Our first thoughts when we wake in the morning are not about terrorism. Instead, we're thinking of tasks awaiting us at work, errands we must get done after work, or arrangements still needing to be made for family activities on the weekend. It is this preoccupation with daily routine that seems to disrupt, if not dislodge, our focus on terrorism.

Besides, some people considered these terrorism alerts utterly useless anyway, saying: If the enemy decides to stalk us, get us in his scope and fire away, there's nothing we can do about it. Que sera sera!

Transferring this fatalism into the spiritual realm, these same people think that God's protection is no better than what some of those referees in so-called professional wrestling provide. Now, if you've ever seen the WWF at its incriminating worst, you know that all kinds of barbaric behaviors occur, which these buffoon referees never seem to see—or stop! But caricaturing God this way isn't fair. For if the Bible tells us anything, it tells us how the guiding, guarding presence of God can stop sin from perpetrating its harm. Check out Psalm 91 and see all the provisions promised for the opposition Christians may encounter.

More than terrorism, it is sin—and the sponsor of it, Satan—that generates our greatest opposition. Defending our self from that, and doing our part to defeat this opposition when it launches its assaults, can be quite an adventure. Honesty and accuracy require us now to report on the damage this opposition can cause.

The Crushing Burden of Guilt

One consequence of sin, alluded to already, is an unawareness of its presence. G.D. Watson remarked:

> We have purposes and drifts and tendencies and biases and bents in our nature that we are unaware of ... human beings would be frightened to death if God were to show ... all the details and driftings of their nature that they are not aware of ... There are latent principles in us that God sees will in a few years work out our absolute destruction.[1]

The fact that sin will bind and blind the soul it inhabits is not a fact often considered.[2]

Counselors of every description will tell you that the number-one problem they deal with is guilt. What keeps this guilt in place, often, is our unwillingness to deal with it. We know the genesis of this avoidance goes all the way back to the beginning of the human race. What was the first thing Adam did after he sinned? Hid! And what was the second thing he did? Lied! And what was the third thing that he did? He started blaming everyone in sight—including God!

The modern transgressor today is really no different, in that he, too, will keep his distance from the Lord, deny personal culpability, and choose to blame parents, spouse, the environment—anybody, everybody—but certainly not himself. The symptoms, and they appear often, reveal the source, a self seduced by Satan.

In this day of victimized thinking in which a person's wrongdoing is habitually attributed to some wounding from the past, the "blame game" has become quite the fashionable response. But while this response may engender sympathy from others, it won't engender healing from heaven. "Truly it is an evil to be full of faults," Pascal observed, "but it is a still greater evil to be full of them but to be unwilling to recognize them."[3]

Regarding man's propensity to dodge an avalanche of scriptural evidence exposing his guilt, the German theologian Reinhold Niebuhr offered this assessment:

> Luther rightly insisted that the unwillingness of the sinner to be regarded as a sinner was the final form of sin. The final proof that man no longer knows God is that he does not know his own sin. The sinner who justifies himself does not know God as judge and does not need God as savior.[4]

To deny the obvious, or to acknowledge it with no emotion, is really frightening. In some ways it's like talking to a sociopath who can commit the most heinous crimes, and yet be quite unmoved by it all. This person can give a bloodcurdling account in the most matter-of-fact way, as if it had no more significance than going to Starbucks to get a latte. Upon hearing such an account, we are left to wonder, "Is this really a *person*? How can anyone on the planet think like this?"

Actually, we have all defended self in sociopathic ways. The hard heart, the contaminated conscience, the enthroned self, will instinctively react this way. But we may be so spiritually insensitive, we may not know it. What may be horrific in the eyes of God may mean next to nothing to us. So one need not focus on criminals only to see this principle at work; it shows up in less dramatic ways, too.

Addressing this phenomenon, A.W. Pink wrote:

> Because particular persons are not swearers, morally unclean, drunkards or thieves, they are very apt to imagine they are far from being wholly

corrupt; in fact, they consider themselves good and respectable people. These are described in Proverbs 30:12: "There is a generation that are pure in their own eyes, and yet is not washed from their filthiness." However irreproachable may be the walk of the natural man, his nature is polluted and his heart thoroughly defiled. And the very fact that he is quite unaware of his vileness is sad proof of the blinding power of indwelling sin.[5]

It would be better for sin to be exposed, and for the scum of guilt to be acknowledged, than for a clueless assessment to kick in and dismiss the case prematurely. Reacting to this problem, the Puritan theologian John Owen said that a major pastoral burden of his ministry is "to convince those in whom sin evidently hath the dominion that such indeed is their state and condition."[6]

Sadly, such a condition is unfortunately common. And were this an episode only, perhaps encouragement could come easily. But it is an epidemic! Sin reigns, and guilt rules.

The Chill of Isolation

A second consequence of sin is a loss of intimacy with God. This point was dramatically illustrated at Calvary.

On the town's garbage heap just outside Jerusalem, three crosses were erected, and upon each cross a criminal was hung. A larger-than-usual crowd soon gathered, riveting their attention on the center cross.

There, the Nazarene turns his head one way and then another, conveying by these multiple motions considerable physical pain. In an attempt to breathe better, the Galilean suddenly lifts himself by arching his back. But the attempt to solve one problem only creates another, as the nails start to tear his flesh. A spasm of pain immediately results, thus dictating a return to his former position.

As bad as this physical pain was (Cicero called it the most cruel punishment known to man), there was yet another suffering that day, one inflicting a much more grievous wound. This particular suffering had to do with the perfect fellowship enjoyed between Father, Son, and Spirit throughout the eons of eternity. There had never been any tension between them! Their greatest joy, always, was each other!

In his poem, "The Creation," James Weldon Johnson has God saying, "I'm lonely. I'll make me a man." In truth, God was never lonely—not during precreation days, nor during all the days that followed. Theologians correctly assert that God doesn't have any needs; for all his needs (if we can even use that word) are forever and gloriously satisfied within the Trinity.

It was on this day, though, that Jesus' greatest desire, his fellowship within the Godhead, was about to be disrupted. By taking upon himself the sins of the world, Jesus saw the weight of that hideous heap bring a reaction from heaven that proved to be the most painful part of his suffering.

Far greater than what the nails, the thorns, and that spear could ever produce was the unfathomable suffering Jesus bore when the Father turned his back and the Holy Spirit took his flight. The resulting cry—"My God, My God, why have you forsaken me?"—conveyed an agony too deep for anyone to comprehend. For sure, the piercing shriek of that cry made it clear that Jesus was hardly doing a devotional on the twenty-second Psalm. This cry was nothing less than the consummate agony of hell!

David Brainerd wrote in his now-famous journal how the cross of Jesus completely changed the lifestyle of savages. Ministering to the Indians in upper state New York, Brainerd said, "I never got away from Jesus and him crucified; and I found that when my people were gripped by this, I had no need to give them instruction about morality."[7] Drinking, gambling, stealing, murder—all ceased, as did those less notorious sins, once the cross of Jesus came into view. This makes perfect sense, actually, for one can't love Jesus and still cultivate a fondness for what necessitated his death.

Now, if God reacted so decisively against sin even when his dear Son was involved, do we honestly think that sin's attachment to us will result in a less decisive reaction? This can never be! Repeated and unrepented sin will always cut off our fellowship with God! Yes, the *relationship* will remain (for a believer), but the *fellowship* won't.

Giving insight about this issue, Andrew Murray said:

> The loss of God's presence is always due to some hidden sin. Just as pain is nature's warning of some hidden pain in the system, defeat is God's voice telling us there is something wrong. He has given himself wholly to his people. He delights in being with them and revealing in them his love and power. Therefore, he never withdraws himself unless they compel him to do so by sin.[8]

True, while the manifestations of his presence may be temporarily withdrawn for faith-strengthening, love-pursuing purposes, his fellowship will not be withdrawn unless sin compels this. Even a little sin, if willingly indulged and protracted by practice, can block the presence of God.

Richard Jefferies illustrated this point when he told of an experience he had while sitting near his window one night waiting for a certain star in the southern sky to appear.

> The dusk came on, and grew deeper; but the star did not shine. By and by, other stars less bright appeared, so it could not be the glow of the sunset which obscured the expected one. At length he began to doubt the accuracy of his own knowledge; when, suddenly, a puff of air blew the branch of a pear tree, a leaf moved, and there was the star behind the leaf.[9]

Just as a constellation can be hidden by a branch, and its brightest star can be hidden by a leaf, so, too, one strategically-located sin can effectively block the presence of God.

To those who entertain sin and continue to welcome its pleasures, this question must be asked straight away: Do you prefer the pleasures of sin to the pleasures of being in fellowship with God? This is a legitimate question. Because given the premise that welcomed sin and fellowship with

God are mutually exclusive, you are going to have to make a choice. So let there be no delay! The presence of the Lord can return to your dry and dreary soul, if you make the decision to keep company with sin no longer.

In his typically tender way, F.B. Meyer gave this assurance: "When so far as we know them we have put away our sins, or at least are steadfastly resolved to be rid of them, we may count on an ungrieved Holy Spirit; and this will always mean the consciousness of our Savior's presence."[10] Can there be any pleasure greater than that?

The Anguish of Self-Inflicted Harm

A third consequence of sin is known to us all, frustration. Proverbs 13:15 declares, "The way of the transgressor is hard." Hellishly hard! Those little shortcuts we take, those clever compromises we conceive, those manipulative schemes we execute, never work in our favor—at least not when the final tabulations are made! Sin *always* demands a price—and sometimes an exorbitant price!

Numbers 32:23 sums it up well, "Be sure your sins will find you out." You may think you have gotten away with it; and for a while you may also think life couldn't be better. But the Baptist preacher R.G. Lee had it right when he said, "There's going to be a payday someday!" That little spark of sin may have flared without starting a fire, but just know that ignition *will* come, and with it, destruction!

Do you recall what the Lord said to Saul on the road to Damascus? "Saul, Saul, how hard it is to kick against the pricks." What a vivid word picture this is! The pricks refer to wooden poles strategically fastened to the legs of an ox, each with sharp points attached to the end of the pole. So if the ox is tempted to go in a wayward direction, this instrument could be used to correct his course. But sometimes the ox, determined to go his own way, vented willful frustration by kicking against the pricks. The result? You know what it is: greater pain to the ox!

Similarly, if we pursue a course that God has pointedly cautioned against, we, likewise, are being as dumb as an ox—and in the end, we are only hurting ourselves! Addressing this point in a somewhat unusual way, Philip Yancey described a situation where this cause-and-effect dynamic seemed not to be the case.

> In the movie, *The Last Emperor*, the young child anointed as the last emperor of China lives a magical life of luxury with a thousand eunuch servants at his command. "What happens when you do wrong?" his brother asks. "When I do wrong, someone else is punished," the boy emperor replies. To demonstrate, he breaks a jar and one of the servants is beaten.[11]

This insulation from harm, so insolently enjoyed by the last emperor, isn't extended to us, obviously, because our sins do have repercussions! In fact, it is a spiritual law that offers no amendment: To indulge sin is to see its harm boomeranging back. In the terse words of Proverbs 8:36, "…he who sins against me wrongs his own soul." Thus, the British pastor J.H. Jowett warned, "All sin works towards decline, insipidity, impotence, and night."[12]

Within the heart of man are possibilities and purposes that could bring eternal satisfaction to his soul. But sin has a way of ripping these inbred purposes out of a man's heart so he can no longer do what he was made to do. According to Tozer, "Sin has made man like a bird without a tongue. It has within itself the instinct and the desire to sing, but not the ability."[13] Keats described what happened to a nightingale that had lost its tongue: Unable to express its deepest instinct, this songless bird died of suffocation.

And so it will be for that person who chooses sin and not God: With horrified gasps he will finally see on that last day the cruelty he brought upon his own soul. All through an endless eternity he will suffer a self-loathing that screams, "Why did I do it? Why was I so insane to reject Jesus? Why did I ever choose sin when it never did that much for me in the first place?"

The Sensing of Insecurity

A fourth consequence of sin is a loss of assurance. In the first epistle that bears his name, the Apostle John declared this to be the case when he wrote, "Now by this we know that we know him, if we keep his commandments." But what if we don't keep his commandments? Since this condition describes many people, let's flip the premise and see where that leaves us.

In doing this, we discover that for those drifting in the deadly currents of an ongoing sin, there is this nagging, gnawing suspicion that their salvation isn't real. Even if they have a theology that informs them otherwise, a lamentable loss of assurance will continually plague them anyway. Accordingly, as God becomes increasingly distant, all that was once precious will fade in its impressions and diminish in its impact. Later, there may even come this dizzying disorientation, this almost surrealistic symptomatology that God himself isn't real—which of course he is, but because of permitted sin it will seem as if he isn't.

I can't begin to tell you the number of times I have been called to some church member's home only to hear a confession ending with the words, "I don't think I'm a Christian, after all." As it turned out, the evidence indicated otherwise. Nevertheless, for this person it *felt* as if salvation was lost. Why? Because this is what sin will do! Repeated sin will produce an agonizing suspicion that salvation was never received, that all these church-going years have been a fraud.

F.B. Meyer helped explain this dynamic when he wrote, "Obedience and faith are two aspects of the same posture of soul; as you obey, you are able to believe; as you believe, you can obey."[14] Remove either one of these dynamics and the other one will surely suffer.

The Forfeiture of Joy

Closely associated with this loss of assurance is a corresponding loss of joy. Martyn Lloyd-Jones observed, "Assurance is not essential to salvation, but it is essential to the joy of salvation."[15] According to Dr. Jones, "You cannot know the joy of the Lord until you are perfectly certain that all is well between you and God."[16]

Interestingly, when David finally repented and came back to the Lord, one of the first things he prayed for was a restoration of his joy (Psalm 51:12). Joy is that serene and supreme confidence that God, no matter what the situation, is both willing and able to show himself strong on our behalf. And while it is true that joy, first and foremost, isn't an emotion; it's also true that joy can escort the heart to exhilarations not commonly known.

Unfortunately, the loss of joy comes as no great surprise to many Christians, because, quite frankly, they expected their joy to leave. To them, joy is a fickle friend, a somewhat fleeting commodity, the presence of which cannot be sustained on this side of heaven. So the prospect of muddling through long seasons without joy is, to them, totally predictable.

But is this what Jesus said? No, Jesus talked about our joy being full (John 16:24)—which means that on scale of one to ten, we're all the way over to a ten, to the kind of joy that erupts into fervent, radical worship!

Perhaps you've had experiences where emotionally, all ambivalences dissolved as you were caught up in ejaculatory praise. In John 17:13 Jesus spoke of his joy being available to disciples. *What*? A believer can have the same joy Jesus has? And not just a little dab of that joy, but a joy so extensive it will totally fill that person?

Imagine how different our worship would be, and our family life, our work, and witness would be, if this joy did indeed become ours! Why, this dynamic would change everything! To miss out on such joy, then, is hardly a ho-hum, what-else-is-new fact of life. For the one fact that must not be overlooked is that if Satan can steal our joy, he can steal the vibrancy from our witness, once contagious in its appeal.

Many of us have acclimated ourselves to a life that has more teaching than testimony, perhaps thinking this sorry state of affairs is inevitable. But is it? Consider again what Scripture is offering: a joy that is full, a joy that is lasting, a joy no man can take away (John 16:22).

So what does this say about the rise and fall of our emotions being normative for a Christian? Isn't this assumption—the Christian's emotional life will be similar to that of the non-Christian's—just another overly-reductionist view contrived by an unbelieving church?

In its quest to avoid triumphalism, and all those indicators of the supernatural promoting it, the church keeps telling people how emotions aren't to be trusted, how joy isn't the same thing as happiness, how we all have these valley-bound days, and why we can't stay on the mountaintop. But even though there is some truth in these assertions, in aggregate, and by design, their conclusion is really false. Because if the Bible teaches anything, it teaches how to bring the mountain into the valley! So if indeed that can be done, then to be without joy must mean *something is wrong*! Something that can't be explained away by mounting a case against the inferiority and unreliability of emotions.

According to legend, Satan was once asked what he missed most since falling from his former high estate in heaven. Satan answered, "I miss most the trumpets in the morning."

Oh, the vitality of divine life! The utter joy of heaven with all its matchless thrills! The repeated summons of the trumpet to yet another climax of grandeur and glory! Such will be forever forfeited, though, by every soul who keeps company with sin.

The Shut Down of Faith

A fifth consequence of sin is extremely serious—an inability to launch out in faith. Once again, the Apostle John crystallizes the point for us:

> Beloved, if our heart does not condemn us, we have confidence toward God. And whatever we ask we receive from him, because we keep his commandments and do those things which are pleasing in his sight (I John 3:21, 22).

So what is the basis of our confidence? The fact we don't have a condemning heart, the fact we have been keeping the commandments, the fact that by doing those things, we please God. But what if the reverse is true? What if our heart *can* make a case against us? And what if the alarm of conscience *is* going off? If we deliberately continue to disobey God, will we still be able to launch out in faith under those conditions? No, we won't; for the presence of guilt will shut down our faith. Therefore, without any announcement declaring this shutdown, an internal awareness will inform us that a faith launch is impossible—so why bother to try?

This is an extremely vulnerable position to be in, because the Bible tells us four times the "just are to live by faith." According to these verses, all of life is to be a series of faith transactions, whereby the believer crosses the bridge of faith in order to secure the blessings of grace (Romans 4:16; 5:2). But if the bridge of faith is down, and if life-goals are now being pursued in some other way, then the needed grace supply will be out of reach! Consequently, all God is offering, and all he holds out to us in his promises, remains in his unreachable hands.

Having valued our sin more than we valued the blessings of grace, we put ourselves in a place where faith couldn't function, where God's grace supply couldn't reach us. So you tell me: What kind of calculation went into that evaluation? The Bible speaks of abounding grace, the kind of grace that puts us over the top (II Corinthians 9:8), the kind of grace that rewards us with an unexplainable, ever-expanding peace (II Peter 1:2). But we in our Olympian wisdom thought sin offered more? This is crazy!

Listen, there is only one bridge to God's grace supply. Only one. Therefore, the irrationality persuading us to sabotage our faith bridge makes no sense—and is this the mindset we want?

As we've just seen, sin has many devastating consequences: It puts us under the crushing burden of guilt, it exiles us from the presence of God, it catapults us into a life of futility; it causes us to lose our assurance, our joy, and even our faith. Of course, all of this is toxic to the believer! And that's why Hannah Whitall Smith declared: "Besetting sins are to be conquered; evil habits are to be overcome; wrong dispositions and feelings are to be rooted out, and holy tempers and emotions are to be begotten."[17]

This assignment from the Lord—dislodging sin from core to circumference—is actually a survival pursuit, once one finally sees the extreme danger sin portends.

Sin, the stalker of every baby and the destroyer of every godless life, is nothing short of horrible. J.C. Philpot, who preached in nineteenth-century London, lamented sin's assault by saying:

> Sin is my hourly companion; and my daily curse. Sin is the breath of my mouth; and the cause of my groans. Sin is my incentive to prayer; and my hinderer of it ... Sin spoils every pleasure; and adds a sting to every pain.[18]

Alexander Whyte, the Scottish preacher of the nineteenth century who specialized in the doctrine of sin, made this wise and useful observation:

> *God chastises sin by means of sin.* He employs the remaining sinfulness of the sanctified heart as his last and his best instrument for reaching down into the depths of the heart in order to [affect] its complete discovery, complete correction, and complete purification. There is no tyranny so terrible, there is no invasion and captivity of the soul one thousandth part so horrible and so hated of all God's saints, as is their captivity to their own sins.[19]

Once discovered and uncovered, though, a deep resolve will well up in the believer's heart, declaring, "It *must* not be! And it *will* not be!" Sin shall have no dominion over us (Romans 6:14).

Such a resolve would certainly please the heart of God. In this regard, Goethe, the German philosopher, once said that "If I were God, the world of sin and suffering would break my heart." Well, it does break God's heart! But it won't be until it breaks our heart, too, that sin's alternative, the life of obedience, will become an immensely appealing option.

And just imagine how good we would feel, if we remained obedient even when hell rages against us. Why, if that became our legacy, it would be an inspiring adventure story well worth telling!

Reflection Questions

1. Of the six consequences of sin identified in this chapter, which has hurt you the most? Which has hurt you most often? And which has hurt you most recently? Please explain.

2. What insight presented in this chapter most motivates you to eliminate sin from your life? Please explain.

Chapter 10

Defective Obedience—Part I

John Bunyan's classic, *Pilgrim's Progress*, describes the journey to the celestial city every believer must take. The journey isn't always upward and onward, though, for there are those times when we regress instead of progress. Such times insert chapters into our life story we really don't want.

One reason many people like biographies is because they have a way of disclosing chinks in the armor—certain imperfections of thinking, certain undesirable deeds—with which we can easily identify, and to which we have also succumbed.

In order to present its characters in a more positive light, one might think that biblical biographies would gloss over personal defects. But, no, due to Scripture's sensitivity toward sin (a factor often omitted in secular biographies), no false aura of glory encases any of its biographies.

Noting this fact, Alexander Maclaren wrote, "Scripture never blinks the defects of its heroes. Its portraits do not smooth out wrinkles, but, with absolute fidelity, give all faults."[1] Accordingly, decisions that never should have been made, and thoughts that never should have been entertained, are brought into full view. Never to glorify them! And never to excite prurient interest! But for the sole purpose of giving accurate and needed insight.

As we further contemplate the obedience God cherishes, the obedience essential for being good, we do need to be aware of certain examples that are defective in source, motive, or method.

When examined more closely, obedience has shades of gray that black-and-white simplicity often overlooks. Penetrating this misconception, the devotional writer Andrew Murray observed:

> The inward work of God is hindered by bad men through their obedience to earthly passions; by good men through their striving to be good in their own way, by their natural strength and a multiplicity of seemingly holy labors and contrivances.[2]

God may extend mercy toward these ill-advised attempts, but as the venerable Lightfoot once put it, "The mercies of God are never recorded in Scripture for man's presumption, and the failings of men never for imitation."[3]

The scriptural examples we will consider now, although negative in nature, can still be beneficial to us if they alert us to "zigs" and "zags" of behaviors that should be studiously avoided.

We often think of obedience and disobedience in black and white terms, wherein the motives, the response time, and the commitments of each are thought to be either uniformly commendable or uniformly objectionable. What sometimes manifests, though, is more complicated than that.

As an astute observer of human behavior, Solomon suggested as much when he wrote about spiders in palaces (Proverbs 30:28). The palace, of course, represents that which is splendid, ornate, exquisite, and highly esteemed. The spider represents that which is loathsome, repulsive, perhaps deadly, and certainly out of place. A spider in the palace? The proper response for this is obvious, is it not? Take the broom and get rid of it!

Even in the church, where splendid character shows forth in one of her leaders, this phenomenon of "the spider in the palace" may sometimes be observed. T. De Witt Talmage, the nineteenth-century American preacher, said, "A well-developed Christian character is a grand thing to look at ... You say, 'How useful that man must be!'" If only that observation were *always* true, but, no, further observations offer a different testimony. According to Talmage:

> ... you find, amid all his splendor of faculties, there is some prejudice, some whim, some evil habit that a great many do not notice, but that you have happened to notice, and it is gradually spoiling that man's character ... Others may not have seen it, but you are anxious in regard to his welfare, and now you discover it ... a spider in the palace.[4]

This odious fusion where good blends with evil, and obedience blends with disobedience, is certainly not inevitable, nor is it irreversible; therefore, this mixed-morality morphing is worth our attention.

There are many models of obedience considerably more varied than our unexamined thinking has somehow supposed. Hence, there's a need to become better acquainted with these models, if for no other reason than to achieve earlier detection of our susceptibility to encroaching evil. One such flawed-obedience model might be called delayed obedience.

Delayed Obedience

In Matthew, chapter 21, verses 28-31, Jesus tells a parable of two sons commissioned by their father to do an important task. Son number one in this parable, perhaps possessing what psychologists today would call an oppositional defiant disorder, flat out refused to go. In sharp contrast with his brother who said, "I go, sir!" this son made it known he had no attention of doing what the father said. So with a stomped foot and a turned back he hardened his resolve. As time passed, however, son number one began to have second thoughts. Perhaps his conscience began to bother him, or perhaps his deeper feelings for the father began to emerge. Whatever the real motive was, son number one finally did what his father had asked him to do.

So what's wrong with this response? Shouldn't we only look at the bottom line—that is, the eventual outcome—and let it go at that? No, we shouldn't; for a serious failing about the delayed-obedience model is this apparent notion that instructions from God are negotiable. But why would anyone ever think that? If Jesus taught us to do on earth precisely the way it is done in heaven, then wouldn't it be true to say that in heaven the angels wouldn't even think of negotiating with God?

Check it out. The consistent testimony of Scripture is that whenever God speaks, the angels obey—*always*! Is this because they don't have a choice, because angels are like robots? No, angels have *full* access to intellect and volition; yet they obey God—instantly—every time!

This scenario perhaps confuses us, because we assume that if the mind and will are involved, moral compromise is inevitable. But on this point, as with many others, we must examine our presuppositions further. To have a will doesn't mean (as we have supposed) being in the middle, equipoised between good and evil. On the contrary, the sanctified will gets out of the middle and is all the way over on the side of good.

Moreover, consistent adherence to good doesn't mean that the will has been coerced, as compliant-child responses often are. For instead of responding to pressure, the sanctified will responds to principle; and instead of doing so grudgingly, the sanctified will does so with pleasure.

Tozer spoke of how "angels live through a thousand serene millenniums without feeling the slightest discord between their desires and the will of God."[5] And when one then adds to this discussion the amazing fact that God did something for us he never did for the angels (having died for us on Calvary's cross), this notion of negotiating with God becomes all the more unreasonable.

Scripture says we are bought with a price and that we are not our own (I Corinthians 6:19, 20). So whim, mood, convenience, and our own ideas should not be factors in our daily decision-making. All such intrusions should be suddenly and summarily withstood as a fresh appreciation of the blood stirs our heart to grateful obedience.

We must remember that at the time we received what Jesus did for us on the cross, we signed our life over to him. II Corinthians 5:15 clearly makes this point when it says, "... he died for all, that those who live should live no longer for themselves, but for him who died for them and rose again." So what part of this verse do we not understand?

As we think about the heart of our Father, we know he would never tell us to do anything that would bring destructive harm to us. For every word he says, even those words that seem grievous and at the time inflict some pain, are good words, once the panoramic perspective of heaven is clearly in view. Furthermore, not to seize the moment with full obedience may mean, for us anyway, that the opportunity will be lost—or, if not that, the intended blessing will be greatly reduced.

Just know: When delay follows truth, so, almost always, does disobedience. For precisely this reason, once God's truth has been made known, we mustn't allow our claim for more time to tempt us into an internal debate. It simply makes no sense for human reason to elevate itself above divine revelation, especially when one knows the Author of truth and the reliability of his words.

Such supposed scrutinizing of the Father's instruction is really masking the rumblings of a rebellious spirit, which, during this ill-advised delay, are going to gain momentum for an eruption of evil. Scripture says, "Today if you will hear his voice harden not your hearts ..." (Hebrews 3:15). It was in this regard that A.B. Simpson declared:

> There are some things which in their very nature must be done quickly or they lose their effect. There are processes that will bear slow, deliberate action, but there are great decisions that must be instantly made, and advance movements that must be carried forward as the walls of a fortress are stormed by swift and sudden assault.[6]

Delayed decisions, even if the decision itself is right, offend God and hurt us, especially if such delays are an equivocation of his clearly understood will.

Displaced Obedience

A second model of obedience to be avoided is what might be called displaced obedience. It is in the Old Testament, sometimes called the storybook of the ages, that we learn more about this type of obedience.

One day the Lord told King Saul to destroy the people of Amalek—utterly, completely, permanently! This called for every man, woman, boy, and girl; every ox, camel, donkey, and sheep; all humans, all animals, to be executed in terminal judgment. The assignment for this, given in the 15th chapter of I Samuel (verses 1-3), couldn't have been more clear—the day of reckoning had finally come!

About such a day as this, when mercy is withdrawn and judgment is ordered, F.B. Meyer warned, "... there are moments in our lives, irrevocable moments, when we take steps that cannot be retraced, when we assume positions which we cannot retreat, when results are settled never to be reversed."[7] In the words of Scripture, "What is written is written."

With regard to Amalek, there were two reasons prompting this divine order: one theological and the other historical. Scripture sets forth the theological reason by using a metaphor: the cup of iniquity being full (Genesis 15:16). What this metaphor conveys is the fact that the evil people do may be perpetrated for a time without any direct, divine intervention. But if the indomitable patience of the Lord is to no avail, and if the cup of iniquity continues to fill, there will come that day when the opportunity for repentance is withdrawn and divine retribution is unleashed. Such a day had now come for Amalek.

History records how the people of Amalek vexed Israel from their early days in the wilderness. The hostility that began there didn't end there; for this hostility—through murder, rape, pilferage, and plundering—continued without mercy, and without cause. Finally, after three centuries of this abuse, time ran out for Amalek, as the One to whom all vengeance belongs announced that Amalek was to be removed from the face of the earth!

This total destruction of Amalek was not an assignment to be taken lightly, obviously. Yet, inexplicably, King Saul *didn't* do as he was ordered. Instead, he allowed King Agag to live and his property to be preserved. Equally grievous to God was the fact that Saul decided to keep some of the enemy's livestock as spoils of victory, as plunder for profit—despite the Lord's command to destroy all!

When confronted by this failure to obey, Saul had his excuses fully rehearsed. Responding to the prophet Samuel, Saul said, "It was the greed of the people that forced my hand! Their insistence just couldn't be stopped, Samuel! Besides, what a fine offering to the Lord: this splendid herd of livestock!"

Scripture reports that when the prophet heard this sheepish recitation of excuses, he took no stock in it. So, with unflinching resolve, based on a supernatural revelation, the prophet ignored everything this truth-twister said.

Failing to persuade the prophet, Saul finally admitted that yes, he had sinned—and in so saying, that seemed to be the extent of it! There was no remorse, no regret for offending God, no sorrow for putting the safety of God's people in jeopardy, no grief cracking his voice, no tears brimming his eyes. Instead, with an alacrity that was alarming, Saul pivoted from this small point about sin with equally false and facile words as he sought a full and unconditional pardon from the prophet—*which did not come*!

During the night previous to this visit, God told Samuel all that Saul had done. And, sure enough, when Samuel came into the presence of the king, confirmation of this sin immediately came to the prophet's ears when he heard the bleating of sheep—and to the prophet's nose when wafting winds carried the odor of this preserved livestock. Samuel therefore *knew* that none of what Saul was telling him was true. Infuriating to Samuel also was that he knew it before the first syllable came from Saul's lying lips!

During this fateful meeting, Samuel declared that Saul's days as king were coming to an end, for God had decided another man, a better man, would replace him!

Deposed? Replaced? Why, Saul couldn't accept that! So from that day forward, Saul became the king who wouldn't give up his throne. Adopting this as his fixed and irreversible agenda, the royal backslider then launched a campaign of supposed obedience, whereby he hoped to reverse God's decision to remove and replace him.

Obedience? Fine, Saul decided, he'd demonstrate obedience! Lots of obedience! Impressive obedience, too! Enough obedience, in fact, to regain divine favor!

With this sudden zeal—unwanted by God and unwarranted by circumstances—Saul assaulted the peaceable people of Gibeon—to the point of *their* extinction from the earth! Apparently, the rationale for this ruthless assault was rooted in an incident that occurred a short time after Israel entered the Promised Land.

After crossing the River Jordan and commencing the campaign to conquer Canaan, Joshua made an ill-advised covenant with the people of Gibeon, a covenant that allowed them to live among the people of Israel (Joshua 9:3-15). This covenant was not as God would have had it; nevertheless, a covenant was a covenant, so there was no going back on that now! Not, that is, until this sudden flash of idiocy, this flush of supposed purity, converged into this monstrous zeal to do the imagined bidding of God.

Displaced obedience! The failure to obey God in one matter was followed by the decision to more than make it up to God in another matter. All this, mind you, to compensate for the original disobedience!

Displaced obedience may also involve replacing clearer instructions that are recent with instructions from the past that are now dubious. What we see in Saul, on display forever, is supposed obedience: deficient in motive, delinquent in time, and destructive in deed.

Still on the statute books at that time was a law calling for the death of witches and other practitioners who consulted evil, supernatural powers. Well, with his memory suddenly revived, and his indignation instantly ignited, Saul launched an attack on this small part of the population, too, with a zeal no more holy than the manipulative motives that inspired it.[7] The result of this zeal? The swords flashed, the blood flowed, the cries for pity went unheeded as Saul refused to extend to others the tolerance he reserved for himself!

None of this supposed obedience, singularly staged for heaven's viewing, worked, of course. For while God is always pleased to see improved behavior following genuine repentance, this was not what Saul was offering. What he offered was really displaced obedience with an undisturbed rebellion at its core! Had not the prophet already told this king during that last visit when a verdict against him was announced that rebellion is like witchcraft? So why this flexibility with truth? Why amend the clear assignment God had given?

Rather than deal with what amounted to witchcraft in himself, Saul decided to externalize the issue by attacking the witchcraft in others! And further: Instead of responding with obedience where God told him to apply it, Saul opted for *other* places, *other* issues (less costly to himself, as it turned out) where compliance to the command of God was easier.[8]

To those less knowledgeable of the facts, sudden flurries of obedience by a follower of God may impress. But this is not the kind of obedience that God wants. And neither is, what may be called, debated obedience.

Debated Obedience

Luke, chapter 5, verses 1-9, provides the account of Jesus preaching from Peter's boat as the crowds gathered near the shoreline. This was pretty heady stuff for a formerly common fisherman! Not only had the Messiah selected Peter to be a disciple, but now the Master was in need of Peter's boat to do kingdom work!

We can only imagine how all this transacted. As Peter positioned himself behind the Lord that day, taking in the entire scene (which included a vast multitude looking his way), perhaps a surge of self-importance began to make its appeal. And perhaps, too, Peter began to envision the much larger crowd *he* would one day rule once the Lord ushered in the kingdom.

Mindful of what was happening to Peter, the Lord concluded his sermon that day by giving Peter the command to launch into the deep. When reading the biblical narrative further, it becomes obvious from Peter's response that this instruction made no sense to him *at all*! So, verbalizing his ambivalence out loud, Peter articulated his objections to the Lord with very little restraint!

Yes, eventually, and reluctantly, Peter finally agreed to do what the Lord had told him to do. And, yes, Peter never responded like son number one did—in that Peter's resistance, though felt and expressed, never took the form of a flat-out refusal. Nevertheless, even this resistance is something to be examined.

What was Peter thinking? That Jesus didn't know what he was talking about? That his command was ill-considered, utterly flawed, and therefore compliance would be a complete waste of time? This was precisely what Peter was thinking!

To himself, Peter reasoned, "Lord, when it comes to preaching, performing miracles, and revealing all that is true in the spiritual world, no one knows what you know. But, Lord, when it comes to fishing, you're looking at an expert! I have fished these waters for years! And unlike carpenters such as yourself, I know where and when the fish bite. And it isn't now! And it isn't where you're telling me to go!"

Silence ... after which the Lord's strong and insistent stare eventually made its point! Peter then yielded to the Lord's bidding and launched out into the deep; at which time it seemed as if every fish in that sea was in a race to get into Peter's boat! Not only were the nets breaking (because there were so much fish), but both Peter's boat, and another boat called in to help, almost sank due to this deluge of fish!

Interestingly, Peter's response was not what might be expected. Instead of being excited about all the fish (and perhaps pledging the Lord to a repeat performance: same time, same place, next week), Peter got down on his knees and confessed what a sinner he was.

How revealing! Peter didn't pursue a business partnership, as many in his position might have been tempted to do. No, of all things, Peter asked the Lord to get away from him.

So why did Peter respond this way? He did so because this experience traumatically toppled Peter from his inordinately high view of himself and his much-too-low view of the Lord. In a flash, this sudden and shocking insight enabled Peter to see that Jesus indeed was like none other ... that Jesus' control over nature credentialed him as being far more than a man ... that the authority due the Master was such that Peter should have never, ever doubted *anything* Jesus had to say!

Even today, academicians will arch their eyebrows in skepticism if a scriptural perspective addressing them is surfaced. With a confidence that can only be labeled absurd, they'll clear their throats (to get attention) and then venture their contrary thoughts with an air of superiority.

Joining these musings of modern education are business men who think that while Jesus can be trusted with issues of the soul, they don't really need him for their business. Holding a similar view, other professionals think that while the words of Jesus are needed in the spiritual realm, they don't need his advice in their area of their expertise.

But don't you see? By trusting what the Bible tells us not to trust (our own understanding), we will not seek what we so desperately need (if only we had a modicum of sense to see it), the wisdom of the Lord—a wisdom that applies even to that area of life where we think ourselves most proficient!

There are, to be sure, other ways that supposed obedience gets skewed. And that's why we mustn't end our consideration of this subject at this point. Rather than race through this analysis by hurriedly stacking every example of defective obedience in one pile, let's undertake a personal inventory that deals with what we just discussed.

Delayed obedience ... is that going on in your life?

Displaced obedience ... would the Holy Spirit be concerned about such a substitute in you?

Debated obedience ... is this a dynamic still at work in your life?

If any or all of these defective examples of obedience are yet present in you, please deal with these issues now. The adventure ahead won't turn out right if you stay in an information-gathering mode, yet never let the truth you're learning convict you, and change you.

Reflection Questions

1. What example of a "spider in the palace" comes to mind when you think about yourself? You need not disclose this to others, but do deal with it before the Lord, and then be prepared to share the fact of that with others in your group.

2. Of the three defective examples of obedience discussed in this chapter, which one has most troubled you in the past (however recently), and how was this dealt with?

Chapter 11

Defective Obedience—Part II

The reason the hymn writer said, "Trust and obey, for there's no other way" is because there isn't. If we won't trust the Lord enough to obey him, our life will be one of continual frustration. And what kind of adventure is that?

The perpetually-sinning Christian is, perhaps, the most frustrated, and frustrating person on earth! Think about it. His refusal to come under lordship means he isn't pleasing God; and his refusal to sell out to Satan means he isn't pleasing the underworld. Of course, given all these conflicts, he isn't pleasing himself, either.

Oswald Chambers wrote, "Whenever you obey God, his seal is always that of peace, the witness of an unfathomable peace, which is not natural, but the peace of Jesus." Chambers went on to say:

> Any problem that comes between God and myself springs out of disobedience; any problem, and there are many, which is alongside me while I obey God, increases my ecstatic delight, because I know that my Father knows, and I'm going to watch and see how he unravels this thing.[1]

The confidence that can be ours when we obey God is in sharp contrast with the frustration will be ours when we don't. While one might think that any sane person would want peace, and not frustration, the record shows: Intelligent people—and, by society's standards, respectable people—forfeit what is better, and do so for an extended period of time.

The life of deliberate disobedience may not be the life you chose, yet it seems that something short of obedience has somehow gotten into the picture. Exactly how this occurred may not be altogether clear to you at this point, and that's why other obedience approaches should be examined.

In the previous chapter we saw three examples of defective obedience, examples where the lines blur, where gray becomes the prominent color, and where a given behavior is neither black nor white.

In this chapter we want to continue this examination, by checking to see how a lack of moral clarity can sneak in even when obedience seems to be the objective.

Distorted Obedience

A fourth model of obedience to avoid is distorted obedience. We see an example of this in Genesis, chapter 12, where God's calls Abraham to leave his home, Ur of the Chaldees, and to leave all his family as well. Though not disclosed at that time, the land where God was directing was about a thousand miles away.

In response to this call, Abraham promptly made his departure from Ur with none other than nephew Lot in his entourage. When reading this, we are tempted to do a double take! Because hadn't God just told Abraham to leave all the family behind? So why is nephew Lot coming along?

This inexcusable exodus eventually proved to be a disaster, as the corrosive effects of compromise became evident soon enough. The outcome caused Abraham, Lot, and company to stop five hundred miles short of their eventual destination—and to remain there for decades!

There were other problems, too! The herdsmen of Lot and Abraham began to quarrel so vociferously that the two kinsmen and their respective entourages had to separate. In a statement oozing with prophetic overtones, Scripture reports what happened next. Preferring gold to God and fortune to family, Lot "pitched his tent toward Sodom."

No, he didn't immediately move into this city (utterly corrupted though it was); he just started moving in that direction. Seeing all the lush fields where his cattle could graze and all the enticing amenities of city life, Lot got closer and closer and closer, until he eventually became a full-fledged citizen! And—what do you know?—he then became mayor of the city!

What followed in years to come was a catastrophic cascade of fire and brimstone raining down on Sodom and her sister city, Gomorrah. A rescue attempt by the angels to save Lot and his family could have succeeded. However, Lot's wife didn't make it—and it was all her fault!

Even Abraham got dragged into this; first, by going to war to help free Lot—in alliance with these wicked cities, mind you! And second, by standing in the gap for Lot while interceding against an impending judgment from God.

None of this was according to the will of God! And had there never been this partial obedience in the first place, Lot might not have lost his wife—and indeed his very soul!—in that very wicked city. Scripture says of his tenure in Sodom: He was vexed every day.

G.D. Watson commented on the one who "will obey the Lord on nine points and rebel on the tenth. He has partial obedience."[2] This business of editing God, of picking and choosing what we will obey and what we will ignore, is as immoral as it is high risk. Addressing this precise point many years later, the Lord told Joshua not to depart from the Word, to the left or to the right (Joshua 1:7), because consistent obedience is prerequisite to good success.

You can always be sure that once selective obedience gets into the picture, as it is in so many lives today, "good success" diminishes as an outcome—and, if not reversed, fades into oblivion. This truth was amply illustrated centuries before in biblical history. Instructions had been given to the brothers, Cain and Abel, regarding the proper way to worship the Lord. The acceptable offering, they were told, was to be a first-fruits offering that conveyed God's priority over their lives.

The Bible specifically says that what Abel gave was in the "first fruits" category (Genesis 4:4). But with Cain that comment wasn't made. Cain, the first liberal, thought worship didn't have to be undertaken in any particular way; so, like many "open-minded" people today, Cain thought he could worship the Lord the way Cain thought best, so long as he was sincere. Instead of a sacrifice representing the first and best, Cain came waltzing into worship with some nice juicy tomatoes. Ooh, la la! What state fair wouldn't give Cain a nice prize!

With this "palsy walsy" view of God and Cain's absolute abhorrence toward any form of dogmatism, Cain was shocked to find his enlightened flexibility renounced by the Lord. And in a sign of what would escalate much later between these two perspectives, Cain, the supposedly enlightened one, lashed out in horrifying hatred against Abel, the devoted follower of God's word.

The Lord later warned Cain that sin, like a lion, was perched at the door ever ready to pounce! And sure enough, pounce he did, rendering Cain a vagabond on the earth. His life, in years to come, hardly resembled the good success promised Joshua (Joshua 1:8). So much, then, for distorted obedience!

A Forced Obedience

A fifth model of obedience to avoid is what might be called forced obedience. An example of this is Jonah. A. B. Simpson said, "We see in Jonah a man who obeys and serves God as long as it suits him, but is a stranger to that obedience which knows no choice except the Lord's will."[3]

You know the story. God called Jonah to minister to the city of Nineveh. But, no, Jonah ran just as fast as he could in the opposite direction! From Tarshish, he traveled to Joppa and not to Nineveh. This meant Jonah went about two thousand miles off course.

Nineveh, built by Nimrod on the east end of the Tigris River, was a very formidable city. According to archeologists, the walls surrounding this city were ten stories high—and, get this—were sufficiently wide for three chariots to drive on top, side by side! Within these walls were garden plots and cattle fields! This city was so big—sixty miles in diameter—it would take a traveler back then three days just to journey across it! No wonder, then, that in Israel and in other countries beyond, there was this three centuries-old fear of Nineveh, that menacing city from the East, lurking to expand its borders!

While Nahum (Nahum 2:8-13; 3:4-7) and Zephaniah had preached *against* Nineveh (Zephaniah 2:13-15), Jonah was the first told to preach *to* Nineveh. God's call to Jonah actually consisted of three words (Jonah 1:2)—"arise" (a word that calls for readiness, a word that summons to action), "go" (an evangelism word, if not a missionary word) and "cry" (a word that simply means to preach with passion). Arise, go, cry—those three words represented Jonah's marching orders to this capital city in the Fertile Crescent.

Saying "thanks, but no thanks," Jonah went down to Joppa. And to track his itinerary further (both geographically and spiritually), this rejection of the Lord's assignment meant Jonah went down, down, down, in every respect. First, he went down to Joppa, then he went down into the ship; and from there, he went down into the sea, then he went down into the fish, and finally he went down into Sheol! This itinerary, descriptive of many running from God, results in a continual downward spiral until finally reaching rock bottom.

Jonah was eventually vomited onto the very shores God had first directed him. But what kind of a testimony is that? This bile-drenched prophet not only caused that miraculously prepared fish to gag but many others as well who later heard this story of forced obedience.

Not too surprisingly, one can check out the Hall of Fame chapter in Hebrews and never once see the name of Jonah. Though he preached one of the greatest revivals in biblical history, this omission isn't too difficult to figure out. Because what is there to commend in Jonah's example? Why should his name be revered? And why *shouldn't* it be removed from even footnote status?

The seeming erasure of Jonah from historical memory is further documented in the New Testament. Because when Jesus began his ministry, one of the charges against him was there had never been a prophet from Galilee. But this wasn't true. There had been a prophet from Galilee. According to II

Kings 14:25, Jonah was that prophet. However, he was forgotten because his forced obedience isn't worthy to be remembered, except perhaps as a pattern to be vigorously avoided. Join Jonah? Why, no one should do that!

Our last report on Jonah was that he begged God to let him die. Reflecting on this request, A.B. Simpson writes, "We see in Jonah the picture of a man who wants to die when he is least prepared to die."[4] It seems that every calculation he made was wrong! This, regrettably, is the lamentable legacy of forced obedience.

External Obedience

Another model of obedience to avoid is what might be called external obedience. The best illustration of this is the Pharisees. While the Pharisees haven't enjoyed good press in our day, the enormous respect they had in the eyes of their contemporaries is a historical fact.

During the intertestamental period—those four hundred years between Malachi (the last Old Testament book) and Matthew (the first New Testament book)—the Pharisees came into existence. A major factor in their ascendancy was their exemplary devotion to God's law—a devotion strongly contrasting with the Sadducees who were fast forsaking the religious in favor of the political.

The Pharisees codified what all the other religions, and people of no religion, think—namely, that to get to heaven, you have to be good. But as the most compelling articulators of this position, they became the targets of the most stinging words Jesus ever spoke. Jesus' warnings not to do alms before men, and not to orate long, pretentious prayers in the marketplace, addressed the Achilles heel of the Pharisees—external religion! Jesus even called these religious leaders a white-coated sepulcher—that is, a good paint job on the outside with nothing but death on the inside!

The fastidious righteousness of the Pharisees prompted the publishing of hundreds of new laws. On this point, Philip Yancey writes: "Pharisees and teachers of the law competed with one another in strictness. They had atomized God's law into 613 rules—248 commandments and 365 prohibitions—and bolstered these rules with 1,521 emendations."[5]

This elaborate breakdown of God's law was motivated by the belief that every one of these laws could be kept; and that by doing so these religious leaders (and any others who would follow in their steps) could pass God's inspection with flying colors!

To demolish this confidence, Jesus delivered the Sermon on the Mount, declaring over and over, "You have heard it said unto you ... but I say unto you ...." What followed was not a repudiation of what the law said, but a clarification of its intended meaning. In this way, Jesus pitched the standard sky-high, much higher than where the Pharisees had pitched it.

Then Jesus dropped a bombshell! In Matthew 5:48, he declared, "You shall be perfect, just as your Father in heaven is perfect." This, by design, left his hearers stunned, stupefied, speechless! Perfect? Why, nobody can be that!

Precisely so! And that's why the external obedience of the Pharisees was doomed from its inception. Our goodness can never ever be good enough; that road will get us precisely nowhere! What we *all* need, every one of us, is a Savior! A Savior who can do more than polish our rough exterior, a Savior who can change us from the inside out.

The reason Pharisaism has never died out, though no such group officially exists today, is because it really appeals to our pride. Pharisaism contends that this pull-yourself-up-by-the-bootstraps effort is the way to go. Harder, faster, better is its motto. This view was put forward then, and still motivates today, because of one deeply-held conviction: that by diligence and discipline you *can* make it! But can you?

We hope we can, and we want to think we can, but the Bible says we can't. On this point, Scripture offers an astonishingly radical perspective: The person determined to impress God with many good works doesn't have one good work to his name (Matthew 7:18). Not one!

One might think that because grace sounds so much better than works that the rush would be on to switch roads and obtain this grace. But the reason this hasn't happened is because grace affirms we're so bad off we *have* to have it! We have no other recourse! Other than the grace of God, there is no viable option!

Well! Because men prefer approval, rather than grace, they're still grinding it out, much like the Pharisees of old. The approval men still seek—embedded as it is in external obedience—is an unseemly quality, a quality so abhorrent that A.B. Simpson was forced to expose it:

> It should be your aim and mine, not so much to win the love of others as to be worthy of it; not so much to be esteemed as to be worthy of esteem; not so much as to bind ourselves to the hearts of men as to stand so high and glorious that we will draw them to us as the magnet draws steel. It is better to be than to seem ....[6]

Any obedience that has the ulterior motive of impressing others is false.

Fleshly Obedience

A seventh kind of obedience to avoid is fleshly obedience. This is the kind of obedience Paul described in Romans, chapter 7. Lamenting the civil war struggle inside, Paul said of this man that what he wanted to do, he didn't do; and that what he didn't want to do, he did. This is a struggle well-known to many.

But how could a man who loved the law, and desperately wanted to please God, find himself slam-dunked into abject defeat? The reason this occurred, the Bible tells us, is because of the mistaken notion that says: If God gave a command, the committed person can obey it. But can he? No, he cannot, a point Jesus made very clear in John 6:63 when he said that the flesh (meaning our self-life) profits nothing.

Unfortunately, these words have fallen on deaf ears. No one has believed Jesus on this point! Not in the beginning, anyway, and not for a long time thereafter. Instead, the optimistic assessment prevailing insisted that self can do a lot—not everything, mind you, but still, a lot! And so many years were wasted making the effort.

Self-reliance has been so deeply ingrained in us from our growing-up years it became the instinct of habit. *We* thought, *we* chose, *we* did—and trusted our innate abilities to accomplish our goals. In doing all this, we found a culture that admired our efforts.

And should these resources prove insufficient at times, we *then* asked God to help us. Well, this "God of the gaps" dynamic—wherein we trust ourselves, mostly, and God (if it really comes down to that), *sometimes*—is not an arrangement agreeable to God. One reason it isn't is because it credits the competency of our capacities more than it ever should. Scripture says that we are not to lean on our own understanding. Yet we do lean on it—most of the time! Scripture also says to be strong in the Lord and in the power of his might. Yet we undertake almost everything with our *own* abilities.

In doing so, we don't think we're rivaling God. To the contrary, we know we need God! *But* ... what we don't know is how much we need him. And what we also don't know is how to access his strength.

It is not until we experience the futility of this way of life—finally seeing the obedience God does require and our own inability to comply with it—that we will then experience what the man in Romans 7 experienced, defeat. With our confidence suddenly shattered, we will finally seek from God what we had never sought before: a level of living where holiness isn't discounted, but is both accessed and activated.

The typical Christian today is stacking zeros on heaven's scorecard, totally unaware that the man Paul described eventually got out of this Romans 7 dilemma; and when he did, the victory was so complete he never returned! Just how he did this is exceedingly important, so we'll discuss this later.

In contrast to all these other attempts to obey, the goal—reachable and doable—is this: a delighted obedience.

A Delighted Obedience

In Psalm 40, verse 8, we are given words Jesus spoke just before he became a baby in Bethlehem. Drawing back the curtain of time while allowing us to peer into eternity past, Scripture lets us eavesdrop on this conversation between Jesus and the Father.

Have you ever wondered what they said to each other when Jesus was about to leave heaven to become a human on earth? The emotion at such a departure, due to the unfathomable suffering Jesus would endure, had to be intense.

According to Scripture, this is what Jesus said, "... Behold, I come; in the scroll of the book it is written of me. I delight to do your will, O my God. And your law is within my heart." You'll notice from Jesus' perspective there was no conflict with the Father's will—only a desire to do it! Though obedience would extract an extraordinarily high price, there were no moaning and groaning and "please-don't-make-me-do-this" petitions. And why not? Because for Jesus, the assignment wasn't duty—it was delight!

Worth noting here is that this delight wasn't just rooted in the futuristic perspective of how good it was going to be once the whole ordeal was over, but was rooted also in a present-tense desire to please the Father. Reinforcing this delight was this astute recognition that God's plan was good in every way, and that to change the plan in any way would produce something less, and not better.

The Bible says that Jesus learned obedience. This statement puzzles people, causing some to ask, you mean Jesus didn't know how to act? No, he knew the principles; what he later learned, though, came by doing, by applying these principles. The transition between these two states wasn't one from immorality to morality, but one from principles known to principles practiced as a human being.

One example of such learning occurred at the temple when Jesus was a boy. G.D. Watson writes:

> When he stayed behind his father and mother in Jerusalem with the doctors and lawyers, his whole heart was on beginning right there and doing the work of his ministry—teaching and explaining God's Word. He saw the doctors of divinity were all blind as bats; and a great many of them are yet. He saw that the Church was starving and dying for spiritual light, and his little heart reveled in unfolding these things ... And yet

he found out after being corrected by his mother, under the instruction of the Holy Ghost, that his time was not yet ....[7]

So indelible was this lesson, Jesus articulated it years later when his ministry was launched at Cana, and later still when his ministry led to Calvary. In each instance, sensitivity to the Father's timing was very much on the Master's mind—to the point he could see no green light for the wedding miracle until persuaded of the Father's timing, and could see no red light for the cross once he knew, for a certainty, the time had come. Always, the timing of what Jesus said and did, as well as the approach used in each instance, was governed by the Father.

A summary point worth considering is this: The delight that inspires obedience, as well as the delight that issues from it, can supply and sustain habits of holiness. Hudson Taylor spoke of this lifestyle, saying: "The Lord Jesus received is holiness begun; the Lord Jesus cherished is holiness advancing; the Lord Jesus counted upon as never absent would be holiness complete ...."[8]

Holiness has begun for every believer, of course. But ask yourself these questions: Has it *continued*—and is it now on pace for completion? Hudson Taylor is right: If we cherish Jesus, our progress toward manifested holiness will steadily continue. And further: If we also believe he will supply what he summons, our advances will see the finish line soon enough.

But where the finish line is nowhere in sight and our progress toward it is barely discernible, then delighted obedience, the kind Jesus showed us, is obviously missing. Hence, we're at great risk for wasting our life.

Consider, as we conclude, this very sobering question. If Jesus were to give only one message to you today, what would it be? Would it be "Repent"? Or would it be "Thank you"?

For many in the church, the message would be repent! But it doesn't have to remain this way! Instead of a distorted obedience, a forced obedience, a fleshly obedience, or an external obedience, there can be instead a delighted obedience—a heart at peace with itself and in harmony with the Lord.

This can only occur, however, once a biblical how-to-ness for properly obeying the Lord is both taught, understood, and acted upon. To that end, we will continue our fact-finding survey of the dynamics of obedience, properly undertaken, as well as the dynamics of sin, improperly permitted.

Reflection Questions

1. Of the eight models of obedience presented, which is the least representative of you? The most representative of you? And the most recently exhibited in your life?

2. As you think about these different models of obedience, connect one of these with a pivotal decision you made, and then explain the difference this decision made in your life.

3. Answer the last question posed in this chapter: If Jesus were to stand before you, what would he say—repent? Or would he say thank you? Please explain.

Chapter 12

Motivations for Goodness—Part I

Biographies that are honest, biographies that dig out the facts and disclose what is true, reveal their subject "with warts and all" (to use Cromwell's words). Unlike the sordid biographies that only tease and titillate, biblical biographies instruct and clarify.

It would be a mistake to identify too much with the failings of others, or to draw a sick comfort from their reported mistakes. This is why, whenever the Bible discloses spiritual failures, it never appeals to prurient interests or to a promotion of pride. The primary purposes are these: to give a warning and to raise hope.

Every Christian has experienced a time during his or her relationship with the Lord when the motivation to be good was in decline. Perhaps you are in such a time right now, chug-chug-chugging along on two cylinders instead of eight. If so, this experience is teaching you that joylessly cranking it out, as you function more on instinct than on inspiration, is not a desirable way to live.

Having nothing but vapors left in your tank, you are sadly conscious of the fact that the excitement that accompanied your conversion is fast becoming a distant memory. It may even seem as if an invisible canopy has descended, that moves whenever you move—locking you in and keeping God out. Call it normal. Call it inevitable. But what are you supposed to do when motivation is gone? Can any real progress be made when this occurs? Once motivation disappears, the outcome, most likely, isn't going to be good.

The enigma of declining motivation, toward God and toward the goodness he espouses, is captured somewhat in selected quotations from J.I. Packer. In one place, Packer writes:

> God has implanted a passion for holiness deep in every born-again heart. Holiness, which means being near God, like God, given to God, and pleasing God, is something believers want more than anything else in this world.[1]

Only a few pages later Packer observes: "The pursuit of holiness is very evidently a Christian priority, but it is one believers today commonly neglect."[2] Just two pages later Packer says, "... holiness is a neglected priority throughout the modern church ...."[3] And only two pages after this Packer declares, "The relative eclipse of holiness as a main evangelical concern is little short of tragic."[4]

But how can a "passion" fall into neglect and a "priority" experience eclipse? If truly a passion, and rightly a priority, neglect is the one thing that won't happen! Actually, the only way one's motivation for holiness can decline is if passion is quenched and priority is reordered. But this corrupt coalescing of negatives should never deteriorate the inner life of a believer. And should this ever occur, repentance becomes a nonnegotiable imperative.

The Refreshing From Repentance

The first thing we should recognize is that while dry times are statistically normal, they are not inevitable. So instead of thinking that what we're going through is just a part of life, we should let another message register in our brain, and it is this—*something is wrong*! And the most likely factor accounting for this condition is sin.

According to Scripture, sin destroys our intimacy with God (I John 1:6), hinders our prayers from being heard (Psalm 66:18), prevents the Lord from helping us (Isaiah

59:2), and banishes us to the dryness of the desert (Numbers 14:34, 35). Therefore, the next step needed should be more than apparent—repent!

Charles Finney, the preacher and professor of nineteenth-century America, maintained his intimacy with God by dealing with sin whenever he first sensed its presence. At the first sign of spiritual dryness—however slight, however diminished by degree—Finney expedited a quiet time with God, determined to discover what was wrong. He would go to a solitary place (usually in a wooded area) and "pray through" until that which was alien to his spirit was identified, uprooted, and removed.

Because Finney refused to tolerate dryness, a powerful anointing came upon him. Indeed, so extraordinary was this anointing that one day Finney walked into a factory, unknown and unannounced, and three hundred workers fell flat on their faces. Why? Because a powerful momentum surged in Finney's life! This anointing, attributable to his decisive response to the cooling of spiritual temperature, was also triggered by his heartfelt repentance. At the first hint of personal wrongdoing, Finney aggressively dislodged the sin.

A lot of people are on a spiritual roller coaster these days. The highs, the lows, the sudden turns, the sickening declines, are recounted by believers with heads nodding in agreement and with moistened eyes communicating complete understanding. Yet, the question must be asked: Why must this be such a familiar experience?

Jonathan Edwards, another great preacher and professor, said he was converted when he was five years old and never backslid. Charles Spurgeon, perhaps the greatest preacher ever, said he never went fifteen minutes without experiencing the presence of God.

So how did these men do it—by being perfect? No, not in that way; they did it by reacting *immediately* to the first indication of sin in their lives. Finney, Edwards, and Spurgeon found a blessing when they repented, a blessing far better than anything sin had to offer. Does this not intrigue you? Well, let's learn more about this blessing by checking out the book of Acts. The account about to claim our attention occurred soon after the church was born.

Not long after the Spirit manifested at Pentecost, Peter was preaching to the Jews from Solomon's Portico when he made this most remarkable statement: "Repent therefore and be converted, that your sins may be blotted out, so that the time of refreshing may come from the presence of the Lord, and that he may send Jesus Christ, who was preached to you before, whom heaven must receive until the times of restoration of all things ..." (Acts 3:19-21a).

Now the "restoration of all things" is talking about the Lord's establishment of the millennial kingdom. The stunning message Peter delivered that day promised that Jesus would come back immediately and wrap this whole thing up. That's right, bring history to a close—*if* these Jews would only accept Jesus as their Savior!

This would mean, prospectively, there would be no destruction of Jerusalem, no loss of their homeland, no scattering of the Jews among the nations, no Hitler, no Middle East hatred, no terrorism. Think of it: All these terrible times could have been avoided, if only these Jews had accepted their Messiah that day.[5]

Admittedly, there is something of a mystery here, because, on the one hand, the Lord's return to earth is a date certain, known only to God. In fact, the Greek word for "times" in verse 19 is the word *kairos*, which means a fixed, determined time, a time not even Jesus knew while he was on earth. But on the other hand there is a sense in which the Lord's return is closely associated with Jewish repentance, a factor clearly predicted in prophecy.

In Zechariah 12:10, the Lord declared, "And I will pour on the house of David and on the inhabitants of Jerusalem the Spirit of grace and supplication; then they will look on me whom they pierced. Yes, they will mourn for him as one mourns for his only son, and grieve for him as one grieves for a firstborn."

On that coming day when the blinders will be removed, Zechariah tells us that the Jews will see at last who Jesus really is. At which point, overwhelmed by their centuries-old rejection of the Messiah, their hearts will break, their tears will flow, as these Jews, the beloved of God, are brought to repentance!

Of course, the Jews aren't the only ones who have suffered more than they ever needed to suffer; others are doing the same thing today. And about these people, George MacDonald writes:

> Some people will endure an immense amount of misery before they feel compelled to look for help, from where all help and healing comes. They cannot believe that there is truly an unseen mysterious power, until the world and all that is in it has vanished in the smoke of despair; until cause and effect is nothing to the intellect, and possible glories have faded from the imagination.[6]

Just why people would wait so long, even until their world collapses, is difficult to understand. But, though the hour is late and the price for keeping one's distance from God has been high, the Lord will graciously accept those who turn to him today, just as he will accept the Jews who turn to him just before history comes to its convulsive conclusion.

In Zechariah 13:1, the Lord declares, "In that day a fountain shall be opened for the house of David and for the inhabitants of Jerusalem for sin and for uncleanness." This, we know, is a fountain that the believer today has experienced. It is a fountain that changes everything inside us!

How great is the mercy of our God to wash away our sin and make us clean again. Neither the psychiatrist nor the psychologist can do anything like this! Mental health experts are more likely to minimize the whole thing by telling us our failings are normal and that what we really need to do is to accept ourselves as we are. But even when they say this much, they're only accommodating our belief system with professional tolerance. Deeper down, they resist anything that looks like blaming or judging. So if they said what they really think, they'd say there's no need at all for the fountain Zechariah described.

Now notice what comes next: After this repentance by the Jews, Zechariah 14:4 says: "And in that day his feet will stand on the Mount of Olives, which faces Jerusalem on the east ...." This speaks of the return of Jesus to the earth! And this will occur when? At the time the nation of Israel repents before the Lord! So, given the fact this time is soon approaching, I didn't want to extract only the pastoral counsel found in Acts 3:19 without first alerting you to the broader context of what was declared. Repentance brings Jesus on the scene—in that future day, as well as today!

Now back to our agenda at hand: what to do about the spiritually dry times? The antidote to this dryness is what Scripture calls "the times of refreshing from the presence of the Lord." The Greek word used for "refreshing" means rest, respite, cool. So what image does that conjure up? The Bible tells us that Adam walked with God in the cool of the day. This indicates a time of unbroken fellowship, a time when Adam's intimacy with the Lord was sweet and strong.

So if we want the dry times to be over for us, we must first repent by coming to this fountain. For it is only there that all the scum encrusted on our soul can be washed away by the force and flow of this fountain's waters. Again, there aren't a lot of options here. Unless we come to *this* fountain, a fountain that will enable our floundering faith to bloom, that soul-sapping dryness will remain on the scene.

The Protection of Conscience

Another motivation for being good deals with the need to protect our conscience. In Romans 13:5, we are told to submit to our governmental leaders "for conscience sake." You see, if properly protected and programmed, conscience will serve as a moral compass, as an ethical radar. However, if the alarm of conscience is ignored, there will come a time we won't even hear it.

The Bible identifies gradations of conscience. For example, there is the "good conscience" (Acts 23:4), a conscience programmed with God's Word, a conscience that rings its alarm exactly when it should at a Spirit-empowered volume that can't easily be ignored.

Now, while most of us aren't exactly thrilled when our alarm clock begins to ring, it is we who set those clocks the night before, and did so because we knew we needed the assistance the alarm clock brings. That alarm clock, like our conscience, disciplines us. Yet, while we do need it to work, we aren't always thrilled when it does.

As with alarm clocks, so with the conscience: There are different levels of quality. Some clocks are accompanied with FM music, snooze alarms, pulsating lights, and even vibrators. Other alarm clocks hardly work. In fact, you might as well not use them because the alarm is too soft and short to get the job done. Recognizing how these various outcomes can occur, spiritually, the Bible describes the various types of conscience a person can have.

Those possessing what the Bible calls "a good conscience" will hate evil and love righteousness. Yes, love and hate are strong words. Nevertheless, Richard Baxter, the seventeenth-century English Puritan, was right when he wrote, "Love Christ and you will hate that which caused his death." You will absolutely hate it!

But many of us have had our moral sensitivities numbed by a deteriorating culture. Billy Graham observed how matters that would have been morally objectionable a decade or two earlier are more commonplace and accepted now. This is largely attributable to the inundating ways that the entertainment industries have sabotaged our culture. These cultural contaminants have caused us to take in stride that which the Lord himself stridently resisted.

Let's face it! Not too many people today *hate* evil. They may disagree with it, and on selected issues offer their opinions against it. But generally they don't hate it—unless, of course, a particular evil brought intense, personal pain!

Whenever most people see sin and the perpetrators of sin, there isn't a passion for evangelism, or a resolve to disciple God's people. Instead, a much milder response occurs, one that has no resolve to turn the tide against sin. So the infiltration of worldliness into the church continues!

The tolerance enthroned in the church was effectively taken to task by A.W. Tozer. In his book, *The Divine Conquest*, Tozer wrote, "Throughout the entire New Testament a sharp line is drawn between the church and the world. There is no middle ground."[7] In today's church, however, this line has been virtually erased. People attending church seem almost as worldly as those who never come.

Their respective lifestyles, when examining each aspect, aren't all that different.

Compounding this problem, church attendees will invite friends to join their spiritually-anesthetized and morally-compromised congregation. In his book, *Faith Beyond Reason*, Tozer lamented their dysfunctional conscience and absent God. "If angels can weep, they must weep salty tears upon seeing a proselyte who has never really met the Lord making another proselyte who will also never meet the Lord."[8] Though they join some church, what neither one of them join is Jesus.

The second type of conscience the Bible identifies is a "weak conscience" (I Corinthians 8:12). This refers to the wrongly programmed conscience of a believer who holds to convictions that didn't come from God's Word. Sort of like the alarm clock that doesn't go off at the right time, this conscience sounds its alarm whenever there is dancing, card-playing, movie-going, or exertion of energy on the Sabbath. Typically, the person with this type of conscience has a "dos" and "don'ts" checklist in his back pocket, which, in his mind, has the status of Scripture. Having a warped view of God and a reduced vision of life, this person confronts anybody, anytime, anywhere, who isn't complying with this checklist!

Lacking wisdom in his approach and grace in his spirit, a poor advertisement for the faith is often exhibited, because—by majoring on the minors, and then hounding the church to follow this agenda—the false impression is given that the thundering of Sinai is echoing in the church still, and that the gentle slopes of Zion are entirely too easy to climb.

There was a time in Paul's life when he had this kind of conscience, a time when he was rounding up Christians and hauling them off to jail. So sure that he was right in this endeavor and that these Christians were wrong in their theology, Saul sought to eliminate them! But as for himself—well, he didn't need any grace.[9] Summing up Saul, at least during this period of his life, A.B. Simpson said:

> Paul was not so much a bad sinner as a good one.
> He was a moral man, a righteous man, a

blameless man, a conscientious man, a religious man, a most earnest worker for the religious cause in which he believed. There was no loose joint in his harness where the arrow of conviction could enter. He had lived before God "in all good conscience" (Acts 23:1), unto the day of his conversion. Such a man is very difficult to reach. Our appeals roll off like water. God's severest warnings found no lodging place in his armor-plated soul.[10]

Why? Because his supposedly good conscience was wrongly programmed! Later, when his conscience was rightly programmed, Paul assessed himself as having been "the chief of sinners." What a turnaround! Such a radically different perspective! Clearly, despite similarities, the weak conscience and the good conscience are not at all the same!

A third type of conscience described in the Bible is the "evil conscience." This is the conscience greatly harmed by indulging evil—whether in the past (but not dealt with biblically) or in the present (and not dealt with at all). John Bunyan said conscience can become "stony, benumbed." It can be "bribed, deluded, muzzled."[11] Alexander Maclaren observed, "The more a man goes wrong, the less he knows it. Conscience is loudest when it is least needed, and most silent when most required."[12]

The world's value system has contaminated conscience to a considerable extent, so that what Scripture forbids is now tolerated, and what Scripture commands is now ignored.[13] Hence, without any internal debate or any filtering discernment, the rationalizations of men have replaced the revelations of God.

In his book, *The Set of the Sail*, Tozer says: "Morally, the world is like a bombed city. The streets are blocked, the buildings lie in ruins, and the wounded and homeless wait for the healing service of men who can help them in their distress."[14]

But how can anyone enmeshed with worldly thinking offer this help? The answer is, he cannot. You've heard the old bromide, "let your conscience be your guide." Well, if yours is a weak conscience or an evil conscience, this won't be good advice. Because if it's a weak conscience, the decision made may seem so right and yet be horribly wrong.[15]

Unfortunately, there is much to indicate that a majority of our population has an "evil conscience," a fact they would vehemently deny, although a survey of their opinions, and a study of their lifestyles, will prove this *is* the type of conscience they have.

The last type of conscience identified by Scripture is a "seared conscience" (I Timothy 4:2). Horatius Bonar said, "A seared conscience is the sinner's heritage." Offering a similar perspective, Oswald Chambers wrote, "A bad man can be perfectly happy in his badness. This is what a seared conscience means."[16] Speaking of such a man, Thomas Watson wrote, "He thinks his conscience is good because it is quiet."[17] And sadly this isn't a rare occurrence! Dr. Dale Yocum declared, "Millions of people have silenced the inner voice until it never condemns them."[18]

The seared conscience or "shipwrecked conscience" (I Timothy 1:19) often involves Satan or demons. Accordingly, this type of conscience is dangerously close to the point of no recovery. In fact, so entrenched are these "doctrines of demons" ministered by "deceiving spirits" (I Timothy 4:1) that the takeover of the conscience extends beyond mere confusion, or even willful sin; instead, the conscience itself, which should have served God, is now in the hands of Satan. *He* is its programmer—not self, not the world, but the personification of all evil, Satan.

Now, if a Christian doesn't want this to happen, he or she must recognize that the indulgence of sin will invariably damage one's conscience. Therefore, one's capacity to discern and defense evil will be gone. In this regard C.S. Lewis observed:

> When a man is getting better, he understands more and more clearly the evil that is still in him. When a man is getting worse, he understands his own badness less and less. A moderately bad man knows he is not very good: a thoroughly bad man

thinks he is all right. This is common sense, really. You understand sleep when you are awake, not while you are sleeping. You can see mistakes in arithmetic when your mind is working properly: while you are making them you cannot see them. You can understand the nature of drunkenness when you are sober, not when you are drunk. Good people know about good and evil; bad people do not know about either.[19]

The prospect of losing conscience to the enemy of our soul provides a strong incentive to turn away from sin. Because if we welcome sin, and thereby allow our conscience to be destroyed, we won't see what we need to see, nor feel what we need to feel. Such an outcome would be like a pilot's instruments giving faulty information. Of course, no pilot wants to navigate a plane if the plane's instruments have gone haywire. Once "up" seems "down," and "down" seems "up," a catastrophe is about to occur!

The Deterrence for Imaging Evil

What may also help the believer become good, and I mean consistently good, is a proper recognition of the dangers of sin. Jesus likened sin to serpents and scorpions—that is, something deadly, something that can hurt you when you least suspect it.

If you were told that there's a scorpion in your bed, would you shrug it off and go to sleep in undisturbed tranquility? No, you'd be out of that bed *immediately*! And you wouldn't return to bed until that scorpion was found, removed, and killed!

Similarly, if you were to hear a hissing nearby, would you dismiss the hissing as meaningless and inconsequential? No, you'd drop everything *at once*, determined to locate the whereabouts of that snake!

So how have you remained comfortable with sin in your life? Most likely you've done this by accepting the lie that sin won't hurt you. To yourself, and perhaps to others, you have said, "I can handle it. There's no reason to worry." But it is precisely this minimizing that sets you up for failure!

For once sin is minimized, plans to avoid it are seldom made; and if made, are soon ignored. However, to take Jesus at his word means bringing these negative images to mind every time sin comes near you.

Do you think this form of aversion therapy might help? Extending this line of logic, we recall how the Bible calls Satan a thief, a liar, and a murderer. Now, if a known thief were coming to your house, wouldn't you be hypervigilant in your attempts to protect everything you possess? And if you were in conversation with a notorious liar, wouldn't you suspect the veracity of everything he said? And if a cold-blooded killer were in your neighborhood, wouldn't you want to stay as far away as you possibly could?

So why aren't Christians more avoidant toward Satan? It's incomprehensible, really! Whenever he knocks on the door, what do they do? They invite him in! And whenever he makes his little sales pitch, what do they do? They take him at his word! And whenever he leads them straight to destruction, what do they do? They turn to *him* for help!

Sound crazy? Well, it is! Sin and Satan are nothing but bad news! Sin can establish a stronghold so formidable it can't be budged, much less dislodged. II Peter 2:14 describes those who "cannot cease from sin, enticing unstable souls. They have a heart trained in covetous practices ...." You see, by repeatedly saying "yes" to every temptation that presented itself, these decisions eventually became them; hence, they could no longer choose against their preference.

But you say, "Can't the Lord intervene and help these people to change their ways?" We could wish the Lord's intervention would result in a successful turnaround. However, Jesus challenged us to "remember Lot's wife" *for a reason*. It is we, and not just biblical scholars, who must remember her, because it is we who must keep ourselves from the disobedience that leads to death.

You will recall that messengers from heaven were dispatched to rescue her. Angels strongly implored Lot and his family to leave Sodom at once, and not to look back lest they be consumed in the fiery judgment. So what does Lot's wife do? Well, first, she was reluctant about leaving this notorious city. Second, she expressed no gratitude for the rescuers who had come to save her. And, third, she did exactly what the angels told her not to do—she looked back! Apparently, the longing in her heart proved stronger than impending judgment so that not even the sight of fire and brimstone could melt her heart.

And would you say that you have had experiences like this—less dramatic, to be sure, and certainly not as life-threatening? Yet, haven't you also ignored warnings while at the same time fostering evil desires? Concerning people like this, J.C. Ryle observed:

> ... there is always some darling evil habit, which they cannot tear from their heart. Hidden worldliness, or covetousness, or lust, sticks to them like their skin. They are willing to see all their idols broken, but this one. If you are such a one, I say to you this day, Take care: "Remember Lot's wife."[20]

In the end, she died a bizarre death, symbolic of the fact she had lived a bizarre life. Somehow, she just couldn't give up what she knew would destroy her. *But* is she alone in this example? Is she the only one who has lived this way?

When examining the story of Lot's wife, one has to wonder if many in the church are just like her, because notice: According to Scripture, full salvation that day required following God's messengers to the mountain, as Lot did. Merely getting out of Sodom wasn't the salvation God was offering. Yet, many there are who remain in the plains with Lot's wife—halfway between Sodom and the mountain of deliverance. And perhaps this is so because pulpits wrongly proclaim this is the best we can hope for: an exodus from Sodom, with Sodom's sin still controlling our hearts.

This story repeated when God got Israel out of Egypt, only to see Israel with Egypt still in their hearts. As Lot's wife got no further than the plains, that generation of Jews got no further than the wilderness. Similarly, Christians today who accept only half a gospel (imputed righteousness but not imparted righteous) will likewise incur a futile, unsuccessful journey and needless judgment. Why? Because all this halfway stuff is false in its theology and tragic in its consequence.

Peter likened this phenomenon to a dog returning to its vomit, or a washed pig returning to the mud hole. So include these images in your aversion therapy: the dog slurping up what he regurgitated, the pig wallowing in the mud from which it had been retrieved, Lot's wife looking with longing on that the Lord was judging. Granted, these are negative images, but negative images serve as warnings—warnings that God uses to send a jolt of motivation.

What we've seen so far in this chapter are three motivations for obedience, each strong in its appeal. Will you consider once again the contribution of each?

1. The refreshment of soul that can come whenever sin is repented from—don't you want this?
2. The protection of conscience that results whenever truth is heeded and not hushed—don't you also need this?
3. The alarm that goes off whenever biblical images of sin are projected onto our mental screen—isn't this a strategy you need to use more?

Getting your heart right by repenting, your head right by instilling God's truth, and your will right by seeing how dangerous sin really is, goes a long way toward living a life of consistent obedience.

Reflection Questions

1. Describe the last time you experienced the refreshing of the Lord's presence following repentance?
2. What kind of conscience do you currently have, and why do you think this is true?
3. Which of the aversive images Scripture suggests best addresses your experience with minimizing sin?

Chapter 13

Motivations for Goodness—Part II

George Eliot, the nineteenth-century British author, made the observation: "... what makes life dreary is the want of a motive."[1] And she was right! To live without purpose, without drive, and without hope is to trudge the way of the beast while still having the heart of a man.

To appreciate this fact as we should, we would do well to contemplate the alternative to a life with motivation, even if it isn't true. What if the Bible furnished no motive, but in the spirit of a drill sergeant only fired out commands? Or what if we had to comply with commands that didn't make any sense, or had to march in lockstep to orders that were obviously harmful to us?

What God says makes total sense, though, and is always beneficial. He is never the author of random thoughts or capricious commands. Indeed, the life he designed for us is better than any alternative we could ever devise!

Another hypothetical alternative is this: God could have demanded snap-to obedience on the sole basis of authority, requiring us to trust his wisdom without explanation; or to trust his power without demonstration. But, no, God supplied enough motivations to make obedience immensely appealing and, conversely, to render disobedience hideously repulsive. That he did so underscores our immense value in his eyes. The considerable respect God willingly accords us is foundational to the motivations he provides us. Given this context, a full consideration of these motivations is certainly in order.

The Reality of Hell

Perhaps no motivation is as repulsive to the human spirit as the biblical doctrine of hell. Not wanting to believe such a place exists, or that anything we do might send us there, we minimize the seriousness of sin, dismissing all these warnings of judgment as well-intended hyperbole. Responding to this reaction, Horatius Bonar, the nineteenth-century Scottish pastor, wrote:

> If sin be but a common scar or wrinkle to be erased from the soul's surface by a few common touches, if pardon be but a mere figure of speech, meaning God's wide benevolence and good natured indifference to evil, why tell of wrath, fire, the never dying worm and the ever rising smoke? Does God love to torment his creature by harsh words or fill their minds with images of woe he does not intend to realize?[2]

Hardly that! Sin *is* serious! Its consequences are serious! And God is very serious about every warning he ever gave!

Nevertheless, in the "feel-good" atmosphere of today's church—where the positive is emphasized and the negative is ignored—hell is simply not on the agenda. The modern mind hardly bothers with (what it calls) terroristic texts. Instead, a smiling Savior is presented and not some livid Lord executing vengeance. Taking to task the mush and gush that exudes from these weak, breathy, pink-cheek preachers, Tozer scolded:

> Unfortunately, the ten-cent-store Jesus being preached now by many men is not the Jesus that will come and judge the world. This plastic, painted Christ who has no spine and no justice, but is a soft and pliant friend to everybody, if he is the only Christ, then we might as well close our

books, bar our doors and make a bakery or garage out of our church buildings.[3]

Tozer is absolutely right: This sort of Jesus will never triumph over evil! Nevertheless, with their glad-hand evangelism, preachers will market Jesus without uttering a syllable about hell. Check out the sermon titles in the newspaper, or the book listings at your Christian bookstore, or the sermons you hear on the radio. Have you heard a sermon on hell lately?

The likely reason you haven't is because history can't get over the fact that the most tender lips that ever spoke had the most to say about hell. Yet, despite the Lord's insistence that judgment is coming, we seem to be living in some sort of collective denial.

The question that has to be answered in this regard is this: Is hell to be disregarded as a primitive doctrine that we moderns, possessing higher knowledge, should rightly ignore? A.W. Tozer addressed this question in his book, *Man, the Dwelling Place of God*.

> Whatever is stated clearly but once in the Holy Scriptures may be accepted as sufficiently well-established to invite the faith of all believers; and when we discover that the Spirit speaks of the wrath of God about 300 times in the Bible, we may as well make up our mind to accept the doctrine or reject the Scriptures outright. If we have valid information from some outside source proving that anger is unworthy of God, then the Bible is not to be trusted when it attributes anger to God. And if it is wrong three hundred times on one subject, who can trust it on any other?[4]

To suppose that our sense of morality is higher than the morality of God is actually wicked to the core.

As for the Apostle Paul, well, he trusted Scripture on this point and was thus strongly motivated by the reality of hell. In II Corinthians 5:11, Paul declared, "Knowing therefore the terror of the Lord, we persuade men ...." The collective "we" used in this verse could have been used again to say, "What we don't do, and would never think to do, is participate in a conspiracy of silence and keep quiet about the dangers of hell! The reality of eternal judgment should never be ignored!" What God reveals must be reckoned, always, as well-established holy truth.

"The terror of the Lord?" You won't hear about that in today's church, will you? Churches sanitize this dark, horrible reality by portraying God as a virtual bystander to this dreadful, terrifying outcome—*if* such an outcome is even possible, they wonder.

In this same mode of flexible thinking, the church will spin multiple rationalizations, saying, for example, that God didn't want people go to hell; hell, they would remind us, was created for the devil and his demons. Besides, God did all he could do to keep people from such punishment! But, alas, there were those who ran through every stop sign, who declined every offer of help. So what was poor God to do? He tried!

Offering further proof, people quote that verse which says God takes no pleasure in the death of the wicked. Now, while everything said is completely true, it is not a truth that is complete; for the Bible has much more to say on this subject. For example, Psalm 2:4 says the Lord will laugh at the wicked and "shall hold them in derision." Can you imagine what *that* would be like: to have God laughing at you?

II Thessalonians 2:11 declares that God's response to the practitioners of deceit will be to "send them strong delusion that they should believe the lie." So how would you like it if God totally removed his truth and left you duped by a delusion?

II Thessalonians 1:8 says that when Jesus and his mighty angels come "in flaming fire," they will be "taking vengeance on those who do not know God, and on those who do not obey the gospel of our Lord Jesus Christ." Vengeance—from Jesus? This seems incongruent with that image of Jesus many moderns embrace. For how could the gentle shepherd with the flaked-out lamb on his shoulders ever terrorize those who rejected him?

In his book, *The Holiness of God*, R.C. Sproul offered a clarifying perspective on this subject by passing on an observation from a theologian in our day:

> Hans Kung, the controversial Roman Catholic theologian, writing about the seemingly harsh judgments of sin God makes in the Old Testament, says that the most mysterious aspect of the mystery of sin is not that the sinner deserves to die, but rather that the sinner in the average situation continues to exist.
>
> Kung asks the right question. The issue is not why does God punishes sin, but why does he permit the ongoing rebellion of man? What prince, what king, what ruler would manifest so much patience with a continually rebellious populace?[5]

Yes, God is patient, but as he said before the flood: His Spirit will not always strive with man (Genesis 6:5)—and he didn't! The cataclysmic judgment that came—long mocked by scorners and jeered by scoffers—came with sudden force. And will it ever come again? God says that it will. He declared the day will *surely* come when the Lamb will bare his teeth, and when those who misread his patience will seek in vain to escape his wrath.

According to the prophet Joel, the Lord shall roar out of Zion on that day (Joel 2:1f.), and the heavens and earth will shake! When God does come swooping down with vengeance, it will not represent a sudden change of mood or a deviant altering of disposition, because Psalm 7:11 says that "God is angry with the wicked every day."

In his book, *The Guilt of Sin*, Charles Finney explained:

> God is not angry merely against the sin abstracted from the sinner, but against the sinner himself. Some persons have labored hard to set up this ridiculous and absurd abstraction, and would fain make it appear that God is angry at the sin, yet not at the sinner. He hates the theft, but loves the

thief. He abhors adultery, but is pleased with the adulterer. Now this is supreme nonsense. The sin has no moral character apart from the sinner. The act is nothing apart from the actor. The very thing that God hates and disapproves is not the mere event—the thing done in distinction from the doer; but it is the *doer himself* ... The sinner himself is the direct and only object of his anger.[6]

And for this reason, the sinner doesn't just go to hell; he is *cast* there![7]

With this view of the Lord's terror clearly in mind, Paul became passionate in his desire to witness to the lost. Given the very real danger these people were in, Paul could do no less than warn of God's holy wrath.

In contemplating Paul's perspective, you might ask yourself: What would I do if there were a fire next door? Would I wait until the next commercial before meandering over to see who in the family burned to death? Of course I wouldn't do that. I would rush right over, quickly assess the danger, give urgent warnings, and do whatever else I could to rescue people still in danger.

But if hell is a lot worse than any house fire, why are we so complacent to warn people of this far greater danger? To Paul, the reality of hell, the terror of the Lord, were so real they strongly motivated him to witness. And we would keep our silence?

Should this be our continuing response, what explanation will we give on that last day when that acquaintance of ours, or that friend, or that relative, asks us why we never said a single word about their impending peril? How could we *know* what's coming but say nothing about it?

The issue at hand is not whether or not there is a hell. There *is* a hell; and just because people don't believe hell exists doesn't mean they're not going there! What it does mean is that there's a lot rationalizing going on. Underscoring this point, G.D. Watson declared, "Every human being, civilized or savage, has the consciousness of sin, whether confessed or unconfessed, and every soul has an intuitive dread of some awful future calamity in consequence of sin."[8]

The issue for the believer is this: In what way will the reality of hell motivate him or her to witness; and, further, to live a life credible enough to offer a witness?

The doctrine of an eternal hell—the destiny of which is to be determined during our brief life on earth—is loaded with powerful motivations for how we should live our lives. Could it be, though, that despite the terrors of hell, we will continue to drift in the currents of the day—watching TV, taking in the latest movie, preoccupied more by our hobbies than we are with the Lord? But if we do this, how will all this wasted time be regarded when it comes to helping a friend, or a loved one, make the most important decision he or she could ever make?

To be sure, hell isn't the best reason for someone to come to the Lord, nor is it the best reason for someone to live out a witness for him. But it is a legitimate reason, compelling in its implications and strong in its motivations.

Augustine's observation—that the person who fears hell fears burning and not sin[9]—may well be true, just as this same person is more repelled by God's judgment than compelled by God's love. Nevertheless, truth even at the low rung of the ladder can lead to higher truth. The fear of hell can stop one in his tracks and redirect toward a better course. This does need to happen, too, because as Thomas Watson wisely put it, "It is the highest point of prudence to make preparations for another world."[10]

The Compulsions of Love

In this same chapter, the Apostle Paul cites another motivation for being good when he declared, "For the love of Christ compels us ..." (I Corinthians 5:14). This ongoing desire to please Jesus, to become a channel through which his blessings can flow, can inspire us to make sacrifices we wouldn't otherwise have made. When moved by this compelling love in his own life, the Apostle Paul declared, "... I will very gladly spend and be spent for your souls, though the more abundantly I love you, the less I am loved" (II Corinthians 12:15).

Whenever one is always the giver and another is always the taker, there is, in that kind of relationship, a big challenge. To give so much, only to be appreciated so little, can tempt an "I'm-out-of-here!" announcement. But what sustained Paul when he was repeatedly taken for granted was this overriding desire to bless Jesus most of all. So, instead of calculating who owed what to whom, and instead of seeing if there was enough reciprocation to balance the account, Paul played his life to the Lord, fully realizing *that* account could never be balanced. The Lord's love toward him was always—always!—far greater!

Many Christians speak carelessly when they profess in their verbally facile way their supposed love for other Christians. However, God sets forth criteria in his Word that clarify whether this love is as professed. For example, I John 5:1 says, "... everyone who loves him who begot, loves him who is begotten of him." This means that if you love God for enabling you to be born-again, you will also love the ones he loves, others who were also born-again.

Regarding this point, F.B. Meyer said it well: "If the Lord Jesus is the center of our heart-life, we must inevitably be drawn into fellowship to all those to whom he is also first and best."[11] Sentimental blather may profess great love for other believers, but notice how the next verse measures the authenticity of this love: "By this we know that we love the children of God, when we love God and keep his commandments."

Now, here's the point. If a believer comes to church each Sunday, cooled down in his love for the Lord and compromised in his behaviors during the week, *that Christian will hurt other believers*. Why? Because worship has a stereophonic character, wherein meaning is picked up all around. A believer who brings cold water to church will be dampening the witness God wants him to give; whereas the believer who comes to church spiritually hot will contribute to an incendiary atmosphere that helps ignite the faith of others. Our assignment, then, is this: To bless other believers by bringing the Spirit's fire when we gather, rather than bringing that which may douse the little flicker of faith others have left.

When measured by this criterion, can we truly say that we love the people of God? Or does our spiritual decline, and our distancing from others, say precisely the opposite? Remember, friendliness isn't the same thing as fellowship.

The Investment of Trust

Another motivation for goodness can be found in the fact God trusts you. In I Timothy, chapter 1, verses 12 and 13, the Apostle Paul said, "... I thank Christ Jesus our Lord who has enabled me, because he counted me faithful, putting me in the ministry, although formerly I was a blasphemer, a persecutor, and an insolent man ...."

I wonder if you can identify with this verse. Can you look back on a past that you're not proud of, yet rejoice where God has now brought you? You may not be a pastor or a missionary like Paul was, but has the Lord given you a unique opportunity to witness for him? By having given you this opportunity, the Lord is telling you, "I know you're going to handle this assignment well. I know you're going to bring me glory."

When I was in elementary school my mother used to tell me that she knew I was going to be a good teenager. Whether this was a calculated move on her part, I can never be entirely sure. But I believed then, and do so today, that she meant what she was telling me.

There were a few times during teenage years when I was tempted to do something clearly wrong. But what stopped me each time was the fact my mother's trust meant a lot to me; so I decided to resist the temptation and do what was right.

On one occasion another mother in the neighborhood was visiting with my mother expressing dread about what these upcoming high school years were going to bring for her son. As it turned out both mothers were right. Each had accurately predicted how their respective sons would do in high school. And in retrospect I can't help but wonder if the granting of trust in one case, and the withholding of it in the other, had something to do with these eventual outcomes.

For God to express his belief in you, telling you that you are his person, and that he knows you'll undertake your responsibilities well, has to encourage you to try even harder, because you want his confidence in you confirmed! For sure, the very last thing you want is to disappoint him.

The Bible does tell us that the Spirit of God can be grieved by a believer (Ephesians 4:30). Grieve, as we know, is a love word; it causes deep hurt. You wouldn't want to wound the one who has done so much for you, right? Instead, you want to honor him who trusts you, and trusts you every day. This motivation leads to heartfelt obedience.

The Infusion of Joy

We often think that acceptance of the Lord's will leads to hardships, and that yielding to temptation leads to satisfaction. Now, while Scripture does talk about "the pleasures of sin," it adds these ominous words, "for a season." *For a season* sin extends pleasure. *For a season* sin offers an easier way. However, as time passes and the hooks of sin sink in, an entirely different outcome emerges—one far worse than what we bargained for!

The broad road narrows. The road widely traveled loses its appeal. Sin extracts its price! The devil takes control! This is exactly why the road *less* taken, the narrow road of consistent obedience, is much to be preferred.

In John 15:10, Jesus said if we keep his commandments we will abide in his love. In the next verse, Jesus declared that the by-product of consistent obedience is a joy that remains, a joy that is full. So apparently the real choice is between abiding joy and temporary pleasure. It is in his wonderful book, *Our Own God*, that G.D. Watson clarified the distinctions between these two qualities.

> Joy is deep; its fountains are hid in the depths of the spirit; it pervades the interior nature like the law of gravity that silently abides in every atom of the earth.
>
> Pleasure is on the surface. It deals with the senses and is the gratification of our outward nature. Joy is calm, like the placid river, or the quiet unspeakable wealth of the gorgeous sunset, or the

entrancing contentment of looking from a lofty mountain over a magnificent landscape. Its very nature is to quiet and soothe the inward parts of the soul. On the other hand, pleasure is stormy; it agitates the faculties like the wind ruffling the sea ....[12]

By invoking images of nature to illustrate more profound spiritual realities, G.D. Watson helped us see the stark contrasts between joy and pleasure. Joy is deep and abiding; pleasure is shallow and fleeting.

Have you ever considered this latter outcome—a joy that remains, a joy that is full? To *always* have full joy would seem to be impossible, right? Just ask the mental health experts, or the average citizen on the street, or even yourself, for that matter. Virtually everyone will tell you such joy is impossible, that life has its ups and downs, that emotions cycle through with mountain-top highs and valley-bound lows. Even Scripture tells us that "many are the afflictions of the righteous." So, fullness of joy—always? C'mon!

Well, this is one of many instances where God's thoughts are not our thoughts—*until we get a revelation on this*! So instead of dismissing Jesus' words, or explaining them away, we should ask God to reveal how the words of Jesus are true. Apparently, there *is* a way to get the mountaintop into the valley. Not eventually—many months or even years later—but immediately, and with full impact!

As we attempt to replace our thoughts with the Lord's thoughts, we recall Jesus saying that he and the Father will dwell in us and will manifest themselves to us *if* we keep his commandments. Here, manifestation means we're going to experience the felt presence of the Lord! And this is a critical factor, because Psalm 16:11 declares "... in thy presence is fullness of joy." (Psalm 16:11) To access his presence, therefore, is to access his joy.

The psalmist gave another clue about accessing the Lord's joy during difficult times when he said, "I have set the Lord always before me." By contrast, what we tend to do is to set the problem always before us; or, if not that, we set our thinking about the problem always before us. But to set the

Lord always before us—with a contemplation of *his* love, *his* resources, and *his* promises—brings an entirely different result! Instead of a nosedive into defeat and a subsequent takeover of our emotions by the enemy, the presence of God will minister deep comfort, calming peace, and, yes, jubilant joy! What a powerful motivation for goodness, then! Think of it: to have an ongoing experience of joy instead of being on the emotional rollercoaster we've been on!

A potential trap needs to be identified, however; for Jesus is our God, and not joy. Always, our passion, must be for him and not for this blessed by-product of joy. Otherwise, if our real goal becomes a thrill-seeking adventure, idolatry will intrude. To fixate on elevating feelings is to succumb to the mentality of our drug-taking culture, about which J.C. Ryle was correct to caution:

> True holiness, we surely ought to remember, does not consist merely of inward sensations and impressions. It is much more than tears, and sighs, and bodily excitement, and a quickened pulse, and a passionate attachment to our own favorite preachers and our own religious party ....[13]

R.A. Torrey, the Spirit-filled preacher who influenced continents for Christ, was by his own admission a man who wasn't much immersed in feelings. His temperament was more that of a lawyer, or a professor, and not one characteristic of the typical evangelist. Yet, it is unquestionably true that the Spirit filled him for his evangelist's calling just as the Spirit filled R.A. Torrey's more emotional colleague, D.L. Moody. The joy in each man was different in its expression but, arguably, not in its depth.

The Power of Our New Nature

As encouraging as these words of Jesus are on this topic, many will shrink back from the promise made, saying that if joy is based on consistent goodness, I'm sunk!

To them, the life of consistent goodness seems unattainable, and therefore it's only natural to slack off.

While greyhounds may chase the mechanical rabbit they're never going to catch, people don't function this way. Unreachable goals discourage us, deter us, and soon enough derail us. So why run if we're always going to lose?

What most hinders our pursuit of consistent goodness, though—even more than discouragement—can be identified in one word, self. The self that masquerades as our true identity, greeting us at every turn, is depicted well by the House of a Thousand Mirrors found in the Palace of Wurtzung. J. Gregory Mantle described it this way:

> You enter—a thousand hands are stretched out to meet you. A thousand smiles greet your smile, a thousand eyes will weep when you weep, but they are all your hands, your smiles, your tears. What a picture of the selfish man! Self all around, self deceived, and he is deceived.[14]

Even when self seeks to quit her ways and finally follow God, the escape from self's governing grip isn't easy. Hudson Taylor gave this account from his own life experience. "I prayed, agonized, fasted, strove, made resolutions, read the Bible more diligently, sought more time for meditation—but all without avail. Every day, almost every hour, the consciousness of sin oppressed me."[15] To read Hudson Taylor's biography is to become impressed with the magnitude of his effort and the frustration of the outcome.

With much sympathy, F.B. Meyer wrote words that speak to our hearts:

> We, too, may be traversing at this very hour battlefields which have been sadly marked by defeat. Again and again we have met the foes of our peace in mortal conflict, only to be repulsed. Our hopes have been dashed to the ground and our banners rolled in dust and blood. We meant never to yield again, but we did yield. We meant that that solemn vow should be kept, that holy resolution carried into effect; but they were shivered in pieces. We have been overthrown by

our adversary, and overpowered in spite of all of our efforts ....[16]

Is there no escape, then? Indeed, there is! Hebrews 8:10 provides a truth that can put an end to discouragement and defeat. Setting forth one of the major tenets of the gospel, this verse declares we have a new heart inside us, a heart that already has the laws of God written on it. Amplifying this truth, G.D. Watson wrote, "Every part of Jesus' life—the various traits of his life, the various instincts of his life, the various heart-longings of his life—is implanted in the heart that is born-again ... The Holy Ghost implants within you the new life, the Divine life ...."[17]

This means that if we become filled with the Spirit, our new nature (this new heart) will rise and release. And when it does, we will exhibit the very qualities the laws of God require. Here's the point: Since our new nature is fully capable of producing everything the law commanded, the goal of believing and behaving is not out of reach, as we have thought. The power for fulfillment is already inside us!

Contemplate further the marvels of the new nature. When departing heaven to come to Bethlehem as a baby, Jesus told the Father that "Your law is within my heart" (Psalm 40:8). Now, if this were true of Jesus then—which of course it was; and is also now true of us, as Scripture declares it is—that has to mean that what we have inside us is the very life of Jesus (Colossians 3:4)! And what a tremendous difference *that* makes!

So if you're in a time right now when your "want to" doesn't want to, this has to mean you're functioning in your flesh—a way of thinking, feeling, and doing that you can and must relinquish. By switching tracks, and by getting into your new nature, these problems of inadequate desire, wrong thinking, and too-little willpower will be overcome. What will instead manifest are the nine parts of the Holy Spirit's fruit (Galatians 5:22, 23).

Just know that God isn't calling us to a way of life we can't enter. When God told us to be holy like he is holy, he meant it! The Greek word for "holiness," *hage*, is a combination of two words. G.D. Watson pointed out: "The word *ge*, always in the Greek Testament means earth, and the prefix *ha* is the strongest negative, and means *no earth.*"[18] The word "Adam," then, literally meant "red earth." *But* God took Adam out of us and put the new nature in us! And this new nature is the very life of our Lord.

Once this new nature is activated, we are *immediately* dead to sin and alive to God. This is always true of the new nature. However, it is not true of those not functioning with new-nature capacities (even though they possess new-nature capacities). Offering his own testimony, Dr. Martyn Lloyd-Jones said:

> I lose my sense of hopelessness because I can say to myself that no longer am I under the dominion of sin, but I am under the dominion of another power that nothing can frustrate. However weak I may be, it is the power of God that is working in me.[19]

This means: The victory we thought we couldn't have is well within reach!

There may be times when it appears that God's power in our lives has been thwarted, and that in some way God is now against us. Roy Hession said:

> A guilty conscience always makes a man feel God is against him and that anything adverse that happens to him is some sort of punishment. That is just not so. We must really take seriously that word 'God was in Christ reconciling the world to himself, *not imputing their trespasses to them*'.[20]

From time to time, Satan will try to gain an advantage over us by telling us that some new sin has been imputed to us. But the Bible says that *all* our sins were imputed to Jesus.

What will help us return to the orbit of new-nature living is the realization of how highly God regards this new nature, and thus will act consistently and creatively to put us back on the path of its intended destiny. Roy Hession explained:

Jesus Christ is the Redeemer of lost men and lost situations, whether the situation has been wrong half a lifetime or only a day. When he moves in to redeem, he not only forgives the sins we confess but also overrules for good the whole situation in which we have landed ourselves! Yes, and when he starts doing this sort of thing he does so in style. He often gives back to a man far more than he forfeited so that the repentant sinner cannot go on blaming himself but is lost in wonder, love and praise for all that grace has done ....[21]

Offering similar counsel, Jessie Penn-Lewis wrote: "If you do miss step with your Lord, trust him, by the skillfulness of his hands to put you in step again, and do not whip yourself with vain regrets but continue in his love and leave yourself entirely to his keeping."[22]

How motivating this restoring grace from God! A life that seemed impossible at first, the life of consistent goodness, can indeed be a major part of our biography. But for that to occur, we must allow all these motivations for obedience to have their intended and inspired effect.

Perhaps you recall the movie based on the old television show, *The Addam's Family*. If so, you'll recall that each member of this family exhibited strange qualities no one would ever want to imitate! In real life, all who are members of the first Adam's family will also exhibit qualities that aren't exactly desirable. And these aren't just humorous qualities, or strange qualities; they are deplorable qualities! Detestable qualities!

But when we got saved, we were taken out of Adam's family and put into Jesus' family! Therefore—because we are not who we used to be—we don't have to live as we used to live.

Clearly, the motivations for obedience are many, and, as Scripture and history amply confirm, they are real. In aggregate, these motivations strongly encourage righteous living by inspiring and invigorating our mind, by enlisting and enlivening the will, and by lifting and leveling our emotions. All that is within us is thus harnessed by heaven, so as to drive us ever onward to the life eternity honors. What an adventure!

Although it is good to be reminded of all these motivations, there is much truth in Count Nicolaus Zinzindorf's words, "I have but one passion. It is he; it is only he." And what did this passion produce? It produced the stirring faith of the Moravians, an eighteenth-century movement that quite literally began a one hundred year prayer meeting. With hearts aflame by their love for Jesus, the Moravians sped the gospel to may lands. And, remember, it was they who led to the Lord an unsaved missionary named John Wesley, through whom England was later mightily impacted by the once great Methodist denomination he began.

The cold orthodoxy of Europe turned into fervent piety once this wealthy count named Zinzendorf found his formerly dead heart gripped by one great motivation—to live his life for Jesus! Just that. Nothing else mattered!

Could you say the same: "I have but one passion. It is he; it is only he." Could you say that? Just know that when your motivations reduce to that, the increase of God's goodness in your life will become a persuasive testimony to many people.

Reflection Questions

1. How has the reminder of hell impacted you? In what specific ways will you be different?

2. In reflecting on what constitutes a true love toward believers, what is the first change God wants you to make?

3. What change of thought did you have when contemplating the joy God said we can have?

4. Do you think God trusts you today? If so, why would he? And if not, why wouldn't he?

The Hero: Overcoming All Odds

*James Bond is fiction
Spider Man is fiction
The Terminator is fiction
Sean, Toby and Arnold all play characters from fiction
The Apostle Peter, however, was real!*

And who more than Peter could have said:

*No one is perfect…
We all make mistakes…
I may not want to, but I sin every day
I just can't help it!
To err, is what? Oh, yeah—human!*

Yet, it is this same fallible Peter who became a spiritual hero. Though his past defeats are legendary, the life Peter later experienced was remarkably different. So different that with much credibility Peter was able to convey a message which, in earlier years, would have resulted in snickers and sneers. But having experienced the transforming power of God, Peter declared:

*Be holy, just as God is holy
Purify your souls
Show forth the praises of Him who has called you out of darkness
Sanctify the Lord God in your hearts
Be partakers of the divine nature
Giving all diligence, add to your faith virtue
You shall never fall*

In the end, Peter became more of a hero than any of those revered in fiction books. He lived a remarkable life, a life above the downward drag of sin, a life people at that time saw, and people today say is impossible.

Chapter 14

Consistent Goodness—Part I

We all love hero stories—David defeating Goliath, Samson bringing down the temple, Elijah calling down fire from heaven. However, all these stories feature episodes in the physical realm. What God desires more is heroism in the spiritual realm. And not just occasional episodes; what he really wants is an ongoing pattern of spiritual boldness.

Amazingly, the life of consistent goodness—which was unknown to David, Samson, and Elijah—has now been made possible through the new nature. People with skeptical mindsets may say that only a "saint" can live a life like that. But not even this claim is true, because the missionary, the monastery-dweller, and the monk also experience moral failure. So where *do* we turn to find a credible example?

What would make the case, I suppose, is if some regular guy, whose rough edges were common knowledge, demonstrated the radical difference the new nature can make. A change like *that* would certainly get our attention!

Well, to find such a man, one won't have to look any further than the first disciples, and particularly the most prominent among them, Peter. Surprisingly, it is from Peter that we learn how to live a consistently good life.

Given the blunders of Peter, who would ever think that sustained righteousness would be on display in his life? The pitfalls of Peter have been recounted so many times we've discounted him as a likely leader for righteousness training. Yet, Scripture tells us "the rest of the story" as it presents, by example and teaching, the victories Peter later experienced.

Peter's earlier mistakes, many and major, are easy to identify with. But later, a new and improved Peter emerged on the scene. And it is what he said then that will now claim our attention.

In the second epistle from Peter, the first chapter, we see astounding claims about sustained righteousness. What makes these claims all the more impressive is that they are accompanied by practical "how-to" instructions, each meriting our closest attention. For who wants the downward drag of the soul to continue even one more day if the provisions to prevent this decline are immediately available?

Contrary to what has happened to others, and to what we've been thinking is true of us, sin is not inevitable. Believers can get out of this "I-sin-every-day" thinking. These disastrous detours can be bypassed. We can *remain* on the road of sustained obedience.

According to Peter in verse 10, "If you do these things, you shall never stumble." What things? Well, beginning with verse 5, Peter details exactly what "these things" are. So let's check them out.

> And besides this, giving all diligence, add to your faith virtue; and to virtue knowledge; and to knowledge temperance; and to temperance patience; and to patience godliness; and to godliness brotherly kindness; and to brotherly kindness charity (II Peter 1:5-7 kjv).

Seven commendable qualities are listed here, but the question begging to be answered is: Why would we need to add anything to our faith? Scripture says in I John 5:4 that faith is the victory, so why would we need to add anything to that? In reply, consider this question: What does James 2:17 say about the kind of faith that remains alone, the kind of faith that has nothing added to it? It is dead! And what good is dead faith? Yes, our salvation is secured by faith alone; but if this faith is really of God, it won't remain alone. There will be other virtues added to it—and energized by it! This is the launching pad for consistent righteousness.

Faith is not some religious decoration for display. Making this point, Charles Spurgeon likened faith to a sword, and not one simply for show! He said this sword:

> ... was not made for presentation on a gala day, nor to be won on state occasions only, nor to be exhibited upon a parade ground. It is a sword that was meant to cut and wound and slay; and he who has it girt about him may expect, between here and heaven, that he shall know what battle means ....[1]

The faith that adds on, then, is not one of chronology, such as numbers on a page, but one of continuing conflict that culminates in many victories.

The Greek word for "add," *epichorego*, conveys the needs supplied for a musical chorus—the instruments, the performers, the assistants, the conductor—everything essential for a splendid performance. In his book, *The Holy Spirit* (volume 2), A.B. Simpson said, "... chorus into your faith and life these beautiful graces; bring them all into tune, and work them out in harmony and praise, so that your life shall be a doxology of joy and thanksgiving."[2]

Interestingly, the etymology of this word also includes the idea of choreography. The word picture here can depict a Greek dance, where one dancer holds the hand of another, and then another—fainting right, swirling left, with hands clasped high, as each moves through the ranks of this ensemble in festive jubilation. The simple point being: The dance of obedience isn't undertaken by one dancer; others take part in this dance, too.

The Case for Courage

The first dancer mentioned is called "virtue" in the King James Version of the Bible, but is better translated as "courage." Alexander Maclaren acknowledged the critical contribution courage makes to obedience, saying, "Courage, springing from the realization of God's helping strength, is indispensable to make any man, in any age, live out thoroughly and consistently the principles of the law of Jesus Christ."[3] Acceptance of God's principles will always require the courage sufficient to implement them.

Soon after penning these words, Peter was crucified upside down! His uncommon life had resulted in an uncommon death! But well before that, his life of victory meant uncommon pressures designed to force a discrediting retreat. Peter's courage, however, refused retreat!

Paul Billheimer, in his book *Destined for The Cross*, described the hostile atmosphere confronting the early church by quoting a man who had thoroughly researched this issue.

> Norman Grubb tells us that in the early centuries of the church, when Christians faced the common threat of martyrdom, the elders of the church were asked this question before hands of consecration were laid upon them: "Art thou then able to drink of the cup which I am about to drink or be baptized with the baptism with which I am about to be baptized?" To which they answered, "I take on myself scourgings, imprisonment, tortures, reproaches, crosses, blows, tribulation, and all the temptations of the world which our Lord, and Intercessor, and the Universal and Apostolic Holy Church took upon themselves."[4]

To join the church in that day involved more than signing a decision card, being welcomed by a friendly pastor and shaking hands with church members after a worship service. No, to acknowledge you were a follower of Jesus in that day meant you were willing to face an intensely hostile world—*come what may*!

William Barclay, a University of Glasgow professor, tells of how the courage commended by Peter won over a man who later became a great church leader himself.

> Tertullian was one of the greatest of the early Christian fathers. They say that, at one time, he

may well have been the attorney general of the Roman Empire. He was certainly a lawyer, and he was so impressed with the dauntless courage of the Christians whom he prosecuted that he enquired what made men like that, and he became a Christian.[5]

Though the fires of persecution got red hot during these persecutions, the courage of believers, even in the flames, glowed even brighter! This, the Lord used as a powerful witness! Eusebius, the fourth-century church historian, recounts the torture inflicted upon believers: Bones were broken, teeth knocked out, bodies devoured by blood-thirsty beasts. Eusebius then writes:

> Some of them, after scrapings and rackings and severest scourgings, and numberless other kinds of tortures, terrible even to hear of, were committed to the flames; some were drowned in the sea; some offered their heads bravely to those who cut them off ... others were nailed to the cross ... with their heads downward, and being kept alive until they perished on the cross with hunger.[6]

Do understand that the connection between faith and courage is essential; because if we don't add courage to our faith, our faith won't stand strong when it undergoes its most stringent tests. Sometimes, we think that if we'll just put our faith in God, heaven will open up, its power will cascade down, the barriers that had been blocking the blessing will topple over, so that—finally and fully—all that we had been believing God for will fall nice and easy into our lap. But this is hardly a scenario where courage is needed.

Reminding us when courage was intensely needed, Scripture recounts: the taunting of Goliath, such as David faced; the rampage of intimidating giants, such as Joshua faced; the gathering of a menacing army, such as Gideon faced; the foaming madness of a wild man, such as Jesus faced when this terror of the countryside raced straight toward him during those pre-dawn hours following a harrowing night at sea. So, yes, there *are* times, scary times, when courage is needed.

Some people think courage is a fickle friend, a fleeting commodity, in that sometimes you have it and sometimes you don't. But is courage the fortuitous outcome of favorable circumstances, a bold temperament, the right-time-of-the-month bio-rhythms, and an upbeat mood swing? Courage is hardly as elusive as that, especially for the child of God.

The Bible says Asa "took courage," that Jehosaphat "took courage," that Paul "took courage." A quaint manner of speaking, you say? Perhaps so, but when God offers courage, we have to decide if we'll take it, or if we'll settle for a low vision, a small assignment, continuing defeat, and an extended exile from the fulfillment God intends for our life.

If only we'll do as Asa did, as Jehoshaphat did, as Paul did, and "take" courage, courage will then take us into the dreams God has for our life.

The usual way this plays out among many believers is this: Failing to believe courage is there for the taking, they panic, they retreat (in a way that is not spiritual) so their eventual exodus is without the leadership of God.

In contrast with the absence of courage is a counterfeit of courage. You will recall that when God told Joshua to be of a "good courage," the idea of a not-so-good courage was clearly suggested.

For example, the courage that takes confidence in its own resources may win some victories, such as Sampson did, but in the end it will go down in terrible defeat, just like Sampson did. So if we don't want to be playing Captain Courageous on a high seas adventure from which we'll never get back, we need to be sure that the courage we add to our faith is good courage.

G.D. Watson eloquently described this courage:

> The courage which can stand alone with God, that not only can face numberless foes, but endure patiently the desertion of friends, the misunderstanding and criticisms of other Christians, to take up a task that all others regard

as hopeless, to take a stand that is denounced as insane delusion, to discern victory through dark, dense battle clouds where all others see nothing but defeat, to work patiently without one word bragging on the work, to pray on, press on, weep on, fight on day and night, through love or hate, with friends or foes, whether encouraged or denounced, requires a celestial courage that is born out of the heart of Jesus ....[7]

Athanasius, the fourth-century bishop from Alexandria, stood strong in his defense of Jesus (and a right understanding of the Trinity), and for that he was banished from his post and exiled from his country.

One day a colleague said to him, "The whole world is against you!" To which the beleaguered bishop replied, "Then it is Athanasius against the world."

Commending this kind of courage, A.B. Simpson exclaimed, "No man can have God's highest thought and be popular with his immediate generation. The most abused men are often the most used. The devil's growl and the world's sneer are God's marks of highest honor."[8]

The Need for Knowing

The second quality we need to add to our faith, if ours is to be a consistent goodness, is knowledge. The Bible says God's people are destroyed because of a lack of knowledge (Hosea 4:6). In this regard, F.F. Bosworth said it well: Faith begins where the will of God is known. This makes perfect sense. For how can there be a faith-launch, if the principles for deploying this launch aren't understood?

Now, because knowledge is added to faith at this point—*after* one has become a Christian, and *after* aroused opposition by the enemy—this knowledge has to be more than entry level, how-to-become-a-Christian knowledge. So what kind of knowledge is this? The Greek word suggests that this knowledge is able to discern what even the brainiest brains could never discern. Permit this explanation.

The acquisition of any knowledge worthy of attainment requires time, and often a considerable investment of time.

No one can dabble in the things of God and expect to have something valuable added to his faith. However, as one makes himself available to God in faith, asking God to reveal what the human mind would conceal, a supernatural impartation of divine truth can then occur, wherein God shows the believer what on his own he could never see.

For example, in Ephesians, chapter 1, we find Paul praying that God will give a spirit of revelation and knowledge so that the eyes of our understanding would be enlightened, thus enabling us to know three things. And would you notice them? 1) The hope of his calling, 2) the riches of our inheritance, and 3) the greatness of God's power toward us (Ephesians 1:17-19). These three things, about which most Christians know very little, are essential to believers today.

Do you know the calling God has for your life? The Bible says God created before the foundations of the world the good works he wanted you to walk into (Ephesians 2:10). But do you know what these good works are? Many people, Christian people, can be on this earth for several decades and still be almost clueless about what God wants them to do. As a result, they meander through life without any sense of vision or mission.

There were three major facets of God's plan for Paul's life, all three of which were revealed before Saul became Paul in a dramatic conversion experience. In checking this story out, we learn God didn't observe Paul for a while and then, "playing things by ear," give Paul an assignment based on a current need of the church. No, God knew exactly what he wanted Paul to do *before* there was a church, and *before* Paul even became a Christian.

God has a clear plan for your life, too, the discovery of which will bring immense satisfaction; and if completed, a strong sense of accomplishment. Remember, you are hardly an afterthought to God, left to take up space and be a consumer. God formed you with a distinct purpose in mind.

Interesting to note here is that the three-part assignment God gave *didn't* line up with Paul's assessment of himself. This should inform us that we can't take a test on our gifts and passions and then, on that basis alone, decide how we should minister. These tests can be helpful when they assist discovery of what God put inside us. However, we shouldn't overload what these tests were intended to do by interpreting them as God's final answer for ministry direction. These tests are *human* instruments that summon *human* reflection; so it would be a mistake to trust them too much.

According to Scripture, Paul became so stubborn about the ministry he thought he should have, he debated with God—and in the temple no less! During this full-on debate Paul presented all the reasons his ministry should be to the Jews and not, as God was telling him, to the Gentiles. Paul was a Pharisee, a member of the Sanhedrin, a student of Gamaliel, a Hebrew of the Hebrews, a former persecutor of the church and now a preacher of the gospel. So why couldn't God see this? Paul was the perfect choice for a leadership ministry in Jerusalem!

As the biblical record makes clear, Paul had to get a revelation on this point; and until he did so, he kept trying to reverse the priorities of God's plan for his life. Paul actually stood God's plan on its head—making God's last priority the first priority—and thus Paul became a sidelined saint, having no ministry until he would accept God's assigned ministry.

One wonders if other Christians have also missed God in this way. Without revelation knowledge in our life, we, like Paul, will waste a lot of time; and, also like Paul, we'll experience many needless frustrations.

So, yes, faith is a good thing, but it is important to add the kind of knowledge that directs the investment of our faith. Further delineating what kind of knowledge this is, Paul's prayer in Ephesians chapter 1 focuses on the need for a revelation of the believer's resources. Most believers, sad to say, know almost nothing of this knowledge. Consequently, they do what little they can—with good intentions, no doubt—but not with the results God had in mind.

Once a believer does get revelation knowledge, that believer will be put in the grip of this revelation—to the extent he simply has to have what God is offering! Prior to God opening one's eyes, all this talk about the believer's resources will likely be words that the mind quickly disengages from. Why? Because it takes a definite act of God opening our eyes before we can really know the supply of God. This is a supply Scripture calls a "mighty power," the very power that raised Jesus from the dead, a power "far above" anything the devil has (Ephesians 1:21), a power that resides in us this very moment.

Do you have a revelation knowledge of God's power inside you? Or does such talk about "power" float out of the real world where you live?

Imagine if you did get a revelation of this power. What might the difference be? Why, the difference would be between meager results of dubious duration and a lasting work of God that has glory written all over it!

Jesus said the church was to be built upon this rock. Upon what rock? Upon the rock of a revelation knowledge of Jesus himself, a knowledge that sees him as our Savior, Sanctifier, Healer, and coming King. Upon this rock, Jesus said, he would build his church, against which the gates of hell could never prevail.

I would submit that this knowledge, this discernment, is absolutely critical for lasting effectiveness in God's work—and that's why we must add it to our faith! We must vividly see what Jesus is personally and uniquely offering *us*. There is a certain capacity and a prescribed direction, each being absolutely essential to our eventual success.

Encouraged by this direction, and now aware that courage is needed to follow it, we are better prepared to learn the next needed steps for consistent goodness. These steps will be disclosed in the next chapter.

Reflection Questions

1. Is there a situation in your life where courage is exactly what needs to be added to your faith?

2. Are you asking God to give you the kind of revelation knowledge Paul prayed for in Ephesians, chapter 1? If so, what are the results so far?

Chapter 15
Consistent Goodness—Part II

Many Christians think that living a consistently obedient life—a good life, a pure life, a holy life—is bound to fail, even for a Christian. The standards, they think, are too high, the opportunities to sin are too many, the flesh is too strong. Some Christians even say they can't make it through a day without sinning.

Another factor contributing to our losing battle against sin is the belief that we have two natures—one good and one not so good. Each of these natures, it is believed, alternately and frequently expresses itself. People may not want to sin, yet frequently they do. And the main reason they do is because of this ongoing conflict between the old nature and the new nature.

To be stuck in this kind of thinking is to operate with diminished efforts, accept reduced goals, and succumb to moral defeat. J.C. Philpot observed, "What a mere shallow pretense to vital godliness satisfies most ministers, most hearers, and most congregations!" It's as predictable as it is obvious: Those who believe a believer has two natures—one good and one bad—are going to behave the way they believe.

In 1885 Robert Louis Stevenson wrote, *The Strange Case of Dr. Jekyll and Mr. Hyde.* Convinced of the dual nature of man, the author created a character, Dr. Henry Jekyll, who, in the author's estimate, wasn't as strange as some people think.

Jekyll invented a drug that could change a man from good to bad, and another drug that could completely reverse this change. Using these drugs to experiment on himself, Jekyll produced a very bad man, whom he called Edward Hyde. While in a drug-induced state, Hyde committed multiple crimes, even murder. But no one ever suspected Hyde. That's because he turned back into Jekyll, this well-regarded doctor who kept company with intellectual elites. His refined appearance seemed to ward off suspicion.

After a while, the drug wasn't needed for Jekyll to become Hyde. The evil side of this man's nature began to dominate, so that by the end of the story the good doctor died as the evil Edward Hyde.

Those who think Jekyll and Hyde depict human nature even after one becomes a Christian do much damage to themselves. Their belief actually becomes a self-fulfilling prophecy. To say a man has two natures makes no sense, biblically. For either a man is regenerate or he is unregenerate; he is not both. Yet, because this two-natures view prevails in the church today, the call to holiness is muffled, muted, stifled, and eventually silenced.

A.B. Simpson said, "This contentment with inadequate and imperfect progress in the life of holiness is, I repeat, a scandal to the church of the First-born. The whole weight of Scripture is against such a thing."[1] Continuing his commentary, Simpson observed, "Our error today is that we do not expect a converted man to be a transformed man, and as a result our churches are full of substandard Christians."[2] Even Seneca, the Roman philosopher, said, "I would I were not so much bettered as transformed."[3] It is regrettable that this aspiration of a Stoic has not taken hold in God's church.

In his book, *Paths to Power*, A.W. Tozer wrote:

> To any casual observer of the religious scene today, two things will at once be evident: one, that there is very little sense of sin among the unsaved, and two, that the average professed Christian lives a life so worldly and careless that it is difficult to distinguish him from the unconverted man.[4]

But what if a Christian told you he had a nature just like God's, that he had escaped the corruption of this world, *and* that he now knew how to never stumble again in his walk with God? Sound too good to be true?

Many people would dismiss such talk as the excited faith of adolescent theology, or as the ivory tower faith of a theologian more acquainted with theory than life. But what makes these words entirely credible is that they come from a person who had made his share of bonehead blunders.

The name of the man who said these things was Simon, later renamed by the Lord, Peter. Now, Peter knew as well as anyone how fallible the flesh could be! And he also knew, *by experience*, how formidable the enemy's attacks could be!

What makes Peter's words even more shocking to us are these staggering, almost unbelievable, assertions about having escaped the corruption that is in the world through lust. Escaped? We don't know anyone who escaped! They *all* struggle, and do so until the day they die. So how did Peter overcome?

Well, he tells us how by setting forth three factors: It is by having 1) divine power, 2) divine promises, and 3) a divine nature. Now, if language means anything, and if Peter has any credibility, these words have to get our attention!

In his book, *A Larger Christian Life*, A.B. Simpson asserts, "There is no single paragraph in Scripture that more profoundly unfolds the depths and heights of Christian life than the first 11 verses of Second Peter."[5] Again, Peter's words are not the rash words of a religious fanatic, but are eminently practical words, rooted in the realism of tested and proven faith.

Peter identified seven qualities that need to be added to our faith, two of which we considered in the previous chapter, and three more we'll consider in this chapter. But first we must stress the role *we* are to play in this.

You will notice that Peter doesn't just say add these seven qualities. What he actually says is we are to add them "with all diligence" (II Peter 1:5). So to those having an "automatic pilot" view of the Christian life—wherein this "let go and let God" theology[6] gets distorted to mean that once a person becomes a Christian he'll float into the heavenly city just as easy as you please—Peter's words about "all diligence" duly correct and, of necessity, redirect.

A.B. Simpson pointed out, "There are some things which if done at all must be done audaciously. A cavalry charge cannot be made with caution and timidity. When once the order is given it must be all charge and nothing else."[7]

This "all diligence" approach Peter commends stands in contrast with an occasional effort, made only if a burst of inspiration happens to strike. Instead of this "goose-bump" motivated obedience (which can be here today and gone tomorrow), Scripture says we're to obey in season and out, whether we're feeling good or not, and whether things are convenient or not. Whatever the situation, whatever the mood, no license for laziness should ever be granted.

Ruth Paxson, the twentieth-century American committed to the deeper life, wrote:

> The only cure for self-will is a deliberate, determined choice to do God's will in all things, at all times, at all costs. It is to have one's heart firmly fixed upon the doing of God's will as the rule for daily life and to permit no exception to this rule.[8]

The etymology of the word "added," seen throughout this passage in Peter, includes the idea of a generous supply, such as a rich benefactor might give to a project for which he strongly cared. Assuming, then, this context of a caring God, we are to give ourselves with the same utter devotion, and not in any occasional, halfhearted, nonchalant way. God's commitment should inspire ours!

If you look up the word "will" in a concordance, you'll see more than 4,000 citations, occupying more than twelve pages. This indicates that our will is exceedingly important to God. Indeed, the surrendered will, the sanctified will, are actually indispensable to consistent goodness.

In her book, *The Sea Around Us*, Rachel Carson described a microscopic vegetable life called plankton. Plankton—having no destiny of its own and no power of its own—can drift thousands of miles, from one ocean to another. Just like plankton, many Christians are drifting in the capricious currents of this world, seeming to have no will of their own.

Soren Kierkegaard, the Danish theologian, told a story about people like this. It is a story about a flock of geese milling around a filthy barnyard, imprisoned by a high wooden fence. One day a preaching goose came into their midst, and, perching himself on an old crate, admonished these geese for being content with their confined, earthbound existence. He then recounted the exploits of their forefathers who spread their wings and flew the trackless wastes of the sky. Expounding this point further, he talked about the goodness of their Creator who had given them the amazing ability to fly—even to faraway places!

As he spoke, the geese nodded their heads approvingly, appreciating and applauding such eloquent words from the preaching goose. But then—never looking over the fence, nor making the first attempt to flutter their wings—they went back to their waiting dinner, for the corn was good and the barnyard secure.

Likewise, we today can hear about God's power enabling a life beyond what we've ever known. However, if our next move is to choose the familiar over the superior, what are we really thinking—that these words about power are the hype of heaven? But why would we ever think that? Isn't the power God promises, and the new nature he gave, enough to live a consistently good life?

In one sense, yes; but in another sense, no. Because to live this kind of life we're going to have to exercise *our* will. Henry Scougal, the Scottish devotional writer from the seventeenth century, made this point in quaintly written words: "We must not lie loitering in the ditch and wait until Omnipotence pulls us from thence. No, no: we must bestir ourselves and put forth ourselves in our utmost capacities ...."

In the words of the apostle, we must "give all diligence." A halfhearted effort occasionally and feebly given will never achieve what God promises. That which *will* yield what he promises requires first giving all that is within us.

A Time for Temperance

The quality of temperance is the third add-on to our faith recommended by Peter. Some translations call this quality, self-control, but that can be a bit misleading, inasmuch as self should never be trusted to control anything. So let's do some theology here.

The spirit re-created in the believer at the time of conversion is where the life of God indwells, and where our new nature resides. Jessie Penn-Lewis wrote: "So many of God's children do not know that they have a 'spirit.' They live in the 'soul'—that is to say, in their feelings, in their sense life, in their minds; but as to what is 'spirit,' they do not know."[9]

But they must be made to know! For the life of Jesus is found only in that domain! This inner sanctum, having the fruit of the Spirit already, has now been made perfect; and, as such, is the rightful governor of all our attitudes and actions. The soul, however, is a different proposition entirely. When one becomes a Christian, that doesn't mean contaminated thinking is immediately deleted, that a weak will is instantly made strong, and that certain feelings are suddenly made pure. No, the progressive aspect of salvation involves getting our soul under the control of our spirit.

G.H. Lang pointed out what a major project this revamping of old thoughts and ways can be when he wrote, "It is fatally easy to bring over into our post-conversion period the thoughts and ways of our pre-Christian days, even as Israel brought into the wilderness, the ideas, lusts, ways they had followed before redemption."[8] Much of their earlier thinking remained fully intact. Therefore, once Israel began a new life, continuity with their old life in Egypt had to be ended and not just amended.

For that to occur, however, the people of God needed to cross the Jordan (which means death) before they could ever live the life God had promised them (the faith conquests in Canaan). Wilderness-bound people can never experience such a life! And yet many, vainly, are still trying to do so even today.

On the negative side, there are certain excesses God wants the believer to avoid. The typical indulgences—

alcohol, smoking, drugs, overeating, oversleeping, overspending, illicit sex and other addictive behaviors—don't require much commentary, except to say if we don't keep adding to our faith, we may very well succumb to one of these formerly conquered sins.

Remember, the only thing a believer has to do to sin is nothing. If a believer just cuts himself some slack and briefly vacations from the straight and narrow, the sin he once mastered will come back to haunt him. And this will occur—because sinning is inevitable? No, not for that reason! The forces of temptation are never greater than the resources of grace! But, to obtain victory, this grace must be used!

In this world, the believer must swim against the tide, paddle upstream, struggle against the onrush of a strong and steady current. If we reduce the effort—well, downstream we will go! Again, the only thing necessary for sin to regain control is the inertia of an undisciplined life—however brief, however slight.

There are other ways one can lose balance, too. Plotting this loss of our balance, the enemy may change tactics by allowing us to go in a direction he had been opposing. We had been pressing, pushing, and driving ourselves with all that we had, when suddenly—the enemy gave way, stepped back, and watched us fall flat on our face!

The sudden disappearance of opposition meant that our momentum took on a greater speed with a greater-than-anticipated force. Hence, with arms flailing, feet scrambling, and the most chagrined expression on our face, we ended up looking foolish—and becoming vulnerable.

An uncommon experience, you wonder? Actually, this kind of thing occurs in the ministry all the time. For example: pastors serving their people to the point they neglect their families; evangelists traveling the globe as if they don't have a family; missionaries making sacrifices they never should have made precisely because they do have a family.

This same problem can also be seen in some church members. Instead of cultivating relationships with their children and nurturing long-neglected marriages, church members will attend too many meetings at church. Then, when family life fractures, they wonder how something like this could have happened to people so faithful—not realizing that it happened precisely because they were "so faithful."

Dallas Willard observed that a major enemy to our intimacy with God is our service for God. We find it easy to maximize service and minimize the time we spend in bible study and prayer. Oswald Chambers wrote, "The whole basis of modern Christian work is the great impulsive desire to evade concentration on God. We will work for him any day rather than have him work in us."[11]

Instead of letting our service *to* God flow from a daily renewal *in* God, the service we offer runs on its own steam, only to pass boundaries that should have been recognized.

One man felt the call to pray for long hours into the night, night after night. He prayed for the heathen in Africa, for the Hindus in India, for the Buddhists in China, for the materialists in Japan. But then one night, sensing a divine interruption, this man seemed to hear God say, "George, why don't you go to bed. I'll watch the world for the rest of the night." You get the point, don't you? Even in ways that are good and godly, we can still lose balance.

Jesus withdrew from the multitudes for this reason, recognizing his need for rest. Of course, when he did so, there were still needs to be met—one can always count on that being true! Nevertheless, a person can only do so much. Wisdom will require discernment and balance.[10]

Balance, you say—but what exactly is that? Well, it's making schedules that declare God's priorities. It's recognizing limitations when they do exist. It's not overloading in one area of our life to the exclusion of another area. It's seeing how overcomitment may be as big a problem as under-commitment is.

Temperance—which is God's ability to order our life so we exhibit what A.B. Simpson called "the power of poise"—is a quality already in us, inasmuch as it is a part of our new nature. From the domain of our new nature is a resident source indispensable for the activation of any fruit. However, we need to utilize what is in us, adding it to the faith also in us, so we can better protect ourselves from a senseless stumbling and a foolish fall.

The Purpose of Patience

A fourth quality Peter says we should add to our faith with all diligence is patience. Patience is the decision to keep faith on the job. Patience means to rely on the divine supply.

Whenever we find ourselves in a difficult season, in a time when prayers seem unanswered and problems are without solution, the temptation to take things into our own hands can become very strong. Samuel Chadwick observed, "The saddest thing in Christian workers is they despair too soon."[13] And having done so, inferior methods, designed to alter outcomes and end the frustration, become attractive. We see this lesson illustrated in the Old Testament.

The Middle East is a boiling political cauldron today, all because Abraham and Sarah tried to help God in ways contrary to his will. For years, they had been waiting for God to give them a baby. But with the passing of years and no baby on the scene, Sara (which was her name at the time) got this idea that the baby could come some other way—just send in her handmaiden, Hagar, to be with Abraham for a night. That way, through this much younger woman, the long-awaited child could come! But the result, we now know, was Ishmael, through whom the Arabs descended. Yes, God loved Ishmael, as did his father, Abraham. Yet, history, ancient and modern, chronicles the long conflict between the Arabs and the Jews. The heartache has been tragic!

Whenever we set aside faith and take matters into our own hands, drastic outcomes will likely occur. Forgotten at the time we act this way is the fact God has his own solutions, which are infinitely preferable to ours. But we forfeit these solutions if we substitute our wisdom for his.

Another temptation that comes during a season of challenge is simply to give up. We can make the decision to end the anguish of waiting by casting our faith confession aside and letting our dream go. There's a spiritual law in play here: Because whenever the pressure is on, we are going to cast something. We'll either cast away our confidence in God (Hebrews 10:35), or we'll cast our cares upon God (I Peter 5:7).

This tension between faith and sight can be quickly terminated by joining the wrong side of the struggle, sight.

Hebrews 10:35 urges believers not to do this, saying that our confession of faith, if maintained, offers a great reward. Despite this passionate plea, though, and despite the promised reward the Bible says can be ours, people become discouraged anyway and cast away their confession in the same manner they throw out the trash.

A much better way to relieve this tension was given by Peter! When we cast our care on the Lord, Peter said, the burden soon shifts from our shoulders to the stronger shoulders of the Lord. This brings welcome relief in mere moments.

There's no use denying that pressures can be unbearable sometimes, especially if we're handling these pressures by ourselves. God knows that; and because he does, the Lord doesn't want us managing the pressures of life by ourselves. True, the pressure may remain for a while; God won't solve every problem instantly. *But* a greater capacity to handle the pressure will be offered by the Lord right away.

These times of waiting and wanting can be very difficult for even the strongest Christian. So why does God require all this? He desires it because, whether patience takes the form of waiting or the form of endurance, it develops something in us so supremely important that God speaks of it in the most amazing way: Scripture says, "Let patience have her perfect work that you may be perfect, entire, lacking nothing."

Wow! According to this verse in James, patience has the capacity to release every blessing of God intended for the believer on this side of life. What an astonishing stack of superlatives! Perfect! Entire! Lacking nothing! These three descriptors refer to a life that other people would envy.

Consider, by way of contrast, the alternative to patience. What would happen if God answered every prayer request we made the same day we made it? Why, if this were the case, our spiritual muscles would never grow. In fact, bestowed blessings too-soon given could even harm us. G.D. Watson addressed this point when he wrote:

> Were we allowed to measure off the kind of blessings we should have, we would probably

have them of too low an order and we would have them come prematurely. The very blessings would surfeit and ruin us, and render us utterly incapable of the sweetest and deepest joys for which we were created.[14]

This is a point the Spirit of God touched on when he inspired the words, "Beloved, I pray above all things that you prosper and be in health, even as your soul prospers." Take soul prosperity out of this equation, and the result of these other blessings may well be a disaster.

Every wise parent knows that overindulging the kids with toys is not a good thing. Likewise, God knows there are conditions that need to be met, a timing that needs to be considered, in order for his intended goodness to *remain* good in our lives.

Something of eternal value comes into our souls whenever we wait on God, endure when it is difficult to do so, cast ourselves upon him with a greater intensity than we've done before, and in the process discover insights about God that bless us more than what we first asked to receive when all this waiting began.

In his book, *The Practice of Godliness*, Abraham Kuyper said, "Patience does not sparkle in the sunlight of the day. It glows in the darkness with an inner light. It glows in the night of suffering ... when the soul wrestles in deepest distress."[15] And I would submit that the glow of this kind of testimony is reason enough to add patience to our faith. Remember, a macadamia tree takes five to seven years to produce nuts but then it produces nuts for the next 100 years. A Chinese bamboo takes five years and five weeks to sprout from the ground, but then in the next five weeks it grows 90 feet tall.

As in the natural world, so in the spiritual realm: Patience has its immense rewards! This is exactly why we must let patience have her perfect work, because, in the words of Vance Havner, "He who waits on God loses no time." But he who refuses to wait loses the Savior's supply. And this may result in being overcome in a way that no amount of time can possibly reverse.

The Goal of Godliness

The next quality Peter tells us to add to our faith is godliness; and by this he means giving diligence to those disciplines that increase our intimacy with God—prayer and bible study, chief among these. A.B. Simpson defined this quality of Spirit as "the upper chamber, the observatory, where we look up and out upon the heavens, where we meet and know God ...."[16]

There's simply no way we can remain patient, sustain faith, add courage, get control of self, and grow in knowledge unless we are regularly meeting the Lord in the Word.

Brief and occasional times with God may fit an acquaintance relationship—but not an intimate one! Just as the Jews required fresh manna every day (yesterday's manna would never do), we too need a fresh revelation from God. To receive *daily* "manna" is always critical to what we want "manna-fested."

This is why Peter said we're to desire the sincere milk of God's Word in the same way a baby desires milk. So how does a baby desire milk? You know the answer to that question! When the time for feeding comes—and the baby knows exactly when this is—the milk better be there or everyone around will hear about it! And yet, without a peep of protest, there are Christians who will forgo God's Word for days and even weeks—to the detriment of their souls!

By allowing the Bible to gather dust, the resulting consequences are sadly certain: fear will return, sin will return, the heart will become hard, the mind will become dense, and the will (the ultimate decision-maker) will become feeble in its resolve. It is simply impossible to escape these consequences if we neglect the feeding of our spirit.

You and I need wisdom for daily living that can only come from the Bible. The wisdom that enchanted Rome—appealing to one's desire to weigh, sift, and sort out—is nothing when compared to the wisdom found in God's book. Aflame with divine revelation, the Bible chases away the cobwebs of confusion as it sets forth title deeds to eternal life. God-breathed in its source and God-honored in its outcomes, Scripture is crucial to anyone who would live a consistently good life.

More than any book of the month, this book of the ages is imperative for the release of God's blessings. So instead of being an optional enrichment, Jesus tells us we're to *live* by every word that proceeds out of the mouth of God.

To think God's Word and act on God's Word is critical to becoming godly. Moreover, godliness itself is critical to success in our journey. Because the more we know about God, the less likely it is we'll fall or stumble.

Sure, the trials of our life can be challenging, but this is exactly when the Bible will help us the most. As Leonard Ravenhill put it, "The Bible was written in tears and to tears it will yield its best treasures. God has nothing to say to the frivolous man."[17]

It is the *treasured* word hidden in our hearts that will keep us strong, especially when temptation makes its most enticing appeals. But what do you suppose will happen to the occasional Bible reader when the enemy of his soul launches a full campaign against him? John Bunyan summed it up well. "Either this book will keep you from sin, or sin will keep you from this book." There is going to be a breakthrough or a breakdown. One or the other. And it all depends on who we are listening to: the devil, who deceives in order to destroy; or God, whose truth will set us free.

"If you continue in my Word," Jesus said, "*then* you will be free" (John 8:31). Did you get that? Continue! Because the day you stop, the very day bible study ceases to be a cultivated habit in your life, is the same day you will find yourself on sin's great decline, going faster and further away from God than you ever imagined your once bible-taught soul could go. Don't let that happen to you! And if it's already happening, the time has come to stop it—now!

To Peter that night in the garden, Jesus said, "I have prayed for you that your faith fail not." Do understand that if we're to avoid the failure Peter said could be avoided, such prayer is needed for our faith, too. As E.M. Bounds put it, "Only those who obey have the right to pray."[18]

But the reverse of this is also true: Only those who pray will have the power to obey. Prayer, rightly undertaken, touches our spirit with God's Spirit, thereby releasing a power to do his will—no matter what the opposition, no matter what the need. Fully realizing this fact, Satan is intent to keep us from praying. T. Austin-Sparks wrote, "The focal point of all the enemy's attention and strategy is the prayer-life of the believer. If he can destroy that ... he has gained the day, defeated the saints, and frustrated the ends of God."[19]

So, big question here: Has he gained the day and defeated *you*, all because of prayerlessness?

Properly exercised, prayer puts us in the presence of God—and this needed nexus is imperative! Because it's impossible to keep one's gaze on the Lord and at the same time look with desire on sin. It is as we look to the Lord, Scripture says, that we will be changed into his image and live a life that goes from "from glory to glory" (II Corinthians 3:18). This glory-to-glory journey will then enable us to do what we couldn't do before: to run from sin's clutches just as Joseph did, saying, "How can I do this thing against God?"

Conversely, the first condition necessary for sin to gain an advantage over us is *blocking the presence of God*. Aware of this serious and salient fact, the enemy of our soul wants to keep us: 1) from meeting the Lord in the Word; and 2) from spending time with God in prayer. Why? Because the devil wants our image of God to grow dim, our last revelation from him to grow stale, our will to weaken, and our spiritual temperature to drop.

Once the presence of God has been blocked in our lives, the opportunity to sin becomes wide open. Open, not just in the sense of a possibility, but in the sense of being instantly inhaled by sin, as if it were sucking siphon rendering you vulnerable, powerless, defenseless and soon defeated.

Consistent goodness? That *can* be our testimony, according to Scripture. But not if we're trying to accomplish this through our self-life! And not if we're infrequent in the time we give to increasing our intimacy with God!

In summing these principles up, would you not agree that there are no alternative approaches more effective than what Peter identified: temperance, patience, and godliness—all added to our faith? When each of these virtues is isolated for study and examined for its benefits, it becomes clearer that what Peter presents is hardly a grab-bag of "do-goodism" carelessly tossed our way. For each virtue links to the other, and in aggregate enhances the wisdom for doing exactly what the inspired apostle said. Affirming the worthiness of this outcome, A.W. Tozer said: "As the excellence of steel is strength, and the excellence of art is beauty, so the excellence of mankind is moral character."

This isn't a side issue; it is *the* issue. Our supposed belief in God matters little if there isn't the proof of a transformed life.

Reflection Questions

1. In giving an overall assessment of your spiritual progress, how would you rate your exercise of willpower?

2. What have you been casting recently—your confidence in God? Or your cares upon God?

3. Of the three qualities to be added to your faith discussed in this chapter, which one have you added with the most success, and which one have you added with the least success?

4. Are you, at this point, inspired to live a life without stumbling? Or are you more inclined to doubt that consistent goodness is possible?

Chapter 16
Consistent Goodness—Part III

Do *you* think it's possible to escape moral corruption? Most people don't. They think that in this world, wrong desires and all the ruination it brings will be a fact of life. However, the Apostle Peter said there *is* a way to escape the corrosive effects of sin. According to the Apostle, it is a major mistake to accept the consensus view: namely, that we're only human so sin is bound to have inroads into our life.

Accommodating conventional thinking on this point, the cry of the psalmist—"Search me, O God, and see if there be any wicked way in me"—isn't heard much today; and there are at least two reasons for this. First, Christians don't want an update reporting the evil in their lives. Second, discovering the obvious doesn't exactly require a supernatural searchlight. As Keith Moore puts it, calling on divine omniscience to discover sin is a like a country boy searching for dirt with a microscope! Why bother? Sin is everywhere! The primary reason for this being: this mistaken notion that our inner resources are inadequate for the battle.

But why would we ever think that? If left with inadequate resources, as so many have concluded, what does that say about how the Lord equips us? That the Almighty won't share his might with us? That the battle he left us to fight is a losing cause? That heaven is our only refuge? That being human means frequently losing to the great enemy, sin.[1] Yet Peter says we can get past this "being-only-human business" and become instead a partaker of the divine nature. So if Peter is right, then the chains of sin *can* be broken and the flight of ever-soaring righteousness *can* begin.

Whoa! We've reached a fork in the road on this one! It is here, at these widely-diverging crossroads, that we must acknowledge the direction Scripture bids us to take is almost universally rejected by others—educated or not educated, religious or not religious, disciplined or not disciplined.

The message Peter shares in this chapter is likely to be blocked unless we first confront the notion that God's standards are too difficult for any of us to comply with. E.M. Bounds said, "There is no denying that the unrenewed man cannot obey God."[2] But once a man becomes a Christian, receives a new nature, accesses the enabling power of God, the whole situation changes—and to say otherwise only contradicts the Bible and slanders God!

Persuaded by this fact, E.M. Bounds penned both a probing question and a compelling conclusion:

> Is he so arbitrary, so severe, so unloving that he issues commandments that can't be obeyed? The answer is that in all of Scripture not a single instance is recorded of God having commanded any man to do a thing that was beyond his power.[3]

But as long as we think God's commandments are "impossible ideals"—worthy in the way they instruct, noble in the way they inspire, but unattainable, after all—we'll filter what God is saying and start spewing these utterly inane observations about "no one being perfect" and "all of us having our weaknesses." The disastrous effect of this perspective is that we will feel no expectation—and hence no obligation—to obey God *always*.

Charles Finney emphatically refuted what many Christians believe when he wrote, "It is a dangerous error to inculcate that Christians sin daily and hourly. It sets the door wide open for false hopes and fills the church with the victims of delusion."[4] Dr. Dale Yocum insisted "that sin is a foreign element in the constitution of man."⁵ So removing that which is foreign shouldn't be out of the question.

Besides, the world has seen enough contradiction. As Oliver Wendell Holmes observed, "... there are plenty of praying rogues and swearing saints in the world." Mishmash morality is widespread! Yet if the gospel is what it claims to be, it must offer a greater victory than envisioning only a one-day-escape to heaven. Heaven, remember, has *already* performed a heart transplant sufficient for a complete renovation of our moral life—now! Therefore, it is by drawing on what was deposited in our new nature that we can exhibit, not indwelling sin but the indwelling life of our Lord.

Challenging the assumption that freedom from guilt (and not freedom from sin) is all God offers, the Mishnah declared, "If anyone says to himself, 'I will sin, and the Day of Atonement will expiate it,' the Day of Atonement does not expiate it."⁶ We seriously distort the biblical message by overloading our expectation for future forgiveness in this way. What about an expectation for present deliverance? Is there a sustainable solution that works today *and* tomorrow?

The heart that perpetually sins, the heart that deeper down expects this sorry outcome, need not be cavalier in manner or insincere in motive to succumb to sin. Sheer ignorance may account for this failure.

To overcome this ignorance, then, we must remember two resources mentioned by Peter, which, in tandem, are sufficient for a major upgrade of our moral life. These provisions—the power of God and the promises of God—warrant further consideration.

Resources for Change

While identifying God's resources for victorious living in chapter 1, Peter first refers to—notice his words in verse 3—"the divine power" God gave to believers. Now, we all know how feeble our efforts can be, but if—somehow, some way—we could tap into divine power, this would change everything! Ephesians 3:20 says of God that he is able to do exceeding abundantly above all that we ask or think, according to the power that works in us." Now, if we access his power in the way Scripture stipulates, God will be faithful to manifest, produce, deliver, bless, meet the need, show himself strong, and bestow his favor.

Yet, to properly access this power it is important to differentiate between holiness and obedience. Holiness is a gift, suddenly acquired; obedience is an achievement subsequently empowered by that gift. Further clarifying this issue, Samuel Chadwick offered this correction:

> Another mistake made by many earnest Christians about holiness is that it comes by a gradual growth in grace and by a steady progress of spiritual discipline. They are always growing toward it, but they never get into it—always struggling and striving to attain, but never entering into possession. The positive expectation is always seen to be afar off, and they die without having possessed it. The hopeful future never becomes the positive now ... But holiness does not come by growth; neither is it identified with growth ... Growth is a result of health; holiness is health.[7]

This truth was set forth in a previous chapter where we discussed imparted righteousness. This righteousness, what we may also call holiness, is characteristic of the new nature (Ephesians 4:24). It is a marvelous capacity *suddenly* deposited at conversion, then *suddenly* released when the Spirit fills. Without this Spirit-filling and the subsequent righteousness-release from our new nature, obedience is doomed.

This has been the sad story most Christians have lived. Using simple language to set forth profound truth, Samuel Brengle wrote, "A man may grow in his coat, but not into his coat; he must first get it on. Just so a man may 'grow in grace,' but not into grace."[8] All attempts to obey God must draw on the life of God resident in the new nature, and must then depend on the Spirit of God for a fresh release of this holiness. Scripture clearly states that before any behavioral change, we must first put on the new man (Ephesians 4:24).

To miss this one critical point is to misunderstand everything Peter says about consistent goodness! Nailing this point down, Augustus Sabatier, a French Protestant theologian from the nineteenth century, elaborated on this distinction:

> It is not enough to represent the Spirit of God as coming as a help for man's spirit, supplying strength which he lacks—an associate or juxtaposed force, a supernatural auxiliary ... There is no simple addition of divine power to human power in the Christian life.[9]

The divine power, like holiness, is a part of the new me, the new nature. By faith, I access this holiness, and then I trust "the divine power" to manifest holiness in me. Moreover, in the words of C.T. Studd, this holiness is "... not the sickly stuff of talk and dainty thoughts and pretty words; we will have a masculine holiness, one of daring faith and works for Jesus Christ."[10] It will be the kind of holiness we saw in Jesus Christ.

But how do we do that? Well, instead of soaring into some ozone layer of spirituality with all of its supposed tingles and thrills, Paul gives autobiographical advice when he writes in II Corinthians 12:10 this principle: "For when I am weak, then I am strong." Now this shouldn't be too hard for most people, right? All we have to do is to be weak.

Are you weak? If you are, don't run from this condition to seek a puny strength of your own; just stay weak. But in that weakness acknowledge, what many people never personally acknowledge, that you have no resources of your own to get the job done. Not even the new nature can be activated entirely on your own. It is the Spirit who inhabits your new nature who must assist its release. And this doesn't happen automatically. What must precede is our own weakness acknowledged and our own faith extended.

Whenever Brother Lawrence succumbed to sin, he immediately told the Lord, "This is what life in my own strength produces, Lord. I need you to rise above this." For Brother Lawrence, there wasn't any shock about what self can and can't do, because self was never viewed as a source for victory anyway. So instead of wasting time by attempting what would never work, Brother Lawrence clung to Jesus with a determined dependence that refused to be denied! By doing this, he made a power connection with God, through which the formerly elusive victory could then manifest.

According to the Apostle Peter, divine power isn't reserved for some unusual, once-in-a-lifetime crisis. It has a wider application, pertaining to "life and godliness." Life refers to our circumstances; godliness refers to our character. So whatever we have to face, inside or out, is amply provided for by divine power.

And just here we should note that God's power isn't used against us to compel and coerce, but instead is provided for us to use. F.J. Huegel said, "God does not exercise his sovereignty over the wills of men, forcing them by the sheer weight of omnipotence to believe, to obey; forcing them to be good. Morality on such an artificial basis wouldn't be worth the snap of your finger."[11]

In his book, *The Divine Conquest*, A.W. Tozer likened coerced compliance to one who "is still an outlaw at heart even though he may be yielding grudging obedience to the sheriff who is taking him to prison."[12] Similarly, Samuel Chadwick wrote:

> There can be no virtue in compulsory obedience. If a thing is done because it cannot be helped, what reward is there? If obedience is yielded only to force, what merit is there in obedience? If the march is at the point of a bayonet, there is no room to boast over marching. If we trot to avoid the prod, it is hardly reasonable to speak of the necessity as virtue. The value and preciousness of virtue are in its voluntariness. There is no virtue in necessity, no religion in compulsion, no credit in obedience that has no choice.[13]

By both manner and method, the provision of God's power is offered in a much different way. And while we can miss it through ignorance or avoid it by choice, there is still in every believer a resident power to obey—a power we all need! Powerless religion leaves a man exactly where he was before he acquired religious language: still in bondage to sin. Such a man may know Jesus as Savior, but Tozer asks the questions:

> Is justification from past sins all that distinguishes a Christian from a sinner? Can a man become a believer in Christ and be no better than he was before? Does the Bible offer no more than a skillful Advocate to get guilty sinners off free at the day of judgment?[14]

Surely it does! There is a power, Peter tells us, that does more than get men technically free while still leaving them in bondage. This power will set people free from sin, self, and Satan—now!

Peter also tells of another provision God made for us—"great and precious promises." These promises are called "great" because of their number (there are 7,487 promises, an amount sufficient to address every circumstance we'll ever face). And these promises are called "precious" because of their incomparable value. These blood-covenant promises boost our faith, eliminate confusion, make clear God's will, comfort our emotions, steady our will, and fire-up our imagination.

As we then go out on a limb to claim one of these promises, faith will cause our new nature to rise and release. Hence, we become, in Peter's words, "a partaker of the divine nature"—to the extent we escape "the corruption that is in the world through lust." This makes sense, doesn't it? For once the new nature surges to take control, temptation, in whatever form it presents, will lose its power precisely then.

Now, we can glide along on such sublime thought and suspend critical thinking while we do so—but doing something like this predicts our peril! So, wanting to avoid such peril, I now want to infuse this discussion with a high dosage of reality.

The media, the pulpit, and even our own experiences argue that succumbing to sin is a somewhat regular occurrence that happens because it is inevitable. Okay, we acknowledge that argument, recognize that oppositional thinking as we set forth this common viewpoint. But what must also be recognized is that God's ways are not our ways, and his thoughts are not our thoughts—which is why the Bible is needed to correct erroneous thinking!

Inspired by the Holy Spirit, Peter says that if we do the things that he sets forth in this chapter, we will never stumble. Never? Why, history is replete with people backsliding! Even A.B. Simpson spoke honestly about this.

> Many have promising beginnings in the life of consecration, are sealed by the most real and glorious manifestations of the divine presence, grace and power. But these beginnings have afterwards been followed, through lack of vigilance and obedience, by gross error, spiritual declension, soul-deceiving sin and even disobedience, worldliness, weakness and what seemed to threaten even final apostasy.[15]

When examining various types of sinners, Scripture discloses obnoxious ones, like the Pharisee who congratulated himself for not being as bad as others; as well as the obtuse ones, such as the rich young ruler who asked, "What lack I yet?"—before then turning his back on Jesus and refusing to become his disciple. In between these two extremes, the obnoxious and the obtuse, many people live their pathetic lives as they repeat the cycle of confessing, repenting, trying to do better, but failing again. This cycle can be stopped, however, if we add to our faith what Peter says should be added.

Kindness and Love

The next two qualities that should be added to our faith are brotherly kindness and love. Both these qualities are outwardly directed, affirming A.B. Simpson's observation, "The cloister and the cell are not the finishing rooms for holy character." And neither is the library or the schoolroom! While education and contemplation are worthy endeavors, the outcome of these endeavors must be translated in our interactions with people, some of whom who are not always congenial and receptive. Hence, kindness must grow in the harsher climate; and love, sometimes, must endure the assaults of the angry.

If there is a distinction between these two qualities, and perhaps there is, that distinction has more to do with the recipients of these virtues than with the nature of the qualities themselves. I say this because in I Peter 1:22, Peter talks about "the love of the brethren," and in I Peter 3:8 he tells us to "love as brethren." Therefore, love and brotherly kindness are inextricably linked, although love extends to those who are not in the family of God.

D.T. Niles said that God's interest is the world, and therefore we need to get interested in what he is interested in—the world! A.T. Pierson declared, "One must fall in love with the world to be possessed with the missionary spirit."[16]

The "holy huddle" that isolates itself from the world and implodes by self-absorption dynamics is not the example given by our Lord. The Bible says he grew in favor with man—not the backslapping, joke-swapping, hail-fellow-well-met kind of favor, but a favor owing to his genuine and godly caring for others. Going where religious people wouldn't go, Jesus became a friend to the sinners; and in so doing, shocked onlookers set their tongues "a wagging." These tongues were also wagging when the prostitute passed by or when the drunkard stumbled into town. Condemnation, from them, was unfortunately common.

In that day and this, it's quite easy to criticize, to heap scorn, to spread rumor. But A.W. Tozer said, "Always it is more important that we retain a right spirit toward others than we bring them to our way of thinking, even if our way is right."[17] To vent criticism achieves nothing—which is why the world has never built a monument honoring a critic.

Jesus developed a reputation for socializing with the notorious. His heartbeat for evangelism moved him to make connections, to build bridges, to establish relationships. There is, after all, a need to "Immanuelize" before we evangelize: to be *with* before we speak *to*. Rattling off a testimony in trophy-hunting evangelism is not of God.

The personal benefit of releasing God's love to the world was conveyed well by the poet:

> I sought my soul, my soul I could not see;
> I sought my God, but God eluded me;
> I sought my brother and I found all three.

We see an example of this benefit in our Savior. Yes, Jesus experienced the blood-sweating dread of Gethsemane, but once love locked in, the anguish lifted. Thereafter, Jesus was in full possession of his soul, striding masterfully across the garden as the soldiers thundered into his midst. Determined to please God most of all (but determined also to love the disciples), Jesus gave himself completely. During the arrest and the execution that followed, we see nothing of Gethsemane's anguish reappearing in Jesus. Why? Because love brought this kind of anguish to an end.

The Bible says that faith works by love. Love gives the energy, the purpose, the resolve to do what faith sets out to do. And this is why love must be added to our faith.

In his book, *Rumors of Another World*, Philip Yancey tells of a visit he made to what was formerly called Burma. The person inviting him said, "When you speak to pastors, you should remember that probably all of them have spent time in jail because of their faith." So Yancey asked if he should talk about one of his books, *Where Is God When It Hurts?* Or, *Disappointment with God?*"

"Oh, no, that's not really a concern here," he said. "We assume we'll be persecuted for faith. We want you to speak on grace. We need help getting along with each other."

Isn't that interesting? These leaders had withstood the intense pain of undeserved persecution, yet when it came to fellowship, a more difficult challenge presented. This is often the case in churches with a stable membership: The opportunity to frustrate or irritate is likely to occur. All these fellowship-robbing grievances—something small but something remembered—can be avoided if we endeavor to keep the unity. But if we don't keep the unity, these grievances will fracture fellowship, resulting in an atmosphere that is ugly both to the world and to the Lord.

The willingness to offer kindness to a stranger has its unique appeal, obviously, but to offer kindness to one we know so well and can take for granted so easily, is another proposition entirely—especially if there's an unattended wound festering underneath! The broad smile that flashes when we greet a stranger seems to suddenly disappear whenever a certain church member crosses our path—or even crosses our mind! So isn't kindness also needed here?

The Consequences

Having now considered the seven qualities Peter tells us to add to our faith, we are now ready to consider the consequences for doing so. In verse 8 we read: "For if these things be in you and abound, they make you that you shall neither be barren nor unfruitful in the knowledge of our Lord Jesus Christ." This is a negative way of stating a positive truth, namely: These principles work! They get results! They produce observable behavioral change!

Notice the keyword—*if*. By premising everything on this word, Peter followed the example of his Lord who said, "If you have faith ...." "If you do what I command you ...." "If you love me ...." "If you ask anything ...." "If you can believe ...." On and on it goes: if, if, if!

R.G. Lee observed:

> What royal roads "if" opens up for us to travel. And what palace doors "if" throws open wide. And what treasure chests "if" unlocks. And what light "if" radiates ... And what unknown continents "if" discovers. And what glorious affirmations "if" declares.[18]

Jesus said, "If any man hear my voice ...." "If any man serve me ...." "If any man keep my saying ...." "If any man would follow me ...." It all hinges on that one little word, "if."

While it is true that God is omnipotent, he has put a big "if" in your life and mine—several "ifs," in fact. Therefore, the life we live, and the success we have, is going to be determined by how we respond to these "ifs." Life changes dramatically when an "if" becomes a "done."

The premise for the promise also includes the requirement that these things be *in* you. Notice: not just in your head, where many ideas pass through without consequence, but in your heart—valued, treasured, and acted upon! You can't just dabble in your approach to the Christian life: Scripture says these principles must be in you *and abound*.

When first hearing these words, we may think the standard is being lifted yet higher and higher. But this misses the point! What Scripture is really telling us is that we *can* have abounding courage, abounding knowledge, abounding godliness. Instead of a punitive-parent "must" embedded in this message, there's a nurturing-parent encouragement. Do you see the positive message here? The believer's resources are immense!

One could wish that life would be so easy and accommodating that courage isn't going to be needed. But Jesus said, "... in this world you will have tribulation"—the kind of tribulation that will try the soul and pressure its surrender if courage doesn't stand in the gap! Again, the blessing heralded here is that tribulation *can* be overcome, and *will* be overcome, if a God-supplied courage is used.

Thinking this not to be the case, some people complain, "Well, I've done all I know to do." Perhaps so, but maybe they don't know enough. *Abounding* in the knowledge of God is a critical factor.

The biggest enemy most people have is self. But wouldn't you agree that abounding temperance would do the job if only this were added to their faith? Once self is denied and defied in God's way, major problems go away.

The discipline that delights to spend time with the Lord is also a huge problem for many people. But this battle, too, can be won, once an abounding godliness moves with momentum in one's life.

Similarly, patience, which seems to be in short supply these days, won't ever fade away once an abounding diligence is given. So instead of patience being overcome, patience itself will overcome the inferior motives attacking it.

And as for kindness and love—well, these too can abound in our lives. Notice: not just trickle, not just spurt, but according to Scripture abound! This word "abound" is emphatic in the Greek, suggesting a lavish supply, a generous giving.

For all this abounding to occur, however, there must first be diligence—in the words of Peter, "giving all diligence." Sporadic effort, given whenever the mood strikes or a burst of inspiration comes, won't ever be enough. Those worthwhile pursuits assigned by God demand more.

Do we really think that Jesus lived the life he lived without intense effort? Do we think his righteousness was simply transposed from heaven? Dale Yocum asked, "Was his perfection of manners and morals a mechanical performance in which it was impossible for him to be tried, tested, exhausted, or perplexed?" No, Yocum answered, the life Jesus lived "was characterized by an incessant carefulness."[19] And this, I submit, would be synonymous with Peter's words, "giving all diligence."

"All diligence" includes and implies a refusal to compromise. Other options may be viable, perhaps for lesser problems, but the requirement of wholehearted diligence is indispensable to eternity endeavors. For his part, A.B. Simpson encouraged this aspect of diligence that is unwilling to welcome evil, when he wrote:

> Let us beware how we tolerate a single sin, how we leave an enemy in the land, how we make terms with any forbidden thing, how we enter into alliances with the world, or let its spirit touch our fondest affections."[20]

The pulpit has long focused on the disobedience in the wilderness that lasted almost forty years. What has drawn far less attention is the disobedience in the Promised Land *that lasted ten times as long*! How utterly disgraceful was this long, drawn-out rebellion coming from God's people! What a stunning incongruity—sinning in the Promised Land! Rebelling in the midst of rewards! Yielding to defeat after they just won! How could this be?

In his book, *The Land of Promise*, A.B. Simpson answered.

Many have promising beginnings in the life of consecration, are sealed by the most real and glorious manifestations of the divine presence, grace and power. But these beginnings have afterwards been followed, through lack of vigilance and holy obedience, by gross error, spiritual declension, soul-deceiving sin, and even open disobedience, worldliness, weakness, and what seemed to threaten even open apostasy.[21]

What God's people allowed in the Promised Land brought consequence much worse than what came to their fathers in the wilderness. Worse, not only in duration of time, but also in the degree of debauchery permitted. Even though the advantages God's people had were far more than enough to avoid what happened, the tragic end to this story was—*they lost the Promised Land*! Completely lost it!

This sad-but-true story never needed to happen! But it played out the way it did because there wasn't the initiative needed to stop it. *What they knew, they didn't do.* So with inertia present and initiative absent, their spiritual descent became more rapid than they ever thought it could be.

Maybe you have also experienced the shock of spiritual decline in which you almost felt like a bystander witnessing your own tragedy. And maybe, too, in the midst of this, you asked God to stir you up. *But* God is telling you and me to stir our own selves up. We have asked him to keep us from the harm of the evil one. Yet I John 5:18 says a believer can keep himself so the wicked one touches him not. Don't you see? The stirring, the keeping, the abounding—so much of this depends on *us*, attributable to the fact that we will reap what we sow.

Should this stirring, keeping, and abounding effort not materialize, Peter warns: "... he that lacks these things is blind, and cannot see afar off, and has forgotten that he was purged from his old sins." In assessing each negative listed here, it must first be pointed out that the blindness mentioned is a willful blindness. The Greek word conveys the idea of deliberately closing one's eyes. John Milton summed up this situation well when he said, "There are none so blind as those who will not see." As to why any person would choose this condition, given the fact the devil can make mincemeat of a blind person, is hard to fathom.

Actually, there are two types of sight problems we should consider. One is myopia, seeing only what is near, only what is at hand; and an example of this is Lot's wife. Instead of seeing Sodom's corruption eating away at her soul, she loved the life she had in Sodom—so much so she didn't want to leave it! And therefore, contrary to the angel's instruction, she looked back with a longing heart for all Sodom stood for.

You know what happened then: Judgment came and instantly destroyed her! Listen, the dynamics triggering this judgment are not to be forgotten! We must "remember Lot's wife," Jesus said, and the myopia that corrupted her heart. Yet, despite the Master's call for us to remember, multiple millions today are just like this woman: caring nothing about the things of God, and everything for what the world has to offer.

Remember, how one views life—the frame of reference used, the code of ethics employed—determines the choices made and the outcomes faced.

Myopia puts too small a frame on the picture, focusing on immediate gratification rather than eternal consequences. But there is another sight problem that bears mentioning, hyperopia. The person with this problem is overly focused on the future. An example of this is the fool the Bible talks about who set his eyes on "the ends of the earth" (Proverbs 17:24). To see only the faraway future, only the eventual outcome and the final consummation, is a sure way to "miss it" in life.

One lady became clinically depressed when her study of various millennial theories persuaded her that her children were going to have to go through the tribulation. *What*?! Really? A less extreme version of this malady can be seen in the husband always working for his future and therefore having little time for his family. Likewise, perfectionists can only enjoy themselves when the goal has been reached and all is going well. Before then, enjoyment is minimal.

The Bible conveys a different message, however: that we're not to despise small beginnings, that we're not to give excessive thought about tomorrow, and, yes, that a blessing doesn't have to be in full bloom before we can enjoy it.

Now, when the Bible says "... let those who have eyes to see, see," it assumes that many lack the sight needed to respond properly to God's Word. Even a Christian can find himself so blindsided by some distraction that the greatest fact of all—the salvation of his or her soul—fades into insignificance.

James Thurber said, before anyone dies, he should find out what he's running from and also what he's running to. Those with spiritual blindness, however, really don't have a clue about either question; and therefore they meander through their entire lives without purpose or direction.

In concluding this passage, Peter repeats the words he gave earlier, "give diligence." Again: If we want the favorable results promised in this passage, then diligence, rightly applied and rightly supplied, is a nonnegotiable.

Admittedly, some care very little about a life of consistent goodness. Samuel Brengle wrote:

> It is one of the strange contradictions of modern Christianity that every church holds so lightly the importance of its creed that it extends the right hand of benediction to every other; and thus there is a tacit understanding nowadays that it doesn't much matter what you believe, so long as you profess to believe something.[22]

Brengle went on to say that those serious about consistent goodness were "preserved from this false charity and the chaotic indefiniteness and confusion which comes from it" because of aroused opposition to what they believed. This opposition came "not only from the intellectual apologists for existing systems, but from the thousands whose half-hearted service and unwilling consecration it has condemned."[23] Clearly, the motivation for this opposition was to defend lower standards, so as not to feel judged by living at that level.

People reacted strongly against the holiness message in Brengle's day (the nineteenth century) and do so today.

Astutely, Brengle counseled, "Do not think you can make holiness popular. It cannot be done."[24] Similarly, Dr. Dale Yocum declared, "A life of holiness and spiritual power is an open rebuke to men of this world. The more evident the holy character, the more fierce the antagonism will be."[25]

The fire of holy living will itself draw fire, even from the church. The half-gospel the church proclaims, which is little more than a détente with darkness, insists that sin's power cannot be broken in this life. Some even say that the more God reveals himself, the more we see the depths of our sin and the strength of its hold on our lives. But according to the esteemed G. D. Watson, "Such a statement is false, for Scripture and experience prove that God can so purify and fill the human soul, that it is conscious of being freed from sin, and possessed with the living presence and holiness of Christ ...."[26]

To further motivate us, I Peter 5:10 identifies the very achievable prospect that should encourage our diligence: "you shall never stumble." That word "never" offers so much hope, for no one is likely to win a race if he keeps stumbling while running it. But to hit our stride with skill, and to run with grace and win—oh, my!—*that's* what God has in mind!

So to that end he has told us in his Word just how this victory can be ours. Consequently, we, like Peter in his day, can become a spiritual hero today—living what hardly anybody does live, a consistently good life. That's heroism!

When assessing the various types of heroism, we acknowledge there is the heroism of the moment—this can get you a headline in the newspaper or acclaim on TV. Then there's the heroism of a lifelong struggle—this may result in a holiday honoring your achievement, or history books lauding your importance. But from God's perspective there can be no greater hero than one who lives a consistently good life.

Peter did this—and you can do it, too. Moreover, when you do, the reward that'll be yours will be far better than any headline or holiday.

To further persuade you of just how good these rewards will be, we will take up this subject in the next five chapters. And by doing so, we will further explore how utterly intriguing goodness can be.

Reflection Questions

1. How has a deeper intimacy with God blessed you with manifesting holiness?

2. How has the experience of claiming a divine promise helped you to be pure?

3. What was it like for you when you lost sight of your eternal cleansing?

4. What do you *really* think about living a holy life without stumbling?

The Romance: United at Last!

*The King marries ...
The bride is greeted with royal fanfare ...
A celebration begins that would make a White House extravaganza look like a Salvation Army soup kitchen.
Crowns are given ...
The presentation of awards begins ...*

And you call this fiction? No, what the Bible describes is utterly real! The "happily-ever-after" ending is true!

Chapter 17

Rewards for Goodness—Part I

"Happily-ever-after" endings are embarrassingly trite to the person who prides himself as a realist. These endings provoke either a raised eyebrow of skepticism or a bemused smile of condescension. What the realist values more is the kind of observation Shakespeare made when he wrote, "The evil men do live after him; the good is interred with their bones," and the observation Thomas Gray made when he wrote, "The paths of glory but lead to the grave."

Such high doses of smack-down realism appear intellectually honest, utterly urbane, impressively erudite, insightfully shrewd, and cutting-edge in its sophistication. This is why critics will smirk at "happily-ever-after" endings by calling them predictable, simplistic, and formulaic. Wand-waving, star-sparkling outcomes, they say, are for children.

C.S. Lewis, Professor of Medieval and Renaissance Literature at Cambridge University, took to task the critics' perspective by pointing out that the fairy tales left on our nursery floor are more realistic than the books we read in adult years. According to Lewis, the beasts and witches in these fairy tales foreshadow the way evil will finally manifest; only they do so, he said, not with exaggeration, as these elitist critics claim, but with remarkable restraint.

Scottish professor James S. Stewart agreed with Lewis. According to Stewart, our Bible depicts this life and the next with sound and sage descriptions. Stewart contends:

The Gospel is quite shattering in its realism. It shirks nothing. It never seeks to gloss over the dark perplexities of fate, frustration, sin or death, or to gild unpalatable facts with a coating of pious verbiage or facile consolation. It never side-tracks uncomfortable questions with some naïve and cheerful cliché about providence or progress. It gazes open-eyed at the most menacing and savage circumstances that life can show ... The very last charge that can be brought against the Gospel is that of sentimentality, of blinking the facts. It is devastating in its veracity, and its reality is a consuming fire.[1]

As for these scoffed-at stories that imagine endings of delight—what, with rainbows shimmering and angelic voices singing—sugar-coated optimism isn't really the problem. The real problem is an imagination that is too tame, too tentative, too timid. For what could possibly stretch the mind more than marriage to the Son of God! And ascending to heaven's throne! And becoming co-inheritors—can you imagine?—of all that *God* owns!

Living in some stately castle in rural England may be nice, but to dwell where planets swirl, stars sing, and meteors flash—all with such varied and astonishing brilliance—is quite beyond what a finite mind could ever imagine! And just think: Ever ready to do our bidding at that time will be—some silver-clad knights riding white horses? Think bigger! At our constant command, Scripture says, will be magnificent angels, supernatural beings more awesome in appearance and more stupendous in strength than an entire army of knights. Why, one look *at* these angels will cause their knees to quiver, and one look *from* these angels will cause their armor to melt.

When it comes to contemplating future rewards, Christians tend to minimize what realists openly deny. For some reason, which scrutiny can never support, Christians think that this entire reward scenario is beneath worthier and nobler aspirations. Consequently, they deem the motivations of love and gratitude admirable, but this motivation for rewards as somewhat unseemly.[2] Clearly, though, this is not what Jesus thought. In fact, Jesus was so excited about the rewards he declared more than once that when he returns he's bringing the rewards with him!

So are our motivations higher than his? And are our aspirations higher than those of the apostles, who likewise contemplated these rewards with strong anticipation?

There's nothing imaginary about the rewards, nor about Scripture's portrayal of the end of history. So if we want a wisdom that lines up with the thinking of the apostles—and more importantly with the mind of the Lord—we would do well to drop these unexamined opinions of ours and start focusing, with teachable hearts, on God's rewards.

Reflections on the Rewards

As we start our consideration of the rewards, certain questions immediately come to mind. For example, is everyone's experience in heaven going to be the same? That is, will the people faithful to the Lord down here be accorded the same life in heaven as the ones who compromised their convictions and got in bed with the world?

Responding to this question, Dr. A.J. Gordon wrote, "I cannot think of a final divine reckoning which shall assign the same rank in glory, the same degree of joy, to a lazy, indolent and unfruitful Christian as to an ardent, devoted, self-denying Christian."[3]

Commenting on the humanism that infects our culture by handing out prizes to all and makes distinctions among none, G.D. Watson observed, "Most people regard the heavenly state as one of perfect equality in all things. The fact is, the Scriptures reveal that there will be far more ranks and degrees among the people in heaven than on the earth ...."[4] Further clarifying this point, Watson said, "The saints in heaven, infants or apostles, are all equally pure ... but in growth there is variety and multiplicity."[5]

Those who served the Lord with sacrifice are going to receive greater honor, and hence an enhanced capacity for heaven, than those who blended with the rest of the world and did next to nothing for God. A.B. Simpson declared, "God is not going to throw away his crowns and thrones on those who have lived for earthly rewards."[6] They may get what they sought on earth, but they won't get God's rewards.

If there is any doubt about differences of rewards, one need only recall Jesus' words about those who would be "great" in the kingdom as compared with those who will be "least." Moreover, the Lord's words about "first" and "last" also communicate the great gamut of differences that will exist between the experiences the faithful will enjoy and the corresponding experiences carnal Christians will have.

While this perspective does make sense, it also raises understandable questions, namely: Will these differences in rewards incite jealousy? That is, will the person walking around in a baseball cap remain content even when he sees other believers wearing splendid crowns?

To partially answer this question, it must be pointed out that rewards aren't always tangible in nature. We understand the significance of these rewards better by thinking in terms of differing capacities to enjoy God, and differing capabilities to worship and serve God. Some will have a thimble-size capacity; others will have a barrel-size capacity. The person with the thimble-size capacity, however, will have no idea what the barrel-size capacity is like, any more than a dog appreciates an evening stroll in the same way his master does.

Yet, while these capacities do differ, satisfaction is experienced by both. Not the same satisfaction, when one is measured against the other, but complete satisfaction when it comes to fulfilling these respective capacities. Remember, there is *always* an immense satisfaction attached to God's rewards, sufficient in their appeal to change the direction of one's life.

Just how motivating these rewards can be is documented in Hebrews, chapter 11, where we read: "By faith Moses, when he became of age, refused to be called the son of Pharaoh's daughter, choosing rather to suffer affliction with the people of God than to enjoy the passing pleasures of sin ..." (verses 24, 25).

Commenting on these pleasures, J.C. Ryle, the nineteenth-century bishop, provided this background of life in Egypt when Moses was alive.

Egypt was a land of artists—a residence of learned men, a resort of everyone who had skill, or science of any description. There was nothing which could feed the lust of the flesh, the lust of the eye, or the pride of life, which one in the place of Moses might not easily have commanded.[7]

Reflecting further on the momentous decision Moses made, A.B. Simpson wrote:

He said one eternal "No" to the world and one everlasting "Yes" to God. He gave up a throne and a crown, and chose his lot among the afflicted people of God ... There is a choosing, there is a refusing. There is a "Yes," there is a "No." Beloved, have you spoken the decisive word? Have you said "Yes" to God without reserve? Have you said "No" to the world and sin and self?[8]

In reading this account from Scripture we might be tempted to ask, "Moses, why would you decline a position that would have made you next in power to the Pharaoh of Egypt, the most powerful man on earth? And why would you cast your lot with the dredges of Egyptian society, those low-down Jewish slaves?"

But rest assured, Moses knew exactly what he was doing! With clear calculation, his entire life pivoted on one prevailing thought—indeed, a life-changing thought that was disclosed in verse 26, where we read: "Esteeming the reproach of Christ's greater riches than the treasures in Egypt; for he looked to the reward."

By saying Moses "looked to the reward," that had to have been an expression of faith because none of these rewards were tangibly evident. There were no pictures of what they looked like, no documents describing their function, no oral tradition explaining their appeal. Nevertheless, Moses made the most important decision in his life based entirely on these anticipated rewards. And with that as his goal, none of earth's enticements dissuaded him.

Moses gave up power, prestige, pleasure, and preeminence, choosing to identify with the used and abused Jewish slaves. What's more, he did so not because of love and gratitude only; Scripture says another factor proved decisive. Providing all the motivation Moses needed was one inducement, one incentive: an overriding desire for God's rewards. This one, all-important conclusion propelled Moses into a life so legendary, so inspiring, it is still revered today. And chances are, if we saw what Moses saw, we'd make some stunning decisions, too!

Now, if the rewards of God are potentially this motivating, what do you suppose Satan would want? Exactly what he's got—a bunch of believers who never give a thought about the rewards! Isn't it true that the values church members hold, and the decisions they make, as well as the goals they adopt, are all processed *without* God's promised rewards imprinting the soul?

Yet, what's going on today wasn't true in the early church. The biblical record makes it quite clear that those believers thought a lot about the rewards!

So, wanting what God has to say on this subject to become a frequent feature in the theater of your mind, let's examine what the Bible has to say about the rewards. And in doing this, let's get to the bottom line first: What are we going to get? Heaven, yes; Jesus, yes; but in terms of the rewards, what?

Perhaps the best way to understand what these rewards are is to consider what the Bible has to say about the crowns that will be given. Thomas a' Kempis wrote, "The Lord has many lovers of his crown but few lovers of his cross." This observation is true in a limited sense, perhaps, if occasional sighs for a happily-ever ending in heaven qualify. But in reality most Christians know very little about the crown the Lord will give.

Actually, there are five crowns the Lord will give, all described in Scripture—each for a different accomplishment, each with a different reward, and none assured simply because someone is a believer. So can it be truly said that Christians *love* these crowns, if they haven't yet learned the precise reward each crown represents? To be honest, aren't their vague impressions of the crown directly traceable to a lack of interest? Interest will spike, however, once these rewards are more fully explored. So let's do that next by discovering what each of these five crowns represents.

The Crown of Gold

First, there is the crown of gold, spoken of in Revelation 4:4, where we read: "Around the throne were twenty-four thrones, and on the thrones I saw twenty-four elders sitting, clothed in white robes; and they had crowns of gold on their heads."

We know that thrones and robes speak of royalty and purity, but what do these crowns represent? In answering this question, it should be pointed out first that the crowns for these elders are not at all the same crown worn by the Lord. The Greek word to describe his crown is *diadema*, from which we get the word diadem. However, the Greek word used to describe the crowns these elders wore is *stephanos*. *Stephanos* crowns were given to victorious athletes, to the ones who ran and won, to those who fought and conquered, to those who resisted and persisted in certain valued endeavors.

Now, in the material world, gold is that which man most treasures. So what is it in the spiritual world that is treasured the most? Worship! Right? Nothing comes before that! Those receiving the crown of gold, therefore, are going to be given an extraordinary capacity for worship.

In saying this, we come upon a most important truth. God's rewards are not mere adornments for public display; they represent instead a range of supernatural capacities for divine service. G.D. Watson said the "rewards for good works will decide our station and rank in the kingdom, and our degree of glory and usefulness in the ages to come."[9]

The capacity to minister to the Lord in worship was often hampered on earth. Too often this trial and that sin, this trouble and that worry, clogged it all up. But can you recall a special time of worship when the Lord filled you— indeed, almost overwhelmed you with his presence? This is what the crown of gold portends! One support for this view is the context of the passage itself where this crown is mentioned. Upon reading the passage, we see there is a praise service going on. These elders are ecstatic! Though all are serious men, each is seriously in love with Jesus!

In verse 8, the Lord receives effusive praise for his holiness. In verse 9, he receives glory, honor, and thanks. And in verses 10 and 11 we read:

> The twenty-four elders fall down before him who sits on the throne and worship him who lives forever and ever, and cast their crowns before the throne, saying: "You are worthy, O Lord, to receive glory and honor and power; for you created all things, and by your will they exist and were created."

The ejaculatory worship erupting from their hearts is something we wish would more frequently and fervently come from our hearts. How much we desire for mind, will, and emotions to be so captured that all we can see, think about, and never get enough of, is Jesus!

Have you ever tried to pray but couldn't? Many of us know what it is like to come to a worship service so dry inside that nothing much could happen. Well, the crown of gold means no more rollercoaster rides—up on the mountaintop a little, down in the valley a lot. Instead, it will be all mountaintop! That's what this crown enables.

Some people wonder what the casting of crowns means. One thing it doesn't mean is that we're giving our rewards back: "Thank you, Lord, but we're not worthy to receive this; so you take it." Such an idea would be wholly inconsistent with Scripture, since the Bible makes it clear that these rewards are given on the basis of our works (I Corinthians 3:8; Revelation 22:12). So did God make some error in judgment? Is it even possible that, somehow, contrary to what *he* thought, we weren't worthy of this crown? Obviously, that can't be true; and since giving back this crown, or any other crown, would mean losing the capacity each reward entails, doing something that wouldn't make any sense. Keep in mind: Though *we* get the reward, the Lord is rewarded by our reward. So why stop this?

There are some Christian leaders who talk about giving their crown back to Jesus. Their talk is only that, for no one is going to be giving a crown back.

When I was in elementary school—a private, religious school in the state of Florida—our principal would burst into tears during almost every chapel service, declaring that he was going to give his crown back to the Lord. It was almost like clockwork, tempting those of us who didn't have our heart in the right place to look at our watches and bet when the "I'm going to give my crown back to Jesus" comment was coming. As it turned out, the principal was caught in a major embezzlement scam that became front-page headlines in our city. So apparently he wasn't yet in that place where he was giving everything back to Jesus.

Well, then, if the casting of these crowns doesn't mean returning rewards to Jesus, what does it mean? In reply, it should be noted that in Scripture only this crown gets laid before the Lord; this isn't true of the other crowns. Apparently, there is something about this crown that must be utterly yielded to the Lord; and perhaps this is so because this particular crown represents something Lucifer once had.

In her book, *Rejoice*, Debbie Roberts wrote:

> Lucifer was the leader of the heavenly choir who sang at the dawn of creation. His anointed ministry was to cover God's throne with worship and praise. He was clothed as a priest with all precious stones, and he had the workmanship of all tabrets (rhythm), pipes (harmony), and viols (melody), in him on the day he was created.[10]

While no one could sing like Lucifer could, the Spirit-filled believer today is instructed to make melody in his heart to the Lord. But can he or she ever do what Lucifer did? In his book, *Victory over the Devil*, Jack Taylor said of Lucifer:

> He was in all probability the nearest one to the throne of God. He reflected as no other created being the glory of God. Lucifer was not only a musician, but he was music in himself ... he was

such a musical instrument that he could break into a sound which resembled that of a thousand perfectly coordinated orchestras.[11]

There was something magnificent about Lucifer's anointing for worship! This spectacular anointing added beauty to spirit and splendor to soul—enough beauty, and enough splendor, to bedazzle thousands of angels!

Seeing for themselves that astonishing brilliance and that ravishing beauty emanating from this anointed cherub, a third of heaven's angels made the decision to choose Lucifer over God. Imagine that! Even in the gleaming glory of the highest heaven, they thought Lucifer superior.

Really? *Angels* did this? How could any sane person do this? If you must know, it's because the glory accorded Lucifer was too marvelous to describe and too sensational to ignore. Waves of glory, rising and swelling, higher and wider, surrounded and penetrated with staggering impact! Apparently, to be in the presence of such glory was enough to overwhelm wisdom and give birth to pride.

Lucifer became so intoxicated with himself, he reasoned, "Another God? Well, sure, why not? Isn't that what we have already?" In fact, so blinding was his glory, and so heavy was his stupor, Lucifer concluded it was high time for him to start receiving what he had been giving! Thus, the great rebellion began.

Significantly, by the time we get to the book of Revelation, we see the worship of heaven as glorious as ever. However, to assure this rebellion will never happen again, these crowns are laid before the throne—not in disavowal, but in submission.

The Imperishable Crown

A second crown the Bible identifies is the imperishable crown. I Corinthians 9:25 says, "And everyone who competes for the prize is temperate in all things. Now they do it to obtain a perishable crown, but we for an imperishable crown."

Here, the contrast is made between the wreath an athlete won that would only wither and die, with the crown the servant of God will obtain, which will never wither and die. Hence, I Peter 1:4 described this crown as incorruptible, undefiled, that fades not away, now reserved in heaven for you. Isn't that good? When commenting on the riches of this world, people often say you can't take it with you, which is true. But when it comes to God's greater riches, this verse tells us you *can* send it ahead. And by doing so, you make sure it's there by the time you arrive!

During the days of the New Testament, crowns were given for winning an athletic contest or for performing an important service. These crowns were then worn at banquet celebrations or when entering the temples of their gods. So in seeking to understand what this crown is, we proceed on the assumption that surely Scripture would have chosen a different symbol if there weren't some connection between what this crown meant to the world in that day and what it would mean to the believer in the future.

For example, the crown of the athlete—what does that represent? Exhilaration! What do we see when television cameras visit the locker room of the winning team at the World Series or at the Super Bowl? We find men jumping up and down, grinning from ear to ear, unable to find words to express their thrill! As these men look back on their lifelong dedication and the near torture they had to go through to achieve their victory, they can't celebrate this victory enough! This is the great victory that all the doubters and critics said would never come!

So as the big game approached, the overriding thought (magnified by advertising) was that this one game would determine everything! The champion of the world would be crowned! Accordingly, the publicity buildup for this game would dominate TV viewing at home and water-cooler conversations at the office. No matter one's gender or generation, this grand interruption to normal, everyday life was strongly felt. Never mind the immediate rewards of fame and fortune, the accolades of history were there for the taking! Think of it: Every neon light could go dark one day, but *their* name would shine on forever!

Lost in all this enthusiasm, though, was a convenient forgetfulness of one fact: This *same* game—so special and unique, supposedly—was going to be played again next year ... and the next year ... and the next year.

Nevertheless, caught up in all the hype, crowd frenzy and ticket scalping were there to greet the game. The band played, the flag flew, the crowd roared—and then ... it was over! The victory party ended ... the television cameras were turned off. And in sharp contrast with all the hoopla, this great moment of glory became a trivia question.

What felt so good, and at the time seemed so important, ended—well, abruptly. So what did these athletes then do? Wanting desperately to regain what was ever so briefly theirs, these athletes proceeded to give every effort they could give to get back to the top.

How sad to see discarded heroes of the past languishing in the shadows, vainly attempting a comeback. But in contrast to the diminishing satisfaction these athletes experience, the Bible assures us that God's rewards will never fade. The ecstasy, the exhilaration, the feeling that this is just too good to be true, won't ever go away!

Chances are, those old trophies of yours commemorating past accomplishments are only collecting dust now. Oh, you may glance in their direction from time to time, but that hardly recaptures the feelings of glory, or replicates the thrill you originally felt. At best, there's but a brief flash of memory, so dulled by the years you often decide not to indulge it.

By contrast, God's rewards are so satisfying, so thrilling, and so utterly beyond what you ever thought you would get, you will *never* get over it! Exhilaration!

As previously mentioned, the crown was also given to someone who performed a faithful service for the king. This is a little more difficult to correlate with the rewards of God, because the reward for government service today may be little more than a letter of commendation. Offsetting this impression are the Lord's words about our reward being "great." Well, then! That one word "great" stirs the imagination!

Do you remember the story of the fellow who picked up a tramp walking a dusty, desert road? As is turned out, the tramp was the eccentric billionaire, Howard Hughes. And due to the help he received that day, Hughes gave this man, Melvin, one million dollars!

To ourselves we may think, "What luck! I wish I had a benefactor like that!" But in truth, we do! This is why, whenever opportunities to serve our God present, we should snap these opportunities up with great eagerness, knowing the reward-earning capacity attached to each service will be supremely compensated by our extravagantly wealthy God.

Crowns, we noted, were also worn by men of honor at the banquet. Granted, there are some people who don't like parties, but chances are these same people can think of at least one party they attended that was so good they didn't ever want it to end! And when it did end, as all parties must, they later wished, "If only all of life could be like that great party we had Friday night!"

In truth, there aren't many gatherings where the chemistry among attendees would trigger this response. But did you know that God is going to throw a party—and that *you* are going to be an honored guest?

The party God will host won't be some starchy, formal, black-tie affair, such as world leaders host in their respective capitals. In our country, Presidents will wine and dine celebrated people at a state dinner party. However, the Messianic banquet of our Lord is going to make one these White House extravaganzas look like a Salvation Army soup kitchen! The festivity, the fellowship, the fulfillment the Lord has planned for us will far exceed all expectations.

We must also note that the wearing of the crown into the temple depicts another reality reserved for the believer: our entrance into the presence of God. This, when we read Isaiah and John, may seem like a fearful prospect, one triggering an Isaiah-like "woe is me!" confession, or a falling to the ground that may render us, like the Apostle John, almost dead.

But remember, our sins at this point, and the nature that produced them, will be history; for we will have been elevated into the bridehood of Christ. Hence, we will be spared the anguish of discovered sin (sin more horrible than we had ever imagined), but instead will hear the Lord praise *us* (I Corinthians 4:5).

Can you even imagine what it will be like to have God sincerely and effusively praise you? Oh my! The blessing of *his* words will never lose its power!

The imperishable crown, then, is the exhilaration of winning the greatest contest ever, the commendation from the greatest benefactor ever, the appreciation of the greatest party ever, and the acclamation from the greatest person ever. So whenever you think of the imperishable crown, just remember these earthly things: winning the Super Bowl, a million dollars from Howard Hughes, being honored by the White House, and becoming a person even the greatest person on earth would praise. Then, multiply all that by near infinity and you'll have some idea of what the imperishable crown entails.

As mentioned at the outset, there are other crowns besides these two, crowns that we will examine in the next chapter. Each crown we study adds to our understanding of God's rewards. So as we continue to examine these crowns, let's ask the Spirit of God to help us see what Moses saw; and to see them in such a way that we, too, will make life decisions based on God's rewards.

What often blinds us in this matter is our satisfaction with the familiar, even if the familiar is rooted in sin. Lamenting the way that the morphine of sin dulls our spiritual sensitivities toward the life to come, G.D. Watson wrote:

> Soon—oh, so soon!—we are to stand right in the blazing realities of God, and eternity, and all of our faculties are hardly half-awake. Do we often think of that inexpressible hour when we shall gaze on our precious Jesus for the first time?[12]

Let us long for that day! And cultivate even now a vision for that hour! Because apparently just a glimpse of these rewards will cause us to desire them with all our hearts! And, really, it is this desire, this commitment to the Lord, that the good life is all about.

Reflection Questions

1. Think back on the time you were most recognized, most appreciated. How did this appreciation affect you?

2. Imagine the scene: the Lord of glory praising you .... How will you respond?

3. How did this chapter increase your motivation to obey God?

Chapter 18
Rewards for Goodness—Part II

One of the strongest motivators for determining human behavior—for encouraging good and becoming more like God—is rewards. This is especially true if the rewards are greatly valued, and even more true if, before these rewards are given, a time of waiting excites the imagination.

The proliferation of award shows today discloses something deeply embedded in human nature—the desire for our efforts to be appreciated! The music world gives the Grammy. The television world gives the Emmy. Broadway gives the Tony. Hollywood gives the Oscar. Country music has its own award show, gospel music has theirs, the cable networks have theirs, the soap operas have theirs—why, these gala celebrations fill the calendar! And we haven't even mentioned the awards given by the literary world, the academic world, the athletic world, the business world, and a host of other industries that offer their night in the spotlight. These annual affairs of coveted acclaim abound!

The desire for appreciation is largely rooted, I suppose, in our childhood. It was during these years when the slightest improvement of behavior became a celebrated event: whether tying our shoes correctly, coloring within the lines, or eating all our dinner. When we were young, praise and recognition were commonly given. The unintended consequence of this, perhaps, is that some people were conditioned for excessive approval-seeking in later years. But in sharp contrast to these childhood years, much of what we do in adult years goes virtually unnoticed. We can be productive year in and year out, yet hardly anyone notices!

Not wanting to be overlooked like that, and certainly not wanting to be taken for granted, there is something resident in most of us that sends signals for some measure of recognition. Though these signals may not be strong and may not be frequent, they are sufficiently strong and frequent to communicate a desire to be honored.

It is true that when the faithful employee is given a watch after forty years of service, this isn't exactly the honor the human heart desires. Who wants to work all those years just to get a watch?

Trophies aren't much better (despite the press coverage preceding the ceremony and the party that follows). And, frankly, other attempts to honor also fall short. For example: what students do for their teachers at the end of the year, or that barbecue the team holds for their coaches, or even those hall-of-fame ceremonies at the end of a career.

One might think that at least for these hall of fame inductees the crowds would be huge and the publicity enormous. But, no, these poorly attended events often become a "filler" column, a short article buried under the fold on some back page in the newspaper.

In drawing conclusions about these and other attempts to reward, the comment of Charles Williams, the British poet and novelist, quickly comes to mind: "It is as pleasant as it is unusual to see thoroughly good people getting their deserts." Often, the recognition that comes to even the best of humanity is much less than it ought to be.

Mindful of all these failed earthly attempts to honor, one wonders if these failures will be replicated in heaven. Is the ceremony going to be a "yawner"? You know the scene— the dutiful speeches, the corny jokes, the polite, perfunctory applause. Is heaven's awards banquet going to be like that?

In Luke 6:23, Jesus indirectly answered this question when he said, "Rejoice in that day and leap for joy! For indeed your reward is great in heaven." Well, now! In promising a leaping joy, do you get the idea that these rewards are going to be stunning, staggering, stupendous, and altogether awesome? And when Jesus said "indeed," a very emphatic word, and then added the word "great," an uncommonly strong word, the Son of God elevated our thoughts about these rewards to sky-high expectancy.

Keep in mind that when God created the world, he said it was "good." So if the whole world, with its breathtaking views and marvelous resources, only merits a "good" from God, one has to wonder what "great" must mean.

Whatever it does mean, it was cause for Jesus to say "be exceedingly glad" about the rewards to come (Matthew 5:12). And in saying all this, the Lord couldn't have raised our expectations any higher.

More than once the Bible reports Jesus saying that when he comes back, he's going to be bringing the rewards with him (Revelation 22:12). Apparently, Jesus is so excited about what he's going to give, he can't wait until we join him in heaven—he wants to do this right away!

So, to answer the question earlier asked: Far from being a cheap, chinchy, calculating rewarder, the rewards the Lord gives will thrill and fulfill beyond anything we can imagine!

Most Christians know very little about the rewards. What God is so excited to give never influences a decision, never gets mentioned in a prayer, never becomes a feature attraction in the theater of their minds. In fact, if someone were to ask, "Should a Christian do what he does for a reward?" most people would think there is something unworthy about that. The only worthy motive for serving God, in their minds, should be gratitude. But as lofty as that might sound, it isn't biblical! These rewards, after all, are God's idea! So we shouldn't be shifting attention from what *he* conceived and is so excited to give. Remember, rewards were ordained by God to motivate the believer to obedience!

In the previous chapter, we discussed two crowns that some will receive at the time God rewards: the crown of gold, which has to do with an increased capacity for worship; and the imperishable crown, which refers to peak experiences in the anointed life. In this chapter we will examine three other crowns. And in doing so, we will see how each of these crowns adds dimensions to the recipient's life in heaven that are distinctive from what others, without these crowns, will experience.

The Crown of Righteousness

A third crown identified in Scripture is what II Timothy 4:7-8 calls the crown of righteousness.[1] Commenting on this crown, the Apostle Paul said:

> I have fought the good fight, I have finished the race, I have kept the faith. Finally, there is laid up for me the crown of righteousness, which the Lord, the righteous Judge, will give me on that Day, and not to me only but also to all that have loved his appearing.

Here, as in I Corinthians, chapter 9, reference is made to the sports world and, more specifically, to the accolades that come to those who triumph.

The struggle for any winning athlete is intense, as it was for Paul in the race God had him run, and as it is for you in the race that God designed for you to run. These struggles—for Paul, for you—are not haphazard, but are predictable, given the difficulty of the race. Similarly, all who aspire to please the Lord will also be confronted by formidable opposition—generated by Satan, or other sinners, or self.

It is comforting to know that these struggles are in some sense "Father-filtered," in that there is a design imposed upon them. Though some of what you're facing was never sponsored by God, ultimately, God superintends the process so it will yield what it must for your eternal good.

At the time certain challenges present, you may not feel so good, yet even what opposes you *can* bring you an appreciable advantage. Helping us to grasp this truth, A.B. Simpson wrote:

> The very hardships that you are enduring in your life today are given by the Master for the explicit purpose of winning your crown. Do not wait for some ideal situation, some romantic difficulty,

some far-away emergency; but rise to meet the actual conditions which the providence of God has placed around you today.

Your crown of glory lies embedded in the very heart of those things—those hardships and trials that are pressing you this very hour, week, and month of your life.[2]

As Paul faced each struggle—not as a victim, but as a more-than-conqueror—he did so with his eyes on a future reward. Yes, he wanted to please Jesus. Yes, he wanted to spread the gospel. And yet the biblical record doesn't omit this fact: *Paul was also looking forward to "that day."* Providing more insight into this, A.B. Simpson declared:

> The prospect of this glorious day was the inspiration of Paul's own faith and hope in the midst of all his trials and discouragements, and in view of it he would utter that magnificent boast, "I know whom I have believed, and am convinced that he is able to guard what I have entrusted to him for that day" (2 Timothy 1:12). "That day" was to him the day of days, the day on which all accounts should be balanced, all losses regained, all wrongs righted, all sacrifices repaid, and all tears forever wiped away.[3]

Martin Luther once said, "There are only two days on my calendar: Today and that Day."

In contemplating what "that day" will bring and what this particular crown honors, one must first check out the premise for its distribution by asking: Have I fought a good fight? Or did I take it easy, preferring to coast while accommodating all the desires of the soft life? Did I actually *run* the race, redeeming the time and making every moment count? Or did I, without purpose and drive, just meander through life with no vision or mission directing me? In taking this little inventory, we should also ask ourselves: Did I finish the race, accomplishing what God wanted me to do?

Or was I one of those people who couldn't even figure out what God wanted me to do? Then, when completing this internal inventory, we should ask: Did I really love his appearing—imaging it and being motivated by my vision of it? Or, for me, did long seasons of time slip by without any thought of the Lord's imminent return crossing my mind?

It is imperative that the answer to each question comes from the Lord—not from the Accuser, and not from yourself. Two words help us track our progress in this assessment—accomplishment and affection. And when you think about it, these two words are closely connected! Why did Paul *accomplish* what he did in the race completed and the fight won? Because of his great *affection* for Jesus! And why do so many others do so much less? Because of their diminished affection for Jesus!

The phrase Paul uses in his magnanimous attempt to include other recipients for this award is actually a very strong phrase, "to all that have *loved* his appearing"—referring of course to that day when Jesus returns to receive his own from the earth. G.D. Watson said, "There is something in believers looking for the second coming of the Lord which puts upon them a character of faith and watchfulness ...."[4]

True, there are other Christians who want the Lord to return, but not because they're so in love with him. What motivates them, I'm afraid, are all the defeats and disappointments they're facing. So, from their perspective, the sooner God wraps this whole thing up and gets them out of here, the better!

But to "love his appearing" has to mean more than a pitiful desire for a rescue. For the ones who *really* love his appearing are yearning for a sweeter and deeper fellowship with him now. Because they love him to this extent, therefore, they're determined to honor the Lord's arrival with years and years of dedicated service.

There's another group of Christians who could care less about the rapture. These people are so caught up with daily life, and so enticed by all the things this world has to offer, they are in no hurry to leave. Apparently, as the poet put it, the world is too much with them.

With typical candor and insight, Tozer accurately described their condition.

> God has set eternity in our hearts and we have chosen time instead. He is trying to interest us in a glorious tomorrow and we are settling for an inglorious today. We are bogged down in local interests and have lost sight of eternal purposes. We improvise and muddle along, hoping for heaven at last but showing no eagerness to get there, correct in doctrine but weary of prayer and bored with God.[5]

Love his appearing? Why, people in this condition scarcely think about it! Oh, they may have enough theology in their brains to agree that the return of the Lord will be a blessed event. But this is only an occasional thought, and not one that imprints their hearts or in any sense directs their lives.[6] Pressing this point as it deserved to be pressed, A.B. Simpson asked, "Beloved, is our heart in the hope of Christ's return? Are our affections clustered there? Are our ambitions in the skies? Are our investments, our plans, our pursuits all tending to that imminent event?"[7]

Those who do love the Lord's appearing are committed to getting his work done *before* he comes! Therefore, while being engaged in this world, they are not enmeshed with this world; and while enthralled with heaven, they are not enticed by earth. It is these people, and these people alone, who will receive this third crown.

Notice next how Scripture speaks of this as a crown *of* righteousness and not *for* righteousness. This implies a boldness attributable to our righteousness (that is, to our right standing before God) that knows how to receive from God. Remember: The Bible says we are to come boldly before God's throne so we can obtain (Hebrews 4:16).

What enables this commanded boldness is the knowledge we are pleasing to God, that we belong in the Throne Room of the universe, that what God has for us is actually due us, legally, in the jurisprudence of heaven (because of the righteousness embedded in our new nature).

So recipients of *this* crown are the ones who embraced their identity in the Lord and successfully functioned in the authority God gave them to exercise. It is precisely because they do please God that they can be used by God.

Could it be, then, that the ones receiving this reward will enjoy a greater sense of God's pleasure toward them, just as they did on earth? While toddlers sense this pleasure on one level as it is gratuitously offered by adults, those brought to maturity in the Lord will experience God's pleasure on a greater level, due to spiritual attainments that merit his eternal reward.

Again, those wearing this crown will have a greater faith to receive *from* God and thus will have greater assignments to accomplish *for* God throughout the eons of eternity.

Also noteworthy, since love seems to be the premise of this reward, are the reciprocal dynamics of receiving and returning the Lord's love. This receiving and returning will be much elevated for those who wear this crown of righteousness.

Some Christians today will *say* the Lord loves them—that is, if their view is requested whenever this topic surfaces in conversation. And because theology credentials what they say, there *is* a measure of believability in their words. Yet other people will see in their eyes and hear in their voice something else: a deep-seated ambivalence with very formidable blockages. Something in them seems to block the receiving and returning of the Lord's love.

There are many reasons for these blockages, none of which we will attempt to identify or explain at this juncture because more the point at present is the fact these blockages do exist. It is sad, but contrary thoughts about the Lord's love are deeply embedded in many Christians today. This is why, whenever they do say something about God's love, their words have no accompanying emotion.

These parroted words, these vacant emotions, are so unlike the Apostle John, who just couldn't get over the fact of how much Jesus loved him! But instead of being overwhelmed by this love, as John was, and giving themselves with abandon to it, like John did, all the intangibles declare that restraint is evident and that emotional reservations are prominent. Their words say one thing; their eyes say another.[8]

Has enough been said at this point to make you realize that this is a problem hindering you? If you're journeying through life with your foot on the brakes—especially when it comes to personal testimony and praise for the Lord's love—put this problem at the top of your agenda for attention and solution. Come to the Lord now, and to those friends of his who can help you resolve the deep-seated ambivalences that are restricting your experience of God's love.

Once you begin to target this issue, honesty will uncover thoughts you didn't know you had and feelings you wish you didn't have. But remember, a loving God will bring you through all this so you can then experience on earth what those who will receive this crown in heaven will experience—a more rapid cycling of the receiving and returning of the Lord's love.

Scripture's testimony about the Lord's love for us should be more decisive in our thought formation than is often the case. And perhaps no thought can more quickly clear this issue up than that articulated by Thomas Watson: "Holiness is God's image; and God cannot choose but love his image where he sees it."[9] Similarly, Stephen Charnock encouraged, "If you be new creatures, you are the delight of God. It is impossible but God should have the most tender respect to his own likeness ...."[10] If you'll learn to claim this truth for yourself, the Lord's love will be more real to you.

Alexander Maclaren wisely observed, "If I am to love God, I must be quite sure that God loves me."[11] So *why* does he love us—because he is love? No, even God knows that answer won't work. *The ultimate reason he loves us is because his image and likeness are at the core of our being!* Remember, God loves what he gave! And what he gave was his righteousness, now imparted into our new nature (Ephesians 4:24)! But if you don't know who you are (the new nature resident in your born-again spirit) and think of yourself instead in terms of all that has happened in your past, then it is that confusion which will prevent you from understanding why God loves you.

You may think that loving the person you imagine yourself to be makes no sense. And you will be right; it doesn't. But once you understand that you have one nature, not two, and that this new nature totally defines you, you can then respond to A.B. Simpson's profound encouragement:

> Let us abide in the love of Christ. Let us persuade ourselves that he loves us infinitely and perfectly, and that he delights in us continually, and is wholly committed to us to carry us through and fulfill in us all the good pleasure of his will. Let us not think that we must wring from him, by hard constraint and persuasion, the blessing which our faith compels. Rather he has set his heart on our highest good and is working out for us, in his loving purpose, all that we can receive of blessing.
>
> Lying like John in his bosom, let us each reckon ourselves to be the disciple whom Jesus loved. Like Enoch, let us claim by faith the testimony that we please God, and looking up with confidence we shall find his responsive smile and benediction. The true secret of pleasing God is to trust him, believe in his love to us, be artless children and count ourselves beloved of God.[12]

Those who do follow Simpson's advice will find themselves, soon enough, in that number this crown rewards—those who look with longing love for the Lord's appearing.

The Crown of Glory

A fourth crown Scripture discusses is the crown of glory. I Peter, chapter 5, verse 4 says, "And when the Chief Shepherd appears, you will receive the crown of glory that does not fade away." Now, this is a promise made to laborers in the church, and more specifically to the elders who feed and lead God's flock. Having the title of an elder isn't the critical factor here. The focus instead is on nurturing God's people.

It isn't always easy to serve in God's church. Some people get their feelings hurt: They misunderstand, they presume motive, they say things they should never say. And so from them there isn't even a hint of bestowed glory upon their leaders.

Referring to this distressing reality, the Apostle Paul once said, "... the more abundantly I love you, the less I am loved" (II Corinthians 12:15). And Paul wasn't alone in this experience! Many church leaders today can easily identify with this statement. But the good news is that what church members take for granted, God will richly reward.

The word "glory" in I Peter 5:4 means to reveal, to disclose, to boast; it is even described as a "weight"—not in the sense of a burden, but in the sense of something very important and significant. Accordingly, this crown refers to an increased ability to discover the wonders enmeshed in the essence of God. The Bible never says that we will know everything there is to know about God the moment we enter heaven. The greatest joy of heaven will be these continuing discoveries we will all make about our God!

In focusing on what is yet to be discovered about the unfathomable essence of God, G.D. Watson made an interesting observation.

> No angel mind that has been gazing for countless ages into the glad perfections of God could begin to tell us of the infinite bliss that God has in seeing his own glory, in understanding the riches and perfections inside his own bosom.[13]

And since no one is more fascinating than he, and no one can enthrall our enraptured attention more than he, this preoccupation of eternity will cause those who have this crown to light up in the reflected glory they are accessing. Precisely what constitutes this experience isn't completely clear on this side of heaven. However, even on this side of heaven, we know what it is to discover a truth about God so exciting we can hardly contain ourselves.

Faber said, "Eternity will not be long enough to learn all he is, or praise him for all he has done." Thomas Goodwin wrote: "When we see God to the full, we shall be so in love with him that the heart will never turn off from him. That 'fullness of joy,' those 'rivers of living water' will carry the soul away with a torrent forever."[14] Talk about the love boat ... this trip will be much better!

For those elders who labored in the Word, and even for untitled people who did the same thing to build up the Lord's body, God is saying there is going to be this reward of seeing with greater insight what the Bible (a sufficient revelation, but not an exhaustive one) was beginning to disclose.

G.D. Watson reminded us that there are two kinds of love for God—the love of gratitude and the love of excellence.[15] Gratitude is important, of course, and there are many reasons for encouraging it. But to love God because of his excellence is an even higher form of love. Those inheriting this crown will delightedly and expansively enjoy this love. That will be their reward: this ecstatic rapture as they gaze upon God!

The distinction of this crown from the previous crown is seen in its more exclusive focus on the essence of God, whereas the crown of righteousness rewards rights and privileges from the Lord that were properly exercised. For many years, teachers of the Word, whether they were officially recognized by the church in a salaried position or not, studied the person of God almost like a jeweler examining a diamond.

You are familiar with such inspections. First the diamond is placed under the light, then it is turned slowly and slightly, in one direction and then another, so trained eyes can detect every nuance of value. Then, with each discovery made, we hear an excited utterance and, still later, another burst of exuberance as previously undetected qualities are discovered.

In the 19th chapter of Revelation, where we read about the Marriage Supper of the Lamb, we are told in verse 12 that Jesus has a name that no one knows; only he knows it. Commenting on this verse, A.B. Simpson said, "... it means that after we know of Jesus there is still much we do not know. There is a mystery still hidden in his infinite heart and all that he is yet to reveal to us is far greater than even what we now know of his power and love."[16] G.D. Watson wrote, "He will give us, as his sons, access into his inner life, and admit us, as the Psalmist said, 'into the white ivory palaces' of his own being."[17]

Oh, the depths of his riches and glory! Plummeting into these depths, those with this crown will search, will discover, and then, breaking surface, will emerge to proclaim the greatness of their God!

Each discovery thrills! Each proclamation encourages! And the good news is that this will not be an assignment exhausted in eternity! In all the rarefied splendors of heaven, there is nothing that will further enhance eternity's joy than this anointed ability, this rewarded proficiency, that sees the beauty of our God.[18]

Those of us who don't understand art can't see all the beauty in a picture, or in a sculpture. And the same principle holds true when it comes to God. The more we understand God, the more we'll see his beauty. What remains hidden to others will be made known to us.

The Crown of Life

A fifth crown the Bible talks about is the crown of life. James 1:12 says: "Blessed is the man who endures temptation; for when he has been approved he will receive the crown of life which the Lord has promised to those who love him."

Prior to this verse, James lists six stages of temptation—that is, a deliberate solicitation to evil, something straight out of the pit loaded with tantalizing appeal! What Satan is offering seems so attractive! So you may think that to decline the offer is to lose out in a big-time way. But here God is saying "Child, you won't lose out. Resist Satan and I'll give you (literally this reads) *the* crown of *the* life. By taking this fact into account, you won't have a hard time turning Satan down.

In Revelation 2:10 we see the same truth from a different perspective. Instead of temptation, the challenge in view is persecution—a persecution involving much more than some personal slight, or some intended affront that hurts you. Actually, something far more grievous is inflicted.

Speaking from heaven to the Church at Smyrna, the Lord Jesus says:

> Do not fear any of those things you're about to suffer. Indeed, the devil is about to throw some of you into prison, that you may be tested and you will have tribulation ten days. Be faithful until death and I will give you the crown of life.

Commentators accurately observe that the Church at Smyrna was one of only two churches Jesus addressed that received no criticisms, no warnings, but only praise. That's because this church, a persecuted church, had withstood—without compromise—the onslaughts of Satan.

You may say, "Satan isn't attacking me. I'm not being persecuted!" Yet, with axiomatic assurance the Bible tells believers today that the godly shall be persecuted (II Timothy 3:12). This isn't a matter of geography (this could happen to you if you live in North Korea or Saudi Arabia); because those who say what Jesus would have them say, and do what Jesus would have them do, are going to find themselves the targets of hell's fury, no matter where they live. Let's face it: Our world hasn't changed a bit! And human nature hasn't improved, either! It is a spiritual law, therefore: Every godly person is going to be persecuted!

This won't happen to the compromisers, though, to those chameleon-like Christians who fit in with both the church *and* the world. Attack them? Why? They're hardly worth hissing at! Their lives are so lukewarm it makes Jesus sick (Revelation 3:16).

By contrast, Satan loves the counterfeit Christianity these believers model. So, yes, by all means, let them go to church! Satan will gladly go with them! And while there, his eyes will brighten, his interest will peak as he asks: Is there a business meeting scheduled?

Now, the apparent reason people compromise is to secure some perceived advantage for themselves. The advantage could be quicker access to something desired, or, perhaps, being spared from something not desired. Not everything will be negotiable to them; but, disturbingly, a lot of things will be. For their enticed hearts are all too ready to deal! Consequently, while a rare few believers are battered pillar to post, other Christians enjoy life on easy street. Addressing this unsanctioned lifestyle, F.B. Meyer said:

> Ah, friends, what are we living for? Are our pursuits bounded by the narrow horizons of earth and limited to the fleeting moments of time? Are we constantly engaged in lining as warmly as possible the nest in which we hope to spend our old age and die? Are we perpetually seeking to make the best of this world?[19]

People who live this way pay no price at all for their faith! So what is heaven's perspective on this? Simply this: If that's what they choose, then (to quote Jesus) "they have their reward."

But for the Christian whose name is known in hell, and for that one who came under attack and wouldn't back down, God will more than make it up to him or her. Just how he will do this isn't exactly revealed in Scripture. Perhaps, instead of a "one shoe fits all" approach, this will be done on an individual basis. God may tailor the "extra" he will do for the uncompromised believer according to this believer's unique tastes. Yes, all believers will experience eternal life, but there is something more this believer will receive. The God of great surprises will find a way to reward all that this believer lost when he resisted that temptation and endured that persecution.

This, by no means, completes the survey of God's wonderful rewards.[20] In the book of Revelation there are seven specific statements about overcoming that also yield information about our coming rewards. Thomas Watson pointed out, "To show fully what a believer's gains are at death were a task too great for an angel; all hyperboles fall short of it; the reward of glory exceeds our very faith."[21]

Yet, faith can still set its sights on these rewards, even though our knowledge at this point is partial. In seeing only this much, though, it certainly becomes clearer why Moses made the decision he did. For once a believer—any believer—

gets a vision of these rewards, it will cause him to look at life in an entirely different way, and thus help him make decisions he might not have otherwise made.

All that you are going through now—which could have been avoided had you given preference to self instead of devotion to God—is being watched by the Lord, even if it is being ignored by the world. And at your disposal during this time is his multidimensional grace of God, sufficient to see you through—and I mean all the way through, and not just to the end of that besetting temptation. Accordingly, A.B. Simpson declared:

> Yes, we are forging our crowns day by day. We are weaving out triumphal robes. We are making out eternal destiny. We are settling into our final place. And the glory which the Master is preparing for each of us, he is working in us now ...."[22]

One can only add: How vitalizing is this vision! How it steadies our will and strengthens our resolve!

But, for so wonderful a reality to materialize in our future, we must reorder our priorities now in order to gain God's greater pleasure.

Reflection Questions

1. This chapter acknowledges the desire for recognition, often stemming from childhood years, that may express itself in adult years as a legitimate desire for the honor God says believers should give one another. How do these thoughts resonate with you?

2. Which of the three crowns discussed in this chapter has the most appeal to you? Please explain.

Chapter 19

The Reaping of the Rewards—Part I

If you remember those pop quizzes teachers gave, you remember the groan that chorused through the classroom whenever one was announced. But what if a pop quiz turned out to be the final exam? Why, had that happened, the groan would have become an unhinged roar! What would be far worse, though, is if the final exam of our *life* were to be completely unannounced! To have never said a word about so serious an event as this just wouldn't be fair!

No one wants to be caught off guard, right? Especially if far-reaching consequences may result. Therefore, Scripture openly announced to believers that "we must all appear before the judgment seat of Christ ..." (II Corinthians 5:10).

Actually, there are two judgments Scripture tells us about: the Great White Throne judgment, which is for lost people (Revelation 20:11-15), and the Bema Judgment, which is for saved people. At the Great White Throne judgment a declaration of *condemnation* will be pronounced. At the Bema Judgment a decree of *commendation* will be announced.

The word "*bema*" refers to a raised platform upon which dignitaries summon recipients for honor. Even in Corinth today, tourists can see the *bema* located near the Greco-Roman marketplace. In Paul's day, the Isthmian games were held in Greece on alternate years to the Olympics. At the conclusion of these games the athletes who were victorious appeared before the *bema* to receive their crowns.

So with this background in mind, Scripture speaks of a coming day when the Lord will award *his* crowns. These crowns, however, will bestow an honor that is higher than any that can be given on earth.

According to Scripture, it is our works that will be on trial at the Bema Judgment Seat of Christ and not our life (I Corinthians 3:13). At that time, and at that place, each work will be examined in open (not in secret) to assess what kind of work it was. Based entirely on this examination, the rewards will then be given.

This may surprise you, but nowhere does Scripture say that everyone who goes to heaven is even going to get a reward. G. D. Watson writes, "The Apostle John shows us the difference between the Book of Life, which simply registers the names of those who are saved, and tells us that there are other books, out of which the great and small are to be judged according to their works" (Revelation 20:12).[1] Apparently, some Christians will only be cited in the first book.

As for the other books, if there be any good works, they won't be examined randomly or selectively; instead, the entire body of our works will be judged. So in this respect, Jesus' judging isn't at all like the judging that goes on at the county fair. At the county fair, Aunt Minnie will enter her largest pumpkin in the vegetable competition; and Uncle Harold will enter his roundest, pinkest pig in the livestock competition. Yet, Aunt Minnie grew more than one pumpkin; and Uncle Harold raised more than one pig.

In their respective attempts to win the coveted blue ribbon, Minnie and Harold will select and submit only the best of what their labor produced. But it won't be this way at the Bema Judgment. Selections and submissions aren't going to be the name of game, because at this setting *all* our works will be judged.

One has to wonder, even if it's mere speculation, what it would be like if we could select only our best work and put that forth for God's inspection. If this were possible, we could rivet our attention on just one episode or one area of our life, then live the rest of our lives with no thought about God's standards being followed. Under this arrangement, it wouldn't matter if other areas of our life were in bad repair.

This preferred agenda of ours would certainly speed up the rewards ceremony; because if only selected samples are judged—well, good news, that wouldn't take very long! Well, maybe it wouldn't, but do remember: God can render split-second judgment for everyone and everything. Besides, what's the hurry? Eternity is a long time. This prophetic event isn't caught in the vortex of a time crunch.[2]

If the judging of our works were like the judging at the county fair, only rare exhibits of excellence would be put forth: at best, small slice-of-time actions, as if these represented our entire life. But this arrangement would lend itself to considerable distortion, and perhaps to a false elevation of self-esteem.

For example, a golfer may take pride in being able to hit the ball out of the sand trap and into the hole, even if he achieves this only twice out of a hundred attempts. Likewise, a tennis player may boast of a wicked crosscourt backhand shot that will send a puff of chalk skyward for the winning point—game, set, match!

Well, in his dreams, maybe; or perhaps he got a shot off a like that in practice once. But shots like these—from the golfer or the tennis player—are hardly a part of their regular repertoire. Besides, confusing rare excellence with normal performance results often in a tennis racket slammed onto the court, or a golf club wrapped around a tree.

To avoid distorted thinking like this, the Judge of all the earth will judge every work you and I ever did. Horatius Bonar addressed this point with eloquence when he reminded us that "a holy life is made up of a multitude of small things."

> It is the little things of the hour, and not the great things of the age that fill up a life ... Little words, not eloquent speeches or sermons; little deeds, not miracles, nor battles, not one great heroic act or mighty martyrdom, make up the true Christian life ... The avoidance of little evils, little sins, little

inconsistencies, little follies, little weaknesses, little indiscretions and imprudences, little foibles, little indulgences of self and of the flesh, little acts of indolence or indecision or slovenliness or cowardice, little equivocations or aberrations from high integrity, little touches of shabbiness and meanness, little bits of covetousness or penuriousness, little exhibitions of worldliness and gaiety, little indifferences to the feelings or wishes of others, little outbreaks of temper, crossness, selfishness or vanity—the avoidance of such little things as these go far to make up at least the negative beauty of a holy life.[3]

Affirming this perspective, G.D. Watson wrote, "There is no better way in the world to test every trait in a soul than by little things. Every Christian duty, every grace of the Spirit, every privilege in life is being proved and manifested to the eyes of God and angels in things so small we seldom take thought of them."[4]

By examining all, there can be no complaints about the Lord judging one part of the record and not that part we preferred his eyes to see. By judging everything, God reinforces the principle that all aspects of life are important: every part and particle, every word and deed, every intent and outcome, every aspiration and accomplishment—the motive, the method, the glory—all will undergo full inspection! Nothing will be accorded one ounce of weight, or one penny in value, that is in any way less than what his all-knowing mind will accurately assess. On this point, Scripture raises a rhetorical question that needs no answer: Shall not the Judge of all the earth do right?

That this Judge will be sympathetic, yet impartial, is a point A.W. Tozer addressed in his book, *And He Dwelt Among Us*.

> ... there will be no dodging, no whimpering, no whining, no crying on our wrists and saying, "But Lord, you didn't understand." He does understand, because he became one of us and

walked among us. Never was a tear he did not share; never a bitter disappointment he did not feel; never a grief he did not suffer; never a temptation that did not come to him; never a critical situation that he was not in.[5]

Consequently, there will be no need for more affidavits, more testimony, and more proof, since the Judge we will one day stand before knows all and understands all.

We wish we *could* place complete trust in the judiciary systems of our world; we really do. However, just as the judiciary in Jesus' day was exposed for its corruption, this same kind of corruption extends across nations and hemispheres today, at times giving a bad name to that animal from "down under" called the kangaroo.

I don't know why the shenanigans of corrupt lawyers, lying witnesses, and "bought" judges should tarnish the name of one of God's most unusual creatures. The kangaroo shouldn't be libeled for what these unscrupulous men from the judiciary have done.

During some of the more sensational trials in history, we have seen high-priced lawyers use their legal cunning to beat the system and get their guilty clients off. But the histrionics that might impress a gullible jury, and the financial inducement that might impress a bribable judge, will never impress God. In his book, *The World's Last Night*, C.S. Lewis describes the perfect Judge rendering his verdict:

> ... it will be infallible judgment. If it is favorable, we shall have no fear; if unfavorable, no hope that it is wrong. We shall not only believe, we shall know, know beyond doubt in every fiber of our appalled or delighted being, that as the Judge has said, so we are: neither more, nor less, nor other. We shall perhaps even realize that in some dim fashion we could have known it all along.[6]

This was a knowledge that was accessible, had we wanted to obtain it. It was what some call "actionable knowledge," the kind of knowledge that could redirect our course and keep us out of jeopardy. Lacking this knowledge drives many toward doom.

So, if what will be revealed on that last day is largely knowable now, wouldn't it make sense to retrieve this truth from the deeper recesses of our soul where we often—with no spirit of reverence and no motivation for obedience—hide it? To continue such a charade means that one day we will be exposed as an ostrich without sand.

Suggesting a better processing than the one commonly employed, C.S. Lewis advised:

> We can, perhaps, train ourselves to ask more and more often how the thing we are saying or doing (or failing to do) at each moment will look when the irresistible light streams in upon it; that light which is so different from the light of this world—and yet, even now, we know just enough of it to take it into account. Women sometimes have the problem of trying to judge by artificial light how a dress will look by daylight. That is very like the problem of all of us: to dress our souls not for the electric lights of the present world but for the daylight of the next. The good dress is the one that will face that light. For that light will last longer.[7]

To deliberately deceive one's self really makes no sense if this deception is going to be exposed one day, and if the consequences then measured out are going to devastate willingly-deluded souls.

Darkness in the Church

One would think that this superior light would have had an unhindered flow in the church, informed as it should be by the Word of God, and assisted as it could be by the Spirit of God. One would also think that, aided by this light, a different set of values would have been on display, at least in the church. Regrettably, this has not always been the case. Instead, the church struts its own version of the ambitious

CEO, its own version of the charming performer, its own version of the cautious politician, its own version of the slick salesman.

Choosing to be a caboose on the world's train, the church has often been reduced by a pathetic imitation of worldly ways, wherein its values prevailed and God's values were scarcely to be seen. Commenting on this sad state of affairs, A.W. Tozer wrote of a world where the Son of God was judged while those respected in both religious and political circles triumphed.

> Our Lord died an apparent failure, discredited by the leaders of established religion, rejected by society and forsaken by his friends. The man who ordered him to the cross was the successful statesman whose hand the ambitious hack politician kissed. It took the resurrection to demonstrate how gloriously Christ had triumphed and how tragically the governor had failed.
>
> Yet today the professed church seems to have learned nothing. We are still seeing as men see and judging after the manner of man's judgment. How much eager beaver religious work is done out of a carnal desire to make good. How many man hours of prayer are wasted beseeching God to bless projects that are geared to the glorification of little men. How much sacred money is poured upon men who, despite their tear-in-the-voice appeals, nevertheless seek only to make a fair show in the flesh.[8]

Such contemptible behavior is discrediting, given the way the shining of heaven's truer light makes it altogether avoidable. In order to find that truer light, and thus get a better perspective on God's rewards, we need to answer some important questions, such as:

- When will we be rewarded?

- For what exactly will we be rewarded?
- How will these rewards be given?
- What criteria will be used?
- What dangers should we be mindful of when it comes to receiving these rewards?

The answers to each question will vary in length; nevertheless, let's answer each question in turn, noting at the outset that some of these questions will be answered in the next chapter.

The Time of the Rewarding

The first question can be answered briefly. Even though there are rewards on earth for those who serve the Lord, namely: a good conscience, the satisfaction of knowing that God is pleased, the camaraderie that comes from serving with others who also love the Lord, the joy of seeing other people being blessed, and even the love that comes to us from these other people—yet our final reward will be different from these valued pleasures, surpassing all of these in its ability to bless. This final, consummate reward will be given after we depart this world and go to be with the Lord.

F.B. Meyer reminded us, "Death is not a state, but a step; not a chamber, but a passage; not an abiding-place, but a bridge over a gulf."[9] And on the other side of that gulf is not some drowsy swoon or cloud-floating euphoria, but a life made even more vibrant by the distribution of these rewards.

There is much significance in the fact that our rewards will be given in glory. There is something of supreme importance that will happen there that enables us both to receive and to profitably use these rewards.

In his book, *Heavenly Life*, G. D. Watson explained:

> ... the redemption of our bodies has a relation to rewards, for it is in our glorified bodies that we are to receive the ocean streams of divine rewards for our faith and service ... we are told that we will be rewarded according to the deeds done in the body, and when we receive our glorified bodies it

will be in those bodies that we receive our rewards.[10]

In contemplating what the glorified ear can hear, the glorified eye can see, the glorified mind can understand, the glorified heart can feel, this exponentially increases the value of God's rewards.

As far back as the Old Testament, we are told exactly when the rewards will be distributed. Isaiah 40:10 declares, "Behold, the Lord shall come with a strong hand, and his arm shall rule for him; behold, his reward is with him and his work before him." The two "beholds" in this verse indicate the extreme importance of each event—the Lord's coming and the Lord's rewarding. Often, we think about the coming of the Lord, but give no thought at all about the rewarding that will soon follow. Clearly, a larger frame needs to be put on this picture.

The fact this verse talks about his strong hand and ruling arm distinguishes this event from the Lord's first coming. Because when Jesus came the first time, he came as God's gentle, sacrificial lamb and not as the ruler of the world.

There is also a distinction between what Isaiah describes and the final scene in heaven. In heaven, there won't be a need to rule with a strong arm; so the subduing indicated in this verse must refer to the establishing of Christ's millennial kingdom. Of significance also: The rewarding in the Isaiah passage has judicial overtones, wherein a deserved punishment will be meted out to those who offended God, oppressed men, and wrongly gratified self.

Isaiah 62:11 links the coming of the Lord with the bringing of his rewards, and it also uses the phrase, "His reward is with him and his work before him." This means all that can legitimately be defined as God's work is going to be rewarded. What the world neglected, or rejected, or never even noticed, and what you became discouraged about and perhaps belittled in your own mind has never been treated that way in the mind of God. Your work, ever and always, is in clear view of the adoring gaze of God, and therefore he is determined to reward you. Indeed, this reward will say a lot about what you will do for God in the future.

Matthew 16:27 says, "For the Son of Man will come in the glory of his Father with his angels, and then he will reward each according to his works." Luke 14:14 says, "... you shall be repaid at the resurrection of the just." I Corinthians 4:5 reminds us that this rewarding won't happen "until the Lord comes." I Peter 1:7 says that praise and honor and glory will break out at the appearing of Jesus Christ. In fact, the last chapter of the last book in the Bible finds Jesus encouraging his church with these words, "And behold, I am coming quickly, and my reward is with me ...."

G.D. Watson pointed out, "There is not one single word in all the Bible about anyone getting his reward at the time of death ...."[11] It won't happen then, but it will happen just before the Second Coming.

Upon examining these verses that speak about the time of God's rewards, we are again impressed with all the "beholds"—an unusually strong word prefacing an important announcement, a word summoning complete and immediate attention. One can almost imagine a booming voice from heaven saying, "Now hear this! Now hear this!"

Given all these repeated calls to give full attention, it becomes all the more amazing how little the church has heard this! Not even the pulpit has sufficiently aroused the congregation's attention to this coming event.

Second, when connecting the dots between the clues provided, it then becomes clear that the rewards will be given not when we die, and not when we return to heaven after the final defeat of Satan, but soon after the Lord snatches his church from the earth, yet before he assumes his reign in the millennial kingdom. The implication of this fact further suggests these rewards will have a strong connection with the tasks and responsibilities we will have during this thousand-year period on earth. The Bible's promise of ruling cities, tribes, and nations certainly fits in here, inasmuch as no such ruling will take place in heaven; nor will it occur on earth prior to the Lord's millennial reign. The first administration obviously occurs during the millennium.

The idea of a coming government headed by Jesus and honored by Jesus has great appeal. For when one considers all the tyrannies and abuses of government, it is no wonder that the older a person becomes, the less impressed he or she is with the political leaders of this world. In the end, they all disappoint, even those more honorable in their intentions and skilled in their abilities.

Such disappointment in government leaders will finally end when the government of the righteous takes over. At that time, every decision will be based on truth, not on expediency; and every decision will be made for benign intentions to bless, and not for self-serving reasons that expand one's political base. Truth, at this time, will no longer be held hostage by evil men—because the liars, the corrupt, and the self-seekers will be displaced forever. Glory to God!

Only those who please Jesus—people full of his wisdom, full of his love—will be allowed to lead. Can you imagine it: A government that always does the right thing in the right way? That is hard to imagine, isn't it?

Perhaps you have wondered why the Lord sometimes puts people with magnificent gifts in lowly places of service. And perhaps you've been tempted to say, or pray, "God, give them a place of wider influence! Give them a place where their gifts can be more fully utilized!"

Responding to this very observation, Samuel Chadwick wrote, "Sometimes there seems to be great gaps between vision and sphere, gifts and opportunity, but there is no caprice and nothing arbitrary in the method of the Spirit."[12] What may be omitted from the picture *we* see is the eternity perspective that discloses what God really has in mind.

In contrast with those who sold their soul for one or two terms in office down here, God is grooming people for a thousand-year promotion so exalted in scope and effective in accomplishments that if world leaders could see it now they would gasp with envy!

A.B. Simpson elaborates:

> There is a day spoken of in the eighth chapter of Romans as a day of the manifestations of the sons of God. It is the day when they will emerge from

their obscurity, and when the King's children who have been in disguise, going to school in the lowly places of trial and suffering, will come forth into the light and appear in all the glory of their royal robes and everlasting crowns.[13]

On that great day, the followers of God, long overlooked and unappreciated, will take their exalted places in the kingdom of God. It is then that their preparation will be utilized. The former impression of a curtain coming down prematurely, bringing to a close a life that deserved so much more, will at that time be forever erased. Simpson writes:

> That day will bring the rightings of our wrongs. That day will pay us the long deferred hire. That day will put us in our right place and displace the sons of pride ... that day will make up for toil and bitter loss. That day will put us in the place for which our talents and merits have fitted us, and from which others have excluded us for so long ... That day will confer upon us, if we are true, rewards so precious and priceless that we will remember our misery only as a vanished dream.[14]

Now, because Jesus said there are many abiding places in the Father's house (John 14:2), these rewards may well include a ruling responsibility, with the aid of angels (I Corinthians 6:2, 3), of an entire planet. Whether the rewards manifest exactly this way, they certainly transcend the time and tasks of the millennial reign and find their greater joy and implementation in what will follow.

The Service to be Rewarded

As our interest in the rewards begins to escalate, it is only natural to ask: What do I need to do to receive a reward? The answer to this question (though many particulars could lead to side-road excursions) can be given more effectively by identifying four broad categories.

First, if we are to be rewarded, we must have had a ministry—a sustained, sacrificial ministry designed to build up the church. I Corinthians 3:9 says "we are God's fellow workers." Granted, the United Nations may have some worthy objectives, but that is not the work of God. Volunteering for the restoration of some historical site may be a fine thing to do, but that also is not the work of God.

While God's economy of vocations is complex—including many more occupations than "religious" ones—the teacher, the mechanic, and the middle management person will only be able to include their vocations in their "ministry" to the extent their efforts, by design and through extended faith, enriched other people's relationship with Jesus.[15] Merely punching a time clock and picking up your paycheck won't qualify.

Suffice it to say that the work God will reward is not *any* do-good activity, but that which was ordained by God, energized by his Spirit, and done for his glory.

We must remember that the Lord already planned the work we are to do, even before we were born. This isn't a work left to whim, or a work to be engaged haphazardly should the mood strike us. The *Lord* must lead! Bringing focus to this discussion, F.B. Meyer wrote:

> It is abundantly sure that the work a man does in this world is not wrought only by the force of his genius, the brilliance of his intellect, or by those natural gifts with which God may have endowed him, but by a something beyond and behind all these—a spiritual endowment which is communicated by the Spirit of God for special office, and which is retained when the character is maintained ....[16]

Any work more indebted to human ingenuity than to divine revelation, having more sweat than Spirit for its method, and more self than God for its motive, will be destroyed by fire (I Corinthians 3:15).

A second thing we can do to merit God's reward is to faithfully and financially give to the Lord. Galatians 6:9 says, "And let us not grow weary while doing good, for in due season we shall reap if we do not lose heart." The context of this passage specifies financial giving to the Lord's work. All the preceding and following verses make this context quite clear. Similarly, II Corinthians 9:6 says, "... He who sows sparingly will also reap sparingly, and he who sows bountifully will also reap bountifully." The outcome is determined by the quality of giving.

Unfortunately, many church members, giving on average about 2% of their income, are stingy in their offerings; so there's no need to itemize what they give on a tax return. Some will give at the "tip" level. In the same way they'll tip a waitress or a barber, they will fork over a little "extra" to God, too—very little as it turns out! The exact amount is too small to remember.

Others will give to the Lord on the entertainment level, their mindset working something like this: If they go to a theater, they'll give. If they go to a ballpark, they'll give. And so, yes, whenever they go to church, they'll also give. These people see their offering as the price of admission—and not a very steep price at that!

Still others will give to the Lord on an emotional level. If a particular song moves them, or a certain sermon comforts them, they will show their gratitude by giving a little more than usual.

Other people are seasonal givers. They give at those special times of the year—Christmas and Easter, especially. Or perhaps—if a child is being baptized, or a grandchild is performing at church—they may, out of the kindness of their little black hearts, decide to give on that Sunday, too.

Rounding out this list of sparing givers are the situational givers. If Mom is about to go into the hospital, or if Dad is up for a special promotion, a better-than-usual contribution, they reason, might just tip the scales in their favor and secure the desired outcome.

In contrast to these sparing givers, the Bible talks about bountiful givers, for whom an awesome reaping will come! Yet we must ask: Is this rewarded reaping going to transact in heaven, or down here on earth? Luke 6:38 speaks of *men* giving unto your bosom, which would seem to indicate a reaping on earth. While addressing this same subject, Jesus spoke of laying up for yourselves treasure in heaven. Clearly, then, because giving is dedicated to the enhancement of the Lord's work, it too will be under review for heaven's rewards.

A third way to be rewarded in heaven is to give ourselves to others in meaningful fellowship. I Peter 3:8-9 declares: "Finally, all of you be of one mind, having compassion for one another; love as brothers, be tenderhearted, be courteous; not returning evil for evil or reviling for reviling, but on the contrary blessing, knowing that you were called to this so that you might inherit a blessing."

To remain in a challenging relationship can be difficult; yet, this is what God has called us to do. We haven't been called to see through our brother, but rather to see our brother through. Indeed, this commitment to our brother is so important that God gave 58 "one another" statements (30 when discounting the duplications) that define, describe, and detail exactly what a biblical fellowship ought to be. To be built up in the unique way "one anothering" achieves is so good, God will reward the effort.

A fourth way to be rewarded, as we've previously discussed, is to faithfully endure persecution. In Matthew, chapter 5, verses 11 and 12, Jesus said: "Blessed are you when they revile and persecute you, and say all kinds of evil against you falsely for my sake. Rejoice and be exceedingly glad, for great is your reward in heaven ...." In contemplating the Lord's words here, we should be careful to keep in mind this word "falsely." Sad but true is the fact that what our enemy says isn't always false. Hearing truth from the lips of an enemy can be painful. But in all probability, the Lord tried to get us to hear that truth in a less brutal way. Foolishly, though, we wouldn't listen! So, finally, the Lord allowed that truth to come from less tender lips—virtually assuring we would finally hear it!

Let's face it: Some people are just obnoxious. But then, when the predictable backlash comes their way, they have the unmitigated gall to wrap themselves in this verse and claim they are being persecuted. Biblically defined, though, persecution must be for the Lord's sake, and not for personal foolishness, or for personality traits that grate on other people's nerves. To have acted offensively was bad enough, but such evil is only compounded by their defense: When still refusing to see their fault, they accuse others.

To those rare few who did live uncompromised lives and did incur the world's wrath, the Bible promises a great reward, one that will make the believer "exceedingly glad"—that is, happier than language can ever convey or experience can ever explain!

At the time the world was retaliating, it may have appeared that God was nowhere around and that his cause had suffered a discrediting defeat. What must be kept in mind, though, is that God will respond to persecutors at a time of *his* choosing. Their cup of iniquity may not be full yet, so the time of God's stored vengeance may be postponed to another day.

Also postponed, though, but certainly not forgotten, is the reward that will come to the ones who faithfully endured this persecution. The Bible says they will be rewarded in a way that far surpasses their suffering.[17] Their suffering may have been great, but their reward will be much greater!

As one thinks about other sufferings intended for believers—self-life crucifixion, the care of the churches, the agony of soul that comes from longing to see people saved, the travail of intercessory prayers, the heartache incurred when building up others in the Lord—all this can be offset by one remarkable thought: The sum of all this suffering, if somehow the mind could comprehend it and objective accounting could quantify it, won't come anywhere near, in its intensity and duration, to the great reward God will one day give.

At the onset of such suffering, our hurt and perplexity were greater than any words could express. But language will fail us again one day when we will be overwhelmed by what God gives. The primary point being: The sufferings will pass; the rewards never will.

Not to be overlooked as valid candidates for God's rewards are people who stood steadfastly during difficult-but-not-dramatic circumstances. Their suffering may not have flamed high in a single episode. Their devotion may not have drawn the attention of the church. Yet, what they did counted for much. A.B. Simpson writes:

There is a reward for the soul winner. There is a reward for the Christian pastor and worker. But there is also a special reward for the man or the woman who has had no great service, and perhaps has won no single soul, but who has stood in the hard place, has kept sweet in the midst of wrong, and in the face of temptation, pure amid the allurements of the world, and simply withstood in the evil day, and having done all, stood at last approved.

On the field of Waterloo, there was a regiment which stood under fire through all that awful day and was not once suffered to charge upon the enemy. It held the key to the position, and again and again permission to advance was asked, the answer came back, "Stand firm." When they had nearly all fallen, the message came back for the last time from their commander, "You have saved the day," and the answer was returned, "You will find us all here." Sure enough they lay a heap of slain on that fatal, yet glorious hill. They had simply stood, and history has given them the reward of valor and the imperishable fame of having turned the tide of the greatest battle of the 19th century. So God is preparing crowns for quiet lives, for suffering women, for martyred children, for the victims of oppression and wrong, for silent sufferers and the lonely victors who just endured temptation.[18]

Just know the Lord is watching everything you and I do. He does this, not like some scowling supervisor anxious to find wrong, but more like a loving grandfather who is always looking for good. Because God is totally good, goodness attracts his attention. That's why he will discover everything that can be rewarded! Better still, the fact the reward comes from *him* will add great significance to its value. By contrast, the rewards that come from others may be tarnished by the way they were given. A.B. Simpson reminds us of a man who was rewarded for great victories on the battlefield—but how discrediting was this presentation!

> Napoleon, in his hour of pride, refused to receive a crown from human hands, but, taking in his own fingers the royal diadem, and placing it upon his head, he exclaimed, "These hands have won; these hands alone shall give the crown of the empire."[19]

How ugly this pride! Frank Sinatra's song, "My Way," may gain the world's applause, but it sounds cheap when compared to the rewarding God will give. These little men can strut on the world's stage and disdain others beneath them. But how different is this really from those less officious ceremonies sponsored by self and conducted by self, wherein the message declared in private chambers is just as arrogant?

Far superior criteria will credential heaven's rewards, inasmuch as the judging won't ever be skewed by bias, the presenting won't ever be marred by pride, and the reward itself will exponentially surpass in value what any man can give.

The fact God rewards—he whose wisdom excels all others and whose love plumbs depths deeper than human eyes can see—invests worth in that reward beyond any than that bestowed by some stooge in a cummerbund, or by some titled person whose place in history is brief and whose impact on history barely causes a ripple.

God stands *above* history—yours and mine and that of the nations—and hands out rewards that will never be duplicated one year later in some other ceremony. Unlike the world's rewards, the rewards of God are forever!

With an eye toward these coming rewards, we would do well to exhibit greater goodness *now*, so it is we who stand in that coveted place of honor, and it is our name pronounced by his sweet lips and resonant voice.

We don't want our names mentioned only in a genealogy that gives date of birth and date of death, as if nothing of significance happened in between. We want our lives to count! We want our lives to have significance and thus to be honored by God!

We know that leaders in today's educational circles scorn grades and any other attempt to distinguish the effort of one student from the effort of another student. In their world, prizes are handed out to all—and therefore mean nothing at all!

As mentioned previously in our study, there will be many ranks in heaven. You should know that the socialistic view of heaven comes from men, and not from God. Of greater value in his eyes is a reward that comes from an intense judging that discerns nuances of value which less scrutinizing eyes would have missed.

To have judged right—without minimizing through ignorance, without elevating through favoritism, and without curtailing deliberation through impulsivity—credentials these rewards in their authenticity, thus enhancing their value for all who receive them.

The very fact there will be rewards means that every moment in life counts. *All* will come before the Lord for inspection; *nothing* will be overlooked. Times for rest and recreation are valid, to be sure, and do contribute to the quality of our work. But good works there must be!

Emphasizing once again the unique contribution each believer is to make, G.D. Watson wrote:

> Each one of us is to believe that we have a place in the mind of God and in his creation, separate and distinct from every other creature ... He does not confound us with any of his other creatures, and has assigned to each of us a special mission and service which no one else can do in just the way God wants us to do it.[20]

Given the principle that whatever is worth doing is worth examining, you should know that at life's end, what you did, and the manner and motive you used in doing it, will be examined by the most brilliant mind, and by the most tender heart. Hence, truth and love will render a verdict no lie can discredit and no inferior motive can impugn.

Just now, it may be as John Henry Jowett described: "The applause of men may not gratify our ears. No worldly garland may be put upon our brow. We may climb unto no high place in the world's esteem. We may stumble along a painful way, we may be continually jostled and elbowed into the rear of the competing crowd ...."[21]

But good news! That is not the way the story will end! The Lord who sees all and sees right will have the last word, and one day—yes, one great and glorious day—that word will be sent forth in his eternal heaven to bless us immeasurably with unending joy.

Reflection Questions

1. Does this teaching about the rewards increase the good you want to do for the Lord? Please explain.

2. As you contemplate what your appearing before the Bema judgment seat of Christ would be like if it occurred today, what changes do you want to make?

3. Of the five services rewarded—ministry, financial giving, fellowship, persecution due to godliness, and standing strong for others in the midst of trial—which one is the Lord speaking to you about the most?

Chapter 20

The Reaping of the Rewards–Part II

John Kennedy, the charismatic President of the United States, is frequently given attribution for the remark, "life isn't fair." While it is doubtful that he was the first to say this, most people can easily resonate with this insight. Citing an instance when the wrong outcome occurred or when a grave injustice was administered, is fairly easy to do.

Yet, this notion that life is unfair is not as true as it may appear. While a given outcome may *seem* unfair if viewed from the more immediate and horizontal perspective; omitted from this assessment, perhaps, may be the fact God was administering a test, the design of which was to promote this person *after* the needed lesson was learned. Another possibility may be that God was dealing with a self-reliant person who needed failure in his life more than he needed success. Besides, the closed door—so disheartening and inexplicable at the time—often leads to another door opening, one that eventually affords a greater satisfaction.

Many factors may account for a disappointing outcome, including the failure to hear God, to obey God, or even the possibility that the desired success may have resulted in considerable harm to one's self or family.

What's needed in assessments like these is a little more humility. We must constantly keep in mind that *our* knowledge is limited, much like Job's was when he darkened God's counsel without knowledge (Job 38:2). To do as Job did, to cross the line of being perplexed by then being strident (if not bitter), means we're assuming much more than we should—at our own peril!

A good rule of thumb is this: No matter how great the disappointment, we should always take God's side—and never blame him! We exalt ourselves way too much if we think our small fragments of finite knowledge can successfully debate an all-knowing God. Whenever we make slanderous charges, such as—"God let me down," "God didn't come through for me"—we're only bringing eternal harm to ourselves. Moreover, this harm could become a satanic stronghold that will arrest spiritual growth for years.

A key factor that will prevent us from drawing wrong conclusions, and from harboring undue resentment toward the Lord, is an awareness that if we frame a picture the way Satan wants us to frame it, we'll draw the conclusions Satan wants us to draw.

In a given slice-of-time action, a terrible deed can be done—something outrageous, hideous, and too horrible to imagine! *But* God says the day is coming when he will take vengeance on perpetrators of evil. These evildoers may have thought they got away with it. The justice of God, however, dictates a major payback. And should grace not be grasped during intervening days, the vengeance that Scripture says belongs to the Lord will cause those he targets to shudder in wild fright when they see it coming, and suffer endless torment after it arrives. So factor that into your assessments of what is and isn't fair!

Just know that answers will be supplied on the other side of life. By then, any perception of injustice attributed to God will suddenly vanish. A.B. Simpson wrote:

> Some day he will sit down with us in that glorious home, and we shall have all the ages in which to understand the story of our lives. And he will read over again this old marked Bible with us; he will show us how he kept all these promises; he will explain to us the mysteries we could not understand; he will recall to our memory the things we have long forgotten; he will go over

again with us the book of life; he will recall all the finished story, and I am sure we will often cry; "Blessed Christ! You have been so true. You have been so good. Was there ever love like this?"[1]

In fact, on that day, this issue of fairness will be totally eclipsed by two realities: the extreme generosity of God toward the believer, and the terrible vengeance meted out to the unbeliever. Richard Baxter, the seventeenth-century Puritan, wrote:

> What an astonishing thought it will be, to think of the immeasurable differences between our deservings and receivings—between the state we should have been in, and the state we are in, to look down upon hell, and see the vast difference grace hath made between us and them—to see the inheritance there to which we were born, so different from that to which we were adopted.[2]

The Judge of all the earth *is* going to do right! And once his sentence is declared, his punishments administered, his rewards distributed, there won't be anyone, anywhere, who will still think that life was unfair! Indeed, if there's any wondering at all about fairness, it will be vocalized in the astonished gasps of those who can't believe that what they did merited such amazing rewards.

Generously Given

Pulling back the curtains of time in order to give us a glimpse into eternity future, the Bible describes how the Lord will distribute rewards. We are made to know, for example, that he will do this generously. Luke 6:38 says that, in response to our giving, "... it will be given to you: good measure, pressed down, shaken together, and running over ...."

Perhaps you've seen cereal boxes much larger than their contents. This bit of deceptive merchandizing is never characteristic of God, because what God gives will be "running over"—words that indicate an overflowing abundance! So there will be no one on that last day who will view his reward with disappointment.

To those who suffered for Jesus and suffered for the gospel's sake, there is the promise of a hundredfold reward (Mark 10:29, 30). This hundredfold reward promised by Mark, as well as the "good measure, pressed down, shaken together, running over" reward promised by Luke, are actually earmarked for the here-and-now. Nevertheless, these verses do say something about the Lord's heart and, correspondingly, about the extent of our final reward. He certainly won't give less in heaven than he gave on earth!

Instead of handing out cheap mementos on that day, and instead of beginning his speech with the acknowledgment that what he is about to give is but a token of his gratitude, we can forget the token stuff! When God gives, he will do so lavishly—and generously! In a manner worthy of his name!

While growing up, my two brothers and I received Christmas gifts from my grandmother on my mother's side, whom we called Nana. Although Nana was a fairly well-to-do woman, one would have never known that by the gifts she gave. She must have gone to a dollar store during an after-Christmas sale to buy what she bought. Consequently, after many years of receiving cheap gifts, we put Nana's gifts back under the tree as soon as we saw her name on the tag. And there those gifts would remain, until, many days later, when we finally had to open them so we could say in our letter to her what we were supposedly thankful for.

Nothing like this will ever happen in heaven! Instead of the obligatory watch and some yawner of a speech, God will reward in an extravagant way.

Astonishingly Acknowledged

When the Lord distributes his rewards, he will also do so in an astonishingly kind way. I Corinthians 4:5 declares that the Lord "... will both bring to light the hidden things of darkness and reveal the counsels of the hearts." What does that sound like to you? To me, it sounds like lower-the-boom time! Yep, better watch it—all those deeds no one else saw, and all those thoughts no one else knew, are now going to get exposed! But would God really do that? He that washed all these sins away with his blood and promised to remember them no more—will he choose at this time to expose his bride by broadcasting her secret sins far and wide?[3]

This verse sets a scenario like that aside by saying, "Then each man's praise will come from God." Whoa! This outcome isn't at all what we suspected! Instead of a gaze resulting in judgment, there will be praise resulting in rewards. A. B. Simpson declared, "All that can be recognized he will cherish, and all that he can forget, he will love to leave in oblivion."[4]

What God will really be revealing on that day are not the sins we feel ashamed of (since those have been blotted out, to be remembered no more). Instead, he will reveal things no one ever knew—those unspoken desires, those noble aspirations, those heartfelt longings for God, those whispered praises and closet prayers. What we forgot, and perhaps never saw come to pass, will be acknowledged by the Lord with expanded commentary and great celebration.

Imagine Jesus praising *you*? Zephaniah speaks of him rejoicing over us with gladness and singing (Zephaniah 3:17). Oh, to be tenderly held by the Lord as he sings a love song to us! I'm telling you—in the whole wide expanse of God's universe—there's no thrill that will even begin to compare with the thrill of receiving effusive praise from God! We will never be the same after this!

And what makes this scene all the more blessed is the fact this will be an individual and not a collective experience. It won't be the whole church courted by our God. It will be you, it will be me, upon whom his adoring gaze will be fixed and to whom his love songs will be offered.

Accurately Assessed

Generously, astonishingly, and now in the third place Scripture informs us the Lord will reward fairly. Matthew 16:27 says he will reward according to our works.[5] I Corinthians 3:8 says he will reward according to our labor.[6] In his book, *God's Eagles*, G.D. Watson said that "the reward will correspond exactly to the action, and also to the magnitude or the weight of the action, and also to the amount of divine love, or of sacrifice, or of faith, or of persecution that has been put into the action ...."[7]

Illustrating the accuracy of God's assessment, G.D. Watson wrote:

> The government in Washington has a pair of scales so delicate that you can put a piece of thin paper on the scales and weigh it, and then write with a lead pencil on that same paper and weigh it again, and the scales will reveal not only the weight of the paper but also the weight of the amount of lead that was put on the paper from the pencil. This is a faint illustration of the way in which God will manifest in the judgment time the character and color and weight and dimension of all the actions and words, and even the thoughts of his people.[8]

The words "according to," frequently asserted when mentioning the rewards, convey proportion, exactness, precision.[9] This quite rightly assumes that the Lord sees all. And that's important; because, as G.D. Watson noted, "The greatest part of a good work is always out of sight, where the soul is working with God in holy prayer and purpose."[10]

Often, it is the flamboyant and sensational which gain the world's attention, but the omniscient eye of the Lord will examine every aspect of even the most modest work of the least known saint. For this reason, Paul Billheimer declared:

> In heaven's "book" the nameless saint in the most remote and secluded spot, completely lost to view, and overshadowed in the battle, is just as important, and if he is faithful, will receive just as great a reward, as the most heralded and gifted leader.[11]

The exactness of this assessment doesn't mean there will be a *quid pro quo* arrangement, an even trade out for reciprocal good; because, while the proportion intended takes into account the quantity and quality of the works being rewarded, it also takes into account the greatness of God's love and the riches of his glory.

The proportion indicated in these verses reflects the relation between works honored and the heart of the one who does the honoring. Every work will bring about a love-motivated reward by an exceedingly rich God! In some way, known only to God, there will be exactness in these rewards corresponding to the criteria used. However, notions of reciprocity and equality are clearly absent from the text. This is because the rewards given will far surpass the works honored. Accordingly, G.D. Watson declared, "The saints will be astonished at the largeness of their rewards."[12]

When men bestow their rewards, dubious criteria are often employed, and contaminated thinking is frequently used. J.C. Ryle pointed out just how much at variance the world's assessment can be when compared with God's assessment:

> ... man knows very little what is great and what is small in God's sight. The history of Nimrod "the mighty hunter" is dispatched in three verses of Genesis, and the history of a Syrian dwelling in tents, called Abraham, fills up no less than fourteen chapters.[13]

This fact shouldn't surprise us, because doesn't the Bible say that the last will be first and the first will be last? Those who received accolades on earth (and perhaps even in the church) may not be as highly esteemed as some nameless, faceless person who served the Lord out of the world's spotlight—but not out of the Lord's fixed and delighted view! That dear woman who gave herself to the hard work of intercessory prayer, a ministry few enter into and even fewer appreciate, may, in the final reckoning, be accorded a place of honor far ahead of some megachurch pastor or globe-trotting evangelist.

Remember, God said his ways are not our ways and his thoughts are not our thoughts. His assessment may be quite different from ours! J.C. Ryle credentialed this truth by an appeal to history.

Baxter, the famous clergyman, was persecuted with savage hostility, and condemned to a long imprisonment by a most unjust judgment. Jeffreys, the Chief Justice who sentenced him, was a man of shameful character without either morality or religion. Baxter was sent to jail and Jeffreys was loaded with honors. Yet who can doubt which was the good man of the two, the Chief Justice Jeffreys or the author of the Christ honoring book, *Saint's Everlasting Rest*?[14]

He whose eyes are too pure to look upon evil, and too sure to overlook our works of righteousness, will surely get it right on that last day.

At any given moment, the extent of one's labor may seem smaller than it really is. Writers such as Blaise Pascal and Oswald Chambers, for example, had their greatest books published after their death. At the time they departed this world, the extent of their labor wasn't known. Well, maybe not by the world it wasn't, but God knew!

The assessments people give, even in the church, may also be far from the truth. One pastor found himself deeply humiliated by a criticizing elder who said—at the communion table, no less—"Only one addition to the church, and he is only a boy." Such meager results reflected poorly on the pastor, perhaps tempting him to doubt his usefulness in God's service. So that evening the pastor called his church to a revival, but no one showed interest; only the little boy came forward to talk to the pastor.

Time passed, the struggle continued, but the story didn't end. It was A.B. Simpson who updated a later chapter in this story.

... one day a distinguished and venerable missionary was being talked about all through the land. He was preaching in the most influential pulpits. He was speaking in the great assemblies. He was dining at the tables of nobles and princes. He was consulting with the British potentate. He had been instrumental in adding half a continent to the British empire, and opening up South Africa to civilization and the gospel. It was Robert Moffat, the prince of missionaries. Before that season was over he had hastened to the Scottish parish and clasped the hand of the minister who had wept one day because of the fact that there was just one member and he was only a boy.[15]

Richard Greenham was one of the most skilled and dedicated pastors the church ever produced. From 1570-1590, he ministered in a small village not far from Cambridge, England. He preached four times a week at daybreak, studied all morning, then went to the fields in the afternoons to minister to his people while they farmed their land. His reputation as a counselor spread throughout the region. People traveled long distances to receive the help he gave. In summarizing this man's ministry, J.I. Packer wrote:

> Yet, for all his godliness, insight, evangelical message and hard work, his ministry was virtually fruitless ... In rural England, in Greenham's day, there was much fallow ground to be broken up; it was a time for sowing, but the reaping was still in the future.[16]

Of course, God knew that! And God also saw every faithful effort this man made! In reality, the lack of results tested this pastor's faith; it did not reflect it. That one family added to the church during Richard's Greenham's ministry will hardly be the sole basis for this man's reward. God's assessment will be far more insightful, and considerably more accurate.

A.B. Simpson recounted another incident that illustrates this principle. He tells of a splendid temple that was built in Constantinople by the Emperor Theodosius.

> Millions of dollars and years of skill and toil were spent upon that cherished enterprise until at last it was ready for dedication. The architect had emblazoned upon its front the inscription, "The

church Theodosius built for God," but when the curtain was removed that covered the facade, to the astonishment of the Emperor, the architect and the crowd of attendant princes and generals, the inscription read, "This church the widow Eudoxia built for God." The ceremonies were instantly stopped and search was made for the presuming widow, but it was days before she could be found, and then it was discovered that she was a poor widow living far out in the suburbs who had done nothing for that splendid sanctuary but simply pull up the long grass from the roadside and spread it over the rough track to keep the beautiful stones as they were drawn to the temple from being scratched and effaced by the rocky road. The Emperor and his advisors, when they found out all about her, wisely concluded that she had not intruded, but that perhaps some angel unseen had changed that record in the night and put upon the front of the temple a little example of the records God is keeping in the books of eternity ....[17]

He who sees all and has the wisdom to assess accurately will render verdicts on that day of days that will astonish many.

Justly Judged

Another characteristic of the Lord's rewarding is the fact he will be just in the judgment rendered. I Corinthians 15:58 says our labor is not in vain in the Lord. Galatians 6:9 declares we will reap if we faint not. Hebrews 6:10 assures us: "For God is not unjust to forget your work and labor of love which you have shown toward his name ...."

A.W. Pink pointed out that the word 'labor' is a stronger word than 'work,' "signifying effort to the point of fatigue."[18] Indeed, God will never overlook the love that labors like that!

In this world, the what-have-you-done-for-me-lately rationale often prevails. In sports, for example, a coach may have won the division title two years ago, but if his team hasn't done as well since, he may be vilified in the press and fired by the owner. But God isn't like that! What you have done will never be forgotten, and will never go unrewarded.

Pete Rose, an outfielder for the Cincinnati Reds, is the all-time major league leader in total number of base hits. And yet this man isn't in Baseball's Hall of Fame. What keeps him out of Cooperstown is his gambling after his playing days were over. Once this gambling came to light, Rose was banned from baseball—a decision that was entirely just. Of dubious justice, though, is the fact the new commissioner of baseball, in cahoots with Cooperstown, then saw to it that a moral clause was adopted that effectively kept Rose out of the Hall of Fame. Is this fair? Shouldn't a ballplayer be rewarded by what he achieved on the field without the aid of drugs?

In contrast to this outcome, Hebrews 6:10 used the word "unjust" to say that God won't let our accomplishments go unrewarded. There will be no backroom deals, no insertion of new after-the-fact criterion. Instead, because justice is at stake here, God will faithfully reward all who should be rewarded.

Publicly Proclaimed

The Bible also tells us that God will reward us publicly. Matthew 6:6 says the Father, who sees in secret, will reward openly. So instead of some personal, informal, off-to-the-side rewarding, God will stage a ceremony before billions of people—and who knows how many angels? To that one who labored in some obscure part of the world, and to that mother who served the Lord in her quiet, faithful way, God will give the attention they never sought, but, once given, they will never forget.

Years ago, there was a television program entitled, "This is Your Life." Ralph Edwards, the producer and emcee of this show, would surprise the person to be honored by contriving circumstances that would bring him or her to Los Angeles. Then, at precisely the planned moment—in a restaurant, or perhaps on the street—Ralph Edwards would thrust a microphone forward and announce that a vast television audience is watching. "For this"—and then he would say the person's name with considerable drama—"is your life!" Hurriedly, the honoree would then be ushered into the studio where a standing ovation awaited, as television cameras broadcast this event to the entire nation.

As you might expect, some well-known person, usually a celebrity, was the honoree. But this wasn't always the case. When I was a boy living in Hawaii, a man who lived a few doors away from me, a Navy doctor, was flown to California to be honored on this show. And what a thrill that must have been!

But what this good doctor experienced that night won't even begin to compare with the thrill that you will experience when God honors you in heaven. Yes, one far greater than Ralph Edwards will summon you front and center, and then will reveal to all the inhabitants of heaven the splendid qualities of your life.

Excitedly Extended

As we've previously mentioned, the giving of these rewards will be done excitedly. Several scriptures have the Lord declaring that when he comes he will bring the rewards with him (Isaiah 40:10; 62:11; Revelation 22:12). Like a parent who wants to bless his child at Christmas, God can hardly wait to give you what he knows will thrill you!

By contrast, have you seen school administrators plod through a graduation ceremony, calling out names with scarcely a smile on their faces? Well, nothing as perfunctory as that will happen in heaven! The only one more excited than you on that day will be the Lord himself!

God is a just God, fully aware that if the picture were to freeze at any given moment, life would seem unfair. It is in this regard that the story is told of an elderly missionary couple forced to return to the states due to ill health. As it turned out, they were on the same ship with President Theodore Roosevelt who was returning from one of his famous game-hunting expeditions in Africa.

As the ship pulled into dock, the bands played and the crowds cheered when their President disembarked from the ship. Meanwhile, this missionary couple got off the ship, unheralded and unnoticed, and found a cheap flat on the east side of the city where they would retire. Apparently, *their* arrival home, after years of service, meant nothing.

That night, the missionary husband said to his wife, "It's not fair! When the President comes home from a pleasure trip, everyone is there to cheer him. But when we come home after forty years of missionary service, no one is there to welcome us."

Not knowing how to answer her husband, the sweet little missionary wife said, "I know you feel hurt. Why don't you turn this over to the Lord in prayer?"

Fine! Her husband decided to do just that! Retreating to his bedroom to pray, he laid it all out before the Lord—the unfairness of a cheering crowd for a returning President after two weeks of fun, but nothing for him and his wife when they arrived home after forty years of service. To this complaint, this great grievance, the Lord spoke but five words that completely changed this man's outlook. The five words from the Lord were these—"But you're not home yet."

Isn't that good? There's going to be a rewarding far grander than what the President received that day! For instead of curious spectators and paid staff, God himself will be waiting at the dock! And accompanying him will be all the angels and citizens of heaven! So when you arrive home, dear and faithful Christian, the celebration that will greet you, and the rewards that will be given to you, will be everything you could have ever hoped for—and more!

A.B. Simpson assured us, "God's bonds are long time ones, and they all accumulate compound interest, and when the day of maturity comes we shall weep with wonder to see the meaning of his hundredfold."[19]

Just a glimpse of God's rewards will excite our motivation to serve him, and will subsequently steady us during those hard times encountered while we do serve him. The Lord is willing to grace our goodness as we offer it, and to reward us later in ways that are exceedingly, abundantly, more than we could ever ask or think. Far more, in fact, than what we thought we should receive when we were holding up our ill-conceived fairness standard.

Fair? Strictly speaking, not really; because what we will receive is more than fair.

Reflection Questions

1. Of the six ways described in this chapter about how the rewards will be given, which one appealed the most to you?

2. In what way has the message "it isn't fair" impacted you in the past? And how has this chapter helped you respond to that message?

Chapter 21

Losing the Rewards

Nobody wants to be a loser. Merging back into the crowd as an "also ran"—a participant without distinction, having a number but not a name—is hardly a welcomed experience. To train and try, only to come up short can be very disheartening. Sure, the hurt feelings will go away, but the memory of it may not.

Even more disappointing than slinking into the shadows is to win in the eyes of the world, only to find out that what you won doesn't mean very much. There have been those who stood on the world's stage, received the world's accolades, and yet, when they made their exit, they did so with disillusionment. The satisfaction they thought they would get never came.

Napoleon, for example, became a world conqueror, a man of power and international fame. But his life came to a close with the lament, "This is my burnt-out hour."[1] There had been a brief burst of glory, but then ... the dust of death!

After surveying all the heaped-up prizes the world had showered on him, Goethe said, "My experience has been nothing but pain and burden, the perpetual rolling of a rock that must be raised up again forever." Apparently, his was the tired tedium of a life without meaning!

Byron, the British poet, seemed to seize life with aggression, demanding its jewels of happiness. So surely he won, you say?[2] Well, Byron himself said this:

My days are in the yellow leaf;
The flowers and fruits of love are gone;
The worm, the canker and the grief
Are mine alone.

But it wasn't supposed to be like that! Such sacrifice and genius! All that discipline and effort! Had not all these men made their mark on the world—but for what?

Henry Drummond answered this question when presenting the claims of Christ to college students. Drummond declared, "I cannot guarantee that the stars will shine brighter when you leave this hall tonight, or that when you wake tomorrow a new world will open before you. But I do guarantee that Christ will keep that which you have committed to him."[3] And not only keep it, he will also richly reward it! So, contrary to what others have experienced, God's promise of satisfaction is not an illusion!

"All your life," C.S. Lewis wrote, "an unattainable ecstasy has hovered just above the grasp of your consciousness." But for what purpose? To tease you? To see it all vanish like bubbles? No, according to Lewis one of two outcomes will occur. Either "you will awake to find, beyond all hope, that you have attained it, or else that it was within your reach and you have lost it forever."[4]

Posited here are two destinies, and both are eternal. To gain the destiny you want, you must live your life for the Lord, running the race *he* set before you, accomplishing the work *he* planned for you to do!

The Theme of Loss in Scripture

John Milton wrote the classic, *Paradise Lost*. The theme of this classic—irretrievable loss: perplexing in its onset, tragic in its consequences—is interwoven throughout Scripture. In Genesis, for example, we see Adam and Eve losing the ideal life God had planned for them. But even before this loss in the garden, there was a far more incomprehensible loss when Lucifer lost a perfect life in heaven!

Can you imagine a magnificent angel becoming a hideous devil, and other angels becoming demons, and the bliss of heaven being exchanged for the torments of hell? All these losses are too great for language to describe, or for the human mind to fathom.

Remember Esau? He ranks near the top of the Bible's losers list! To be the recipient of immense favor, the inheritor of enormous blessing, only to give it all up—shocks the sensibilities of a thinking man! One's brain would have to be fried or scrambled to forfeit one's birthright for a dish of stew! How could he do something like this?

In his book, *The Holy War*, John Bunyan explained precisely how it could happen when he has Diablolus (representing you know who) giving this pernicious piece of advice about the breastplate of iron. Said Diablolus about this part of armor, "It is a hard heart! Keep it on and mercy won't win you, and judgment won't scare you." Not even the Great White Throne judgment will scare, if your rebellion lasts that long, nor the Bema judgment, if you're still resisting the one you call Lord.

And, by the way, there's no denying the fact that the people of God can resist God. Clear evidence of this was on display while the children of Israel were on their way to the Promised Land. There were ten tests en route to this destination. And did you know that God's people failed every one of them?

The exorbitant price for this hardness of heart is now well-known—*forty additional years stuck in the wilderness*! What is not as well-known, though, is what happened to the people of God later. Under Joshua, a new generation finally made it into the Promised Land. But then—you guessed it—*they lost the Promised Land*! And the price for *that* loss was ten times as much—more than four hundred years of misery!

So, given this penchant for losing what's valuable, we shouldn't be surprised when Scripture warns of another loss that could occur. In John's second epistle, verse 8, God's people are warned to watch diligently, lest they forfeit their reward. In Revelation 3:11 we find Jesus telling his church to hold tightly what they have earned, making sure no one takes their crown.

From prehistory to post-history, then, we see this theme of lamentable loss to be a stark reality and not just a potential possibility. Losing heaven, losing Eden, losing the birthright, losing the Promised Land, and one day losing the rewards of heaven—not a commendable history! Nor a desirable prophecy! For who wants to be a loser?

I'll tell you who wants you to be a loser: According to Scripture, a sinister and supernatural force will vigorously challenge every pursuit of God's reward. For if by deceit or defeat Satan can get you to miss out on these rewards, that's exactly what he wants to do. His mindset being: If he can't keep you out of heaven, at least he wants to deprive you of heaven's greater blessings.

Some people say, "Well, as long as I get into heaven, that's all that matters." But that's not all that matters! God wouldn't have said what he said, and Satan wouldn't be doing what he is doing, if these rewards didn't matter. So instead of minimizing these rewards, we need to think about them, and do so in a very serious way.

How Rewards Are Lost

To that end—purposing never to become victims, self-inflicted or Satan-inspired—it is important to examine some of the ways this grand larceny (affecting heaven but transacting on earth) can occur. Woodrow Kroll explains:

> Losing rewards is possible in two ways. We may lose them by default by not seizing the opportunities that are presented to us. But we may also lose rewards by defect, by living our lives in such a way that we do not meet the criteria to qualify for rewards.[5]

Extending this thought while yet narrowing it, G.D. Watson wrote, "Some who desire to be saints of the larger magnitudes, when the testing adequate to those magnitudes are brought to bear upon them, fail, and dwindle down to lesser ranks."[6] Thus, they lose the reward they desired because they failed the test they needed to pass.

It really shouldn't surprise us that Satan is highly intrigued by any plot to steal someone's rewards. After all, Jesus did call him a thief (John 10:10)! So apparently, ever determined to deprive, the devil will plot differing schemes, each designed to keep us from receiving God's rewards.

Now among these schemes is a rerouting of lives from the direction the Lord wanted them to take. Reflecting on this particular practice, A.B. Simpson observed:

> The failure of any man or any people cannot hinder the fulfillment of any of God's purposes. He has other instruments ready; and it is an awful thing when any man, or any church or race are excused by the Lord, or when they let another take their crown.[7]

Colossians 2:18 identified another way rewards can be lost, saying, "... let no one cheat you of your reward." This statement, made while discussing the intrusions of legalism, pinpointed the downside of following spurious standards having to do with food, drink, festivals, and sabbaths (Colossians 2:16). The real danger in these standards is a shift from the Lord's saving work toward one's ability to be good. For under this system of righteousness, one's right standing before God is based not on what Jesus did on our behalf, but on what the believer does to comply with some man-made list. Such a practice generates pride—way too much pride, since as G.D. Watson put it, "We are co-laborers with Christ, but not co-saviors with him."[8]

The legalism of modern times differs in its particulars from the one urged by the Judaizers. The real danger in man-made codes for living is the unwarranted assumption that these codes represent God's thinking, and that they are an adequate summary of Scripture. Who thinks up this stuff? The prideful Pharisee who lives within!

To get suckered into the ways of legalism is to walk a dead-end road, for which there will be no rewards. James S. Stewart said that legalism is "ever seeking to increase its claim upon God by multiplying the regulations and ordinances it proposes to obey."[9] Uncovering the hidden motivation of legalism, Stewart said that "the identification of religion with respectability ... has been a successful method of eluding the cross."[10]

Galatians 1:6 calls this encroachment of legalism "another gospel"—meaning it is no gospel at all! The next verse in this passage speaks even more strongly, calling such a perspective a perversion. In fact, Romans 7:5 goes so far as to say that this flesh-engendered righteousness produces nothing but dead fruit—and what could be worse than a bunch of rotten, smelly, dead fruit?

Wanting us to avoid this trap, Galatians 5:1 says we're to stand fast in the liberty God gave us and not get entangled in a yoke of bondage. But if we do get entangled, thinking we can earn God's eternal favor by our earthly works, the warning of the next verse must be taken to heart: *Christ will not profit us*—not in this life, and not when it comes to bestowing his rewards.

In Mark 9:41 Jesus identified another factor for reward-forfeiture when he said that the one who gave the cup of water in his name would not lose his reward. This implies the cup of water given *without* the name of Jesus will be without reward. Indeed, any act of mercy—however needed and however sacrificially and generously supplied—will not be deemed good in the eyes of God if God himself was effectively left out of this transaction.

While this fact certainly doesn't encourage buttonholing a recipient by "chapter and versing" him or her incessantly, it does mean, minimally, speaking about Jesus to the one you're helping. And that's because "do-goodism" without Jesus disqualifies a work from reward consideration.

To the church at Philadelphia Jesus said, "Behold, I am coming quickly! Hold fast what you have, that no one may take your crown" (Revelation 3:11). You will notice that this particular encouragement to persevere is accompanied by an implied warning that one may lose his or her reward. But how might this occur?

The problem of faithfulness without faith is one way this could occur. People trying to do the right thing in the wrong way will produce nothing worthy of a reward. For without faith, the Bible says, it is impossible to please God (Hebrews 11:6). The governing principle being: To crank out our service *for* God with no real dependence *upon* God will result in a work that can't be rewarded *by* God.

G.D. Watson said, "... with all our learning and skill and experience, we are never to bank on it, never draw a check on it for success ...."[11] For always it is the Spirit of God who must energize our ministry. Yet, despite the importance of the Spirit, Tozer was compelled to write:

> In most Christian churches the Spirit is quite entirely overlooked. Whether he is present or absent makes no real difference to anyone. Brief reference is made to him in the Doxology and the Benediction. Further than that he might as well not exist.[12]

To those parading their good works before others, wanting *their* approval and desiring *their* admiration, Jesus said: "Take heed that you do not do your charitable deeds before men, to be seen by them. Otherwise you have no reward from your Father in heaven" (Matthew 6:1). Given this premise, that deeds done with a wrong motive will forfeit God's reward, it is almost as though God were saying, "You wanted others to see what a good deed you were doing? All right, they saw it—and that's going to be the extent of your reward."

No one wants to stand around God's bonfire seeing his or her works going up in smoke. To avoid this scene, the Lord informed his church of criteria for the rewards, and corresponding criteria that will cause a believer to lose out. This kind of awareness will enable us to do the needed inspecting now, to judge as Jesus will one day judge, so there won't be this terrible loss at the end.

Ways Reward Loss Transacts

Though the loss of rewards is real, we must be careful not to exaggerate it. Some commentators envision a believer's wrongdoing being assessed component by component with the Lord's furrowed eyebrows and frowns frequently on display. But what's worthy in our work can be separated from what isn't worthy without any prolonged prosecutorial rehashing. That God is going to provide extensive commentary about every deed done, every thought welcomed, every motivation pursued, and every opportunity missed, has speculation for its source more than Scripture.

Yes, the Bible speaks of fire, but this is a revealing fire, not a punishing fire.[13] And who knows? In the bright light of *this* fire, the granting or losing of rewards could be revealed instantly.[14] That outcome isn't certain, but what is certain is that these rewards will be consistent with covenant promises. And that includes the obliteration of forgiven sin.

Will there be any shame? The Bible seems to indicate there will be (I John 2:28), prompting this remark from the editorial writer and pastor, A. W. Tozer:

> We'll hardly get our feet out of time and into eternity that we'll bow our heads in shame and humiliation. We'll gaze on eternity and say, "Look at all the riches there were in Jesus Christ and I've come to the judgment seat almost a pauper."[15]

Most likely, such insight won't be imposed upon us through lengthy discovery and fiery prosecution, but instead will become evident in a shorter, if not almost sudden awareness.

Attempting to provide a balanced perspective on this issue, Joseph Dillow offered this comment in his book, *The Reign of the Servant Kings*: "To overdo the sorrow aspect of the judgment seat of Christ is to make heaven into hell. To underdo the sorrow aspect is to make faithfulness inconsequential."[16]

A serious regard for God's rewards is further enhanced by understanding the criteria for obtaining them. The Bible refers to six kinds of good works—three which will not be burned in judgment—gold, silver, precious stones; and three that will—wood, hay, and stubble (I Corinthians 3:12, 13). As we examine each category, we recognize greater-to-lesser valuations in each. For example, gold has more value than silver, and wood has more value than stubble. These differences certainly suggest gradations of rewards. When the rewards are finally given, we will discover that each worthy work was honored, though the rewards for each were not be the same.[17]

Of the six types of works listed, the type most tragic in its rejection is wood. There's not much you can do with hay (except feed horses), and even less that you can do with stubble. But with wood, houses are built, bridges are constructed, many industries are sustained. Indeed, it is precisely because wood is so useful that it will come as a shock to see it rejected. Writing with wisdom on this topic, Hannah Whitall Smith said, "We cannot hope, when that day comes, to conceal our wood, hay, and stubble, however successfully we may have done so beforehand."[18] At the very last we will see the very least—rejected!

How important it is that we should get clear on God's criteria for good works now, well before the time of judgment and possible loss. A.B. Simpson added, "... what a bitter disappointment it will be to look back from the light of eternity and realize how very much God had intended for us, and that it is lost forever."[19]

The Alternative to Losing

But how sweet the contemplation of the alternative when one knows that a great reward is coming! If a believer refuses to coast, refuses to compromise, refuses to get entangled with the affairs of this life but lives his life for the Lord instead, that believer will leave this world with an uncommon anticipation of what awaits on the other side.

By contrast, Bruce Wideman asked:

> Did you ever hear of an atheist saying at the hour of his death: "How glad I am that I can face death as an unbeliever. My soul is quietly resting upon my unbelieving views. All is light. All is joy"?
>
> You have never heard such a testimony from the lips of a dying unbeliever and you never will. Dark, dreary, and hopeless is the way of unbelief.[20]

But for that one who knows Jesus is his Lord, heaven is his home, and the rewards are coming soon, it is indescribably different!

What the rewarding will finally reveal is how the harder way, the way of obedience, the way of goodness in the midst of evil, was in fact the pathway to colossal, stupendous blessings! It's just as Scripture said: The sufferings the faithful endure won't even begin to compare with the glory that will be revealed! According to Scripture, even the smallest sacrifice will receive a great reward.

Amplifying this principle seen many times in Scripture, A.B. Simpson tells the story of a world ruler who, through his actions, illustrated this point.

> It is said that the Great Ivan of Russia used to go amongst his people in disguise and test them. One night he went through the suburbs of his capital and knocked at many lowly cabins as a poor, wandering tramp, asking for a night's lodging and a crust of bread. He was refused from door to door, until at last he came to a humble cabin where a poor man was attending his wife and newborn babe. He opened the door at the knock of the wanderer, kindly invited him in, treated with courtesy and attention, gave him a crude bed and a humble supper and bade him goodnight with great kindness. The emperor lay, sleeping little and thinking much, and in the morning he took his leave amid many thanks.
>
> Late in the afternoon the royal chariot drove to the door and halted. The poor man fled to the gate in great alarm, prostrated himself at the feet of the emperor and asked him if he had caused any crime to cause his displeasure. The emperor assured him that it was all right, and then added, "I have simply come to thank you for your kindness to your emperor last night. He came in the disguise of a beggar to test your love, and now he comes as your sovereign to reward your loyalty. This bag of gold is for your newborn child. As he grows up I will adopt him as my child and give him a place of high and honorable service in

the empire, and if I can be of any service to you and yours, command your emperor."[21]

Simple service to God, seemingly unnoticed at the time it was rendered, will be highly rewarded one day, far beyond any expectation! This is why, if one were to look at the question—to obey or not to obey?—from a strictly selfish point of view, the smartest thing anyone can do is to bend the knee, humble the heart, and ask the same question the trembling and astonished Saul asked that day on the Damascus Road, "Lord, what do you want me to do?"

Failing to ask this question, many Christians today settle for too little, as if God's extravagant rewards weren't understood. In his book, *The Weight of Glory*, C.S. Lewis addressed this sad point with vivid candor.

> Indeed, if we consider the unblushing promises of reward and the staggering nature of the rewards promised in the Gospels, it would seem that our Lord finds our desires, not too strong, but too weak. We are half-hearted creatures, fooling about with drink and sex and ambition when infinite joy is offered us, like an ignorant child who wants to go on making mud pies in a slum because he cannot imagine what is meant by the offer of a holiday at the sea. We are far too easily pleased.[22]

Perhaps our "mud pie" pursuits would end, and perhaps we would wash hands, face, and eyes, if we could see what the Lord is offering us. To that end, A.B. Simpson spoke these words of challenge:

> May God arouse us from lethargy, apathy and trifling. We have a glorious crown to win. We have a living age in which to win it. We have one short life to accomplish. We have the mighty Holy Spirit to help us win the conflict and gain the prize. Let us eagerly desire the best gifts, and let all our being be invested in the one stupendous

opportunity of a life for God, for humanity and for an eternal prize.[23]

There is so much to gain and so much to lose. Oh, what a day! Can you see it in your mind's eye? With excitement in the air, the heavenly-throng now assembles. Overwhelmed with anticipation, they keep saying to themselves, "Today is the day! The day when the great Giver—he who is not unjust to forget our labors of love (Hebrews 6:10)—is going to give his rewards!"

Having experienced such anticipated excitement in his own soul, Edward Payson, that mighty prayer warrior of the nineteenth century, spoke these words on his deathbed, "If men only knew the honor and glory that awaited them in Christ, they would go about the streets crying out, 'I'm a Christian! I'm a Christian! that men would rejoice with them in the blessedness of which they were soon to partake.'"[24]

As you begin to imagine this rewards scene and put yourself in it, what do you suppose you would be thinking as you stand in that assembly? Would you be wondering *if* you're going to be rewarded? And would you wish you had thought about these rewards while you were on earth? Sensing that something awesome is about to occur, would you be excited ... hopeful ... expectant ... a little afraid?

Just know that the day we've been trying to imagine *is* coming. And that is why, in anticipation of that day, you and I need to make some changes. To pump more reality into this perspective, let me now ask you: What if God were to tell you that for one week he was going to watch your life with intense scrutiny and, based on how you lived for him during that week your eternal reward would be determined. How would you respond?

Chances are, you'd start reading your Bible as if it were a treasure map, and you'd start praying to the Lord as if he were your long, lost friend! You might even schedule a meeting with your pastor to find out what you could do for the church; after which, you would check out the poor side of town to see what needs you could meet there. Then you'd go door to door in your neighborhood to witness to anyone not yet saved. And, yes, the check you'd put in the offering basket on Sunday would be the most generous check you had ever given!

In one sense, this flurry of activity would make a lot of sense, given the enormous appeal of God's reward. But what often seems overlooked is the fact God is intensely inspecting our labor for him every day! And overlooked, too, is that our time to serve the Lord, while certainly longer than a week, is actually very short when compared with eons of eternity.

So why are we casual about the work we undertake in his name? Addressing this question, Richard Baxter said it well: If we loiter when we should labor, we'll lose our reward.[25] The great Reformer Martin Luther used to say, "While the devil tempts men, it is the idle man who tempts the devil." So are we going to loiter when we should labor?

Further challenging Christians along these lines, F. B. Meyer said, "There is plenty to do—evil to put down, good to build up; doubters to be directed; prodigals to be won back; sinners to be sought."[26] The assignment is big, the resources are great—*but* the time is short.

Being Ever Mindful of the Rewards

If we want to come to the end of our lives with satisfaction and not regret, this agenda of being and doing good should be constantly on our minds.

Daniel Webster, the Secretary of State under President Millard Fillmore, was eating dinner with a number of prominent people in the Astor Hotel one night when someone asked him, what was the most profound thought he had ever had? In reply, he said that the most profound thought he ever had—indeed, the one that had influenced his life more than any other—was the fact that one day he was going to have to appear before God to give an account of his life.

Not too many people think about standing before the Judge of the universe one day. We think about heaven's homecoming and that blessed moment we first see Jesus. We think about our subsequent introduction to the angels and that emotional reunion with our family and friends. We also think about our glorified state and the perfections of our body. But as for the Bema judgment seat (where our works will be examined to see what kind and how many there were), we scarcely give this a thought.

Helping us anticipate this appearance before the Judge of all the earth, Tozer exclaimed that "all your marked Bibles, all your jolly, joke-telling banqueting Christian friends"[27] will mean nothing to you in that hour when you stand before the Ineffable. The scene will be awesome! The outcome declared that day will affect your eternal future!

What perhaps contributes most to this lack of focus on the rewards is all this talk about grace. To the undiscerning and the self-absorbed, an overload on grace can take the air out of our tires when it comes to motivating good works. With some brevity, then, let's straighten this theology out.

While our admission into heaven is based on grace, the granting and receiving of the rewards is based on something else—works! This may be a somewhat overdrawn distinction, in that saving grace will be accompanied by works, and our rewarded works will be energized by grace. Nevertheless, this is still an appreciable distinction, because what saves us is grace and not the works that follow; and what gets rewarded are the approved works and not the grace that made it possible.

As we focus, then, on the works side of this equation, we are sobered by the account we must give for all our time on earth. Having many decades by our name does present a challenge! Let's see: We ate all our meals on time, we did a pretty good job of sleeping, we seemed to watch all the TV shows we liked, shopped at all the stores we liked, made time for many other recreational pursuits. But were we as routine in our service to God?

F.B. Meyer observed, "Some live for many years but at the end have little or nothing to show for them. Take out the wasted hours, hours of drowsy lethargy, hours of luxurious sloth and self-indulgence, and only a few hours of real life are left."[28] Similarly, G.D. Watson said:

> There are many Christians, it would seem, who miss their true mission in life. Although they may be saved in the end, yet because of lack of perseverance, or by being influenced by other

people's conscience, frustrate the special vocation to which they were called.[29]

Imagine, however, the satisfaction Paul had when he came to the end of his life. This man had done everything God wanted him to do—and he knew it! Is this true of you, I wonder? Are you ready for the rewards? Or are you quite sure that you're *not* ready?

Please settle this question today. Whatever you do, don't leave it unanswered—or wrongly answered. Remind yourself *constantly* that in all the epochs of eternity there will scarcely be a day like that great day when God gives his rewards.

Therefore, the one thing you don't want to do is to lose what could have been, and should have been, yours.

Reflection Questions

1. How might *you* be in danger of losing a crown?

2. After exercising your imagination to envision what the time of rewarding will be like, what impressed you?

3. Are you now willing to ask the Lord, as Paul did with a yielded spirit, "What do you want me to do?"

Chapter 22
What If

G.K. Chesterton, well known for his enormous intellect and his robust imagination, contemplated how different our world would be if all the leaves were black instead of green, and if all the green grass suddenly turned black.

Can you imagine what this would be like? Forget the scientific implications of this color change; think of the aesthetic effect. Would you want to live in a world where black replaced green?

Now add to this scene another color change: the sky and the ocean are no longer blue but a furious red. Can you guess the psychological impact this would have? Why, if the more soothing colors of blue and green were replaced by the harsher colors of red and black, the days of a sanguine personality would be over!

The virtue of "what if" thinking is its ability to open avenues of thought that might not have presented any other way. Our ability to appreciate, and to evaluate, is greatly enhanced with this approach.

We take for granted the prominence of blue and green in nature, simply because these colors are everywhere. However, once we start to think of an alternative color scheme, we begin to experience a much greater appreciation for the colors God did choose.

Exercising this kind of thinking, Tozer said that God could have made functional clouds that "were square and painted battleship gray. They would have been useful, but they never would be nice to look at, and nobody would ever write a sonnet about a gray cloud painted battleship gray."[1] Likewise, Tozer opined:

> God could have made a straight, plain, ugly looking thing and called it a river. It would have worked, fed the fish and done all the things a river could do. But God in his gracious wisdom took his finger and traced the path of the river and allowed it to run around the tree and around the hills and down through the valley. He then surrounded it with beautiful trees, bushes and flowers. He also permitted it to catch the blue of the sky and reflect it as a beautiful mirror.[2]

Aren't we glad that God did all this? A world of square, gray clouds, and straight, unadorned rivers is not the world we would prefer to live in.

Again, by merely contemplating these possibilities, we bring into focus what otherwise would have remained in the blurry background.

What If: Not a Game

The thinking mode that contemplates alternatives is not a game, so as we continue to think in this vein, we purpose to do so reverently, and not in the irreverent manner adopted by participants in the annual occasion Harvey Cox described.

> During the medieval era there flourished in parts of Europe a holiday known as the Feast of Fools. On that colorful occasion, usually celebrated about January first, even ordinarily pious priests and serious townsfolk donned bawdy masks, sang out ditties, and generally kept the whole world awake with revelry and satire.[3]

In further describing this event, Cox admitted that "it did degenerate into debauchery and lewd buffoonery."

Consequently, its termination during the age of the Reformation was welcomed by many people, even those less committed to tradition.

While crass levity serves no good purpose, the ability to imagine a different world, one in which (according to Cox) "accepted values were inverted," may enhance rather than diminish revered and established thought. Even Amy Carmichael, the devout missionary in India, saw the value in this approach. "To understand the force of any Scripture," she wrote, "a good plan is to put it in opposite words."[4] By flipping the premise and seeing where that leaves us, new insights can be gained.

Embracing this rationale, let's now transpose "what if" thinking from the natural world, as first applied at the outset of this chapter, to the ethical world, where the subjects of good and evil are much discussed.

We often gloss over moral assessments, counting them as truisms that warrant no further analysis. For example, one criterion for a good work is that it must comply with Scripture. Well, that sounds right and true, so our minds quickly race past that fact. But maybe we should put the brakes on, back up just a bit, and consider more fully what we too easily accepted.

What if there were no standards? Andre Maurois, the French novelist and critic, wrote, "Why are we here on this puny mud heap spinning in infinite space? I have not the slightest idea and I am quite convinced no one has ...."[5]

Granted, such skepticism may be no more than the regretful residual of bankrupt thinking. But what if we had to discern meaning, and to discern right from wrong by, say, examining nature? Would an inspection of nature provide the standards we need?

"In sober truth," said John Stuart Mill, "nearly all the things which men are hanged or imprisoned for doing to one another are Nature's everyday performances."[6] So apparently the moral instruction we need isn't provided by nature.

Well, then, what if *no* standards exist? None! What if righteousness weren't even an issue? Can you imagine what would life be like if God were like the secular progressives of our day: unwilling to call evil what it is but more inclined to credit "individuality" and "creativity" instead? Or, worse still, what if God left it up to us to create our own code of ethics, requiring only that we be consistent with whatever we conceived? Why, just asking questions like these causes us to appreciate—instantly and immensely—the sanity and security that is ours precisely because God did give us his law. It was necessary for our own moral welfare.

Knowing the value of moral clarity, E.M. Bounds described certain people in his day "... who have no pattern before them after which conduct and character are to be shaped. They just move on aimlessly, their minds in a cloudy state, no pattern in view, no point in sight, no standard after which they are striving."[7]

Ethics without a standard, without a moral compass, without a guiding light, would be subject to ceaseless apprehensions of the heart and constant perturbations of the soul. All without remedy! So, yes, it is indeed good that God gave us his law.[8]

Now imagine what our lives would be like if God had judged us incapable of being moral and thus left us to live our pathetic lives without giving us any laws. True, the rebellious teen-ager might like that arrangement. But then we couldn't call him rebellious if there weren't a standard to rebel against. The evil manipulator on Wall Street might also like this arrangement, as would the gangs that roam the streets at night and the politicians who sell us out for bribes and babes. For under this arrangement people could do what they do without any pangs of conscience! But then conscience wouldn't be needed, and the idea of evil would be obsolete, in a world where moral standards never existed.

What if those who chafe at all the "Thou shall nots" in Scripture suddenly got their way? Would *that* arrangement be better? In his book, *The Gates of New Life*, Scotland's splendid preacher James S. Stewart contemplated this arrangement.

> Of all the doubts which, as Browning puts it, can "rap and knock and enter our soul," by far the most devastating is doubt of the ultimate purpose of God. You may doubt some of the dogmas of

your ancestors, and be none the worse for it. You may doubt a particular article in a creedal statement, and still be on the Lord's side. You may doubt the validity of contemporary fashions in religious thinking, and still have your feet on the Rock of Ages. But to doubt the final purposes of God—which means to doubt the rationality of the universe, and the significance of human experience, and the worth of moral values—is there anything left to live for then?[9]

There is not! The inevitable anarchy that would prevail causes us to shudder to think what our life would be like if God decided we are incapable of morality.

Consider this: What if God later changed his mind about the Ten Commandments and, in a whimsical mood, decided to omit the first five commandments for the western hemisphere and the last five commandments for the eastern hemisphere? Would flexibility like this gain our favor?

Actually, there are several variations of this strand of thought: such as amending God's moral law from generation to generation, or from culture to culture, or from gender to gender. But you get the idea. If the standard constantly shifted, if one group of people played by one set of rules and another group of people played by a different set of rules, how would we then regard those rules? We certainly wouldn't love them, as Paul did, or admire them, as many people today do.

To the degree God's rules keep changing, our regard for them would proportionately diminish. It is with welcomed relief that Martyn Lloyd-Jones reminds us: "The Ten Commandments are the commandments of God to men and women at all times and in all places, and have never been reduced or modified."[10]

Do you see how "what if" thinking—wherein we contemplate alternatives to a given reality—helps us appreciate the constancy of God's standards? While our national laws change with each new session of congress, and the rules of borrowing money change whenever the credit card companies send us a letter to that effect, this isn't how

God operates! What was moral a thousand years ago is moral today; and what is immoral in America is also immoral in Africa.

Here's another possibility for us to contemplate. What if the standards established by God were arbitrary and capricious? For example: God giving prohibitions against swimming, wearing jackets, eating pasta, or getting out of bed after 8 pm on the weekends.

God never decreed commandments like these! His commandments serve an ethical purpose, and thus vastly improve the quality of our lives. Indeed, so sensible and essential are these commandments they incentivize us to keep them. That's why grudging acceptance of these commandments isn't an issue. We instinctively know, at least in our heart, that these commandments are good.

To continue exercising our imagination, we might also ask ourselves, what it would be like if it were possible to bring glory to God by being good *or* by being evil? In this scenario, it really wouldn't matter which you choose, since God is both good and evil. Therefore, just be diligent; because all that really matters is gumption and goals, and not goodness.

By contemplating a scenario like this, we further appreciate that God is holy, holy, holy—and only that! Scripture says his eyes are too pure to look upon evil! In fact, in him dwells no darkness at all!

Yet, how decisively and dramatically our love for God would be altered if he openly entertained evil, or, like the vindictive gods of Rome and Greece, sometimes used that evil against us. That there is no moral vacillation in God is, therefore, just cause for a great celebration! He is absolutely perfect—and will always be so! There isn't the slightest possibility that God will ever resort to evil!

In his classic, *The Knowledge of the Holy*, Tozer offered further commentary on this point:

> All that God is he has always been, and all that he has ever been and is he will ever be. Nothing that God has ever said about himself will ever be modified; nothing the inspired prophets and

apostles have said about him will be rescinded. His immutability guarantees this.[11]

Still, we come to appreciate the immutability of God (and more narrowly, in this instance, the purity of God) when we contemplate, in one way or another, the alternatives.

Talk about love. We take for granted that Father, Son, and Holy Spirit love each other supremely and always function in perfect harmony. But what if they didn't? What if the sibling dynamic of "two against one" found its way into the Trinity?

Given the formidable fact that bringing glory to God is one criterion for determining good, we can see how that criterion would be caught in the vortex of an embattled Trinity, should their fellowship be destroyed, or even disrupted. It is particularly this thought, if we have any apprehension of it at all, that presents the most frightening prospect! How eternally grateful we should be that the governance of the universe belongs to the Father, Son, and Holy Spirit described by Scripture! Such great love!

A.J. Gossip, the nineteenth-century Scottish preacher, used his imagination to invent a dreadful vision of Jesus returning to earth with tears streaming down his eyes to say:

> I was wrong! I was wrong! I thought there was a Father. But I have searched through the Eternities, and can find never a trace of him. Poor little helpless orphaned souls, you must make shift to manage for yourselves as best you can![12]

How terrible the thought! We know Jesus came to this world to declare the will of the Father. But if the Father is an illusion, then so is the will Jesus set forth. Can you imagine the havoc that would be ours today if Jesus weren't indeed seated at the right hand of the Father, as Scripture declares? Why, the gospel we preach would be shredded by this notion! Moreover, all the conclusions we trusted would immediately collapse!

As we view the dynamics of good and evil in Scripture, it is of great significance that every comparison between them represents a sharp fork in the road, wherein good goes in one direction and evil goes in another. Accordingly, when contemplating all these radical changes of direction, we see how good makes our character better and evil makes our character worse. Good benefits; evil harms. Always!

But what if the qualities of good and evil were not so decisively different? What if both qualities could be admired in some ways and impugned in other ways? And further: What if there were an ongoing debate about which of the two is the better course, ethically? True, self-serving people will rationalize morality whenever it is convenient to do so, but we would *never ever* want such equivocation enthroned in the eternal! The fact good and evil, like black and white, are inherently and intrinsically opposite, is cause for celebration. For if it were any other way, mankind would dangerously degrade by adopting despicable lifestyles.

Here's another "what if" to consider: What if there were no judgment at the end of life? What if it really didn't matter what we did on earth? What if God were only concerned that we had a good time? Or what if he were only concerned about our productivity—that is, our industry and our ingenuity? Or what if he were utterly dismissive about *all* of it, and thus brought the curtain down one day, impudently and abruptly, without warning and without review? History over! Forget what happened!

This would mean, in the words of Voltaire, that life is a cruel joke. Because if there were no final accounting, purpose and meaning would be snatched from our lives. However, because life is sacred, the Bible says that we shall all appear before the judgment seat of Christ. Thomas Watson notes, "There is no flying, no absconding, no bribing, no appearing by proxy, but all must make their personal appearance."[13]

We may cringe and even cower whenever the final judgment of our works is discussed, but doesn't this judgment really make sense? That God is a moral being, and that we are moral beings in his image, necessitates judgment. It is precisely because evil is bad that it must be banished; and because good is glorious, it must be honored.

To forego all inspection, allowing what occurred on earth to drift into oblivion, actually cheapens life. For if there is no final judgment, then morality doesn't matter, and becoming like Jesus doesn't matter. Nothing matters in this scenario! Only expedience, pleasure, and productivity do. Never believing this to be true, even for a moment, E. M. Bounds said it well: "God's highest aim in dealing with his people is in developing Christian character. He is after infusing in us those rich virtues that belong to our Lord Jesus Christ. He is seeking to make us like himself."[14] And can life have any higher goal than this?

Our physical appearance, our personal cleverness, our charm, our talent, and all those other qualities the world admires—our wardrobe, our bank account, the kind of car we drive, our sanguine personality—matter little to God. What God cares about is loyalty to his Son, who never changes, and faithfulness to his Word, which shall never pass away.

This, of course, isn't how the university thinks, how the press thinks, or how popular culture thinks. They chase the cheese the world has trained them to chase. Hence, the ruts of routine in their lives run long and deep.

But for what purpose is this chase pursued? After a few ticks on eternity's clock, it's all over! As that 60s song puts it, "What's it all about, Alfie? Is it just for the moment we live?" Why do we do what we do? Where is meaning? Where is there any justification for our existence?

Offering one response, a poet left this epitaph in Westminster Abbey:

> Life is a jest, and all things show it.
> I thought so once and now I know it.

H.G. Wells, the man who claimed so much for the mind, approached the end of his own life baffled and bewildered. The title of his last book, *The Mind at the End of its Tether*, was an open admission that life didn't make any sense to him.[15]

Contemplating this very prospect, the famed poet Tennyson was reported to have said that if this life is all there is "then no God but a mocking fiend created us." And should that be true, Tennyson vowed, "I'd sink my head tonight in a chloroformed handkerchief" and be done with it.

There's really no need for such drastic action because there *is* a profound rationale behind daily life: one that surpasses the thrill of walking the red carpet, standing center stage among dignitaries, or being eulogized at a funeral. The obituaries can say whatever they say. Historians can write whatever they write. Streets and schools and parks can be named after someone in our midst with much ceremony. But none of that will matter much if the flawed assessment of people is all there is.

Besides, how much do people really care? Perhaps for a short while some do. But then time goes by, the waves of history pass over us, and all seems gone forever. That favor we once had, those memories of us that once had meaning—all that gets plowed under as time marches on. The wind blows where we once walked, the cloud hovers where we once stood, the sun comes up but cannot find us.

Reflecting further on this truth, A.W. Tozer wrote:

Who cares about the past generation? If you want to check on that, go out to a cemetery and look around. Who is alive to care about the old man there? There he lies, dead 200 years. Who is alive to care about him? His great-great-great-great-great-grandchildren? They carelessly come with their camera and between jokes and wisecracks, snap old-great-great-great-great-great-grandfather's bent and leaning stone that tells where he lies. Who cares about him? He has rolled around in earth's diurnal turns with rocks and stones and trees, and he matters no more than the rocks on the hillside. Few there are that care when we live, and fewer still when we die, and then nobody cares.[17]

Nobody that is, except God! To him—who sees all and remembers all that was good in us—it matters! And to him, who receives us into his loving presence the very moment we die, it matters a great deal! Every second of our life captured his attention and engaged his heart.

So contrary to what may appear to be the case when gusty winds blow the uncut grass on our grave and when the surrounding solitude seems not to know our name, it is not true to say that the clock simply ran out, that the yawning jaws of oblivion drew us at last with its inhaled breath into deep darkness.

Yes, Scripture reports the words: that man is like a moth, crushed in day "with no one regarding." But it was a lying spirit that spoke those words, and not God (Job 4:19, 20). What *we* do on earth *does* matter! And what matters most of all is the verdict of Jesus the Judge.

Goodness Matters

So will he on that last day say, "Well done, good and faithful servant"? Or will you be sentenced to that place where you will be "well done," because you *weren't* a good and faithful servant?

Putting it another way, will he, the Lord of Glory, say to you, "Enter into your reward"? Or will he, the Lord of History, say, "Depart from me, worker of iniquity, I never knew you"?

Put yet another way, will he, the waiting Bridegroom, say, "You are accepted in the Beloved"? Or will he, the Great Avenger, say that you have a different father, so now you must die in your sins? Not *because* of your sins, you will notice (although there is some truth in that), but *in* your sins—ever oozing its filth, ever pulsating with all that agitates and alienates. Emphasizing the utter seriousness of these choices, G. D. Watson declared:

> The judgment wrath of God against this wicked world is not a metaphor, nor a piece of poetry, but an awful reality; and nothing is more plainly taught in Scripture than the coming wrath of God and the last great conflict against the hosts of sin."[18]

It isn't songbirds that appear on soft, white clouds at the end, but a white horse dashing through the fiery skies with a flight plan to execute holy vengeance.

Modern man may prefer sentiment to truth and feelings to fact, but in his book, *Truths that Transform*, James Kennedy supported Scripture on this point with the following observation:

> The great A.A. Hodge said that all the great church fathers, Reformers and biblical scholars, with all of their dictionaries, lexicons (both Hebrew and Greek), commentaries and systematic theologies, concur that the Scriptures teach an endless punishment of the finally impenitent ... Indeed, it is a mistaken philanthropy that would give any encouragement of escaping the biblical injunction of impending doom to those who die outside of Christ. It is a mock charity which would encourage the impenitent to suppose that there is any chance that God does not mean what he says.[19]

To those who imagine only a temporary hell where pain is inflicted but relief is granted, James Kennedy put forward this scenario:

> ... suppose that a murderer given a life sentence could, after two days, rattle the bars and say to the warden: "Warden, I've had a change of heart. You'll be delighted to know that I'm sorry about the whole thing. I shouldn't have killed all those people. It just wasn't the right thing to do. Please tell the jailor to open the door and let me out because I'll never do that again.[20]

Is this the way it will work? Not according to Scripture! For it is there that we're told it is appointed for man once to die and after that the judgment.

Now, while one can dismiss the doctrine of hell with a sneer and a snort, we must remember that just because a person doesn't believe in hell doesn't mean he won't go there. J.C. Ryle declared, "There is no greater delusion than the common idea that it is possible to live wickedly, and yet rise again gloriously—to be without Christ in this world, and yet to be a saint in the next."[21] Yet, many there are who will live under this delusion until the first blast of hellfire surges with searing judgment and enables tortured sight.

Whether the punishment of hell or the rewards of heaven, our daily decisions should be made with a sense that what we do matters a lot. These days on earth may not always seem significant to us, but just know: Those seemingly incidental choices we made were fully observed by God—as were those times our heart sought the presence of God, the counsel of His Word, the joy of his fellowship, and the approval of him more than all others. Every prayer birthed by his Spirit, every deed done by his love, every extension of faith that said, "I believe you, Lord; it doesn't matter what it looks like"—are a part of the eternal record and will therefore be honored with a permanent reward.[22]

To those who think that what we do on earth doesn't matter (except in ways our fortune is increased and our happiness is extended), God says think again! Because what we do, or don't do, is done under the searching, all-knowing eyes of God, and thus is freighted with eternity in all the consequences it will bring. G.D. Watson wrote:

> The great mass of Christians never get their thoughts any higher than escaping hell and getting into heaven. When we are divinely illuminated, we discover that there are countless degrees of rank and honor and riches and enjoyments that will exist in the heavenly kingdom, and we are now preparing ourselves for just the place we shall occupy in the life to come.[23]

You may minimize your own significance, at times, saying, "There are so many people on this earth, who am I among all these people?" But before answering this question, timid soul, listen to Charles Spurgeon's comment about God:

> ... He has never once taken his eyes off you, and though you be one among so many, yet he has observed you as narrowly, as carefully, as

tenderly, as if there were not another child in the divine family, nor another one whose prayers were to be heard, or whose cares were to be relieved.[24]

Yet sometimes, as an enemy to your own soul, you further minimize your significance by saying, "What I can do is so little. How will my life ever amount to much?" And in asking this question you may be thinking the answer is self-evident: that no amount of effort on your part can possibly make a difference. But the correct answer is the same answer given when Jesus fed the five thousand: Place the little you have into the Master's hands, and allow him to multiply little into much. Just live for Jesus—seeking his strength, his approval. Because one day, if good was your goal and God was your source, you will actually be enthroned with Jesus. With this eternal enchantment in view, A.B. Simpson wrote:

> You are to spend eternity in his palaces and on his throne. You are to be the companion and partner of his mightiest enterprises in the ages to come. Perhaps with him you are to colonize a constellation of space and govern the boundless universe of God. Do you know that he is educating you now to be the fit companion of such a kingdom? Will you let him love you all he wants to and fit you for such a destiny as will someday fill you with everlasting wonder and adoration?[25]

Your answer to that question, dear reader, determines whether the good life is really going to be yours.

Reflection Questions

1. Which "what if" statement disturbed you the most?
2. Which "what if" statement excited you the most?

Subject Index

Adam, 11, 26, 49-50, 87, 92, 93, 134, 176, 198, 200, 225, 318, 363.
Angels
  Compared with man, 49
  Possess mind, will and emotions, 150, 178, 182, 251, 286
  Sent to assist man, 122, 161, 182
  Confronted man, 122
  Will assist the believer's ruling assignment in next life, 294
  Powerful beings, 188, 252
  Number not known, 313
  Always obey God, 150
  Ministered to Jesus, 105, 370
  Will come with Jesus in judgment, 188
  Will come with Jesus in glory, 291
  Will be seen in heaven, 315, 329
  Some chose to rebel, 80, 260, 318
A Kempis, Thomas, 90, 256
Anthropology, 23
Aversion therapy, 182-183

Bailey, A.E., 370, 371, 390
Barclay, William, 208, 376
Baxter, Richard, 40, 177, 305, 310, 329
Barbarism, 10
Bema Judgment, 283, 284, 302, 319, 329, 382-375, 387-388
Bernard of Clairvaux, 108
Billheimer, Paul, 208, 308
Bonar, Horatius, 14, 39, 80, 180, 186, 285
Bonaparte, Napoleon, 299, 317
Boreham, F.W., 88
Boston, Thomas, 43
Bosworth, F.F., 211
Bounds, E.M., 51, 104, 107, 227, 232, 336, 341
Bossuet, Jacques, 40
Brengle, Samuel, 234, 246, 247

Brockett, Henry, 367
Brother Lawrence, 235, 236
Bruce, F. F., 74
Bunyan, John, 87, 147, 179, 227, 319

Calvin, John, 58-59, 385
Camelot, 8
Carmichael, Amy, 335
Carson, D.A., 117
Carson, Rachael, 218-219
Cicero, 136
Chadwick, Samuel, 51, 62-63, 69, 223, 224, 236, 293, 364, 365, 377
Charnock, Stephen, 80, 275, 360, 361
Chesterton, G.K., 32, 33, 81, 333
Chambers, Oswald, 42, 89, 159, 180, 222, 310
Churchill, Winston, 169
Conscience
  Good, 87, 88, 143, 149, 176, 177, 181, 184, 290, 361, 374, 389
  Weak, 178-179
  Evil, 89, 135, 179, 180
  Seared, 180, 336
  Dysfunctional, 10, 31, 33, 108, 111, 116, 126, 176, 178, 181,
Copan, Paul, 39
Cornecilius, 370
Cox, Harvey, 334-355

Dawson, J.W., 52
Death
  Lightly regarded by men, 23, 39, 94
  Openly regarded by Scripture, 128, 252
  Defined as:
    Physical, 183, 189, 367
    Spiritual, 103, 128, 164, 221, 290,
  Consequence of sin, 129, 134, 154
    Administered with vengeance by God, 83, 152,

Subject Index

188,189, 208, 304, 305, 387
No pleasure for unbeliever, 317, 325
No pleasure for God, 188
Joyful only for believers, 281, 328, 381
Determined by choices, 54, 80, 182, 183
Overcome by Jesus, 57
Motivates obedience, 137, 177, 182, 280, 300
  Motivates Christian witness, 190, 208
  Finishing line for faithfulness, 280, 281, 292, 300
Dillow, Joseph, 324
Disraeli, Benjamin, 38
Durant, Will, 29, 32

Edwards, Johnathan, 173
Edwards, Ralph, 313-314
Ethics
  Lightly considered, 24, 336
  Wrongly considered, 16, 32, 36, 39-41, 84, 245, 325
European Renaissance, 24

Faber, 13, 277
Feast of Fools, 334
Finney, Charles, 73, 173, 189, 232, 388

Gillham, Bill, 67-68, 367
Goethe, 145
Golden Age of Greece, 24
Goodwin, Thomas, 277, 373, 382, 383
Good works
  Worldly definitions, 23-25
  Flawed church definitions, 25-27
  Godly definition, 41-44
  Six kinds of works, 324
  Good works not sufficient for salvation, 44, 53, 55, 57, 90, 165

Pride prefers works standard, 57, 323
Specifically designed by God for the believer, 212
Will decide our station in heaven, 257
May be seen after we die, 310
Gordon, A.J., 64, 73, 87, 253
Gossip, A.J., 339
Grace
  Given by God, 71, 281
  For salvation, 54-55, 59, 200, 305
  For sanctification, 39, 67, 69-71, 112, 113, 144, 200, 221, 247 286, 315, 330, 388, 390
  For supply of various needs, 70, 144, 281
  Blocked by pride, 57, 60, 69, 144, 165 166, 178
  Forfeited by ignorance, 176
  Accessed by faith, 144
  Blocked by sin, 144
  Disposition toward others, 63, 178, 207, 240, 388
  Consequence of rejecting, 89, 243, 304, 305
  Abuse of, 238, 243, 330
  Gradual growth versus Spirit-filling, 234
Graham, Billy, 177
Great Ivan, Russian Emperor, 326
Greenham, Richard, 311
Grey, Thomas, 251
Grubb, Norman, 47, 208
Guthrie, Thomas, 86, 87

Hardy, Thomas, 387
Havner, Vance, 81, 225
Hell
  Existence doubted, 39, 186-188, 190-191, 344
  A literal place, 188, 190, 344
  A permanent place, 344
  A place of agony, 137, 191, 280, 319, 344

Subject Index

Associated with Satan, 105, 128, 188
Associated with a lifestyle, 51, 79-80, 86, 344
Opposes judgment, 39
Opposes holiness, 80, 90, 214, 281
Accessed by desires and deception, 94-95, 105, 110
Warranted judgment, 118, 382
The absence of Jesus, 90
Motivates witnessing, 187-188, 190-191
Viewed by believer in heaven, 295
Hemingway, Ernest, 31, 99, 101
Hession, Roy, 199
Hitler, Adolf, 30, 174
Hoekema, Anthony A., 362-363
Holiness
  Defined, 36, 39, 63-66, 71-72, 74, 91, 96, 169, 188, 196, 198, 234, 235, 275, 388
  Resides in new nature, 16, 61, 63, 65-66, 71, 74
  Released by the Spirit, 70, 74, 234
  Released through faith, 235
  Resisted by the world, 80, 247
  Resisted by the church, 67, 216, 246-247
  Translates into obedient lifestyle, 167, 169, 234
  Misconceived, 16, 36, 59, 61, 63, 65-66, 172, 216, 234
    Thought to be humanly possible, 6-7, 63
    Thought to be impossible, 65-67, 167
Holmes, Oliver Wendell, 233
Holyoake, G. J., 31
House of a Thousand Mirrors, 197
Huegel, F.J., 39, 105, 236,
Hughes, Howard, 262, 264
Huxley, Aldous, 11, 15
Hyperopia, 245

Ironside, Harry, 367
Jefferies, Richard, 138
Johnson, James Weldon, 137
Johnson, Samuel, 115
Jowett, John Henry, 140, 301, 359, 360

Kant, Immanuel, 30, 31
Keats, Shelly, 140
Kendall, R. T., 388
Kennedy, D. James, 41, 43, 343, 344
Kennedy, John, 303
Kierkegaard, Soren, 219
Kingsley, George, 11
Knox, John, 375
Kung, Hans, 189
Kuyper, Abraham, 43, 225

Lancelot, 7, 8
Lang, G. H., 220
Law
  Given by God, 41, 287, 336
  Rooted in God—36, 41, 90-92, 168
  Standard for morality, 41, 54,
  Embedded in man, 59, 64, 87
  Wrong way to salvation, 26, 54, 57, 59
  Wrong way for Christian living, 60, 71
  Appeals to pride, 39, 69, 79, 166
  Promoted by the Pharisees, 57-59, 164, 165
  Fulfilled by Jesus, 91, 168
  Commensurate with our new nature, 198
  What if not given, not honored, or capriciously amended, 366-342
Lee, R.G., 139, 241
Lewis, C.S., 12, 28, 41, 44, 94, 180, 251, 287, 288, 318, 227
Lewis, Jessie-Penn, 200, 220
Lewis, Sinclair B., 372
Lightfoot, John, 148
Livingston, David, 87

Subject Index

Lloyd-Jones, Martyn, 141, 199, 337
Louis XIV, 42
Luther, Martin, 57, 67, 87, 135, 271, 329, 366

MacArthur, John, 374
MacDonald, George, 29, 49, 174
MacIntyre, Alistair, 23
Maclaren, Alexander, 91, 126, 147, 179, 207, 275, 363, 383
Madden, Myron, 92
Manchester, William, 58
Mantle, J. Gregory, 197
Markham, Edwin, 52
Marshall, Peter, 13
Mary, Queen of Scots, 375
Maurois, Andre, 335
McGee, J. Vernon, 103
Methodists, 201
Meyer, F. B., 43, 64, 88, 94, 101, 110, 112, 116, 121, 129, 139, 141, 152, 192, 197, 280, 290, 295, 329, 330, 368, 371
Mill, John Stuart, 30, 335
Milton, John, 245, 318
Mishna, 233
Moody, D. L., 196
Moore, Keith, 231
Moravians, 201
Morgan, G. Campbell, 63
Mountains
  Sinai, 26, 41, 54, 55, 87, 178, 389
  Zion, 54, 55, 178, 189
  Moriah, 54
Murray, Andrew, 63, 69, 106, 138, 148
Murray, John, 93
Myopia, 245
Mysticism, 15

New Nature
  Consists of divine life, 39, 70, 198, 233-234
  Resides in re-created spirit, 220, 366
  Can dominate the soul, 73
  Characterized by fruit of the spirit, 64, 223
  Divine life released by Holy Spirit, 66-67, 235
  Fully released in heaven, 73-74
  Suddenly released on earth, 234
  Released through faith, 235, 237
  The believer's only identity, 275-276
  Highly valued by God, 199,
  Enables fellowship with God, 198
  Enables obedience, 56, 63, 65, 68-71, 198, 205, 232, 234, 360
  Ignored or misrepresented by church, 65, 69, 71, 199, 215-216, 275
Niebuhr, Reinhold, 135
Nietzsche, Friedrich, 39
Niles, D.T., 239

Owen, John, 38, 78, 87, 93, 136, 372, 385-386

Pascal, Blaise, 11, 22, 24, 29, 33, 38, 53, 78, 135, 310
Packer, J.I., 31, 49, 65, 87, 172, 311, 384-386, 388
Paxson, Ruth, 218
Payson, Edward, 328
Philpot, J.C., 145, 215
Pierson, A.T., 239
Puritans, 13, 38, 78, 136, 177, 305, 360, 385-386
Pink, Arthur W., 18, 83, 135, 312
Prophecies, 37-38, 374

Ravenhill, Leonard, 81, 227, 388
Revelation knowledge, 213-214
Richter, Jean Paul, 32
Rich, young ruler, 25-26, 53, 189, 238
Rebellion
  Inspired by Satan, 95, 260

Subject Index

Thinks and functions independently, 42
Shocking when on full display, 125, 243
Hides in supposed obedience, 155
Permitted for a season, 189
Will be terminated eventually, 260
May result in eternal judgment, 319
Rewards
  Definition of, 254, 257
  Motivated believers, 255, 256, 264, 269, 315, 325, 344, 345
  Coveted by New Testament believers, 256
  Has extraordinary value, 268, 269, 298, 304, 315, 327
  Never loses value, 262, 300
  Time distributed, 290-292
  Can be forfeited, 320-323
  Opposed by Satan, 320
  Basis for rewards, 220, 253, 256, 258, 278, 281, 284, 292, 294-301, 307, 330
  Rewards not a *quid pro quo* transaction, 308, 309
  Rewards thoroughly examined, 307-313,
  Seemingly good works won't be rewarded, 322-323
  Rewards shouldn't be minimized, 244
Righteousness
  Perceptions of the world erroneous, 1, 12, 22-24, 49
  Jesus' perceptions unlike the world's, 32, 33
  Perceptions of religion in error, 25-27
  Perceptions of the church in error, 25
  Innate, 49-52
  Imputed, 52-59, 62, 68, 75, 76, 183, 199, 365
  Imparted, 62-73, 75, 76, 183, 234, 275, 366
  Inherited, 73-75
  Crown for, 270, 273, 274, 278, 380
Roberts, Debbie, 259
Roosevelt, Theodore, 314
Rose, Pete, 313
Ryle, J.C., 106, 183, 196, 254, 309, 344

Sabatier, Augustus, 235
Satinover, Jeffrey, 85, 86
Stanford, Miles, J., 8
Satan
  Is real and personal, 97, 105, 106
  Was thrown out of heaven, 143
  Now heads an evil empire, 17,
  Is destructive, 50, 97
  uses cruelty, 245, 279, 384
  commits theft, 142, 182, 320
  Must be resisted, 279
  Attacked Jesus, 79, 105
  Attacks the righteous, 99, 107, 108, 113, 115, 211, 228
    persistently, 108, 115
    with forethought, 115, 327
    through ignorance, 95, 256
    through doubt, 93
    through fear, 97
    through compromise, 111
    through the soulish living, 90, 370
    through images, 124, 228, 304, 378
    through others, 50
    through enticement, 104, 107,
      adapts to individual, 104, 114
      inferior to what God offers, 112, 113
  Infiltrates our thought world, 77
    through deception, 35, 199, 227, 279
    through confusion, 25

Subject Index

Infiltrates the church, 280
Destroys conscience, 180
Will be judged, 96, 292
Sauer, Erich, 47, 94
Sayers, Dorothy, 11
Schaeffer, Francis, 36, 84
Scougal, Henry, 219
Secularism, 22, 31
Shaw, George Bernard, 45
Simpson, A. B., 28, 44, 49, 50, 51, 55, 63, 64, 66, 68, 70, 71, 72, 73, 87, 94, 102, 106, 108, 122, 129, 151, 162, 166, 178, 202, 211, 216, 217, 218, 223, 228, 238, 243, 244, 253, 270, 271, 273,, 276, 278, 282, 293, 294, 298, 299, 304, 307, 310, 311, 315, 321, 325, 326, 327, 346, 367, 374
Sin
  Its definition, 13, 42, 43, 72, 78, 89-95, 111, 118, 231
  Its stages, 104-130
  Its inception, 51, 107
    inwardly known, 86, 87
    often minimized, 10, 39, 40, 80, 83-85, 94, 181, 186
    sometimes exaggerated, 215
    requires honest discovery, 78, 83, 94, 110
  Its characteristics
    persistent, 67, 88, 124, 126, 162
    extensive, 196
    deceptive, 93, 95, 110, 124, 126, 135, 238, 264
    pleasurable, 88, 108, 110, 112, 113, 138, 194, 228, 238, 254
    unsatisfying, 22, 94, 126, 139,-141, 144, 145, 162
  Its consequences, 80, 81
    shrivels the soul, 13, 116, 134, 139, 227, 228
    destroys fellowship with God, 137-139, 141, 144, 172, 228
    hinders worship, 137, 257
    dislodges faith, 144
    corrupts the heart, 88, 91, 94, 134, 135
    corrupts the conscience, 88, 174-178
    corrupts culture, 81, 95
    corrupts the church, 177, 178, 217, 232
    gains control, 14, 15, 17, 87, 103, 112, 125, 126, 140, 145, 182, 183, 194, 197, 373
  God's response toward, 39, 57, 68, 90
    patience, 189
    anger, 189, 190, 375
    immediate intervention, 119, 124
  Results of God's response
    penalty of sin removed, 56, 68, 75, 199, 206, 232, 233
    power of sin broken, 62, 69, 72-75, 199, 206, 232, 233
    presence of sin banished, 75, 343
  The believer's response toward
    confession and repentance, 55, 173
    diligence, 77, 78, 112, 129, 136, 173, 221, 226-228, 95-96, 112, 130, 146, 218, 231, 235-236
    seeking God's presence, 55
    activating new nature, 68, 69, 198, 215, 233
Sinatra, Frank, 300
Smedes, Lewis, 389
Smith, Hannah Whitall, 144, 325
Solipsism, 31
Sparks, T. Austin, 228, 370, 381
Sproul, R.C., 74, 188
Spurgeon, Charles, 57, 72, 90, 94, 173, 207, 345
Stevenson, Robert Louis, 215, 379
Stewart, James. S., 16, 59, 62, 251, 321, 336

Subject Index

Studd, C.T., 235
Summum Bonum, 31

Talmadge, T. Dewitt, 149
Taylor, Hudson, 169, 197
Taylor, Jack, 50, 259
Tennyson, Alfred, 341
Tertullian, 208
The Flesh
Types of, 70
  Different than old nature, 67
  Not a part of believer's identity, 367
  Contrasted with new nature, 231, 232, 366, 367
  Contrasted with Sprit-filling, 67, 70, 366, 372
  Extinct in heaven, 74
  Pervasive in the church, 69, 90, 289
  Can be resisted, 198
  Associated with worldliness, 254, 255
  Characteristics of
    Well-intentioned, 68, 166, 167
    Weak, 70, 166, 169, 217, 322, 367, 385
The Holy Spirit
  Resides in new nature, 64, 69, 70, 366
  Possessed by every believer, 69
  Differences between receiving and releasing, 27, 70
  Enables existing righteousness to manifest, 42, 69-71, 198, 207, 327, 385
  Convicts of sin, 89
  Grieved by sin, 137
  Teaches, 103, 238
  Leads, 105
  In perfect harmony with Father and Son, 139, 339
Theology, 23, 27, 35, 66, 141, 178, 183, 217, 218, 220, 273, 274, 330, 368

Thielicke, Helmut, 118
Theodosius, 311, 312
Torrey, R.A., 196
Total depravity doctrine, 50, 51, 385
Toynbee, Arnold, 14-15, 83
Tozer, A. W., 10, 11, 22, 24, 32, 41, 51, 56, 57, 65, 90, 107, 110, 140, 150, 177-179, 186, 187, 216, 229, 236, 237, 239, 273, 286, 289, 323, 324, 330, 333, 334, 338, 342, 375, 388
Trueblood, Elton, 31, 83
Voltaire, 45, 340

Watson, David, 84-85
Watson, G.D., 12, 13, 39, 41, 44, 48, 63, 67, 81, 89, 91, 95, 128, 134, 161, 190, 194, 195, 198, 210, 225, 247, 253, 257, 264, 272, 278, 284, 286, 290, 292, 301, 307, 308, 309, 320, 321, 324-225, 330, 343, 345, 366, 387, 389
Watson, Thomas, 10, 104, 113, 126, 180, 191, 275, 281, 340, 363, 373, 381, 382
Wells, H.G., 341
Wesley, John, 111, 201, 388
Wesley, Susannah, 111
Westminster Abbey, 341
Whitfield, George, 74
Whyte, Alexander, 145
Wideman, Bruce, 325
Wilcox, Leslie D., 69
Will, George 10
Willard, Dallas, 222
Williams, Charles, 268

Yancey, Philip, 59, 139, 164, 240
Yocum, Dale, 180, 232, 243, 247
Zinzindorf, Nicolaus, 201

Scripture Index

Genesis
  1:26, 49
  1:31, 49
  6:5, 84, 189
  8:21, 51
  12: 160
  15:16, 152
  20:6, 119

Exodus
  34:7, 84

Numbers
  14:34-35, 172
  22:18, 109
  22:20 118
  31:8, 128
  32:3, 139

Deuteronomy
  6:25, 59
  28:17-18, 384
  28: 60-61, 384

Joshua
  1:7, 161
  1:8, 162
  9:3-15, 154

Judges
  3:12, 33
  4:1, 33
  6:1, 33
  13:1, 33
  17:6, 33
  21:25, 33

I Samuel
  15:1-3, 152
  16&, 118

II Kings
  5:18, 373
  14:25, 163

Job
  4:6, 92
  4:19, 20, 332

Job (continued)
  9:2, 53
  25:4, 53
  42:6, 92
  38:2, 303

Psalms
  8:5, 49
  48:2, 55

Proverbs
  8:36, 140
  13:15, 139
  14:9, 85
  17:24, 245
  21:2, 35
  21:4, 42
  26:12, 36
  30:12, 135
  30:28, 148

Isaiah
  5:20, 77
  5:21, 36
  6:5, 91
  40:10, 291, 314
  59:2, 172
  62:11, 291, 314

Jeremiah
  13:23, 53
  17:9, 53
  31:33, 64

Ezekiel
  36:26, 64

Hosea
  4:6, 101, 211

Joel
  2:1f., 189

Jonah
  1:2, 163

Micah
  6:5, 103

Scripture Index

Nahum
  2:8-13, 163
  3:4-7, 163

Zephaniah
  2:13-15, 163
  3:17, 307

Zechariah
  12:10, 174
  13:1, 175
  14:4, 175

Matthew
  4:1-11, 106
  5:11-12, 297
  5:12, 269
  5:14-16, 27
  5:48, 165
  6:1, 323
  6:6, 313
  7:18, 44, 165
  16:27, 291, 307
  19:16, 53
  21:28-31, 149
  26:21, 367

Mark
  9:41, 322
  10:29-30, 306

Luke
  3:12, 53
  5:1-9, 155
  6:23, 268
  6:38, 296, 305
  10:25, 53
  14:14, 291
  19:14, 93
  23:18, 93

John
  4:14, 70
  6:28, 53
  6:63, 42,
  7:38, 70
  8:31, 227
  10:10, 320

John (continued)
  14:2, 294
  15:8, 27
  15:10, 194
  16:8, 9, 89
  16:22, 142
  16:24, 142
  17:13, 142

Acts
  2:37, 53
  3:19, 173
  3:19-21, 174
  8:16, 70
  9:6, 53
  10:44, 70
  16:30, 55
  19:6, 70
  23:1, 179
  23:4, 176

Romans
  1:19, 87
  1:24, 89
  1:26, 89
  1:28, 89
  1:32:85
  3:10, 53
  3:10-18, 367
  3:11, 367
  3:19, 54
  3:20, 59
  4:22, 55
  4:16-5:2, 144
  5:1, 84
  5:2, 70, 144
  6:6, 67
  6:14, 72, 145, 385
  7:5, 322
  7:17-21, 367
  7:18, 367
  7:24, 70
  8:2, 64, 68, 70, 385
  8:9, 70
  13:5, 176
  14:23, 42

Scripture Index

I Corinthians
  3:8, 258, 307
  3:9, 294
  3:12- f., 42, 324
  3:13, 284
  3:15, 295
  4:5, 263, 291, 306
  5:14, 119
  6:2-3, 294
  6:9-10, 86
  6:19, 152
  8:12, 178
  9:25, 260
  10:31, 42
  15:58, 312

II Corinthians
  1:14, 382
  3:7, 54
  3:18, 228
  5:10, 283
  5:11, 187, 385
  5:15, 150
  9:6, 295
  9:8, 144
  12:10, 235
  12:15, 191, 277

Galatians
  1:6, 321
  5:1, 322
  5:16, 72, 385
  5:17, 366
  5:22-23, 65, 198
  6:7, 127
  6:9, 295, 312

Ephesians
  1:17-19, 212
  1:21, 214
  2:10, 212
  3:20, 124, 233
  4:24, 234, 275
  4:30, 193
  5:18, 385

Colossians
  2:16, 321

Colossians (continued)
  2:18, 321
  3:1, 112
  3:4, 64, 198
  3:17, 43
  3:23, 43

II Thessalonians
  1:8, 188
  2:7, 77
  2:11, 188

I Timothy
  1:12-13, 193
  1:19, 180
  2:9-10, 27
  3:16, 77
  4:1, 180
  4:2, 177
  4:12, 27
  5:10, 27
  6:18, 27

II Timothy
  3:12, 280
  4:7-8, 270

Hebrews
  3:12, 93
  3:15, 151
  4:16, 273
  6:10, 312, 313, 328
  8:10, 197
  10:35, 223
  11:6, 42, 322
  11:24-25, 246
  12:18-24, 54
  12:19, 54

James
  1:12, 279
  1:14-15, 102
  2:17, 206

I Peter
  1:4, 261
  1:5, 217
  1:5-7, 206

Scripture Index

I Peter (continued)
  1:7, 292
  1:22, 239
  3:8, 239
  3:8-9, 296
  3:10, 78
  5:4, 276
  5:5, 118
  5:7, 223
  5:10, 247

II Peter
  1:2, 144
  2:14, 182
  2:15, 127

I John
  1:6, 172
  1:8, 84
  2:28, 324
  3:4, 84
  3:21-22, 143
  4:4, 374
  5:1, 192
  5:4, 206
  5:18, 244

Jude
  11, 127

Revelation
  2:10, 279
  2:14, 127
  3:11, 319, 322
  3:16, 280
  4:4, 257
  11:15, 54
  20:11-15, 283
  22:12, 258, 269, 314

Endnotes

Chapter 1—Why Good Is Better

1. Thomas Watson, *The Doctrine of Repentance*, (Kindle Edition, 2010; Kindle location: 207-208).
2. A.W. Tozer, *Faith Beyond Reason*, (Camp Hill, PA., WingSpread Publishers, 2009), p.126.
3. Dorothy L. Sayers, *A Mater of Eternity*, (Grand Rapids, William B. Eerdmans, 1973). p.44.
4. James S. Stewart, *The Gates of New Life*, (Edinburgh, T & T Company, 1937), p.177.
5. Blaise Pascal, *Pensees*, (New York, Washington Press Square, 1965), p.109.
6. Commenting on this contrast, John Henry Jowett wrote, "There are two ways of estimating a triumphant life. We may trace the line of external circumstances, and we make an inventory of the material treasures, and the flattering diplomas, and the public honors that have been gained along the way. That road winds by the bank, and ... stretches away through fair suburbs of material comforts, and through gardens of enticing ease, ascending even to lofty eminences of public favor and regard ... But there is another way of judging the failure or triumph of a life. We may follow the line of character. We may register the success of the soul in its mastery of circumstances, in its refusal to be submerged by evil antagonisms, in its preservation of a diamond-like translucency amid engulfing floods of defilement, in its buoyancy in the days of prolonged disappointment, in its quiet and firm ascendency over the beast, in its inevitable emergence from every kind of hostility in increasing majesty and strength." John Henry Jowett, *The Whole Armor of God*, Kindle Edition, 2011; Kindle locations: 1785-1797.
7. A.W. Tozer, *Man, the Dwelling Place of God*, (Camp Hill, PA., WingSpread Publishers, 1997), p.46
8. C.S. Lewis, *The Great Divorce*, (New York, MacMillan Publishing Company, 1973), p.6.
9. G.D. Watson, *Love Abounding*, (Cincinnati, Ohio, God's Revivalist Press, n. d.), p.100.
10. C.S. Lewis, *The Great Divorce*, p.123.
11. F.B. Meyer, "Heman The Singer," located under Sermon Texts on the website sermonindex.net
12. Peter Marshall and Lela Gilbert, *Heaven is Not My Home: Learning to Live in God's Creation*, (Nashville, Word, 1998), pp.32, 33.

Endnotes

13. G.D. Watson, *Love and Duty*, (Salem, Ohio, Schmul Publishing Company, Inc., 1984), p.19.
14. G.D. Watson, *A Pot of Oil*, (Hampton, TN., Harvey Publishers, n. d.), p.108.
15. Horatius Bonar, *God's Way of Holiness*, (Chicago, Moody Press, 1979), p.52.
16. D. Martyn Lloyd-Jones, *Jesus Christ and Him Crucified*, (The Banner of Truth, Edinburgh, 1999), p.15.
17. Ibid. p.16.
18. James. S. Stewart, *Walking with God*, (Vancouver, Regent College Publishing, 2002), p.155.
19. Arthur W. Pink, *Gleanings in the Godhead*, (Chicago, Moody Press, 1975), p.55.

Chapter 2—The Good Life—Part I

1. A.W. Tozer, *Who Put Jesus on the Cross?* (Harrisburg, PA., Christian Publications, 1975), p.170.
2. J.I. Packer, *Knowing Man*, (Westchester, IL., Cornerstone Books, 1978), p.75.
3. A.W. Tozer, *The Radical Cross*, (Camp Hill, PA., WingSpread Publications, 2005), p.132.
4. Pascal, *Pensees*, p.66.
5. John Henry Jowett noted that "our Lord never allowed anything that seemed like sentimentalism to pass unchallenged. He called it to a halt while he questioned its worth." Honorific words, casually uttered by a facile tongue, were routinely returned to the sender for further review. John Henry Jowett, *Friend on the Road and Other Gospel Studies*, Kindle Edition, 2010; Kindle locations: 638-639.
6. A.B. Simpson, *The Christ in the Bible Commentary*, Volume Four, (Camp Hill, PA., WingSpread Publishers, 2009). P.100.
7. Setting forth this contrast between man's morality and God's spirituality, Puritan theologian Stephen Charnock asked, "How excellent is this new creature?" Answer: The new nature has "an excellency above that of the greatest moralist under heaven." *The Works of Stephen Charnock*, (Kindle Edition, 2011; Kindle locations: 1546-1547).

Further expounding upon this excellence, Charnock wrote, "How much therefore should new creatures be esteemed and valued? Is anything, next to God, more worthy our

Endnotes

esteem than that which bears his image? Is anything, next to a crucified Christ, glorified in heaven, more worthy our valuation, than Christ formed in the heart of a believer?" (*The Works of Stephen Charnock*, Kindle locations: 1565-1567).

According to Charnock, the righteousness deposited in the new nature of a believer far exceeds the moral strivings of even a well-intentioned, highly disciplined, vigorous-for-virtue, conscience-attuned, sensitive heart cultivated by mortal man.

8. C.S. Lewis, *The Abolition of Man*, (New York, The MacMillan Company, 1972), pp.56, 57.
9. Will Durant, *The Pleasures of Philosophy*, (New York, Simon and Shuster, 1953), p.73.
10. Blaise Pascal, *Pensees*, p.112.
11. George MacDonald, *The Best of George MacDonald*, (Colorado Springs, CO., Cook Communication Ministries, 2006), p.124.
12. Ibid. p.124.
13. Elton Trueblood, *Philosophy of Religion*, (New York, Harper Brothers, 1957), p.109.
14. Floyd McClung, *Holiness and the Spirit of the Age*, (Eugene, Harvest House Publishers, 1992), p.119.
15. J.I. Packer, *Knowing Man*, p.75.
16. Will Durant, *The Pleasures of Philosophy*, p.93.
17. Helmut Thielicke, *Life Can Begin Again*, (Philadelphia, Fortress Press, 1964), p.ii.
18. A.W. Tozer, *Jesus, Our Man in Glory*, (Camp Hill, PA., WingSpread Publishers, 1987), p.22.
19. G.K. Chesterton, *The Everlasting Man*, (New York, Dodd, Mead & Company, 1925), p.237.
20. Ibid. pp.235, 236.
21. Ibid. p.234.
22. Blaise Pascal, *Pensees*, (New York, Washington Press Square, 1965), p.120.

Chapter 3—The Good Life—Part II

1. Francis A. Schaeffer, *The God Who is There*, (Downers Grove, Inter-Varsity Press, 1968), p.105.
2. Blaise Pascal, *Pensees*, (New York, Washington Press Square, 1965), p.242.
3. Dr. John Warwick Montgomery, among other evangelical

Endnotes

scholars, makes this argument convincingly when he examines the conflict that exist among several multiple norm religions (i.e. in Roman Catholicism, where allegiance is given to both the Bible and the declarations of the Church Fathers; in Christian Science, where allegiance is given to both the Bible and the books of Mary Baker Eddy; and in Mormonism, where allegiance is given to both the Bible and the Book of Mormons, etc.). Examples of multiple norms abound within the so-called church and increase exponentially in the secular realm where multiple norms such as reason, tradition, religion, and philosophy are all used as sources for determining beliefs and values.

The Bahá'í Faith exacerbates this problem to the extreme by combining views from many major religions: Krishna, Abraham, Buddha, Jesus, Muhammad and others are all recognized for presenting valid revelations. Syncretism, the blending of religions, is worse than anything secularists do because it falsely ascribes higher authority to religions created by the devil.

4. Horatius Bonar, *God's Way of Holiness*, p.20.
5. F.J. Huegel, *The Cross of Christ The Throne of God*, (Dixon, MO., Rare Christian Books, n.d.), p.59.
6. Francis J. Beckwith, William Lane Crane, J. P. Moreland, editors, *To Everyman an Answer*, (Downers Grove, IL., 2004), p.109.
7. G.D. Watson, *Spiritual Feasts*, (Salem, Ohio, Schmul Publishing Company, 1991), p.70.
8. Clyde E. Fant, Jr. and William M. Pinson, Jr., *20 Centuries of Great Preaching, Volume II*, (Waco, Word Books, 1971), p.298.
9. Ibid., p.240.
10. A.W. Tozer, *The Price of Neglect*, (Camp Hill, PA., Christian Publications, 1991), p.53.
11. G.D. Watson, *The Seven Overcomeths*, (Salem, Ohio, Schmul Publishing Company, 2007, p.128.
12. C.S. Lewis, *The Problem of Pain*, (New York, The MacMillan Company, 1972), p.65.
13. Anthony Hoekema says that by partaking of the tree of the knowledge of good and evil, Adam and Eve presumed on the divine prerogative for defining each. They wanted to determine the standard of right and wrong; they didn't want God to do this. Anthony A. Hoekema, *Created in*

Endnotes

      God's Image, (Grand Rapids, Michigan and Cambridge/UK, William B. Eerdmans Publishing Company, 1986), p.140.
14. John E. Hunter, *Knowing God's Secret*, (Grand Rapids, Zondervan, 1974), p.71.
15. Oswald Chambers, *Our Brilliant Heritage*, (Grand Rapids, Discovery House Publishers, 1998), p.193.
16. F.B. Meyer, *Tried By Fire*, (Fort Washington, PA., CLC Publications, 2001), p.154.
17. D. James Kennedy, *Truths That Transform*, (Old Tappan, Fleming H. Revell, 1974), p.109.
18. F.B. Meyer, *Christ in Isaiah*, (Fort Washington, PA., CLC Publications, 2001), p.43.
19. Alexander Maclaren illustrated the foolishness of attempting to produce good fruit from a nature that is not good by recalling children playing in the garden: "They stick in their little bits of rootless flowers, and they water them; but, being rootless, the flowers are all withered tomorrow and flung over the hedge the day after." Alexander Maclaren, *Expositions of Holy Scripture, Isaiah and Jeremiah*, Public Domain, Kindle locations: 2295-2296.
20. A.B. Simpson, *The Christ in the Bible Commentary*, Volume Five, (Camp Hill, PA., WingSpread Publishers, 2009), pp. 303, 304.
21. Further distinguishing these two types of morality, Thomas Watson spoke of a "morality (that) shoots short of heaven. It is only nature refined. A moral man is but old Adam dressed in fine clothes." Thomas Watson, *The Doctrine of Repentance*, Locations: 682-683.
22. G.D. Watson, *The Secret of Spiritual Power*, (Nicholasville, Kentucky, Schmul Publishing Company, 2009), p.103.
23. C. S. Lewis, *Mere Christianity*, (New York: MacMillan Publishing Company, 1977), p.124.
24. Voltaire, *Voltaire's Alphabet of Wit*, (New York, The Peter Pauper Press, 1955), p.36.
25. C.S. Lewis saw this issue more clearly, and thus wrote: "There is but one good; that is God. Everything else is good when it looks to him and bad when it turns from him." C. S. Lewis, *The Great Divorce*, (New York, Macmillan Publishing Company, 1973), pp. 87-88.
26. Leonard Ravenhill, *Tried and Transfigured*, (Minneapolis,

Endnotes

Bethany House Publishers, 1982), p.137.

Chapter 4—What God Says about Being Good—Part I

1. Norman Grubb, *Touching the Invisible*, (Fort Washington, PA., CLC Publications, 1941), p.24.
2. Erich Sauer, *The King of the Earth*, (Grand Rapids, Wm. B. Eerdmans Publishing Co., 1967), p.34.
3. G.D. Watson, *Love and Duty*, p.66.
4. Ibid., p.66.
5. J.I. Packer, *Rediscovering Holiness*, (Ventura, California, Regal, 2009), p.139.
6. George MacDonald, *The Best of George MacDonald*, p.108.
7. A.B. Simpson, *The Christ in the Bible Commentary*, Volume One, (Camp Hill, PA., WingSpread Publishers, 2009), p.23.
8. Ibid.,p.35
9. Jack Taylor, *Victory Over the Devil*, (Nashville, Broadman Press, 1973) p. 22.
10. A.W. Tozer, *The Warfare of the Spirit*, (Camp Hill, PA., Christian Publications, 1993), p.82.
11. E.M. Bounds, *Winning The Invisible War*, (Springdale: Whitaker, 1984), p.32.
12. A.B. Simpson, *The Best of A. B. Simpson*, (Camp Hill, PA., Christian Publications, 1987), p.20.
13. Samuel Chadwick, *Humanity and God*, (Salem, Ohio, Schmul Publishing Company, 1982), p.27.
14. J.W. Dawson, *Story of the Earth and Man*, (London, Hodder & Stoughton, 1874), p.377.
15. Blaise Pascal, *Pensees*, p.41.
16. A.B. Simpson, *A Larger Christian Life*, (Ulrichsville, OH., A Barbour Book, 1988), pp.91, 92.
17. In his book, *Humanity and God*, (Salem, Ohio, Schmul Publishing Company, 1982), Samuel Chadwick says, "The New Testament sharply divides all men into two classes, the children of God and the children of the Devil ... There is no intermediate class. The twofold classification is all-inclusive. Every man is sheep or goat, converted or unconverted, saved or lost, a child of light or a child of darkness, quickened into life or dead in sin ...." (p.39). Those who have God's imputed righteousness are deemed good; those without imputed righteousness are deemed evil.

Endnotes

Samuel Chadwick acknowledged the disdain the world has for such divisions. "Divisions so sharp and uncompromising jars upon the susceptibilities of the easy toleration of our times. It lacks accommodation, flexibility and discrimination" (p.39). According to Chadwick, the world insists upon making a point by asking, "Are not men all a mixture of good and bad? Many of the irreligious are personally attractive, while some religious people are decidedly repulsive. Unspiritual men are often scrupulously moral, while others zealous in religion are unscrupulously lax in morality, Yet, the Lord never wavers in his judgment" (pp.39, 40). The two divisions stand. There are those who received imputed righteousness and there are those who rejected it.

18. A.W. Tozer, *Jesus, Our Man in Glory*, (Camp Hill, PA., WingSpread Publishers, 1987), p.136.
19. Charles H. Spurgeon, *12 Sermons For the Troubled and Tried*, (Grand Rapids, Baker Book House, 1975), p.23.
20. A.W. Tozer, *The Warfare of the Spirit*, p.103.
21. Philip Yancey, *So What's So Wonderful About Grace?* (Grand Rapids, Zondervan, 1997), p.234.
22. Ibid., p.234.
23. James S. Stewart, *A Man in Christ*, (Vancouver, Regent College Publishing, 2002), p.247.

Chapter 5—What God Says about Being Good—Part II

1. John White, *The Fight*, (Downers Grove, IL: InterVarsity Press, 1976), p.179.
2. James S. Stewart, *A Man in Christ*, p.248.
3. Samuel Chadwick, *Humanity and God*, p.36.
4. Andrew Murray, *An Exciting New Life*, (Springdale, Whitaker House, 1982), p.68.
5. A.B. Simpson, *Portraits of the Spirit-Filled Personality*, (Camp Hill, PA., Christian Publications, 1996), p.41.
6. A.B. Simpson, *Wholly Sanctified*, (Camp Hill, PA., Christian Publications, 1991), p.31.
7. Ibid,. p.27.
8. Ibid., p.6.
9. Evan H. Hopkins, *Practical Holiness*, (Fort Washington, PA., CLC Publications, 2003), p.9.
10. G.D. Watson, *A Pot of Oil*, p.62.
11. These stages: becoming human, living in full obedience,

Endnotes

dying as the sin-bearer of the world, resurrection, being glorified by the Father, having this glorified life inhabited by the Spirit and then borne by the Spirit into man's re-created spirit.

12. A.J. Gordon, *Rest in Christ*, (Dixon, MO., Rare Books, n.d.), p.8.
13. A.B. Simpson, *The Christ in the Bible Commentary*, Volume Six, (Camp Hill, PA., WingSpread Publishers, 2009), pp.116, 117.
14. F.B. Meyer, *F. B. Meyer*, (Grand Rapids, Baker Book house, 1973), p.81.
15. When Paul speaks of the struggle between flesh and spirit in Galatians 5:17, and proceeds to delineate the works of one and the fruit of the other, the term "spirit" in each instance refers to the new nature and not, as such, to the Third person of the Trinity. This is a view that was held by Martin Luther and C. H. Lenski, among others, since the focus in this Galatians, chapter 5 passage, is on two parallel capacities: our flesh, operating in the soul, and our spirit, which is inhabited by the Holy Spirit.
16. A.W. Tozer, *The Knowledge of the Holy*, (New York, Harper and Brothers, 1961), p.110.
17. J.I. Packer, *Keep in Step with the Spirit*, (Grand Rapids, BakerBooks, 2005), p.34.
18. A.W. Tozer, *The Knowledge of the Holy*, p.113.
19. A.W. Tozer, *The Radical Cross*, p.87.
20. A.B. Simpson, *Wholly Sanctified*, p.6.
21. On page 214 of his book, *God's Eagles* (Salem, Ohio, Schmul Publishing Company, 1989), G. D. Watson wrote: "Some years ago an eminent Greek scholar wrote an article on instantaneous sanctification, and he proved from the Greek New Testament that the verbs which refer to sanctification were always in the aorist tense, to prove an instantaneous heart cleansing in contrast with the slow process of gradual growth." The Bible always depicts the Spirit's filling as sudden, not gradual, whereby the imparted righteousness of God flows from this filling.
22. A.B. Simpson, *Wholly Sanctified*, p.7.
23. G.D. Watson, *The Secret of Spiritual Power*, p.80.
24. A.B. Simpson, *The Christ of the Bible Commentary*, Volume Six, p.29.
25. The old nature has no capacity for God (Romans 3:11); the flesh does (Matthew 26:21; Romans 7:18). The old nature

Endnotes

totally defines a man in this condition (Romans 3:10-18); the flesh doesn't in any way define the essence of a believer (Romans 7:17, 21).

26. Donald L. Alexander, editor, *Christian Spirituality*, (Downers Grove, InterVarsity Press, 1988), p.23.
27. A.B. Simpson, *The Best of A. B. Simpson*, p.67.
28. Miles J. Stanford, *The Complete Green Letters*, (Grand Rapids, Zondervan, 1983) pp. 113, 114.
29. Leslie D. Wilcox, *Be Ye Holy*, (Shoals, IN., Old Paths Tract Society, n. d.), p.257.
30. Contrary to those who believe that the power of indwelling sin will be formidable throughout this life, Bill Gillham observed, "The Bible does not teach that our physical death is God's provision for our freedom." The subduing of sin is a distinct possibility in this life.
31. Samuel Chadwick, *The Way to Pentecost*, p.160.
32. Andrew Murray, *The Ministry of Intercessory Prayer*, (Springdale, Whitaker House, 1984) p.57.
33. These terms are used by Bill Gillham in his very helpful book, *Lifetime Guarantee*.
34. A.B. Simpson, *The Best of A. B. Simpson*, p.57.
35. A.B. Simpson, *The Christ of the Bible Commentary*, Volume Four, p.271.
36. A.B. Simpson, *Seeing the Invisible*, (Camp Hill, PA., Christian Publications, 1994), p.18.
37. The personal agony H. A. Ironside experienced when attempting to pursue sinless perfection is chronicled in his book, H.A. Ironside, *Holiness: The False and the True*, (Neptune, Loizeaux Brothers, 1912) pp.19-40. However, the errors of Dr. Ironside's assumptions are effectively refuted by Henry E. Brockett's book, *Scriptural Freedom from Sin*, (Kansas City, MO., Nazarene Publishing Company, 1941).
38. In his book, *Apostolic Testimonies* (Telfair, PA., Worthy Christian Library, Chapter 7, paragraph 14), A. B. Simpson points out that the scriptural word "perfecting" does not carry with it the idea of sinless perfection. Instead, Simpson writes, "The sense of the word is completing, finishing, carrying forward to maturity that work that has already been begun. The idea is that of the garden which has been cleansed from weeds and planted with seeds, and now it is being carried forward to the fullness of the blossom and the fruit."

Endnotes

39. A.B. Simpson, *The Christ of the Bible Commentary*, Volume Five, (Camp Hill, PA., WingSpread Publishers, 2009), p.316.
40. One can also claim to be perfect, as Paul did, and yet recognize that this perfection isn't complete (Philippians 3:14, 15). F.B. Meyer said this perfection is, "Not faultless, as judged by the white light of eternity; but blameless, so far as his own consciousness is concern." F.B. Meyer, *Our Daily Homily*, Volume 1 (Redding, CA., Pleasant Places Press, 2009), p.6.
41. L.E. Maxwell, *Born Crucified*, (Chicago, Moody Press, 1945), p.20.
42. Charles Finney, *Principles of Holiness*, (Minneapolis, Bethany House, 1984), p.104.
43. John Stott, *Men Made New*, (Downers Grove, IL., InterVarsity Press, 1966), p.102.
44. R.C. Sproul, *The Holiness of God*, (Wheaton, Tyndale House Publishers, 1985), p.40.
45. J.C. Ryle, *Holiness*, (Grand Rapids, Baker, 1984), p.10.
46. On page 91 of his book, *Entire Sanctification* (Salem, Ohio, Schmul Publishing Company, 2000) Dr. Wilbur T. Dayton, Professor of Biblical Literature and Historical Theology at Wesley Biblical Seminary, wrote: "Impute refers to how God sees us and thinks of us. Impart refers to what he gives us or does in us."

Chapter 6—Tracking Sin

1. John Owen, *Temptation and Sin*, (Evansville, Sovereign Grace Book Club, 1958), p.31.
2. Watchman Nee, *Love Not The World*, (Wheaton, Tyndale Publishers; Fort Washington, PA., Christian Literature Crusade, 1986), pp.62, 63.
3. Stephen Charnock, *The Works of Stephen Charnock*, Kindle locations: 1629-1630.
4. Horatius Bonar, *God's Way of Holiness*, (Chicago, Moody Press, 1970), p.21.
5. Horatius Bonar sermon, "The Secret of Deliverance From Evil," Sermon Index.net.
6. Leonard Ravenhill, *Sodom Had No Bible*, (Minneapolis, Bethany House Publishers, 1984), p.23.
7. G.D. Watson, *The Secret of Spiritual Power*, p.89.
8. Vance Havner, *The Best of Vance Havner*, (Grand Rapids, MI., Baker Book house, 1980), p.81.

Endnotes

9. David C.K. Watson, *My God is Real*, (New York, The Seabury Press, 1970), p.23.
10. Elton Trueblood, *The Life We Prize*, (Waco, TX., Word Books, 1972), p.22.
11. Arthur W. Pink, *Gleanings in the Godhead*, p.78.
12. Steven Barabas, *So Great Salvation*, (Eugene, OR., Wipf & Stock, 2005), p.101.
13. Francis A. Schaeffer, *The God Who is There*, p.46.
14. Jeffery Satinover, *Homosexuality and the Politics of Truth*, (Grand Rapids, Baker, 1998), p.32.
15. Ibid., p.35.
16. Thomas Guthrie, *Christ and the Inheritance of the Saints*, (Edinburgh, Crown, 1858), pp.217, 218.
17. R.C. Sproul, *The Holiness of God*, p.114.
18. A.B. Simpson, *The Christ of the Bible Commentary*, Volume 5, p.320.
19. J.I. Packer, *A Quest for Godliness*, (Wheaton, Crossway Books, 1990), p.191.
20. A.J. Gordon, *Fifty Eight A. J. Gordon Quotations* extracted from Northfield Year-book, (Wenham, Mass., Gordon College Archive, 2007), p.139.
21. Clyde E. Fant, Jr. and William M. Pinson, Jr., *20 Centuries of Great Preaching, Volume VIII*, p.217.
22. F.B. Meyer, *Samuel the Prophet*, (Fort Washington, Christian Literature Crusade, 1978), pp.79-80.
23. G.D. Watson, *White Robes*, (Hampton, TN., Harvey Christian Publishers, 2000), p.26.
24. Oswald Chambers, *The Servant as His Lord*, (Fort Washington, PA., Christian Literature Crusade, 1957), p.60.
25. A.W. Tozer, *And He Dwelt Among Us*, (Ventura, CA., Regal, 2009), p.41.
26. C.H. Spurgeon, *Spurgeon on the Attributes of God*, (MacDill AFB, FL., Tyndale Bible Society, n.d.), p.95.
27. Alexander Maclaren, *Expositions of Holy Scripture, Isaiah and Jeremiah*, Public Domain Books, Kindle locations: 1091
28. G.D. Watson, *Coals of Fire*, (Salem, Ohio, Schmul Publishers, n. d.), p.16.
29. Myron Madden, *The Power to Bless*, (Nashville, Abingdon, 1970), p.82f.
30. John Owen, *The Mortification of Sin*, (Feather Trail Press, 2009), p.67.

Endnotes

31. Ibid., p.68.
32. John Murray, *Redemption Accomplished and Applied*, (Grand Rapids, William B. Eerdman's Publishing Company, 1970), p.144.
33. F.B. Meyer, *F. B. Meyer*, p.144.
34. A.B. Simpson, *The Christ in the Bible Commentary*, Volume Two, (Camp Hill, PA., WingSpread Publishers, 2009), p.164.
35. Erich Sauer, *The King of the Earth*, p.19.
36. Charles H. Spurgeon, *The Kings Highway*, (Grand Rapids, Baker Book House, 1975), p.12.
37. C.S. Lewis, *Screwtape Letters*, (New York, HarperCollins, 2001), p.61.
38. G.D. Watson, *God's Eagles*, p.198.

Chapter 7—An Autopsy of Sin—Part I

1. A.B. Simpson, *Wholly Sanctified*, (Camp Hill, PA., Christian Publications, 1991), p.77.
2. Thomas Watson, *A Body of Divinity: Contained in Sermons upon the Westminster Assembly's Catechism*, (Kindle Edition, 2010), p.127.
3. What Satan seeks to draw out is in the realm of the soul. T. Austin Sparks said that this was his target from the very beginning: "The Deceiver assailed the soul—desires, reason, will—and drew this out as a basis of life apart from and independent of God." T. Austin Sparks, *What is Man?*, Kindle Edition, 2012; Kindle Location: 937.
4. E.M. Bounds, *Winning the Invisible War*, p.10.
5. This mission by the angels to bring relief to the battle-weary Christ underscores the severity of the temptations endured. The return of the angels to Gethsemane does suggest that we have underestimated what Jesus experienced in the wilderness.

   Cornecilius exercised his imagination when he painted the picture, "The Temptation of Jesus." A.E. Bailey described the intensity of the struggle this painting depicts: "Jesus, with bloodshot eyes, red eye lids, disheveled hair, has twined his fingers into his beard and with his other hand is gripping his wrist. His eyes are big. They look straight forward. They see nothing, but they reveal an intense consecration upon some internal problem." A.E. Bailey, *Art and Character*, (New York, New York, Abingdon,

Endnotes

      1938), p.77.
6. J. Oswald Sanders, *Satan is No Myth*, (Chicago, Moody, 1976), p.9.
7. A.B. Simpson, *The Christ in the Bible Commentary*, Volume 4, (Camp Hill, PA., WingSpread Publishers, 2009), p.25.
8. J.C. Ryle, *Holiness*, p.4.
9. Andrew Murray, *The Believer's Secret of the Master's Indwelling*, (Minneapolis, Bethany House, 1977), p.40.
10. A.W. Tozer, *The Set of the Sail*, (Camp Hill, PA., Christian Publications, 1986), p.72.
11. E.M. Bounds, *Winning The Invisible War*, p.37.
12. Tony Lane, *Timeless Witness*, (Peabody, MA., Hendrickson Publishers, 2004), p.153.
13. A.B. Simpson, *The Christ in the Bible Commentary*, Volume Two, p.322.
14. F.B. Meyer, *Joshua*, (Fort Washington, PA., Christian Literature Crusade, 1977), p.100.
15. Tony Lane, *Timeless Witness*, p.392.
16. Russell V. DeLong *Mastering Our Midnights* (Kansas City Mo. Beacon Hill Press, 1953), p.51.
17. F.B. Meyer, *Meet for the Master's Use*, (Chicago, Moody Press, 1898), p.57.
18. Thomas Watson, *The Doctrine of Repentance*, Location: 1066-1067.

Chapter 8—An Autopsy of Sin—Part II
1. F.B. Meyer, "He Did Evil Because He Prepared Not His Heart," located under Sermon Texts on the website sermonindex.net.
2. Robert A. Pyne, *Humanity and Sin*, (Nashville, Word Publishing, 1999), p.197.
3. Helmut Thielicke, *Life Can Begin Again*, p.40.
4. Steven Barabas, *So Great Salvation*, (Eugene, OR., Wipf and Stock, 2005), p.183.
5. A.B. Simpson, *The Fourfold Gospel*, (Orlando, FL., Bridge-Logos, 2007), p.287.
6. Thomas Watson, *The Doctrine of Repentance*, Location: 1171.
7. Alexander Maclaren, *Expositions of Holy Scripture Deuteronomy, Joshua, Judges, Ruth, and First Book of Samuel, Second Samuel, First Kings, and Second Kings*

Endnotes

        chapters I to VII Public Domain Books, Kindle Edition, p.171.
8. G.D. Watson, *Love Abounding*, p.44.
9. A.B. Simpson, *The Land of Promise*, (Camp Hill, PA., Christian Publications, 1996), p.171.
10. F.B. Meyer, *Joshua*, p.100.

Chapter 9—The Consequences of Sin

1. G. D. Watson, *Love Abounding*, pp.146, 147.
2. More precision and less confusion would have been achieved had Watson not used the word "nature," but had instead referred to the "flesh," or to internal forces that can pit the soul against the spirit.
3. Blaise Pascal, *Pensees*, p.35.
4. Robert A. Pyne, *Humanity and Sin*, p.150.
5. Ibid., p.181.
6. Professor Sinclair B. Lewis cited John Owen on this point in the book, *Christian Spirituality*, edited by Donald L. Alexander, p.58.
7. James S. Stewart, *The Strong Name*, (New York, Charles Scribner's Sons, 1941), p.94.
8. Andrew Murray, *The Ministry of Intercessory Prayer*, (Springdale, Whitaker House, 1984), p.49f.
9. Steven Barabas, *So Great Salvation*, p.53.
10. F.B. Meyer, *Samuel the Prophet*, p.72.
11. Philip Yancey, *What's So Amazing About Grace?*, p.67.
12. J.H. Jowett, *The Epistles of St. Peter*, Kindle Edition, 2010; Kindle locations: 2663-2664.
13. A.W. Tozer, *Jesus, Our Man in Glory*, p.40.
14. F.B. Meyer, *Samuel the Prophet*, p.214.
15. Martyn Lloyd-Jones, *Life in Christ*, (Wheaton Ill., Crossway, 2002, p.57.
16. Ibid., p.640.
17. Hannah Whitall Smith, *The Christian's Secret of a Happy Life*, (Old Tappan, N. J., Fleming H. Revell Company, 1974), p.62.
18. J.C. Philpot, "More Pearls from Philpot," located under Sermon Texts on the website sermonindex.net.
19. Alexander Whyte, *Lord, Teach Us to Pray*, (Grand Rapids, Baker Book House, 1976), p.107.

Endnotes

Chapter 10—Defective Obedience—Part I
1. Alexander Maclaren, *Sermons on 1 & 2 Kings*, Public Domain, Monergism Books, Kindle locations: 673-674.
2. W.M. Douglas, *Andrew Murray and His Message*, (Grand Rapids, Baker, 1981), p.311.
3. J.C. Ryle, *Holiness*, (Grand Rapids, Baker, 1984), p.264.
4. Clyde E. Fant, Jr. and William M. Pinson, Jr., *20 Centuries of Great Preaching, Volume V*, p.304.
5. A.W. Tozer, *The Radical Cross*, p.34.
6. A.B. Simpson, *The Christ in the Bible Commentary*, Volume Six, p.103.
7. F.B. Meyer, *Samuel the Prophet*, pp.193-194.
8. Exposing Saul's pretentious wrath against the witches, Thomas Goodwin wrote, "Thus did Saul sin. All the religion he had and pretended to in his latter days was persecuting witches; yet in the end he went against this his principle, he went to a witch in his great extremity at last." Thomas Goodwin, *Aggravations of Sinning Against Knowledge*, (Kindle Edition, 2011; Kindle locations: 623-625).
9. G.D. Watson, *Tribulation Worketh*, (Hampton, TN., Harvey Christian Publishers, 2000), p.31.

Chapter 11—Defective Obedience—Part II
1. Oswald Chambers, *My Utmost for His Highest*, (Westwood, NJ., Barbour and Company, n. d.), p.349.
2. Thomas Watson declared: "True obedience is uniform; it obeys one commandment as well as another; it fulfills duties difficult and dangerous ... It is the note of a hypocrite to be discriminating in obedience; some sin he will indulge (II Kings 5:18), some duties he will dispense with .... (*The Great Gain of Godliness*, p.147).
3. A.B. Simpson, *Standing on Faith*, Kindle Edition, 2010: Kindle Location: 1267-1268.
4. Ibid., Kindle location: 1337.
5. Philip Yancey, *The Jesus I Never Knew*, (Grand Rapids, Zondervan, 1995), p.132.
6. A.B. Simpson, *The Christ in the Bible Commentary*, Volume Two, p.253.
7. G.D. Watson, *Tribulation Worketh*, p.28.
8. Dr. and Mrs. Howard Taylor, *Hudson Taylor's Spiritual Secret*, (Chicago, Moody Press, 1990), pp.155, 156

Endnotes

Chapter 12—Motivations for Goodness—Part I

1. J.I. Packer, *Keep in Step with the Spirit*, p.79.
2. Ibid., p.81.
3. Ibid., p.83.
4. Ibid., p.85.
5. I well understand the speculation involved by looking at Peter's words in so singular a way. Other prophecies about Israel—particularly those that predicted the re-gathering of a scattered people—could not come true had the Lord returned at Pentecost or soon after Pentecost. Of course, these other prophecies presuppose Jewish rejection of their Messiah and the subsequent scattering of the people. Nevertheless, an offer can be genuinely made despite an awareness of certain rejection.
6. George MacDonald, *The Best of George MacDonald*, p.97.
7. A.W. Tozer, *The Divine Conquest*, (Harrisburg, PA., Christian Publications, 1950), p.113.
8. A.W. Tozer, *Faith Beyond Reason*, (Camp Hill, PA., WingSpread Publishers, 2009), p.103.
9. A.B. Simpson said of Paul, "There was no loose joint in his harness where the arrow of conviction could enter. He had lived 'in all good conscience before God,' unto the day of his conversion. Such a man is very difficult to reach." A. B. Simpson, *But God*, Kindle Edition, 2101; Kindle Locations: 187-188.
10. A.B. Simpson, *When God Steps In*, (Camp Hill, PA., Christian Publications, 1997), pp.15, 16.
11. *The Speaker's Bible, The Second Letter to the Corinthians*, Edward Hastings, ed., (Turnbull & Spears, Aberdeen, Scotland, 1933), p.19.
12. Alexander Maclaren, *Expositions of the Holy Scripture, Psalms*, Public Domain Books, Kindle locations: 806-807.
13. Documenting this fact, John MacArthur writes: "Ours is the first society since the decaying Roman Empire to normalize homosexuality. We're living in the first generation in hundreds of years that has legalized abortion. Adultery and divorce are epidemic. Pornography is now an enormous industry and a major blight on the moral character of society." John MacArthur, *Leadership*, (Nashville, TN, Thomas Nelson, 2004), Kindle Edition, p.4.
14. A.W. Tozer, *The Set of the Sail*, p.59.

Endnotes

15. When Mary Queen of Scots resisted the arguments of John Knox with the words, "My conscience says not so," the great Reformer answered her, "Conscience, Madam, requires knowledge." And so it does! An ill-informed conscience can lead astray. *The Speaker's Bible, The Book of Isaiah, Volume II*, Edward Hastings, ed., (Aberdeen, Scotland, Turnbull & Spears, 1935), p.75.
16. Oswald Chambers, *Our Brilliant Heritage*, (Grand Rapids, Discovery House Publisher, 1998), p.75.
17. Thomas Watson, *The Great Gain of Godliness*, (Carlisle, PA., The Banner of Truth trust, 2008), p.23.
18. Dale Yocum, *This Present World*, (Salem, Ohio, Schmul Publishing Company, 1984), p.138.
19. C.S. Lewis, *Mere Christianity*, p.87.
20. J.C. Ryle, *Holiness*, p.255.

Chapter 13—Motivations for Goodness—Part II

1. *The Speaker's Bible, The Epistles to the Ephesians, The Epistle to the Colossians*, Edward Hastings, ed., (Aberdeen, Scotland, Turnbull & Spears, 1930), p.37.
2. Horatius Bonar, *God's Way of Holiness*, p.127.
3. A.W. Tozer, *And He Dwelt Among Us*, p.166.
4. A.W. Tozer, *Man, The Dwelling Place of God*, (Camp Hill, PA.,WingSpread Publications, revised 2008), pp.120, 121.
5. R.C. Sproul, *The Holiness of God*, (Wheaton, Tyndale House, 1985), p.153.
6. Charles Finney, *The Guilt of Sin*, (Grand Rapids, Kregel Publications, 1965), pp.84, 85.
7. On page 25 of A.W. Tozer's book, *Echoes of Eden* (Harrisburg, PA., Christian Publications, 1981), Tozer writes: "We must face the fact that when a human has sold himself out to sin and to the mutilating power of iniquity has wrought to make a him to be a devil and not a man, God will no longer love the lost man. Further, it must be said that we ought not to imagine for a second that God is pining over hell and grieving in his heart over lost men in hell."
8. G.D. Watson, *Our Own God*, p.152.
9. Tony Lane, *Timeless Witness*, (Peabody, MA., Hendrickson Press, 2004), p.45.
10. Thomas Watson, *The Godly Man's Picture*, (Carlisle, PA., The Banner of Truth Trust, 2009), p.7.
11. F.B. Meyer, *Samuel the Prophet*, (Fort Washington, PA.,

Endnotes

Christian Literature Crusade, 1978), p.67.
12. G.D. Watson, *Our Own God*, p.108.
13. J.C. Ryle, *Holiness*, p. xv.
14. L.E. Maxwell, *Born Crucified*, p.87.
15. Dr. and Mrs. Howard Taylor, *Hudson Taylor's Spiritual Secret*, p.158.
16. F.B. Meyer, *Samuel the Prophet*, pp.79, 80.
17. G.D. Watson, *Tribulation Cometh*, p.31.
18. Ibid., p.49.
19. Jerry Bridges, *The Pursuit of Holiness*, p.73.
20. Roy Hession, *Our Nearest Kinsman*, (Fort Washington, PA., CLC Publications, 2007), pp.26, 27.
21. Ibid., p.16.
22. Jessie Penn-Lewis, *The Cross of Calvary*, (Fort Washington, PA., CLC Publications, 1996), p.78.

Chapter 14—Consistent Goodness—Part I
1. C.H. Spurgeon, *Barbed Arrows*, (Harrisburg, Christian Publications, 1970), p.69.
2. A.B. Simpson, *The Holy Spirit* Volume 2, (Harrisburg PA., Christian Publications, n. d.), p.158.
3. Alexander Maclaren, *Expositions of Holy Scripture Deuteronomy, Joshua, Judges, Ruth, and First Book of Samuel, Second Samuel, First Kings, and Second Kings chapters I to VII*, Public Domain Books, Kindle Edition, p.105.
4. Paul E. Billheimer, *Destined For The Cross*, (Minneapolis, Bethany House Publishers, 1975), p.45.
5. William Barclay, *Daily Celebration Volume 2*, (Waco, Word Books, 1973), p.181.
6. Eusebius, *The History of the Church*, Kindle Edition, p.175.
7. G.D. Watson, *Spiritual Ships*, (Nicholasville, KY., Schmul Publishing Company, 1996), p.72.
8. A.B. Simpson, *The Holy Spirit*, Volume 1, (Telfair, PA., Worthy Christian Library, Chapter 9, paragraph 22).

Chapter 15—Consistent Goodness—Part II
1. A.B. Simpson, *The Best of A. B. Simpson*, p.37.
2. Ibid., p.68.

Endnotes

3. The Speaker's Bible, *The Second Epistle to the Corinthians*, Edward Hastings, ed., (Aberdeen, Scotland, Turnbull & Spears, 1933), p.54.
4. A.W. Tozer, *Paths to Power*, (Camp Hill, PA., Christian Publications, n. d.), p.39.
5. A.B. Simpson, *A Larger Christian Life*, p.140.
6. The phrase, "Let go and let God" has been falsely maligned by assuming that theologians who spoke this way encouraged passivity. Had those who leveled this criticism done their homework, they would have discovered that passivity was expressly disavowed by those who used this phrase.

   Of course, no phrase can say everything; a phrase may be totally true, while not being total truth. Perhaps the critical spirit could be tempered by not imposing criteria upon a phrase that no phrase could survive.

   To examine what this phrase does say we might ask, is it wrong to tell a believer to "let go"? Saying this is no more wrong than telling a believer to cast his care upon the Lord. And is it wrong to tell a believer to "let God"? Saying this is no more wrong than to tell a believer, "Have faith in God."

   Taken in isolation, the verse that tells us to cast our cares, and the verse that tells us to have faith in God, could just as well be subject to the same unfair criticism that the phrase "Let go and let God" has been subject to. Samuel Chadwick, *Humanity and God*, p.229.
7. A.B. Simpson, *Behind the Veil*, (Telfair, PA., Worthy Christian Library website), chapter 5, paragraph 3.
8. Ruth Paxson, *Life on the Highest Plane*, (Grand Rapids, MI., Baker Book House, 1983), p.321.
9. Jessie Penn-Lewis, Power for Service, (Fort Washington, PA., Christian Literature Crusade, 1998), p.62.
10. G.H. Lang, *Divine Guidance*, (Miami Springs, FL., Conley and Schoettle Publishing Co. Inc., 1985), p.11.
11. Oswald Chambers, *Our Brilliant Heritage*, p.194.
12. Perhaps the most common way of losing balance today is spending too much time in front of the TV. Statistics inform us that parents allow their children to spend, on average, five hours in front of the TV each day. This isn't

Endnotes

just a problem for children, though, because parents watch TV too much as well.

One good rule of thumb to consider—before throwing the TV away with the admission you couldn't control yourself—is to give God as much time as you do the TV. To watch TV for two hours a day, and then give God only a few minutes a day, is bound to have a negative effect on one's thought world.

The sophisticated images crafted by the TV industry provide a huge advantage to Satan, especially when the revelations of God's Word are being routinely ignored, and often opposed. Images, remember, are the choice launchers for Satan's fiery darts. And we're going to plop ourselves in front of a TV set and provide him such a big target?

13. Samuel Chadwick, *Humanity and God*, p.229.
14. G.D. Watson, *Our Own God*, p.104.
15. Abraham Kuyper, *The Practice of Godliness*, (Grand Rapids, Baker, 1977), p.65.
16. A.B. Simpson, *The Christ in the Bible Commentary*, Volume Six, (Camp Hill, PA., WingSpread Publishers, 2009), p.309.
17. Leonard Ravenhill, *Revival God's Way*, (Minneapolis: Bethany House, 1986), p.44.
18. E.M. Bounds, *E. M. Bounds on Prayer*, p.163.
19. T.Austin Sparks, *In Touch with the Throne*, Kindle Edition, 2012; Kindle locations: 275-277.

Chapter 16—Consistent Goodness—Part III

1. A.W.Tozer, *The Knowledge of the Holy*, p.110.
2. E.M. Bounds, *E. M. Bounds on Prayer*, (New Kensington, Whitaker House, 1997), p.158.
3. *Ibid.*, p.155, 156.
4. Charles Finney, *Principles of Holiness*, (Minneapolis, Bethany House Publishers, 1984), p.102.
5. Dale Yocum, *Conformed to Christ*, (Salem, Ohio, Schmul Publishing Company, 1986), p.74.
6. James S. Stewart, *A Man in Christ*, p.235.
7. Samuel Chadwick, *The Way to Pentecost*, (Fort Washington, PA., CLC Publications, 2007), pp.114, 115.

Endnotes

8. Samuel Logan Brengle, *Helps to Holiness*, (Shoals, IN., Old Paths Tracts Society, n. d.), p.15.
9. Ibid., p.61.
10. Robert H. Grundy, *Matthew: A Commentary on His Handbook A Mixed Church Under Persecution*, 2nd edition, (Grand Rapids, MI., Eerdmans, 1994), p.388.
11. F.J. Huegel, *The Cross of Christ, The Throne of God*, p.35.
12. A. W. Tozer, *The Divine Conquest*, (Harrisburg, PA., Christian Publications, 1950), p.105.
13. Samuel Chadwick, *Humanity and God*, p.247.
14. A.W. Tozer, *The Divine Conquest*, p.36.
15. A.B. Simpson, *The Land of Promise*, p.158.
16. Robert, Dana L., *Occupy until I Come*, (Grand Rapids, MI., Wm. B. Eerdmans Publishing Co., 2003), p.285.
17. A.W. Tozer, *Gems From Tozer*, p.78.
18. R.G. Lee, *A Greater Than Solomon*, (Nashville, Broadman Press, 1935), pp.94, 95.
19. Dale Yocum, *Conformed to Christ*, p.94.
20. A.B. Simpson, *The Land of Promise*, (Camp Hill, PA., Christian Publications, 1996), p.171.
21. Ibid., p.158.
22. Samuel Logan Brengle, Helps to Holiness, p.5.
23. Ibid., p.5.
24. Ibid. p.98.
25. Dale Yokum, This Present World, p.50.
26. G.D. Watson*, Our Own God*, p.154.

Chapter 17—Rewards for Goodness—Part I

1. James S. Stewart, *Heralds of God*, (Grand Rapids, Baker Book House, 1972), pp.33, 34.
2. Robert Louis Stevenson was one of those who considered rewards to be an enemy of piety and an insult to virtue. Accordingly, Stevenson wrote, "The world must return someday to the word duty, and be done with the word reward. There are no rewards and plenty of duties. And the sooner a man sees that and acts upon it, like a gentleman or a fine old barbarian, the better for himself." *The Speaker's Bible, The Pastoral Epistles, The Johannine Epistles*, Edward Hastings, ed., (Aberdeeen, Scotland,

Endnotes

Morrison and Gibb Ltd., 1942), p.94.
3. A.J. Gordon, *Ecce Venit: Behold He Cometh*, (New York, Revel, 1889), p. 271.
4. G.D. Watson, *Bridehood Saints*, (Hampton, TN., Harvey and Tait Publishers, 1988), p.99.
5. G.D. Watson, *White Robes*, p.54.
6. A.B. Simpson, *The Christ in the Bible Commentary*, Volume Two, p.147.
7. J.C. Ryle, "Faith's Choice," located under Sermon Texts on the website sermonindex.net.
8. A.B. Simpson, *The Christ in the Bible Commentary*, Volume Six, p.136.
9. G. D. Watson, *God's Eagles*, p.143.
10. Debbie Roberts, *Rejoice*, (Little Rock, Revival Press, 1985), p.49.
11. Jack Taylor, *Victory over the Devil*, p.11.
12. G.D. Watson, *Soul Food*, (Hampton, TN., Harvey Christian Publishers, 2000), p.46.

Chapter 18—Rewards for Goodness—Part II
1. Concerning the crown of righteousness, Florence Nightingale wrote to a friend, "That word strikes me more than anything in the Bible. Strange that not happiness, not rest, not forgiveness, not glory should have been the thought of that glorious man's mind, when at the eve of the last and greatest of his labors; all desires swallowed up in the one great craving after *righteousness* that, at the end of his struggles, it was mightier within him than ever, mightier even than the desire of peace." *The Speaker's Bible, The Pastoral Epistles, The Johannine Epistles*, Edward Hastings, ed., (Aberdeeen, Scotland, Morrison and Gibb Ltd., 1942), p.95.
2. A.B. Simpson, *The Christ in the Bible Commentary*, Volume Two, p.89.
3. A.B. Simpson, *The Christ in the Bible Commentary*, Volume Six, p.40.
4. G.D. Watson, *God's Eagles*, p.266.
5. A.W. Tozer, *The Set of the Sail*, p.93.
6. In this day of instant coffee, microwave dinners, and drive-by restaurants, thoughts of the faraway future are not easily retained. So when modern man asks, "Lord, will you at this time restore the kingdom?" he no sooner looks at his watch, dashes out the door, and then answers as he

Endnotes

goes, "I guess not." Extending prayer, searching prophecy, and considering the signs of the time never factor in. That would take too long.

7. A.B. Simpson, *The Christ in the Bible Commentary*, Volume Two, p.341.
8. In his book, *The Great Gain of Godliness*, Thomas Watson addresses this dilemma on page 138 where he writes: "In this life our love to God is lukewarm and sometimes frozen. A believer weeps that he can love God no more ... but at the day of death ... the sparks of love shall be blown into a pure flame: the saints shall love God ... as much as they are able. They shall love him superlatively and without effect ...."
9. Thomas Watson, *A Body of Divinity: Contained in Sermons upon the Westminster Assembly's Catechism*, (Kindle Edition, 2010), p.72.
10. Stephen Charnock, *The Works of Stephen Charnock*, Kindle Location: 1609-1610.
11. Alexander Maclaren, *Exposition of Scriptures, Psalms*, Public Domain Books, Kindle location: 228.
12. A.B. Simpson, *Wholly Sanctified*, pp.87, 88.
13. G.D. Watson, *Our Own God*, p.35.
14. *The Works of Thomas Goodwin, Volume 1*, (Lafayette, IN., Sovereign Grace Publishers Inc., 2000), p.181.
15. A.W. Tozer, *Whatever Happened to Worship?* (Camp Hill, PA., Christian Publications, 1985), p.87.
16. A.B. Simpson, *The Christ in the Bible Commentary*, Volume Six, p.505.
17. G.D. Watson, *Love and Duty*, p.79.
18. Summarizing a perspective articulated by the Reformed theologian Franciscus Junius (1545-1602), J. Todd Billings wrote: "... there are two types of knowledge of God: archetypal knowledge, which is God's perfect knowledge of himself, and ectypal knowledge, which is knowledge derived from archetypal knowledge but is accommodated to creaturely understanding." J. Todd Billings, *Union with Christ*, (Grand Rapids, MI., Baker Academic, 2011), p.86.

Perhaps the knowledge conveyed to those who possess this crown is more akin to this first type of knowledge, a knowledge of a higher order less mediated in method and less restricted in scope.

19. F.B. Meyer, *Joseph*, (Fort Washington, PA., CLC

Endnotes

Publications, 2002), p.163.

20. Some commentators think another crown is mentioned in Scripture, where Paul refers to the believers at Thessalonica as his crown and joy (I Thessalonians 2:19-20). This crown is variously referred to as the soul-winner's crown, the boasting crown, or the crown of rejoicing. Perhaps this interpretation is correct. It must be acknowledged that in distinguishing one crown from another and attributing distinctive meanings to each, deductive reasoning is often employed, and therefore certainty can be elusive.

    Not every thought set forth about these crowns can be validated scripturally to the extent core doctrines of the faith can be validated. My reasoning for not including this I Thessalonians passage in this discussion about crowns stems from the perception that Paul seems to be saying that these believers are his reward, and not the basis for his reward. Here, as in Philippians 4:1, the crown metaphor seems to emphasize a present tense reality.

    It is true that eschatological overtones can be found in these verses, as well as in II Corinthians 1:14. So, since the double foci of temporal and eternal does exist, it is undoubtedly true that all that Paul invested in these people will be rewarded on that last day. Nevertheless, there is a nuance in the verses cited in this footnote which may place them in a different category from the other verses in Scripture which discuss the rewards and the various crowns God will give.

    Without attempting to press language beyond original intent, the emphasis in these verses seems to indicate these people bring satisfaction to Paul, as the crowns will one day do, but that Paul is not talking about a crown that is distinctive from the other crowns Scripture mentions.

21. Thomas Watson, *A Body of Divinity: Contained in Sermons upon the Westminster Assembly's Catechism*, (Kindle Edition, 2010), p.252.

22. A.B. Simpson, *Portraits of the Spirit-Filled Personality*, p.51.

Endnotes

Chapter 19—The Reaping of the Rewards—Part I

1. G.D. Watson, *Heavenly Life*, (Salem, Ohio, Schmul Publishing Company, 1994), p.76.
2. In contradistinction to the Bema Judgment, Thomas Goodwin speculates that the great White Throne Judgment will be of considerable duration. "The day of judgment will be a long day ...." According to Goodwin, it will involve "the examining of the accounts of all the world, and convincing all mankind, and sending them speechless to hell ...." (*The Works of Thomas Goodwin, Volume 1*, p.525.

   Alexander Maclaren wrote that "every man is ever writing his autobiography with invisible but indelible ink" and that "this autobiographical record which we are busy preparing, which is at once ledger and indictment, is to be read out one day." The reading will be detailed and not condensed. Alexander Maclaren, *Expositions of Holy Scripture, Isaiah and Jeremiah*, Public Domain Books, Kindle locations: 3694-3695/3710-3711.
3. Horatius Bonar, *God's Way of Holiness*, p.110.
4. G.D. Watson, *Soul Food*, p.34.
5. A.W. Tozer, *And He Dwelt Among Us*, pp.164, 165.
6. C.S. Lewis, *The World's Last Night*, (New York, Hartcout, Brace, Janovich, 1959), p.113.
7. Ibid., p.113.
8. A. W. Tozer, *Leaning Into The Wind*, pp.73, 74.
9. F.B. Meyer, *Samuel the Prophet*, p.247.
10. G.D. Watson, *Heavenly Life*, p.72.
11. G.D. Watson, *God's Eagles*, p.102.
12. Samuel Chadwick, *Humanity and God*, p.184.
13. A.B. Simpson, *The Christ in the Bible Commentary*, Volume Six, p.352.
14. Ibid., p.254.
15. Since the "work of God" is closely connected with the gifts of the Spirit, this strongly suggests that our ministry will take place on our free time rather than at our jobs, given the fact that the gifts of the Spirit are not likely to have a free expression during most people's time at work.

    In saying this, I acknowledge painting with a broad brush, and further recognize that a person's paid position may well come into view (at least to some extent) when the

Endnotes

Lord gives his rewards. What must be rethought, though, is the equation of paid work with our ministry. An equation like this can keep a person from undertaking, or even contemplating to undertake, the real ministry the Lord wants him or her to have.

16. F.B. Meyer, *Samuel the Prophet*, p.201.
17. A nondiscerning church tends to lump all suffering in the same category and then wax eloquent about what such suffering produces. However, there are sufferings God ordains and there are sufferings that Satan sustains. The sufferings God ordains include, as we said, persecution, the crucifying of self, the care of the churches (often without appreciation) and an agonizing for the spiritual growth of others, lost or saved, through intercessory prayer and sacrificial service.

    You'll notice that sickness and poverty are not a part of this list, since God calls both of these sufferings curses in Deuteronomy, chapter 28 (verses 17-18; 60-61). Being sick or poor, therefore, was never sanctioned by God, and for that reason these sufferings won't be rewarded by God, unless there were voluntary and godly reasons these types of suffering came upon us, which isn't usually the case.

    Of course, the witness of a godly character will indeed be rewarded even if sickness or poverty weren't understood. A failure to make biblical distinctions about suffering has set church members up to accept what never came from God, or will be rewarded by God. Moreover, by thinking of suffering almost exclusively in these terms, instead of focusing on the suffering God does intend for Christians to overcome, church members today are avoiding what God will reward.

18. A.B. Simpson, *The Christ in the Bible Commentary*, Volume Six, p.205.
19. A.B. Simpson, *The Names of Jesus*, (Camp Hill, Pennsylvania, Wingspread Publishers, 1991), p.91.
20. G.D. Watson, *Bridehood Saints*, p.37.
21. John Henry Jowett, *Things that Matter Most: Devotional Papers*, Kindle Edition, 2010; Kindle Locations: 512-514.

Chapter 20—The Reaping of the Rewards—Part II

1. A.B. Simpson, *The Christ in the Bible Commentary*,

Endnotes

	Volume Two, p.138.
2.	Richard Baxter, *The Saints' Everlasting Rest*, p.58.
3.	In his book, *Knowing God*, (Downers Grove, Illinois, InterVarsty Press, 1973), J.I. Packer argues that God will indeed expose the sins of his bride-to-be at the Bema Judgment seat. Packer states, "The retributive applies throughout: Christians as well as non-Christians, will receive 'according to their works' (p.129). Packer also says: "Paul refers to the fact that we must all appear before Christ's judgment seat as 'the terror of the Lord' (II Corinthians 5:11), and well he might. Jesus the Lord, like his father, is holy and pure; we are neither" (p.133). So the Lord is going to visit terror upon his bride just before the Wedding Feast?

None of this is true, for six reasons: 1) God said he will remember our sins no more—and he won't! 2) It is what we did for the Lord that is being examined at the Bema judgment seat, not the sins we committed against him; 3) Works not comporting with God's standards will not be rewarded, it is true, but there won't be retribution; 4) The term, "the terror of the Lord," can well be translated "the fear of the Lord," and that *is* applicable to Christians; and 5) The term, "the terror of the Lord," (if this translation is retained) doesn't refer to Christians appearing before the Bema judgment. Paul pivots from the Bema judgment scene in verse 10 to contemplate what unbelievers will face at their judgment in verse 11; 6) Packer's repeated assertions of how unholy we are assumes the exact opposite of the I John 4:4 declaration, "greater is He that is in you, than he that is the world," by supposing that the Holy Spirit in us may be greater than Satan but he is not greater than our flesh, and thus we are unholy still. This is not what Scripture says (Romans 6:14; 8:2; Galatians 5:16; Ephesians 5:18). |
| 4. | A.B. Simpson, *The Christ in the Bible Commentary*, Volume Two, p.121. |
| 5. | The observation of the great Puritan John Owen—"... no man ought to look for anything in heaven but what one way or another he hath some experience of in this life"—emphasizes a continuity between this life and the next more broadly based than that of the rewards. Yet, there is a similarity of principle: In some ways our life in heaven will |

Endnotes

be determined by a factoring in of what we sought and got on earth.

6. John Calvin asserted, in his *Institutes of the Christian Religion* (3.14.11,) that "there never existed any work of a godly man which, if examined by God's stern judgment, would not deserve condemnation." However, there is not a single verse in Scripture which makes this point. Calvin's correct teaching on the total depravity of man falls into error if sanctification is minimized and Romans 7 is assumed normative for Christians. God provides the believer with a power over sin, which is more than what many Reformers believe. In their thinking, the progress one can expect is emerging from utter defeat to a stalemate. Such thinking skews their commentary on the rewards.
7. G.D. Watson, *God's Eagles*, p.151.
8. Ibid., p.149.
9. In his book, *Knowing God*, J. I. Packer writes: "The relevance of our doings is not that they ever merit an award from the court—they are too far short of perfection to do that—but they provide an index of what is in the heart—what, in other words is the nature of each agent" (p.131). This notion of unworthy works, which theologian John Owen called "the iniquity of their holy things," is a Puritan thought imported and imposed upon the text and not derived from it. Packer has the verse saying what it does not say: that it is our motives that will be rewarded and not our works.
10. G.D. Watson, *Our Own God*, p.16.
11. Paul Billheimer, *Destined for the Throne*, (Minneapolis, Bethany House, 1975), p.106.
12. G.D. Watson, *Our Own God*, p.106.
13. J.C. Ryle, "Inspiration," located under Sermon Texts on the website sermonindex.net.
14. J.C. Ryle, "Riches and Poverty," located under Sermon Texts on the website sermonindex.net.
15. A.B. Simpson, *The Christ of the Bible Commentary*, Volume Five, p.334.
16. J.I. Packer, *A Quest for Godliness*, p.43, (Wheaton, Crossway Books, 1990), p.43.
17. A.B. Simpson, *The Christ of the Bible Commentary*, Volume Two, p.361.
18. A.W. Pink, *Practical Christianity*, (Grand Rapids, MI.,

Endnotes

Baker Book House, 1975), p.153.
19. A.B. Simpson, *The Christ of the Bible Commentary*, Volume One, (Camp Hill, PA., WingSpread Publications, 2009), p.255.

Chapter 21—Losing the Rewards
1. These words attributed to Napoleon actually came from Thomas Hardy's epic poem, "The Dynasts."
2. James S. Stewart, *Wind of the Spirit*, p.71.
3. Ibid, p.122.
4. C.S. Lewis, *The Problem of Pain*, (New York, The Macmillan Company, 1962), p.148.
5. Woodrow Kroll, *Facing Your Final Job Review*, (Wheaton, Crossway, 2008), p.121.
6. G.D. Watson, *Tribulation Worketh*, p.14.
7. A.B. Simpson, *The Christ of the Bible Commentary*, Volume One, (Camp Hill, PA., WingSpread Publications, 2009), p.255.
8. G.D. Watson, *White Robes*, p.51.
9. James S. Stewart, *A Man in Christ*, p.86.
10. Ibid., p.36.
11. G.D. Watson, *The Secret of Spiritual Power*, p.17.
12. A.W. Tozer, *The Divine Conquest*, p.36.
13. On page 148 of his book, *God's Eagles*, G. D. Watson writes: "We are told in this passage that the fire will manifest everyone's work, of what sort it is, and for thousands of years no one has ever been able to imagine how fire could reveal a man's actions and find the true quality of those actions." But one day, almost a hundred years ago, Dr. Watson accompanied his wife to a physician's office where they sat in a dark room, her arm extended in front of an apparatus that was powered by red hot electricity. Soon after, the physician showed them a slide of the bones in her arm. Speculating that there might be some connection here with the revealing fire at the judgment, Dr. Watson said, "This marvelous instrument of electricity can reveal every part of the human body without burning a single atom of it."
14. Some commentators make much of the vindication a believer may receive when some wrong committed against them is repudiated, and the part the believer actually played in this episode is appreciated with Divine commendation. While it is true that the themes of

Endnotes

vengeance and vindication do have a scriptural underpinning, this aspect of God's dealings with man may be overplayed when inserting it so strongly into the Bema judgment scene.

In my speculation, and that is all this is, I can envision the saints of God concerned not at all about vindication. Even on earth they escaped self to such an extent they forgot the wrong that was done against them—not in memory, but in stirring of the soul which re-presented the pain. Once they float above the clouds and come into glory, the injustices done against them shrivel to near extinction.

The satisfaction vindication is supposed to offer will matter little on that day. The grace that covered my wrongdoings will cover the wrongdoings of any believer that wronged me. So why dig this up?

Discernment at the Bema I understand. Separating what is worthy for reward from that which is not worthy of reward I understand. That there is a painful recognition of loss I understand. But detailing the wrong, providing extensive commentary about the wrong, I don't understand.

15. A.W. Tozer, Sermon Index, Articles and Sermons:: John Wesley Letters, p.18. This comment was made by Tozer to British evangelist, Leonard Ravenhill.
16. Joseph C. Dillow, *The Reign of the Servant Kings*, (Miami, Schoettle, 1992), p.532.
17. In his book, *The Judgment Seat of Christ* (Christian Focus Publications, Geanies House, Fern, Tain, Ross-Shire, IV20 ITW Scotland, Great Britain, 2004), p.85, R.T. Kendall points out the insertion of the word "or" in the NIV translation of this passage. Dr. Kendall then surfaces the notion that a mixture of these materials will be in all believer's lives. Tangential to this observation is a premise that surfaced in the holiness tradition. Authors like Finney and Mahan contended that a given work may be wholly good, with nothing unworthy mixed in. Reformers like J. I. Packer, however, contend that even the best of works will be tainted.
18. Hannah Whitall Smith, *God of All Comfort*, (Gainesville-FL., Bridge-Logos, 2006), p.205.

Endnotes

19. A.B. Simpson, *The Christ in the Bible Commentary*, Volume Two, pp.9, 10.
20. Bruce Wideman, *Flee, Follow, Fight*, (Jackson, Mississippi, Hederman Brothers, 1984), p.142.
21. A.B. Simpson, *The Names of Jesus*, pp.96, 97.
22. C.S. Lewis, *The Weight of Glory*, (Grand Rapids, Eerdmans, 1973), pp.1, 2.
23. A.B. Simpson, *The Christ in the Bible Commentary*, Volume Five, p.221.
24. F.W. Bourne, *Billy Bray*, (Shoals Lane, IN. Old Paths Tract Society, 1937), p.28.
25. Richard Baxter, *The Saints' Everlasting Rest*, (Grand Rapids, Baker Book House, 1978), p.161.
26. F.B. Meyer, *Elijah and the Secret of Power*, (Chicago, Moody Press, 1976), p.119.
27. A.W. Tozer, *The Attributes of God*, Volume 1, (Camp Hill, PA., Christian Publications, 1997), p.173.
28. F.B. Meyer, *Joseph*, p.115.
29. G.D. Watson, *Bridehood Saints*, p.42.

Chapter 22—What If

1. A.W. Tozer, *And He Dwelt Among Us*, p.52.
2. Ibid., p.53.
3. Harvey Cox, *The Feast of Fools*, (Cambridge, Harvard University Press, 1969), p.3.
4. Amy Carmichael, *Whispers of His Power*, (Ft. Washington, PA., CLC Publications, 2001), p.75.
5. Paul Billheimer, *Destined for the Throne*, p.19
6. James S. Stewart, *The Strong Name*, p.257.
7. E.M. Bounds, *E. M. Bounds on Prayer*, p.342.
8. It can be argued that our confusion about morality is sinfully contrived. Lewis Smedes points out: "What Moses brought from Sinai was a morality endemic to the human race, affirmed in conscience as much as it was violated in practice." Lewis Smedes, *Mere Morality*, (Grand Rapids, Eerdmans, 1983), p.10.
9. James S. Stewart, *The Gates of New Life*, p.1.
10. Martyn Lloyd-Jones, *Life in Christ*, p.586.
11. A.W. Tozer, *The Knowledge of the Holy*, p.56.
12. Clyde E. Fant, Jr. and William M. Pinson, Jr., *20 Centuries of Great Preaching, Volume VIII*, p.273.
13. Thomas Watson, *The Great Gain of Godliness*, p.54.
14. E.M. Bounds, *E. M. Bounds on Prayer*, p.323.

Endnotes

15. Clyde E. Fant, Jr. and William M. Pinson, Jr., *20 Centuries of Great Preaching, Volume XI*, p.296.
16. Clyde E. Fant, Jr. and William M. Pinson, Jr., *20 Centuries of Great Preaching,* Volume VIII, p.299.
17. A.W. Tozer, *And He Dwelt Among Us*, pp.113, 114.
18. G.D. Watson, *God's Eagles*, pp. 193-194.
19. James D. Kennedy, *Truths that Transform*, p.124.
20. Ibid., p.97.
21. J.C. Ryle, *Practical Religion*, Kindle, 2010; Location: 7543-7545).
22. On pages 17 and 18 of his book, *Heavenly Life*, G.D. Watson describes with magnificent eloquence the way God will not only remember but also reveal the good that transacted in our earthly life. Watson writes: "The lives of all the saints, long hidden, will then appear, and all their characters, and prayers, and good works, and variegated graces, and numberless shades and traits of experience, will be openly manifested in cloudless light ... The secret fountains in the soul, the processes of our salvation, our repentances, and consecrations, and prayers, and spiritual struggles, and complex movings and experiences, and stages of growth in grace, and efforts of obedience in charity, will all come forth in some way unknown to us but as well-defined about our personality as the qualities of light are untwisted and hung out in the rainbow on a summer cloud when the rain has passed over."
23. G.D. Watson, *Bridehood Saints*, p.99.
24. C.H. Spurgeon, *Charles Spurgeon on the Providence of God*, (MacDill AFB, Fl., Tyndale Bible Society, n.d), p.100.
25. Keith M. Bailey, *The Best of A.B. Simpson*, (Camp Hill, PA., WingSpread Publications, 2006), p.10

www.ingramcontent.com/pod-product-compliance
Lightning Source LLC
Chambersburg PA
CBHW051812090426
42736CB00011B/1446